SOCIAL NETWORK ANALYSIS *and* EDUCATION

For Shannon, Harrison, and Aurelia

"The ties that bind. Now you can't break the ties that bind."

SOCIAL NETWORK ANALYSIS *and* EDUCATION

THEORY, METHODS & APPLICATIONS

BRIAN V. CAROLAN
Montclair State University

Los Angeles | London | New Delhi
Singapore | Washington DC

Los Angeles | London | New Delhi
Singapore | Washington DC

FOR INFORMATION:

SAGE Publications, Inc.
2455 Teller Road
Thousand Oaks, California 91320
E-mail: order@sagepub.com

SAGE Publications Ltd.
1 Oliver's Yard
55 City Road
London EC1Y 1SP
United Kingdom

SAGE Publications India Pvt. Ltd.
B 1/I 1 Mohan Cooperative Industrial Area
Mathura Road, New Delhi 110 044
India

SAGE Publications Asia-Pacific Pte. Ltd.
3 Church Street
#10-04 Samsung Hub
Singapore 049483

Printed in the United States of America

Library of Congress Cataloging-in-Publication Data

Carolan, Brian V.

Social network analysis and education: theory, methods & applications/Brian V. Carolan, Montclair State University.

pages cm
Includes bibliographical references and index.

ISBN 978-1-4129-9947-2 (pbk.)

1. Social networks. 2. Education—Research. I. Title.

HM741.C37 2013
302.3—dc23   2012039567

This book is printed on acid-free paper.

Acquisitions Editor: Vicki Knight
Editorial Assistant: Kalie Koscielak
Production Editor: Laura Stewart
Copy Editor: Kim Husband
Typesetter: C&M Digitals (P) Ltd.
Proofreader: Laura Webb
Indexer: Michael Ferreira
Cover Designer: Candice Harman
Marketing Manager: Nicole Elliott
Permissions Editor: Adele Hutchinson

SUSTAINABLE FORESTRY INITIATIVE
Label applies to the text stock

Certified Sourcing
www.sfiprogram.org
SFI-00341

13 14 15 16 17 10 9 8 7 6 5 4 3 2 1

BRIEF CONTENTS

DETAILED CONTENTS

PREFACE

Without being aware of it until years afterward, the origin of this book can be traced to an assignment that I had in course titled—if I recall correctly—Social Gerontology, an elective I took as an undergraduate sociology major. Around this time, I developed an appreciation for sociology's focus on understanding society in a disciplined way, bound by rules of evidence. For reasons still unclear to me, I also took an interest in education, particularly the social organization of schools and classrooms, which still perplexes me to this day. But I grew somewhat frustrated by the discipline's methodological tools—the analysis of statistical data that treated observations as independent, or the analysis of qualitative data that was strictly bound by context and somewhat limited to telling descriptive stories. There just had to be some middle ground where the precise modeling of individuals' outcomes intersected with the context that gave shape to those very outcomes.

The assignment that first introduced me to this idea was one in which I had to ask my grandfather to keep a log of all his social interactions over the course of one day, in addition to providing other health and attitudinal data. I, too, had to report the same. These data were combined with those provided by the 50-some other students in the class. What emerged from this exercise was not simply an understanding that size and diversity of social networks correlate with a number of outcomes. That point was simple enough. What this exercise made explicit was that individuals both shape and are shaped by the context in which they interact. In hindsight, this was my first cursory experience with social network analysis, one that introduced me to ways in which the precision and rigor of quantitative analysis can be integrated with the richness and description of qualitative analysis. Not only was this a new methodological approach for me, it was a new way of theoretically thinking about and seeing the world: relationships matter.

Fast forward to my years as a graduate student in sociology, and I still did not quite "get" why my dissatisfaction with the theoretical and methodological tools I had learned through my years of course work persisted. I had taken a number of statistics courses that addressed several fancy modeling techniques and surveyed the different designs in which these techniques are employed. I was also afforded many opportunities to learn about an array of qualitative designs, their analytical strategies, and the types of questions that they can address. While these were wonderful courses that reflected the types of sociological research that those interested in education most typically produce and consume, they still neglected to account for the critical role of an individual's relationships with others and how these relationships and the larger pattern in which they are embedded affect that individual.

At this point I was also able to reflect somewhat dispassionately on my own teenage years in a typical suburban high school. It became clear to me that my own adolescent attitudes and behaviors were very much influenced—in good ways and bad—by my closest peers, as well as my (in)ability to interact with peers who floated in different social circles. Similar to the insight I gained from my undergraduate Social Gerontology course, this reflective pause encouraged me to rethink the theoretical and methodological tools that were framing my own emerging research interests in and around education. It was after these first couple of years of graduate studies that things really clicked for me.

It was at this time that I was formally introduced to social network analysis. Working with Harrison White and a number of fantastic students and faculty, I began to recognize that I was not the only one dissatisfied with the reductionist thinking that dominated most quantitative educational research, and social science for that matter. What struck me is that these experiences finally provided me with a formal means for conceptualizing and measuring what my intuition had been telling me for some time. Relationships do matter, and in social network analysis, there indeed existed a set of exciting tools that accounted for their importance. Of course, these tools had been percolating across a number of disciplines for some time, and I was very much late to the conversation. But when I first was exposed to this, it was at a time when the "new" science of networks was exploding across disciplines and in the popular consciousness, resulting in advances that were firmly challenging accepted conceptions about social life. What was odd, however, was that educational research seemed behind the curve in adopting these tools and their accompanying perspective. Educational research was—and still is, to some degree—dominated by the deduction of quantitative research or the induction associated with qualitative research and the tools—the theories and methodologies—that go with them.

This book represents an effort to move past this false distinction and bring the interdisciplinary tools associated with social network analysis to a larger audience of current and prospective educational researchers. In presenting this material, my main intent is to encourage you to consider these tools in light of your emerging research interests and evaluate how and how well they illuminate the social complexities surrounding educational phenomena. Whether your interests lie in examining peers' influence on students' achievement, the relationship between social support and teacher retention, or how the pattern of relations among parents contributes to schools' norms, the tools introduced in this book will provide you with a slightly different take on these and other phenomena. For example, unlike the most common approaches to the quantitative study of classrooms that have treated them as groups of isolated individuals whose behavior and attitudes are influenced by personal and family attributes on the one hand and the characteristics of instruction, teachers, and school organization on the other, the perspective advanced in this book explicitly accounts for the importance of relationships within such formal structures and the informal patterns of interaction that emerge, sustain, or recede.

As noted in the Acknowledgements, much of what is in this text has been cobbled from multiple sources across an array of disciplines. In part, my aim in doing so is to highlight the interdisciplinary nature of social network analysis and broaden the tools that you can bring to your own educational research interests. My contribution is to show how these tools can be adapted so that your theoretically informed vision about the nature of social processes better matches your ability to actually capture them empirically. While considering these tools in your own work, you should also "see" your research interests differently. Much educational research gives primacy to discreet organizational boundaries—the classroom, school, district, and so on—and gives short shrift to the interactions that span these boundaries in various ways and degrees. As you progress through the book, you should appreciate how patterns of stability and change (e.g., why is school reform so hard?) are also attributable to the ways in which resources flow through formal and informal interactions between people—students, teachers, leaders, parents, or others. While organizational boundaries matter, the conceptual sophistication and methodological precision associated with social network analysis allow us to see past these boundaries and focus on the crucial interactions and patterns of interactions that shape outcomes. This foundational insight is a direct result of the pioneering work that was done across these varied disciplines decades ago, and I hope that this text has adequately acknowledged these contributions.

The main intent of this book should be clear. However, there is another reason for writing this book—a reason that is entirely selfish. My years as a sociologist of education have undoubtedly contributed to my personal and professional growth and have given me insights into things that I previously took for granted. However, while my professional interests are still very much grounded in the sociology of education, I am still perplexed by one "finding" from that assignment I had mentioned earlier: My grandfather had a more expansive, more varied, and more dense social network than I had as a happy, well-adjusted 21-year-old undergraduate. How did his ties emerge? What opportunities did they provide? Were his actions at all constrained by these ties? Were these ties at all responsible for his good physical and mental health? I am not sure I know the answers to these questions, but writing this book has encouraged me to think more deeply about the importance and relevance of social networks and the importance of these networks in my grandfather's life.

A NOTE TO READERS: HOW THE BOOK IS ORGANIZED AND WHY

I organized this book into three parts that are intended to accomplish a specific aim. Part I makes the case that social network analysis provides educational researchers with a different way of thinking about and measuring an array of processes and outcomes that explicitly account for the importance of one's relationships with others, as well as the larger pattern in which these relationships are embedded. After making this case and introducing several foundational concepts, Part II focuses on the methods and measures that constitute its empirical tools. I have intentionally tried to dampen the mathematical or computational aspects of the material in these chapters. However, I have been careful not to present this material in a manner that distorts its complexity. The chapters in this section, in particular, were written with a certain audience in mind. Prior to engaging the material in these chapters, you should be familiar with research methods in general and, at the very least, have a level of comfort with basic applied statistics. Part III builds on this material to discuss the ways in which these methods and measures are applied in the context of educational research. The aim of this final section is to bring the text's previous chapters together in a way that provides you with a jumpstart on your network-based studies.

To supplement what is in the text, there is also a companion website available at http://www.sagepub.com/carolan. The resources available at this site include: data files, key terms, slides, and instructions for using general and specialized software applications for social network analysis. I encourage you to explore these resources as you make your way through the text.

I recognize that readers have different styles and preferences. So, to the extent that is possible in such a linear medium as a book, I have tried to allow the chapters to be used in a different order, which may work for readers who already have familiarity with social network analysis. For others, however, it may be best to consider the logic of presentation indicated by the book's table of contents. Finally, I recognize that I have not completely succeeded at perfecting the presentation of such a complex and rapidly developing subject such as social network analysis and its application in educational research. This has been a challenging and, frankly, humbling experience. I would be grateful for any feedback on the book from readers, both students and instructors.

ACKNOWLEDGMENTS

I would like to thank two very influential people whose insights and inspirations continue to motivate me. I only hope that I can serve as such a wonderful model for my own students:

Harrison White, Columbia University

Gary Natriello, Teachers College, Columbia University

Also, I would like to thank my former colleagues at the College of Staten Island, CUNY, and current colleagues at Montclair State University who have been supportive of this work. In particular, I would like to thank those who have served as my department chair during the writing of this book and have afforded me the "space" needed to undertake this task:

Ken Gold, College of Staten Island, CUNY

Kathryn Herr, Montclair State University

Jeremy Price, Montclair State University

Susan Sullivan, College of Staten Island, CUNY

This book would not have been possible without the extensive and thoughtful comments offered by SAGE's excellent pool of outside reviewers throughout the entire writing process. The timeliness of their comments throughout the writing of this book was very much appreciated:

Jennifer Watling Neal, Michigan State University

Philip C. Rodkin, University of Illinois at Urbana-Champaign

Carla Meskill, University at Albany, State University of New York

Carlos Valiente, Arizona State University

Scott D. McClurg, Southern Illinois University

Alan J. Daly, University of California, San Diego

Edward T. Palazzolo, Arizona State University

Tamara V. Young, North Carolina State University

Brenda L. Battleson, University at Buffalo, State University of New York

Vance A. Durrington, University of North Carolina, Wilmington

Donald W. Good, East Tennessee State University

William F. McMullen, Northeastern University

Jianwei Zhang, University at Albany

August E. Grant, University of South Carolina

It goes without saying that the publishing industry has been upended due to a number of factors. However, there is something to be said about the value and importance of a solid, seasoned editorial team. I profusely thank Vicki Knight, who saw the early potential in this book and gently nudged me throughout the entire process, sharing her extensive experience in the craft and business of academic textbook publishing. She has that uncanny knack of making you feel good about yourself while offering a pointed, honest critique. I also thank Laura Barrett, the production editor, and Kim Husband, the copy editor, and Nicole Elliot, the marketing manager. They were sincerely a pleasure to work with.

I have drawn upon a number of published articles and books in preparing this text. I am happy to acknowledge the sources of these articles and books here. I thank the authors for their contributions and thank their publishers for permission to reuse these materials. I have been careful to cite these original sources throughout the text and strongly encourage you to read these articles and books as you will find that they complement much of what is written in these pages.

Specifically, Chapter 1 draws from Wasserman and Faust (1994) and Knoke and Yang (2008). Chapter 2 includes material from Freeman (2004); Mische (2011); Breiger (2004); and McFarland, Diehl, and Rawlings (2011). Chapter 3 relies on Hanneman and Riddle (2011a) and Valente (2010). Chapter 4 includes material from Knoke and Yang (2008); Valente (2010); Marsden (2011); and Wasserman and Faust (1994). Chapter 5 draws from Valente (2010). Chapter 6 incorporates material from de Nooy, Mrvar, and Batagelj (2005); Knoke and Yang (2008); and Hanneman and Riddle (2011b). Chapter 7 also contains material from Hanneman and Riddle (2011b); Knoke and Yang (2008); and Valente (2010). Chapter 8 includes material from Hanneman and Riddle (2005) and Goodreau, Kitts, and Morris (2009).

Chapter 9, too, draws from Hanneman and Riddle (2005); van Duijn and Huisman (2011); and Daly (2010). Chapter 10 draws from Ream and Rumberger (2008); Lin (2001a;

2001b); Burt (2001); Maroulis and Gomez (2008); and Morgan and Todd (2008). Chapter 11 incorporates material from Frank, Zhao, Penuel, Ellefson, and Porter (2011); Valente (2005, 2010); Kreager and Haynie (2011); and Renzulli and Roscigno (2005). Finally, Chapter 12 includes material adopted from Prell (2012); Huisman and van Duijn (2011); and McFarland, Diehl, and Rawlings (2011).

I sincerely thank these authors and publishers—this book would not have been possible without these contributions and permissions.

I would also like to acknowledge Matt Pittinsky and Alan Daly, who kindly shared with me the data that are used throughout the text. This book is better as a result of their generosity. In addition, I am grateful to numerous professors, mentors, colleagues, and students who have pushed my thinking and learning about social networks over the years.

Finally, I would like to acknowledge the encouragement of my parents and the support of my wife, Shannon, and our two wonderful kids, Harrison and Aurelia. Thank you for being the best part of my personal network.

ABOUT THE AUTHOR

Brian V. Carolan is associate professor of quantitative research methods in the Department of Educational Foundations, College of Education and Human Services, Montclair State University. Prior to joining Montclair State University in 2010, he was associate professor of social foundations of education in the Department of Education, College of Staten Island, The City University of New York. He received his BA in sociology from Rutgers University, his MPhil in sociology from Columbia University, and his PhD in sociology and education from Teachers College, Columbia University, in 2004.

Brian has published widely in a variety of areas related to education, including issues such as high school size, grade span configuration, and the social organization of classrooms. This diversity of topical interests reflects his desire to employ methodological strategies from different disciplines to examine phenomena that are of interest to educational stakeholders. Consequently, his work has appeared in diverse outlets including *Social Networks*, *Educational Researcher*, *Teachers College Record*, *Journal of Research on Adolescence*, and numerous others. He currently teaches graduate-level research methods courses to students in the educational and human services fields.

Brian lives in northern New Jersey with his wife, Shannon, and two young children, Harrison and Aurelia. They enjoy all the perks of suburban living, including riding their bikes to school, romping on all local playgrounds, lazy summer days at the community pool, and regular escapes to explore the ins and outs of New York City.

PART I

Theory and Concepts

1

The Social Network Perspective and Educational Research Introduction

"We are surrounded by concentric circles of special interests...However, a person is never merely a collective being, just as he is never merely an individual being."

Georg Simmel (1908/1950, p. 261)

OBJECTIVES

The primary objective of this chapter is to establish a central point in social network analysis: relationships shape a person's behavior and/or attitudes beyond the influence of his or her own individual characteristics. This orienting chapter establishes this point by demonstrating how this theoretical and methodological approach differs from conventional approaches used in educational research, which often views individuals as mere collections of attributes. Upon completion of this chapter, you will be able to (1) distinguish how social network analysis differs from other conventional approaches and (2) weigh its value and utility in the context of contemporary educational research.

THE SOCIAL NETWORK PERSPECTIVE

It is undisputed that a person's sex, age, and socio-economic status, among factors, are critical determinants of one's educational opportunities and outcomes. In fact, the consensus is that these individual-level attributes are responsible for 70 to 90% of the variation in relevant educational outcomes, such as subject-area achievement, graduation, and grade promotion (Bryk & Raudenbush, 1992). Less appreciated, and often unaccounted for, are the roles that one's relationships with others play in shaping these opportunities and outcomes. While most would agree that relationships do matter, most methods and models used in educational research do not properly account for these influences. This absence is odd given that relationships influence a person's behavior above and beyond the influence of one's individual characteristics (Valente, 2010). After all, characteristics such as one's academic history or educational aspirations influence who one knows and spends time with. That is, these characteristics both shape and are shaped by individuals' social networks. Recognizing that these individual attributes are important, social network analysis focuses on the types of relations one has with others and how these relations influence individual and group behavior and/or attitudes.

A social network is a group of individuals and the relation or relations defined on them (Wasserman & Faust, 1994). The analysis of social networks is distinct, however, from the other individual-based approaches that dominate educational research or any other research within the social and behavioral sciences. What makes it distinct is that, in addition to focusing on the individual, the relationships that connect that individual to another are of central importance. Social network analysis, therefore, is not simply an analytical method but a set of theories, models, and applications that are expressed in terms of relational concepts and processes. Relationships defined by connections among individual units—students, teachers, or school districts—are a fundamental aspect of social network analysis. While interest in social network analysis has grown in both the natural and social sciences, a set of agreed-upon principles has emerged that distinguishes this approach from others. Wasserman and Faust (1994) note that, in addition to the use of relational concepts, social network analysis emphasizes (1) individuals and their actions are viewed as interdependent; (2) relational ties between individuals are opportunities for transmission of resources; (3) the pattern of relations among individuals—the social structure—is an environment that can either provide opportunities for or constraints on individual action; and (4) social network models conceptualize structure as enduring patterns of relations among actors.

FOUNDATIONAL CONCEPTS

The social network perspective—that is, its theories, models, and applications—consists of several concepts that are fundamental to an introductory discussion of social networks.

Actor

At the core of social network analysis are the connections among social units and the outcomes associated with these connections. These social units are typically referred to as actors: discrete individual or collective social units. Examples of actors in educational research are students in a classroom, departments within a school, teachers in a district, or parents in a community. The use of the term *actor*, however, does not mean that these units have the ability to "act." Rather, the use of the term *actor* connotes a social unit that is playing a role in a larger social system.

Typically, the social network perspective focuses on collections of these actors that are of all the same type. An example of this would be a set of teachers adapting to a mandated whole-school reform initiative. Collections of actors in this manner are referred to as one-mode networks. However, other methods also allow you to focus on actors that are conceptually different. These two-mode networks consist of two different sets of actors, for example, the relationship between a set of students and the courses they take (Field, et al., 2006). In this example, there are two sets of actors: students and courses. The latter, of course, is an example of a social unit that does not have the ability to "act."

Ties

Ties connect actors to one another. The range of ties connecting any two actors can be extensive. Some of the more common ties used to denote connections among actors in educational research include:

- Behavioral interaction (e.g., talking to each other or sending messages)
- Physical connection (e.g., sitting together at lunch, living in the same neighborhood)
- Association or affiliation (e.g., taking the same courses, belonging to the same peer group)
- Evaluation of one person by another (e.g., considering someone a friend or enemy)
- Formal relations (e.g., knowing who has authority over whom)
- Moving between places or status (e.g., school choice preferences, dating patterns among adolescents)

The ties on which you focus are driven by theoretical and/or empirical interest. But defining what constitutes a tie is a thorny methodological issue discussed in Chapter 3.

Groups

At the most fundamental level, a connection between actors establishes a tie between two actors. A tie between two actors forms a dyad, the basic unit for analysis of social networks. Therefore, dyads are pairs of actors, whereas triads are triples of actors. It follows that a subgroup can be defined as any subset of actors and all the ties among them. Locating and studying these subgroups, whether dyads, triads, or some larger subgroup, has been an important concern in social network analysis and is discussed in more depth in Chapter 5.

However, not all social network analysis is concerned with dyads, triads, or subgroups. For many, the attraction of social network analysis is its ability to model the relationships among systems of actors. A system consists of ties among actors in a bounded group. The concept of group, however, has been treated numerous ways among social scientists. For the purposes of this book, a group is defined as the collection of actors on which ties are to be measured. Following Wasserman and Faust's (1994, p. 19) definition, a group "consists of a finite set of actors who for conceptual, theoretical, or empirical reasons are treated as a finite set of individuals on which network measurements are made."

The limitation to a finite set (or sets) of actors is a simple analytic requirement. Though advances in computing have made it possible to examine ties extending among actors in a seemingly infinite group of actors, analyzing the data in any meaningful way would be problematic. Modeling finite groups is challenging enough, including the identification of network boundaries, sampling, and delineating group membership. These are topics addressed at length in Chapter 4.

Relation

It is unadvisable for you to collect information on just one social tie. Rather, information is collected on multiple ties in an effort to capture the richness of the connections, or lack thereof, among actors. Therefore, you typically measure multiple relations, defined as the collection of ties of a certain kind among actors in a group. For any group of actors, you might measure several different relations. For example, in addition to measuring friendship among adolescents, you might also record the friendships among parents of this same set of adolescents and the curricular choices they make. The important distinction here is that a relation refers to a collection of ties of a specific kind measured on pairs of actors from a specific set of actors. Ties themselves only exist between pairs of actors.

Social Network

Each of the preceding foundational concepts is essential to understanding the social network perspective. Having defined a social network as a finite set (or sets) of actors and the relations or relations defined on them, we can now think of a social network as consisting of three essential elements: (1) a set of actors; (2) each actor has a set of individual attributes; and (3) a set of ties that defines at least one relation among actors. Putting it all together, the social network perspective is one concerned with the structure of relations and the implication this structure has on individual or group behavior and attitudes.

Compared to other research paradigms and their associated methodologies, social network analysis has several distinctive features. These features not only distinguish it from the typical approach that removes the individual actor from his or her context, but they also speak directly to the reasons why the social network perspective provides an exceptional suite of tools to fully explain a wide range of processes and outcomes that are of interest to educational researchers. Together, these features define the social network perspective (Freeman, 2004)

- Social network analysis is motivated by a relational intuition based on ties connecting social actors.
- It is firmly grounded in systematic empirical data.
- It makes use of graphic imagery to represent actors and their relations with one another.
- It relies on the use of mathematical and/or computational models to succinctly represent the complexity of social life.

The historical development of these contemporary features is discussed at the beginning of Chapter 2, which sketches the transdisciplinary history of social network analysis. These four features are applicable to a wide range of social and behavioral phenomena. Because of its wide applicability, the social network perspective can be used to understand phenomena that have historically been of interest to educational researchers.

APPLICATIONS TO EDUCATIONAL RESEARCH

The utility of the social network perspective is best described through an example that employs the foundational concepts just introduced while also previewing some other concepts that will be introduced throughout the text. Throughout this book, many new terms will be used, and a list of key terms is available on the book's companion website available at http://www.sagepub.com/carolan.

Social networks are typically composed of who knows whom, who is friends with whom, or who talks with whom, the different types of ties just discussed. For example, consider Figure 1.1, which shows a hypothetical network based on friendship preferences in a class of 25 elementary school students. Suppose students were asked to list their top three friendship preferences, with each of the three nominations receiving a 1,

0 otherwise. These relations are mapped using widely available social network analysis software, reviewed in the book's final chapter. These maps of social networks are referred to as sociograms and are useful tools to identify certain network properties. Each circle represents an actor, which in this case is a member of an elementary school class. The lines connecting them represent friendship nominations; more specifically, each line connects a pair of students. In this example, the network consists of all 25 class members. This is referred to as the network's boundary.

In this example, the lines are directed; therefore, the arrow shows the direction of the friendship nomination. The thickness of the sociogram's lines does not indicate anything, but it is possible to make sociograms that vary line properties to represent the strength or type of relation. In this case, however, the relationship is either present or absent (binary); the relationship's strength has not been measured. Sociograms are usually constructed in a way that actors who are most central are in the center and their ties are placed near them. For example, Students 19 and 24 appear to receive more friendship nominations than others; hence their central location. There are many ways to arrange actors in a sociogram, as there are many ways to represent actors or their ties. Up to four attributes of each actor can be layered onto the sociogram by altering the color, shape, label, and size of the symbol. For example, boys are denoted as circles and girls as squares. The attributes of the ties can also be altered by adjusting the size and style of the line connecting each dyad.

Central to social network analysis is the contention that one's location in a social structure shapes one's opportunities and outcomes. These locations are referred to as positions, and most people are first interested in figuring out who is at the center. But just as there are numerous ways to define one's position in a network, there is a number of varied ways to determine who is at its center. These dual notions of centrality and position are discussed in Chapter 5. As interesting as it may be to determine which student is most central, it may also be interesting to find out who is on the periphery (those with few ties, for example, Students 10 and 20, who do not receive any nominations) or those who are isolated (those with no ties). While you might assume that being on the periphery of a network is disadvantageous, often these peripheral members have ties to other people within or external to the network in which they may occupy important positions. In these instances, the actor serves as bridge to other groups or networks.

In addition to using characteristics such as gender, it is also possible categorize actors as being members of specific subgroups. However, unless you rely solely on exogenous attributes such as gender or age, defining what constitutes group membership is tricky. Social network analysts have devised a number of ways to partition a network into groups, and these ways are reviewed in Part II. These methods are distinctly different, as they are based on relations rather than on the attributes that one may share with others. In addition, networks can also be divided into distinct positions (also discussed in Part II). Positions are different from groups in that actors who occupy similar positions have similar relations to others but need not be directly tied to each other. Consequently, actors may be identified as being in the same group but in different positions, and vice versa.

This book equips you with the theory and methods used to analyze networks such as the one presented in Figure 1.1. Moving beyond static snapshots such as this, social network analysis also allows you to learn about how attitudes and behaviors spread through networks over time. In other words, do one's friendships change? Does the entire network become more centralized? How rigid is the network's hierarchy? Better yet, assume that in addition to relational data, one also has data on individuals' attributes, such as grade point average. Now, you could ask questions such as, how does being on the outside (periphery) or inside (center) of a friendship network correlate with one's grade point average? Or, do birds of a feather flock together? That is, are students with similar grade point averages likely to nominate each other? Understanding concepts such as centrality, bridging, groups, positions, and homophily enables you to measure and predict how a friendship network changes over time and how these changes relate to outcomes that are of interest to educational researchers. Chapter 5 explicitly addresses this issue by discussing how resources flow through networks over time and how this process influences individuals' behavior or attitudes.

The overall pattern of relationships represented by the sociogram can also be important. Whereas researchers are at times concerned with individual outcomes such as whose friendships remained stable over time, other times the concern may lie with the structure of the entire network and how this pattern evolves over time. Although an individual actor's relations affect his/her opportunities and outcomes, the influence of these relations is shaped by the larger network in which the ties between any two actors are embedded. This pattern is referred to as network structure, and this structure matters in terms of shaping how and when resources flow across the network. For example, the network structure in Figure 1.1 can be described in very concrete ways. Some of these ways include density (the number of ties divided by the total number of possible ties), centralization (the extent to which the ties are focused on one or a few actors in the network), or the number of subgroups (there are numerous ways to identify these). A detailed description of these static complete network properties is presented in Chapter 5.

WHY NETWORKS MATTER IN EDUCATIONAL RESEARCH

The interest in social network analysis across the social and behavioral sciences has grown tremendously in the past 20 years. As this interest has grown, educational researchers have drawn on its interdisciplinary foundations to study a range of phenomena. A brief history of these foundations is presented in Chapter 2, with particular

Figure 1.1 Hypothetical Friendship Network of Elementary School Children Within the Same Class (N = 25). Friendship ties are binary and directed. Square nodes represent girls and circles represent boys. Graphs of complete networks such as this can reveal several interesting network properties, including whether relations are dense or sparse, centralized or decentralized, or whether any individual members occupy strategically advantageous positions.

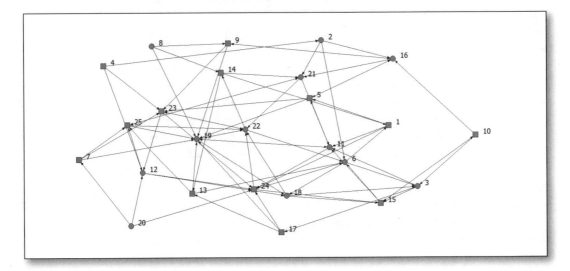

attention given to the advances in the field made by those who have studied educational phenomena. Many topics that have attracted interest from educational researchers can be considered from the social network analysis perspective. Some examples include:

- Diffusion and adoption of innovations (Daly & Finnigan, 2010)
- Social influence (Cole & Weinbaum, 2010)
- Belief systems (Frank, Kim, & Belman, 2010)
- Social capital (Maroulis & Gomez, 2008)
- Homophily (Coburn, Choi, & Mata, 2010)
- Efficacy of interventions (Valente, Hoffman, Ritt-Olson, Lichtman, & Johnson, 2003)
- Small-group dynamics (Katz, Lazer, Arrow, & Contractor, 2004)
- Small-world and scale-free networks (Carolan, 2008a)

These examples reflect the pervasiveness and variation of network-related phenomena. A few of these specific social network phenomena are discussed at length in the book's third and final section, with a focus on the ways in which these network phenomena have been modeled and applied in the educational research literature.

While educational researchers have studied several of these phenomena for quite some time, what distinguishes the studies referenced above is that the explanation includes concepts and information on relationships among actors. As noted by Wasserman and Faust (1994), the social network perspective consists of theoretical concepts that are relational, data are relational, and critical tests of statistical significance use distinct distributions of relational properties. Whether you are interested in the influence of a school's social structure on an individual actor's achievement, or whether certain opinion leaders are critical to the adoption of a reform initiative, social network analysis operationalizes these patterns of relationships in terms of networks and ties among actors. This perspective differs significantly from the ways in which individual or group behavior is typically conceptualized and modeled in conventional educational research. Standard practice usually ignores relational information.

Several hypothetical examples illustrate this. Imagine you are interested in students' behavior in the first year after transitioning to a new middle school, a critical turning point in adolescents' educational trajectories. The first step in the standard approach would be to define a population of interest (fifth-grade students who moved to a destination middle school), assuming a large population, take a random sample, and then collect data on a number of relevant variables (e.g., academic history, socioeconomic status, disciplinary history, sex, etc.). The assumption here is that one student's behavior is independent of any other's. Social network analysis directly confronts this assumption. Anyone who has spent time with early adolescents knows that their behavior shapes—and is shaped by—the influences of others. Moreover, there are many factors that influence the way adolescents behave the way they do (such as attending school on any given day, disrupting the class, etc.). Adolescents often tend to turn to others and either mimic behavior or "act out" in ways to seek approval from select audiences. To best fully capture a description of the student's behavior, you should examine student-to-student relations. These relations might include membership in the same extracurricular groups, the frequency with which they communicate outside of school, joint course-taking patterns, friendship nominations, and others. To fully understand and model the phenomenon of student behavior, you need the relational data inherent to the social network perspective.

Another example illustrates the importance of relational data and how conventional practices do not adequately account for or model these influences. Suppose there is a group of teachers making a decision or trying to reach a consensus. The group may be assigned to select an appropriate textbook for the school's ninth-grade social studies curriculum. Most would be interested in the outcome of this process—what decision has been reached. But focusing solely on the outcome ignores the complex process through which the outcome was generated. One should really look into how members of the group influenced each other in order to make a decision, or, perhaps, not make a decision. The social network perspective allows you to systematically model how these interactions among group members led to the outcome. The influences of any one member are quite critical to the process, and by ignoring them, researchers leave themselves with an incomplete picture of social life. After all, social life is relational, but most social science does not account for these relations.

The reasons for this are varied. But the inability to account for social relations, at least among educational researchers, can be traced to the historical preference for actor-by-attribute data. This refers to the fact that many of the interesting social phenomena that have been examined by education researchers—say, whether a school administrator successfully implements a whole-school reform initiative—have been studied using a framework that removes the actor from its relational context. In this example, the actor is the administrator, who has a number of different attributes that make him or her more or less likely to be successful. These attributes may include one's personality, experience, competence, status, and so forth. This is what is meant by the term *actor-by-attribute*. But what missing from this picture are the relations that this administrator has with others who are critical in shaping how the reform plays out. With actor-by-attribute data, all you have is a set of independent actors, often treated as rows in a data file, who have certain attributes on a number of relevant characteristics, typically organized as columns in the data file. This is the "sociological meatgrinder" in action, removing the actor from his or her social context and assuming that the actor does not interact with anyone else in the study (Barton, 1968, as cited in Freeman, 2004).

Because the social network perspective emphasizes the importance of relational data, the way in which one approaches social network data is upended—the actor-by-attribute approach is conceptually and analytically inadequate. This is an issue discussed in Chapter 4, which focuses on the collection and management of social network data. The collection and management of these data, however, are premised on the idea that actors' characteristics arise out of structural or relational processes. This premise is established in Chapter 2, where the focus is on how the social network approach developed in a way that challenged the conventions that rigidly constrained researchers across the social sciences. Social network analysis and its earliest adherents took on the task of understanding properties of the social structural environment and how these properties influenced observed characteristics and associations among these characteristics. After all, life in and around schools is relational; it's only because, for example, high achievers and low achievers occupy particular kinds of patterns in a school's network in relation to each other that "achievement" becomes an important analytical focus.

RECENT ADVANCES IN SOCIAL NETWORK ANALYSIS

As the importance of relations becomes more widely recognized across the social sciences, the use of social network analysis has grown, especially among educational researchers, a point illustrated at the beginning of the following chapter. The reasons for this growth are varied and have their foundations in a number of advances made in disciplines and fields as diverse as computer science, mathematics, sociology, economics, and public health. These foundations are also discussed in Chapter 2, which presents a succinct review of the historical and theoretical foundations of social network analysis, giving special attention to the contributions of those who have studied educational phenomena through a variety of different disciplinary lenses. As this research has grown—and has become increasingly transdisciplinary— a number of noteworthy and significant research and development areas have been established. This section describes a sliver of theses areas in which social network analysis has made much progress. These recent advances have several implications for educational researchers interested in employing the social network perspective in their own work.

Visualization Techniques

The visualization of social networks has been a core practice since its foundation more than 90 years ago and remains a hallmark of contemporary social network analysis. These images of networks, both static snapshots as well as their evolution over time, are commonly created to develop structural insights and to clearly communicate these insights to others. The use of images to convey social network properties and dynamics experienced three periods of rapid innovation (Freeman, 2004). First is the hand-drawn sociograms developed by Jacob Moreno (1934) to represent relations among children in school. These early images paved the way for the computational approaches for plotting a graph's points and lines. This early history, discussed in more detail in Chapter 2, established the principle that the visualization of social networks communicates the spatial representations among actors and should depict pairs that are proximate in a data matrix as proximate in the image. That is to say, images of social networks should reflect the underlying data. The second phase of innovation moved beyond hand-drawn images and relied on mainframe computers and software to automatically produce graphs. This period throughout the 1960s formally integrated graph theoretic principles into the production of social network imagery. The third and most explosive phase, starting in the mid-1990s and continuing today, does not just produce static images of networks at one point in time but also allows networks to be visually represented as networks—and the actors and relations that constitute them— change over time. Made possible by computational speed, power, and convenience, the animation of both large and small social networks provides new insights into the dynamics that are often of interest to social scientists. A review of several popular network visualization applications as well as best practices in network visualization is provided in the book's final chapter.

Statistical Inference Using Network Measures

In addition to the recent advances made in the visual representations of social networks, there have been several critical developments made in the area of statistical inference of network measures. Most analyses of social networks are, in fact, descriptive (Knoke & Yang, 2008). These descriptive studies are able to make strong, empirically justified statements that demonstrate the static and dynamic properties that are at play within its boundary. These types of studies—and most social network studies fall in this category—aim either to represent the network's underlying social structure through data-reduction techniques or to characterize network properties through algebraic computations. Valente (2010) argues that perhaps the most significant development in social network analysis has been the development of exponential random graph modeling (ERGM), which is introduced in Chapter 9. Statisticians have developed the distributions behind network properties in a manner that has contributed to computer applications that permit the statistical testing of a network's dynamics and evolution. These advances have enabled social network analysis to move beyond description and toward inference: predictions about what will likely happen to a network over time. This set of developments is comparable to the advances more than 50 years ago in terms of understanding the logic of probability and its contribution to the field of inferential statistics. The advances spurred through the developments in ERGM are also introduced in the book's final section, with an emphasis on the p^* models and their ability to explain the presence of dyadic ties as a function of individual- and network-level explanatory factors.

Diffusion

In addition to advances in visualization techniques and statistical inference, both of which have implications for educational researchers, there are several research fronts on which much progress has been made. Diffusion is one of these areas in which researchers have made progress in identifying the structure and process through which attitudes and behaviors flow from actor to actor. Consider the following scenario in which networks play a key role in how an attitude spreads. There is a set of teachers whose relationships are described by a network, indicating who interacts with whom on a regular basis. Presume that any two teachers have a tie or not. Now, consider the introduction of a new student discipline policy. One teacher may enforce the policy if he or she interacts with another teacher who has also decided to enforce it. Also suppose that enforcement of this new policy occurs somewhat randomly, as the chance of interaction might be random and it also might take specific conditions for the enforcement of the policy to spread. Finally, also consider that the chance of any given teacher enforcing the policy increases with the number of others who enforce it. Under what conditions will enforcement of the policy spread to a nontrivial portion of the network? What percentage of teachers will ultimately enforce this policy? How does this depend on the network's structure and the individual's position in that structure as well as one's own individual attributes?

This problem is of obvious importance and relevance to a range of educational phenomena beyond this hypothetical example, including information transmission, opinion formation, reform implementation, participation in programs, and other behaviors. Cutting across studies in diffusion (also referred to as *contagion*) processes is the idea that one's adoption of an attitude or behavior is strongly influenced by the networks of which that person is a part. A more detailed chapter on diffusion theory and how it relates to educational phenomena can be found in the book's third and final section.

Learning

Another research front on which social network analysis has been applied is learning, which is very much connected to the ideas and models used to study diffusion processes. Educational research typically treats learning as an individual outcome, ignoring the messy relational processes through which you form an opinion or an understanding on a topic of interest. Social networks obviously play a central role in the sharing of information and formation of opinions. This is true in the context of one advising their peers on how to solve a math problem, relaying information about what is on the upcoming science exam, evaluating one's merits for inclusion in a peer group, or simply providing information about the location of a classroom. Networks play a key role in shaping opinions, beliefs, and understandings and ultimately in shaping behaviors. Therefore, it is important to have a thorough understanding of how network structure affects learning of all sorts (Jackson, 2008).

Some fundamental questions relevant to educational researchers concern how social networks influence:

- whether students come to hold a common belief about the school or remain divided in opinions;
- which teachers have the most influence over other teachers in the school;
- how quickly students learn; and
- whether understandings on course-related material scattered widely across the class can be aggregated in an accurate manner.

Various answers have been given to these questions, and the book's final section explores some of the basic models that have recently been developed in attempt to provide answers.

LEVELS OF ANALYSIS

Because relationships are the main focus of questions such as those noted earlier, as well as others that lend themselves to the social network perspective, these relationships must be captured in measurement and data collection. There are four distinct levels at which to measure and collect social network data, and this decision is made after you choose the sampling units and relations. Details about the selection of sampling units, relations, and appropriate measures and methods appear throughout the chapters in Part II, but here is a brief summary of the four analytic levels on which you may focus.

First is the egocentric network, which is the simplest level, consisting of one actor (ego) and all the other actors (alter) with which ego has direct relations, as well as the direct relations among those alters. This is referred to as ego's first-order contacts (e.g., friends), in contrast to second (e.g., friends of friends) and higher orders consisting of all the alters of ego's alters, and so forth (Knoke & Yang, 2008). Each ego actor can be described by the number, frequency, and other characteristics of its ties with its set of alters, for example, the density of the ties among its alters (the number of ties present divided the number of possible ties). For example, take a random sample from a population of interest—say, parents who belong to schools' parent–teacher associations—and then ask each (ego) to generate a list of names of other parents (alters) from whom they seek advice about school matters. Then, ask each ego about the nature of his or her relationship with each named alter (e.g., Is this parent's child in the same grade as yours?). You might also want the ego to provide characteristics of the each alter, including gender, age, race, and so forth. The analysis of such ego-level data can therefore focus on questions such as the tendency for parents to seek advice from those who are similar to themselves with respect to an attribute such as socio-economic status (homophily) or whether those egos with high levels of network closure have a better ability to monitor their children's behavior (social capital). This analytic level has elements of both attribute-based social science and relation-based social network analysis (Borgatti & Ofem, 2010). Because of these shared elements, egocentric network research designs are well suited to traditional surveys of respondents who are unlikely to have contact with one another (independence of observations). The 1985 General Social Survey was the first large-scale survey effort that include a battery of items that asked about an ego's alters. More recently, the Educational Longitudinal Survey of 2002, as well as its predecessor the National Educational Longitudinal Survey of 1988, also included a set of questions that asked respondents (egos) about their relations with alters as well as the attributes of those alters.

The next two levels of analysis shift the focus from the ego to the dyad and triad. First, a dyadic network consists of a pair of actors, and the most basic question about a dyad is whether a tie exists between any two actors, and, if so, what are its duration, strength, and frequency? Typical analyses at this level explain change in dyadic relations as a function of the dyad's characteristics, for example, whether friendships between pairs of students split upon transitioning to a new school. Second, triadic analysis focuses attention on groups of three actors. Pioneering work in social network analysis focused on this analytic level and was initially supported by Simmel's (1908/1950) contention that, from a sociological perspective, groups of three are much more interesting. For example, all possible combinations of present and absent ties among three actors generate a set of 16 distinct triad types. An elementary question for empirical social network analysis is the distribution of observed triads among the 16 types, a summary tabulation that is referred to as a triad census (Chapter 5). Research in these triadic structures has focused on sentiment (liking, friendship preferences, animosity), with a concentrated interest in balance and transitivity (i.e., if A likes B and B likes C, does A also like C?).

The fourth level is the one that resonates most closely with what you typically consider social network analysis. Moving beyond the three microlevels noted above, the complete (also referred to as *whole* or *full*) network level focuses on a set of actors and the ties among them in a bounded sample. Working at this level, you select a set of actors to serve as the population for study. Then a few types of ties are measured for each pair (dyad) in the population. For example, you might be interested in a school's teachers and, for each pair of teachers, determine whether they seek help from one another or whether they interact outside of school hours. In this approach, the population of actors reflects some type of group, whether that group is self-defined, such as a group of friends, or an externally defined group that shares some trait or common role, such as teachers in a school.

In general, this approach does not sample in the sense of drawing a random number of respondents from a large population. However, this approach does not necessarily result in a network that is connected (i.e., there is a path of ties from every actor to every other). Instead, what is likely to happen is that the network is split into components: groups of actors that are connected, but these groups are not connected to each other.

There are several strengths of working with complete network data. First, complete network data provide you with an opportunity to examine individual actors, groups of actors, or the entire network. The different constructs that you may measure at each of these levels are discussed in Chapters 5 and 6, which focus on the different ways in which network researchers measure important constructs such as centrality, connectivity, groups, and so on. A second strength of whole network data is that they can incorporate rich contextual information that can be used in subsequent analyses. So, in examining a whole network of teachers in one school, you may want to consider the context in which these relations are emerging, enduring, and receding, especially as the school year progresses and issues arise that trigger these relational changes. There are also several challenges when working with complete network data. The thorniest of these is missing data—the bane of any quantitative researcher. The ways in which social network analysts deal with this issue are discussed in Chapter 4.

It is important to keep in mind the theoretical and analytical distinction among these four different levels of analysis. This distinction will be made clear throughout the text. However, much of what will be presented focuses on the ego and complete levels, as most questions relevant to educational researchers are best addressed at these two analytical levels.

ORGANIZATION OF THE BOOK

This book is organized in a manner that is intended to introduce you to the social network perspective and how it may influence the way in which you approach the study of a range of educational phenomena. The book's organization flows from this objective. Chapter 2 reviews the theoretical and historical foundations of social network analysis, with an emphasis on its use as a powerful tool for empirically studying the dynamic and processual view of schooling that is central to educational theory (McFarland, Diehl, & Rawlings, 2011). Chapter 3 introduces the basic ways in which network data are represented, and the following chapter details how these data are collected, managed, and processed prior to analysis. Throughout both of these chapters, you will be introduced to a variety concepts and notation from graph theory and sociometry. Much care has been taken to gently guide you through these principles without letting oversimplification result in distortion. The mathematics in which this notation is employed comes into play in Chapters 5, 6, and 7, which address issues of what networks "look like" and how they "work." The book's remaining chapters integrate a number of the core issues and ideas that were introduced in the preceding four chapters. This final set of chapters demonstrates how social network analysis has been and can be used to study a variety of different processes that are of interest to educational researchers. The goal of this set of chapters is to provide you with a framework that can be employed in your own work in related research areas.

The progression of the text moves from simple to complex, so it is best to read this text from front to back. Also, given the complexity and richness of the material, I have kept the chapters as succinct as possible. This brevity is in recognition of a number of top-notch general social network analysis texts that go into this material in greater depth. You are encouraged to consult these materials; every effort has been made to direct you to these sources. The final set of chapters focuses intently on one substantive area of educational research that has been studied by numerous researchers using the social network perspective. Here, too, you are encouraged to consult the original sources for details about specific studies that may have been overlooked while trying to maintain the book's intent of serving as an introductory text.

DATA SETS

A small number of network data sets are used throughout the text to illustrate various concepts that are central to social network analysis. Background on each of these data sets is provided, especially the measurements on all relations and individual actor attributes. These data sets are varied but reflect the types of issues that may be of interest to educational researchers. In addition, these data sets are freely available through this book's online supplement and have even been used in a number of published research studies.

Newcomb's Fraternity Members

These "classic" data were originally collected by Theodore Newcomb (1961) from 1953 to 1956 and consist of 15 matrices that record weekly sociometric preference rankings from 17 men attending the University of Michigan in the fall of 1956; data from week 9 are missing. They are also available in UCINET (Borgatti, Freeman, & Everett, 2006), a popular general social network software package reviewed in Chapter 12. A 1 indicates first friendship preference, and no ties were allowed. The men were recruited to live in off-campus (fraternity) housing, rented for them as part of the Michigan Group Study Project supervised by Newcomb. All were incoming transfer students with no prior acquaintance with one another.

Pittinsky's Middle School Science Classroom Friendship Nominations

Collected from students in four middle school science classrooms taught by the same teacher at two points in the school year, these data (reported in Pittinsky & Carolan, 2008) provide opportunities to examine two interesting features of students' social networks. First, because network data were collected in the fall and spring, it provides an opportunity to examine how within-classroom friendship patterns change over time. Second, not only were students asked to nominate their friends, the teacher was also asked to rate who was friends with whom. This provides an opportunity to examine how well the teacher perceived friendship patterns among students and the degree to which this accuracy increased or decreased over time.

Daly's Network of District School Leaders

The third data set used throughout this text is Daly's Network of School District Leaders. Leadership network data were collected at two school districts over 3 consecutive years. For each consecutive year, school district leaders were invited to complete a survey that collected individual demographic information (e.g., gender, ethnicity, marital status, age, years of experiences), 11 different network relationships (e.g., collaboration, confidential, energy, expertise, support you approach, support approach you, work-related issues, input, recognition, best practices, and innovation), efficacy, and trusting relationships. The social network questions asked the participants to assess the frequency of interactions they have with those nominated individuals on a four-point frequency scale ranging from 1 (the least frequent) to 4 (1–2 times a week). The efficacy items were designed based on the Principal Efficacy Scale used in Daly and colleagues (2011) and Tschannen-Moran and Gareis's (2004) studies. The efficacy scale includes 18 items rated on a 9-point Likert scale ranging from 1 (None at all) to 9 (A great deal). The trust scale contains eight items rated on a 7-point Likert scale ranging from 1 (Strongly disagree) to 7 (Strongly agree) modified from Tschannen-Moran and Hoy (2003).

SUMMARY

The social network perspective introduced in this chapter provides a brief introduction to a number of concepts and applications to be discussed throughout the remainder of the text. While targeted toward aspiring and current educational researchers, as well as those who are charged with shaping educational policies and practices, this text will cover a range of research topics that are germane to the field of education. While these topics are diverse—peer influence, social capital, the diffusion of innovations, for example—they all share an emphasis on relations and how these relations can be conceptualized, measured, and analyzed without stripping the individual from the context in which those relations play out. The remainder of this book is dedicated to this focus. In particular, the remaining chapters of this book are dedicated to answering the following question: *How does an understanding of social networks help you make sense of educational opportunities and outcomes at the individual and aggregate levels?* This focus on the distribution of opportunities and outcomes has been a central focus of educational researchers for some time, yet, curiously, the theoretical and analytical tools that they have employed have neglected the relations among actors in context. The remaining chapters redress this shortcoming.

CRITICAL QUESTIONS TO ASK ABOUT THE SOCIAL NETWORK PERSPECTIVE AND ITS USE IN EDUCATIONAL RESEARCH

1. To what degree does the study emphasize one or more of the following: (1) individuals and their actions are viewed as interdependent; (2) relational ties between individuals are opportunities for transmission of resources; (3) the pattern of relations among individuals—the social structure—is an environment that can provide either opportunities for or constraints on individual action; and (4) social structure as an enduring pattern of relations among actors?

2. At which level are the social network data measured and collected: ego, dyad, triad, or complete?

3. What relations have been measured among actors? Why were these relations measured and others excluded?

1. Consider a network of which you are a part. Who are the network's actors? What ties connect these actors? Are there any groups within this network? What relations within this network might be of interest to a researcher? Finally, what makes this collection of actors a social network?

2. Draft a research question that would be of interest to educational researchers that would require the collection of relational data. What relational data would need to be collected? For what reason would relational data need to be collected in order to address this question?

3. Using the same question from the previous response, explain the analytical level at which these data would need to be collected and analyzed.

Borgatti, S. P., & Foster, P. (2003). The network paradigm in organizational research: A review and typology. *Journal of Management, 29*(6), 991–1013.

Daly, A. (2012). Data, dyads, and dynamics: Exploring data use and social networks in educational improvement. *Teachers College Record, 114*(11). Retrieved from http://www.tcrecord.org/content.asp?contentid=16811

Watts, D. J. (2004). The "new" science of networks. *Annual Review of Sociology, 30*, 243–270.

2

Historical, Theoretical, and Analytical Foundations

OBJECTIVES

This chapter provides a concise summary of the interdisciplinary origins of social network analysis, with a special nod to sociology. In addition to introducing you to an array of applications across the social and natural sciences, this chapter will articulate how social network analysis is a both a theory and a method whose potential is great for advancing knowledge of numerous educational phenomena. Finally, despite the recent popularity of social network analysis, this chapter will demonstrate that many of its core tenets were established decades ago by those working within and, more importantly, across a number of disciplines.

INTEREST IN SOCIAL NETWORK ANALYSIS

Public and scholarly interest in social network analysis has grown rapidly in the past 20 years, yet this interest still lags in educational research. The increasing number of applications of social network analysis across a wide range of phenomena has been documented by a number of studies, three of which are noteworthy. For example, Otte and Rousseau (2002) examined social network analytic articles published between 1984 and 1999, and from year to year they show that there has been an almost linear growth in the number of areas in which the social network approach has been applied. Borgatti and Foster

(2003) also report near-exponential growth in the last two decades in publications within the social sciences that use the words *social network(s)* in the title, keywords, or abstract.

However, this growth has not only been across substantive areas, it has also occurred within the broad field of educational research. Moolenaar (2010) reports a similar near-exponential trend when expanding the search terms to include both *social network(s)* and *education*. This growth is easily confirmed with a quick scan of the ERIC database, one of the biggest and most widely used databases that catalogues an array of print content related to educational research. In 1990, there were only six pieces of content that contained the words *social network(s)* in their title or abstract; in 2011, there were 41. Of course, these search strict parameters underreport the amount of content in educational research that relates to social networks, but the point is just the same: interest and applications in the areas of social network analysis and educational research have grown, particularly in the last 5 years. Figure 2.1 shows this trend, chronicling its growth in educational research between the years 1990 and 2011.

While this quick look at its use in educational research indicates that it has become more widely used—perhaps not as widely used as it is in other fields and

Figure 2.1   Publications in ERIC, 1990–2011, with the Term "Social Network" in Either the Title or Abstract. In 1990 there were only six pieces of content that contained the words "social network(s)" in their title or abstract; in 2011 there were 41.

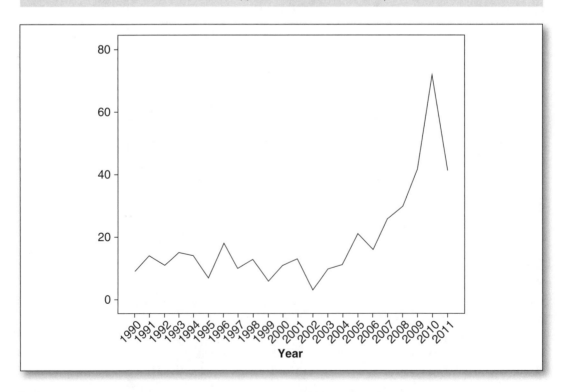

disciplines—this does not, however, indicate that its applications have fully appreci-ated the richness of the social network perspective or the strengths of its analytical approach. In short, the study of social networks has become a euphemism for the study of any group process—for example, teachers collaborating on a curricular inter-vention, school leaders trying to build a consensus for reform, or parents working together to shape school policy. While topics such as these are ripe for social network analysis, several studies that have examined these topics have done so under the label of social network analysis while not leveraging its analytical power and continue to treat actors as mere collections of attributes.

Regardless, this seemingly exponential increase in social network analysis applica-tions across substantive areas has contributed to its acceptance as a "normal" science, described by Kuhn (1962) as a deliberate approach that both identifies puzzles and solves them. Because a normal science is one that results from an ordered sequence of discoveries, it is also cumulative (Freeman, 2004). This cumulative growth is likely due in part to two distinguishing characteristics of the network perspective itself (Borgatti & Ofem, 2010). First, social network analysis is applicable to multiple levels of analysis. In educational research, this analytical lens can be applied to students, classrooms, schools, or districts. This makes it possible to study nearly any type of social system characterized by relations among actors. Second, social network analysis can combine the best aspects of qualitative, quantitative, and even graphical data, which allows for a richer description of social life that is both contextually grounded and empirically rigorous.

This interest has resulted from nearly 100 years of interdisciplinary research—strongly but not exclusively influenced by sociology—that has sought to better under-stand the order beneath the messiness of social life. While social network analysis is becoming an increasingly interdisciplinary endeavor, it was largely developed within sociology and anthropology (Wasserman & Faust, 1994). This is not a coincidence, as social network analysis, sociology, and anthropology share the goal of explaining important social phenomena in terms of how particular units (such as people) are embedded in interconnected systems (McFarland, Diehl, & Rawlings, 2011).

EARLY IDEAS AND PRACTICES

This growing interest in social network analysis is the byproduct of several different forces. As detailed by Freeman (2004), the evolution of social network analysis is a study of a social network in and of itself. Numerous others have reviewed the development of this perspective, both its theory and methods. However, it is worth noting the origins of social network analysis, as the story behind its development and evolution partially explains its current appeal and applicability.

While the intellectual underpinnings of social network analysis can be traced to sociological pioneers such as Comte, Durkheim, and Simmel, its modern applications can be traced to the work of Jacob Moreno in the 1930s. Both brilliant and quirky, Moreno himself is as responsible for the growth of social network analysis as he is for its eventual inability to influence the work of educational researchers.

As recounted by Freeman (2004), Moreno is credited coining the term *sociometry*, the graphical mapping of individuals' feelings about one another. In his most well known work, *Who Shall Survive?* (1934), he explicitly wrote about networks and the effects of two persons and the immediate group. This was demonstrated by showing that an epidemic of runaways at the Hudson School for Girls could be explained by the chains of social relations that connected all those who had left. The argument emanating from this insight was that the social relations among girls served as conduits though which ideas flowed. While the girls themselves may not have had an awareness of location in a social network, it was this very location that determined whether and when they ran away. This work established a defining tenet in social network analysis: Positions in social structure have consequences for the people occupying them.

This work, as well as subsequent collaborations with Jennings and Lazarsfeld published in his nascent journal, *Sociometry*, helped define the four distinguishing features of social network analysis. First, this work has strong structural intuitions—a focus on the embedded patterns of relations within and between groups. Second, it emphasized the systematic collection and analysis of empirical data. Third, this work included graphical imagery as part of its tools; and fourth, there was the use of explicit mathematical models, which helped induce the highest degree of objectivity possible. These are the same four features that continue to define the field (Freeman, 2004).

However, while growth of social network analysis owes much to his insights, he is also partly responsible for dissuading others from adopting and further developing this perspective (Freeman, 2004). By the middle of the 20th century, Moreno had become increasingly interested in therapeutic techniques, including group psychotherapy, psychodrama, and sociodrama, and moved further away from sociometric work. This shift drove early supporters away. In addition, he began to insist that what was then known as the sociometric paradigm had nothing to do with structural research but with strange links to God and psychotherapy. Researchers understandably began to question his entire body of work, and fewer and fewer people paid it any attention. The tentative links between sociology and sociometry faded completely shortly thereafter (Hare & Hare, 1996). So, while Moreno and his collaborators first developed the ideas and techniques of modern social network analysis, they were soon abandoned, and social research was left without a coherent structural approach that modeled actors and their relations in context.

THEORETICAL AND ANALYTICAL BREAKTHROUGHS

However, these ideas were not entirely abandoned, as pockets of researchers across disciplines and institutions continued to develop the paradigm that ultimately became known as social network analysis. Others have provided a comprehensive history of these developments (e.g., see Freeman, 2004, 2011; Scott, 2000). However, it is worth noting that this history is punctuated by several sets of studies that provided the theoretical backbone to structuralism that ultimately evolved into social network analysis.

W. Lloyd Warner and his colleagues at Harvard produced the first set of influential studies in the late 1920s that focused on the study of social structure. Two of these studies are especially noteworthy. The first of these is what became known as the "bank wiring room study," in which Warner and his colleague Elton Mayo explicitly focused on the formal and informal relations among workers at the Western Electric Corporation. Reported in detail by Roethlisberger and Dickson (1939), Warner and Mayo shifted the study from one that focused on the psychological study of individuals to one that stressed the patterning of informal ties among the workers. Data on interpersonal interactions were collected through systematic observation, with six different kinds of personal links measured, including who played games with whom, who traded jobs with whom, and who helped whom, among others. These data were then used to generate graphic images of the social ties among workers. Overall, this work was quite impressive and represented three of the core tenets of social network analysis, with the exception of sophisticated mathematical/computational tools.

The second line of research organized by Warner came to be known as the "Deep South" project, in which he and his team were concerned with the question and degree to which members of various social classes limited interaction to others at similar social class levels. Data were collected from 18 white women regarding which events they attended—an early example of a two-mode network—and were eventually analyzed to uncover who interacted with whom. The book that eventually emanated from his work, *Deep South* (Davis, Gardner, & Gardner, 1941), reflects the same emphasis on social structure that was present in all the work done by Warner's colleagues and students. Again, the only piece that was absent from this early work was an emphasis on mathematical/computational tools.

Both of these influential studies and their emphasis on social structure led to other work at Harvard that continued to shape the work of subsequent researchers. For example, George Homans's *The Human Group* (1950) put both an empirical and theoretical focus on the "chains of interaction" that shape group processes and dynamics. Here, he specifically developed his threefold classification, proposing that frequency, sentiment, and joint activity are all interrelated and how groups emerge and recede is a result of this interrelation. A second influential work that followed was William Whyte's *Street Corner Society* (1943), a rich ethnographic account of the interaction patterns in a community that vividly uncovers a community's social structure. These two examples are in line with the structural emphasis initiated by Warner and others at Harvard. In addition, they helped clarify what sociologists conceptualized as social groups. Still, however, the mathematical/computational tools that would eventually become critical to social network analysis and provide more precision to this conceptualization did not inform this work.

As the structuralist perspective was still in its infancy despite the advances made by these pioneering works, the mathematical modeling of social structure was just gaining traction (Freeman, 2004). This body of research, first at MIT in the 1940s and then more productively at the University of Michigan thereafter, helped develop the mathematical tools that would ultimately be used to represent and test the theories generated by the emerging structuralist perspective. One of these mathematical tools that provided a foundation for social network methods was graph theory. Sociometricians at Michigan, notably Harary and Cartwright, used graph theory to represent social networks and a set of key concepts to study their formal properties. For example, building on Katz and Powell's (1955) work on reciprocity—that is, two actors nominating each other on a given tie—Cartwright and Harary shifted to a focus on groups of three actors (triads) and Heider's (1946) balance theory. This focus included their effort to quantify structural balance propositions and, along with Davis (1967), discussed which types of triads should and should not arise in empirical research (Wasserman & Faust, 1994). This work mathematically formalized Heider's concepts, particularly the core idea that if two actors are friends, then they should have a similar sentiment to a third—that triad is therefore structurally balanced. Around the same time, another big mathematical push to study social networks was occurring at Columbia University. Centered on the work of Paul Lazarfeld and Robert Merton, their work made use of network data designed to produce mathematical representations of social life, notably their work on communication friendship formation (1954).

The mathematical modeling of social structure advanced significantly with the use of algebraic operations to study multirelational networks. Many of these advances can be attributed to Harrison White and his colleagues and students at Harvard who leveraged his background as a theoretical physicist to study social structure and processes and to represent them through algebraic tools. Freeman (2004) describes how many of these students, in fact, later became leaders in social network analysis: Philip Bonacich, Barry Wellman, Marc Granovetter, Ronald Breiger, and others.

Several insights from these nascent efforts highlight their immense influence on contemporary social network analysis. Most noteworthy among these is the development of CONCOR (for CONvergence of iterated CORrelations), which was an early computational attempt to partition actors into positions based on the concept of structural equivalence (this technique is demonstrated in Chapter 5). Structural equivalence, introduced and defined by Lorrain and White (1971), is a mathematical property of subsets of actors in a network. Two actors are structurally equivalent if they have identical ties to and from all other actors in the network. For example, actors A and B are structurally equivalent if both have ties to actor E and both have ties from actors C and D. That is, actors A and B occupy the same position. CONCOR, introduced by White's protégés Breiger, Boorman, and Arabie (1975), was an early effort to apply algebraic properties through computation in order to reveal a network's positions. While more flexible and efficient approaches have been developed in the years since, this approach was used extensively in network research in many fields (e.g., Friedkin, 1984; Knoke & Rogers, 1979). In addition, it should be noted that other programs (e.g., BLOCKER, STRUCTURE, and NEGOPY) that sought to identify actors occupying similar structural positions in a network were also developed around the same time.

While the development of CONCOR represented a major advance in network analysis, White and his colleagues also made further progress in the positional analysis of social networks. One of these advances included the pioneering use of blockmodels to represent network positional systems. Introduced by White, Boorman, and Breiger (1976), blockmodels consist of two components (Wasserman & Faust, 1994): (1) a partition of actors into positions and (2) for each pair of positions, a statement of whether a tie is present within or between positions on each relation. What was critical about this work was that it moved beyond simply identifying positions through structural equivalence and more toward theoretically meaningful statements about positions, the characteristics of actors in those positions, and, most critically, how those positions relate to each other.

Freeman (2004) correctly notes that the biggest contribution from White and his colleagues and students is that they directly confronted the reductionism of the positivists—the tendency to "reduce" individual actors to a collection of attributes removed from context—and the grand theories preferred by the natural and physical sciences. For example, when studying a topic such as teacher effectiveness, most researchers focus on the attributes of the teacher, the teacher's highest degree, use of technology, or test scores of students, for example. By reducing teachers to a set of attributes, positivists neglect the relations among teachers and between teachers and students and how these relations condition their effectiveness as a teacher. In paying attention to those relations, the advances by White and others provided the theoretical and methodological backbone to what was then recognized as structuralism. This view accounted for the web of relations—the social structure—in which actors are embedded that simultaneously constrain and provide opportunities for action. This work became intensely focused on an actor's environment, conceptualized as consisting of other actors and the relationships among them (e.g., collaboration among teachers and supervisory relations between principals and teachers). This focus became the distinguishing feature of what came to be known as social network analysis.

By the end of the 1970s, this theoretical and empirical work was so important that it became impossible for others, regardless of their field, to ignore the idea. This point is reflected in the increase in publications across the social sciences that referenced "social network analysis." This pioneering work was the clearest reflection of the four hallmarks of social network analysis: emphasis on structuralism based on ties among actors, firmly grounded in empirical data, made use of graphical imagery, and was mathematically based. It is not an understatement to conclude that as a result of this work, social network analysis came to be universally viewed as a legitimate set of tools among social scientists.

COMPUTATION AND LARGE-SCALE NETWORKS

Following these advances in theory and modeling were a number of computational advances, without which Wolfe (1978) argues the field of social network analysis could not have developed further. These computational advances ultimately contributed to the analysis of large networks—those with literally thousands or even millions of social units, or even units that were not entirely social in the conventional sense (e.g., Web pages, phone numbers). While early computational tools were concerned with groups, positions, and other related structural properties, a number of other tools sought to provide an integrated suite of network analysis tools, including STRUCTURE, GRADAP, SONIS, and UCINET. The latter is by far the most popular and user friendly and, consequently, has made the biggest difference in the analysis of social networks, especially for those with modest training in mathematics.

While technologies have certainly made the analysis of networks easier and more efficient, there is still a lingering doubt among researchers and the public at large as to whether network analysis yields any novel theoretical insights or simply provides a "new" and flashy way to model the behaviors and attitudes of actors. This doubt has existed in one form or another since its advent.

BARRIERS TO ITS ADOPTION IN EDUCATIONAL RESEARCH

While disciplines and fields across the social sciences adopted and refined the structuralist perspective, its influence in educational research was minimal. While its influence on educational research has certainly grown in recent years, this growth is not at all proportional to the growth exhibited by proximate social scientific disciplines and fields. Why is social network analysis not used as often in educational research as it is used in these other areas?

There are three factors that have muted its influence over the years. The first among these is the dominance, at least in quantitative empirical work, of a psychological orientation to the study of educational processes and outcomes. With a narrow focus on constructs such as learning, psychology's disciplinary focus on individual explanations lent itself to experimental methods that stripped actors from context. For example, the research literature on motivation, especially drawn from the behaviorist tradition, is populated by studies that treat this construct as something that is rooted within the individual. While recognizing the importance of experimental designs that informed this work, this preference shunned the rich contextual description that was a hallmark of early social network analysis. More recently, the U.S. Department of Education's Institute for Education Sciences went so far as to refer to these experimental designs, long preferred by psychology, as the "gold standard" of scientific research (Barnhouse-Walters,

Lareau, & Ranis, 2009). It is difficult to dispute the strengths of these designs, particularly their ability to identify causal effects but these designs have limits when it comes to intentionally manipulating actual social networks under experimental conditions. How can you randomly assign actors to social groups and control for all relevant contextual factors that shape group dynamics? Such designs are perhaps possible but very challenging and maybe even undesirable to execute in the real world of research. It should be noted, however, that there are examples of social network analysis done through experimental designs (see e.g., Corten & Buskens, 2010; Kosfeld, 2004).

Related to this is the seemingly never-ending quest for educational researchers and their work to be considered legitimate. The best way to achieve this legitimacy has been to adopt the pretenses associated with science. For example, the logic of statistical inference and its associated analytical tools were widely employed in an effort to be on equal footing with peers in other social and physical sciences. When not employing experimental designs, generations of educational researchers were—and are still—trained to collect random samples drawn from target populations. These survey methods further removed the actor from context, asking questions about behaviors and attitudes that did not account for the behaviors and attitudes of those with whom they interacted. Because these survey methods relied on responses drawn from random samples, inferences to larger populations could be made. Researchers trained through schools of education adopted these techniques and solidified the importance of randomization and inferential statistics. A quick look at the quantitative research sequence that students take in just about any graduate program in educational research will most likely emphasize these two areas. Because of this, very few educational researchers were trained in linear algebra or matrix manipulation, the mathematics that are necessary to understand the logic of social network analysis. Educational research, at least the research that was most valued by its external constituencies, became a field populated by studies in which actors were removed from their social contexts. For example, rather than being concerned with who studied with whom and how these patterns conditioned one's motivation, educational research focused, rather, on issues such as predicting one's motivation from a set of individual attributes. These different foci are critical to understanding how this shift requires an entirely different way of thinking about educational research. This different way requires a shift in thinking of actors as independent entities, but rather actors who are dependent on others and shaped by context in which they are being examined.

The dominance of psychological explanations of education phenomena and the methods used to study these phenomena (experiments and population surveys drawn from random samples) were aided by the ascendance of popular computer statistical packages such as SAS and SPSS. Such packages allowed educational researchers to further shroud themselves as "scientists." These packages, still widely used to train educational researchers, assist in the rapid calculation of population estimates from randomly—and not-so-randomly—selected samples of respondents. By relying on such packages, accuracy in predicting measures of students' engagement, for example, became more important than understanding how one's location in a social structure influenced those levels of engagement. Regression became the tool of choice and is still the workhorse of most quantitative educational research. Complex models predicting whether there was a significant relationship among variables could be run in a matter of seconds. Educational research became an industry that studied actors, students and teachers alike, using Likert scales that relied on self-reports of behaviors and attitudes. Seemingly all educational research done in this vein consisted of collecting measurements on variables from a random sample of respondents, with little to no thought given to the context in which these behaviors and attitudes emerge and recede. The software applications used to do this type of work reflected the permanence of this paradigm by arranging the data in a tabular format that treated actors (rows) as collections of attributes (columns); hence the term *actor-by-attribute* data.

While these trends were certainly influential in limiting the adoption of social network analysis in education, there was another sentiment that has percolated within and around the educational research community for some time. This sentiment revolves around questions regarding the quality and relevance of educational research (Barnhouse-Walters, Lareau, & Ranis, 2009). This, in part, explains the mad rush for legitimacy that spasms every so often among educational researchers and the institutions that prepare them. It also explains why a portion of the educational research community strongly clings to the experimental and random survey designs that constitute much of the work that has any real import outside of the educational research community. But it is not just concerns about its quality and relevance, it is the historical preference to employ qualitative designs that has limited the adoption of formal social network analytic techniques. There are a number of reasons why educational research has leaned toward these designs, but this preference has indeed hindered the adoption of social network analysis, which on some level provides a nice balance between the rigor of quantitative designs and the rich contextual descriptions inherent to qualitative designs.

In sum, the use of social network analysis in educational research was slowed by an overemphasis on individual explanations of educational opportunities and outcomes, a quest for scientific legitimacy, and a preference for experimental designs that estimate the causal effects of educational "interventions."

THE INTEGRATION OF THEORY AND METHOD

Mische (2011) notes that one of the debates surrounding social network analysis has been whether it consists of a method or a theory. Is network analysis simply a set of techniques for analyzing the structure of social relationships, or does it make up some bigger conceptual framework, theoretical orientation, or even worldview? In an article over two decades ago synthesizing emerging work on social networks, Wellman (1988) argued that network analysis goes beyond methodology to inform a new theoretical paradigm: "structural analysis does not derive its power from the partial application of this concept or that measure. It is a comprehensive paradigmatic way of taking social structure seriously by studying directly how patterns of ties allocate resources in a social system" (p. 20).

From its earliest origins to it most recent applications to large-scale networks, social network analysis has reflected this interdependency between theory and method. This interdependency was made most evident in the advances made by White and his collaborators. It is a theory rooted in relational realism, one of the four main ontologies—explanations for how things come into being—identified by Tilly (2004). First among these is phenomenological individualism, the doctrine that individual consciousness is the primary or exclusive site of social life. Second, methodological individualism is the doctrine that assumes human individuals are the basic unit of social reality but models them within consciousness (economic historians). Third, holism is the doctrine that social structures have their own self-sustaining logics. Fourth, relational realism is the doctrine that interactions and social ties constitute the central existence of social life. Tilly writes that relational realism is best equipped to overcoming the micro/macro gap in analysis because relationships simultaneously form organizational structures and shape individual behavior. It is this fourth one that most closely mirrors the intuitions that support social network analysis and most closely reflects its mid-range theories advanced by White and others.

Employed by Tilly to explain the emergence and resilience of patterned inequality, as well as an array of other social phenomena, relational realism (interchangeably referred to as *transactionalism*) offers you a lens through which the elemental unit of social life is the social relation—a repeated interaction between two or more actors. This confronts the methodological individualism inherent in most social science, emphasizing as it does the dispositions, motives, and calculations of individual social actors. Relational realism, as described by Tilly, also rejects the quest for governing laws to explain large social processes ranging from war, revolution, urbanization, and class formation to the formation of nation-states. Instead, Tilly advocated a careful analysis of social relations, empirical examination of the chains of connections linking persons through time and space in larger compounds of relations. Consider, then, how this approach would view a process such as "school reform."

Relational Perspective

Mische (2011) goes on to note that a broader "relational perspective" within sociology and other social science disciplines has been simmering for the past three decades, often involving scholars who themselves do not use formal network methodology or who use it only marginally in their research. Inspired by such eminent figures as

Harrison White and Tilly, this perspective has taken some of the broader theoretical insights of network analysis and extended them to the realms of history, politics, economics, and social psychology, each of them important disciplines that influence empirical research in education. Fundamental to this theoretical orientation (if it can be called that) is not merely the insistence that what sociologists call "structure" is intrinsically relational, but also, perhaps more deeply, that relational thinking is a way to overcome stale, false dichotomy between structure and agency through a focus on the dynamics of social interactions in different kinds of social settings.

This relational perspective is evident in a number of studies involving educational phenomena. A noteworthy example is McFarland's (2001) exemplary study on student resistance, which clearly represents the relational realism that Tilly employed in his myriad studies of social change. McFarland asks a question that many teachers likely ask themselves numerous times throughout the school day: Why do students defy me? Most explanations in response to this question, especially those offered by critical and resistance theorists, have focused on students' race and class backgrounds (e.g., Ogbu, 1997; Willis, 1977). That is, these explanations focus on attributes that one student may have in common with another and how collections of students who share these attributes are then socially disaffected. While not suggesting that these characteristics are unimportant, McFarland convincingly argues that this is only part of the story. Operating from a relational perspective, McFarland expands his lens to include the informal organization of the classroom, which determines which students have the greatest political opportunities, or rights to discourse, that enable them to use the available social opportunities that task structures define. Social relations and positions define who is most capable of taking advantage of social opportunities created by task structures. Friendship relations serve as networks of local support. Examining 36 classes in two schools over the course of 1 year, McFarland's analysis, which includes a number of student-level social network measures, reveals that students' background characteristics only partly influence students' decision to defy. Students' friendship networks play an important role; the main story is that classroom social networks and instructional formats explain a great deal more about everyday acts of defiance than do background characteristics alone. This example demonstrates that social network analysis represents a shift in the way in which social science, and most educational research for that matter, views how things (e.g., student defiance) come into being and how they work in certain contexts (e.g., classrooms). In addition, this work reflects the four tenets of social network analysis mentioned earlier.

Key Assumptions

Examples of studies that employ social network analysis are also predicated on three assumptions about patterned relations and their effects (Knoke & Yang, 2008).

The first assumption is that social relations are often more important for understanding behaviors and attitudes than are such attributes related to one's background (e.g., age, gender, etc.). For example, in explaining differences in the success of a school-reform intervention, Atteberry and Bryk (2011) emphasize the importance of the density of social relations within a school and the position of key social actors prior to the implementation of the intervention. These structural relations—unlike "fixed" attributes such as gender, race, and age that do not vary in different contexts—exist only at a specific time–place and either disappear or recede when actors are elsewhere. For example, a relation between a literacy coach and a teacher does not exist outside a school setting; likewise, a professional relation between the first- and second-grade teachers does not exist outside that setting. A teacher who does not look forward to going to work and displays no enthusiasm for the job may be a dynamic head of household and committed member of a local governing body. Such behavioral differences are difficult to reconcile with unchanging attributes such as gender, race, and age. After all, these attributes do not change as the teacher moves from one role to the other in the course of her or his day. Actors' relations vary significantly across contexts. The structuralist perspective pioneered by White and refined by Tilly and the development of relational realism sharply contrasts with numerous reductionist approaches that are premised on individual "objects" as the unit of analysis. By positing, and with good reason, that patterns of relations condition social actors apart from their attributes, social network analysis offers a deeper and broader theoretical and empirical explanation for an array of educational opportunities and outcomes.

A second assumption inherent to social network analysis also reflects the integration of theory and method that is a defining characteristic of social network analysis. This second assumption is that social networks affect beliefs, perceptions, and behaviors through a variety of structural mechanisms that are socially constructed by relations among actors (Knoke & Yang, 2008). This assumption motivates a wide array of studies in social networks. For example, social network analysts have focused on the importance of indirect relations brokered by intermediaries, which leads to valuable information for job seekers (Granovetter, 1973), or early access to diverse streams of information for competitive advantage (Burt, 2004). Relations that can be described as either competitive or cooperative influence mobilization efforts for collective action (Sampson, McAdam, MacIndoe, & Weffer, 2005) and maintaining shadow networks for terrorists (Moody, 2006) or drug traffickers (Natarajan, 2000). This assumption encourages social network researchers to uncover the theoretical mechanisms through which relations affect actors and to identify the conditions under which these mechanisms operate in specific contexts. In addition, it also places analytic importance on these relations.

The third assumption extends the idea that social network analysis is a perspective that integrates theory and method. This assumption is that relations are not static but rather occur as part of a dynamic process that is not adequately explained by conventional social theory, nor do the methods most often used by social scientists capture these dynamics. Relations are continually changing as actors interact with others in shifting contexts. In applying an understanding about networks to leverage advantages, actors such as teachers also intentionally or unintentionally transform the relational structures within which they are embedded. For example, Atteberry & Bryk (2010) show how the communication patterns between teachers and the their school's literacy coach affected the successful implementation of a school-level reform initiative. These relations, in turn, altered the flow of information among teachers and created further opportunities or constraints on future interactions and whether the intervention was ultimately a success. These dynamics, as Knoke and Yang (2008) note, reflect the more general micro-to-macro problem in the theory of social interaction (Coleman, 1986). Because social network analysis encompasses both social structure and individuals' agency, it provides the conceptual and methodological tools for linking behaviors at the actor level to larger embedded patterns at the macro level. This third assumption, then, is a direct offshoot of the relational realism advanced by Tilly.

RECONSIDERING THE QUALITATIVE/QUANTITATIVE DISTINCTION

Social network analysis has evolved in a way that marries both theory and method, what Marin and Wellman (2011) refer to as the "social network perspective." But, while it includes elements of both qualitative and quantitative designs, as evidenced by McFarland's (2001) ethnography, questions linger as to whether it is more closely aligned with one than the other. Unfortunately, this divide still polarizes the field of educational research and shapes students' preparatory experiences as they become researchers themselves. It is indisputable that contemporary social network analysis relies extensively on linear algebra and matrix manipulation. After all, one of its distinguishing features is the use of mathematical models to objectively reflect social life. But this does not necessarily mean that it is exclusively quantitative in nature. So what is it?

Subsequent chapters introduce the quantitative techniques that examine the statistical relationships among network and attribute data. While this is an inescapable feature of most contemporary social network analysis, it is critical to recall that actors—students, teachers, schools, and so on—are concrete and observable, or groups of observable actors, such as those occupying the same position or social group. The relations that are of interest from the perspective of social network analysis are usually in the first instance social, cohering together or differentiating concrete entities, rather than simple statistical units (Breiger, 2004). Social network theorists and analysts go as far as to recognize that the inductive modeling strategies of social network analyses—that is, generating big ideas from small observations—are in opposition to the usual canonical assumptions of statistical methods, which prefer a deductive logic that operates from ideas to observations (Levine, 1999).

Undoubtedly, a great deal of progress has been made in the statistical analysis of social networks, including a number of important contributions to the general linear model that take into account the nonindependence among observations and the presence of clear patterns of dependence. These inferential models are introduced in Chapter 8. Nonetheless, social network analysis is difficult to categorize as an empirical strategy that is more quantitative than qualitative. This suggests that it is highly distinctive research perspective that cuts across a number of disciplinary boundaries and traditions (Breiger, 2004).

Because progress has been made in the statistical and substantive analysis of social networks, this has further blurred the line between qualitative and quantitative approaches to data analysis. Typically, social network analysis is a case study, bounded by both time and space. Important contributions to data analysis have combined rich ethnographic work and field observation with application of network algorithms. McFarland's (2001) earlier-referenced work is a great example of this. Therefore, contemporary social network analysis muddles the traditional divide between qualitative and quantitative strategies and includes a mix of strategies, including statistical, algebraic, discursive, and cultural. These diverse strategies require social network analysts to expand their range of theoretical and analytical tools to compensate for the ways in which traditional graduate preparatory experiences fall short.

EDUCATIONAL APPLICATIONS

Social network analysis provides a powerful alternative methodology for studying educational phenomena, but until recently, its ability to fulfill this goal has been severely limited by a number of factors, including computational and statistical power, and the mismatch between classical theory's description of social reality and the ways in which this reality has been empirically studied (McFarland, Diehl, & Rawlings, 2011). What follows is a small sample of areas relevant to educational researchers that have benefitted from the theoretical and methodological advances made by social network analysis. The relational perspective that has matured in concert with the methodological techniques associated with social network analysis has driven these advances.

Social Capital

One area that reflects this relational perspective and has provided much fodder for research in a number of different contexts is social capital. While this theory has been developed and tested in a wide range of contexts, a number of theoretical insights have been derived from work in educational settings. For example, a common assertion in education reform is that you need to create school environments with stronger community in which people are "better connected." This connectedness is viewed as an asset that improves performance by facilitating coordination, trust, and the spread of information—a notion often referred to as social capital (Bourdieu & Wacquant, 1992; Coleman, 1990; Putnam, 2000). Unfortunately, the rhetoric and research pertaining to social capital in schools can easily fall near one of two ends of a spectrum.

On one hand, education reformers are apt to discuss connectedness or social capital in metaphorical terms that, although rooted in the wisdom of clinical experience, often leave underspecified the mechanisms through which social structure impacts student performance. On the other hand, researchers trying to measure the impact of social capital in schools often reduce social relations to a set of variables that capture the properties emerging from interpersonal interactions within a social structure but do not necessarily capture the features of that social structure itself. Consequently, though such studies are very valuable in revealing the association between properties such as perceptions of trust, collegiality, adherence to norms, availability of information and support, and educational outcomes of interest. They usually stop short of attempting to unravel the relational mechanisms responsible for the associations.

However, by providing a way to frame, map, and quantify the relations between people, the social network perspective helps bridge the gap between the mechanisms implicit in reformers' arguments and the empirical rigor required by researchers to draw valid inferences. Through the social network perspective, two different mechanisms have been identified as generating social capital. First is the social closure hypothesis, first identified by Coleman to explain differences in academic achievement between Catholic and public schools. Second is the structural holes hypothesis (Burt, 2004), which contends that those actors occupying bridging roles between distinct groups possess a number of advantages, including early access to information and control over how information flows between distinct parts of the network.

Regardless of the mechanism that you believe is more responsible for the accrual of social capital, the larger point is that this theory is a byproduct of the relational perspective that has emerged over the past three decades of social scientific research. It also provides a much-needed theoretical lens through which empirical reality can be more properly evaluated. This relational perspective has also propelled theoretical developments in other areas that are relevant to educational researchers.

Diffusion

A second area in which educational research has generated theoretical insights through social network analysis is the area of diffusion, particularly how innovations spread through and across organizations such as schools. It is also evident that relational realism has influenced the content and direction of studies within this broad topical area. While the study of diffusion processes—that is, how ideas, attitudes, and behaviors spread from one actor to another—has a long, impressive history (see e.g., Valente, 2005), recent work in and around schools by a number of researchers has contributed to this body of knowledge.

Three studies are noteworthy, all of which focus on the importance of one's network position in shaping diffusion processes and outcomes. First, Frank, Zhao, and Borman (2004) study the way in which the adoption of computer technology in six schools was influenced by one's access to expertise through talk and help. Another example is Coburn, Choi, and Mata's (2010) ethnography that reveals the organizational features of schools that either encourage or inhibit the flow of information across teachers. A third example that focuses on diffusion in schools is Penuel, Frank, and Krause's (2010) study on the critical roles of informal and formal school leaders in advancing reform goals.

Peer Influence

A third area in which social network analysis has contributed to insights that have significant implications for educational researchers is in the modeling of peer influence (also referred to as social influence). There is an expansive literature on social networks and peer influence (e.g., Friedkin, 1998; Friedkin & Johnsen, 2011), which has informed studies ranging from the formation of teachers' attitudes toward reforms (Cole & Weinbaum, 2010) to how the characteristics of friends shape high school students' aspirations and college attendance (Hallinan & Williams, 1990). Building from normative and comparative reference group theory and role theory, this strand of network-based research has sought to explicate the specific mechanisms through which individuals become vulnerable to influence or are able to exert influence on others. Moreover, it has focused on the conditions under which these processes play out. This area of research has much to offer, particularly in regard to how individual student outcomes are shaped by a variety of influences related to the smaller groups with which they are affiliated. For example, the interactions and shared experiences of two students who are assigned to the same academic track increases the likelihood that they will become friends. Since stronger friendships imply greater vulnerability to influence, students are likely influenced more by friends who are in the same track than by those in different tracks (Hallinan & Sorenson, 1985). Such social influences have obvious consequences for individual student outcomes.

These three research areas represent a small sample of the possible areas in which you can use the social network perspective to further advance ideas that cut across the social sciences and be applied to social phenomena in and around schools. However, more broadly speaking, social network analysis can also propel the entire field of educational research in a more productive direction that will ultimately add insights not only to these three areas but also to a number of other areas that are relevant to educational researchers, including trust, culture, and authority.

HOW CAN SOCIAL NETWORK ANALYSIS FURTHER ADVANCE EDUCATIONAL RESEARCH?

There are three potential ways in which social network analysis can advance educational research (for an earlier treatment on this topic, see Frank, 1998). But it can also help the field move past the qualitative/quantitative divide and the methodological individualism and its empirical assumptions of normality and independence that are at odds with classical social scientific theory's description of social life (McFarland, Deihl, & Rawlings, 2011). Undoubtedly, social network analysis will continue to make advances in the areas of social capital and diffusion, especially as they pertain to educational contexts. But there are three broader ways in which social network analysis can further advance the quality, range, and relevance of social science research in general and, more specifically, educational research.

The first potential contribution of social network analysis is its ability to close the gap between sociological theory and empirical reality (McFarland, Deihl, & Rawlings, 2011). As noted earlier, there has always existed a divide between the discipline's theoretically informed vision about the nature of social process and the ability to capture them empirically. For example, some have pointed out that techniques such as general linear modeling distort social scientists' view of the world (Abbott, 1988), and there is a long history of researchers cautioning that many of the basic assumptions of common methods, such as independence and normality, are contrary to classical theory's description of social reality (Emirbayer, 1997; Martin, 2003). Methods such as hierarchical linear modeling (Bryk & Raudenbush, 1992) were originally designed precisely to help close this gap between theory and empirical reality. By allowing variance to be measured at multiple levels, hierarchical linear modeling presents a method more in line with our understanding of the nested relationships of students, classrooms, and schools. By challenging firmly established paradigms and procedures and providing an opportunity to model educational phenomena in ways that better represent the intersection between theory and empirical reality, social network analysis represents another viable alternative to studying social phenomena in and around schools.

In addition to closing the gap between theory and empirical reality, social network analysis can further advance educational research, as there have been numerous statistical breakthroughs and substantial increases in computing power that have allowed for the development of progressively more sophisticated techniques (McFarland, Deihl, & Rawlings, 2011). For example, social network analysis and its related models can now handle millions of actors, and new methods for dynamic and temporal features of networks continue to be at the forefront of the field (e.g., Boyack, Börner, & Klavens, 2009). Much of what social network analysis offers educational researchers, then, is a better means for capturing these complex interdependencies and fluid dynamics than many current and more popular methods are able to.

Finally, social network analysis has the capability to help refine the field's varied theoretical lenses in questions in light of social change (McFarland, Deihl, & Rawlings, 2011).

As statistical tools become more sophisticated and their explanatory power more obvious, they come to be applied to an increasing number of topics. This, in turn, brings about new questions, again often requiring the development of even more advanced tools in order to find answers. It is through these iterations that social network analysis helps educational researchers refine and reconceptualize the very understanding of the social phenomena in which they are interested. You can see this happening within education as many emerging lines of research focus on network aspects of educational and schooling processes. For example, social network analysis and its underpinnings in relational realism have helped reframe teaching and learning by focusing attention on the role of trust (Bryk & Schneider, 2002), relations among teachers (Coburn & Russell, 2008), and the relationship between social capital and student outcomes (Carolan, 2010).

For each of these three reasons—the ability to close the gap between theory and empirical reality, the capacity to deal with complex new forms and amounts of data, and the capability to help refine one's theoretical lenses in questions in light of social change—social network analysis is poised to become an increasingly central set of tools on which educational researchers can draw and, in turn, bring about a paradigm shift from methodological individualism to relational realism.

ETHICS AND SOCIAL NETWORK ANALYSIS

This shift, however, will likely continue to test the ethical boundaries that strictly guide educational research. These ethical issues are both straightforward and complex (Kadushin, 2005). In standard-practice social science research, anonymity or confidentiality are both routinely granted to respondents, informants, and participants in experiments and observations. However, this is problematic in social network analysis in which the respondent not only has to identify him- or herself but also those with whom he or she has ties. Therefore, in conducting social network analysis, it is crucial to do no harm to the participants by (1) emphasizing the voluntary nature of the data collection; (2) disclosing how the data will be used; and (3) disguising the data to maintain confidentiality (Daly, 2010). As the field is relatively new and often misunderstood by members of institutional review boards, further ethical concerns will surface and need to be addressed.

SUMMARY

This chapter provided a brief review of the historical and theoretical foundations of social network analysis. These foundations cut across a number of social scientific disciplines but are firmly grounded in sociology and its emphasis on the importance of relations among actors' bounded social structures (hence the early reference to "structuralists"). The maturation of social network analysis as both theory and method has resulted in a begrudging acceptance that most social science research, especially in a diverse field such as education, needs to conceptually and analytically account for the nonindependence of observations.

CRITICAL QUESTIONS TO ASK ABOUT THE HISTORICAL, THEORETICAL, AND ANALYTICAL FOUNDATIONS OF SOCIAL NETWORK ANALYSIS

1. Before conducting your own social network study, ask whether social relations are critically important for understanding the outcomes in which you are interested. Also, evaluate whether social networks affect beliefs, perceptions, and behaviors through a variety of structural mechanisms that are social constructed by relations among actors. Finally, how will your study exhibit an integration of theory and method?

2. What is the relational perspective and how does it offer a different perspective for educational researchers?

3. How does social network analysis challenge educational researchers who view themselves as more quantitatively or qualitatively oriented?

CHAPTER FOLLOW-UP

1. Search the ERIC database for a peer-reviewed article that has the words *social network(s)* in its title or abstract. Using this article, explain how and to what degree the study reflects the four hallmarks of social network analysis: emphasis on structuralism based on ties among actors, firmly grounded in empirical data, use of graphical imagery, and mathematically based.

2. Using the same article from the question above, describe the study's ability to straddle qualitative and quantitative paradigms.

3. Finally, evaluate how the use of the social network analysis in this same article bridges the gap between sociological theory and empirical reality.

ESSENTIAL READING

Borgatti, S. P., & Molina, J. L. (2005). Toward ethical guidelines for network research in organizations. *Social Networks, 27*(2), 107–117.

McFarland, D. A. (2001). Student resistance: How the formal and informal organization of classrooms facilitate everyday forms of student defiance. *American Journal of Sociology, 107*(3), 612–678.

Tilly, C. (2004). Observations of social processes and their formal representations. *Sociological Theory, 22,* 595–602.

3

Basic Concepts

OBJECTIVES

Building on the introductory concepts briefly noted in Chapter 1 as well as the theoretical and methodological breakthroughs summarized in Chapter 2, this chapter reviews the basic means through which network data and their characteristics at either the ego or complete network level are represented. As such, this chapter provides you with an overview of the foundational concepts that are required building blocks for subsequent chapters. Using a number of graphs and matrices, this chapter emphasizes how network data differ from traditional social science actor-by-attribute data while also sharing some similarities. Because others have covered this material extensively in more comprehensive texts, the emphasis is on directing you to these other sources. To illustrate these basic concepts and provide you with opportunities to work with these concepts, this chapter focuses on one network data set: Pittinsky's Middle School Science Classroom Friendship Nominations (referred to as the "Peer Groups" data set).

REVISITING KEY ASSUMPTIONS

Recall that Freeman's (2004) four hallmarks of contemporary social network analysis include: (1) an emphasis on structuralism based on ties among actors; (2) firmly grounded in empirical data; (3) the use of graphical imagery; and (4) is mathematically based. This chapter incorporates all four of these features by introducing the ways in which graph theory and sociometry are used to mathematically and visually represent the ties among actors that are embedded in an empirical context. The distinctions between these mathematical tools have blurred as computers have assumed a bulk of the analytical responsibilities. The reason for preferencing sociometric over graph theoretic notation will become more evident as the chapter progresses, but suffice it to say that it is the easiest, and perhaps oldest, way to denote properties of social networks.

Regardless of how networks are represented, the collection and analysis of social network data is predicated on three assumptions offered by Knoke and Yang (2008) and noted in the preceding chapter. First, relations are critically important when attempting to explain one's behaviors or attitudes. Second, social networks affect one's behaviors and attitudes through a variety of direct and indirect contacts. Third, relations within and between networks are dynamic. Keeping these three assumptions in mind, this chapter provides an introduction to how the core concepts of social network analysis can be represented and how these representations allow us to see things more clearly.

These concepts will be introduced using the Peer Groups data, which collected relational and attribute data from middle school students in four science classes taught by the same teacher. Keeping with the introductory theme of this chapter, only one network from one point in time will be discussed: student-reported friendship relations among students in one class in the fall semester, the beginning of the school year. Using these data, this chapter will introduce (1) the distinguishing features of network data; (2) the types of variables collected in network studies; (3) how networks are represented as graphs and matrices; and (4) how these representations allow us to analyze network phenomena at different analytic levels. Some of these concepts were introduced in Chapter 1. This chapter goes further by discussing these concepts using sociometric notation and the corresponding logic of graph theory.

GRAPHS AND NETWORK DATA

Social network data at its most basic level consists of at least one relational measure among a set of actors. Substantive concerns and theories that drive a specific network study usually inform which variables to measure and the frequency with which they are measured. For example, the Peer Groups data set was motivated by several questions that shaped the collection of the network data. First, there was an interest in measuring how relations among peers change throughout the duration of the school year. This interest required that data be collected at a minimum two points in time, in this case, the fall and spring of the academic year. In addition, because the analytic focus was on peer relations, Pittinsky asked each student (ego) to rate their friendship on six-point scale (1 = best friend; 2 = friend, 3 = know-like; 4 = know, 5 = know-dislike; 6 = strongly dislike) with every other student (alter) in the class. In addition, the teacher was asked to do the same. This last feature allows the comparison between the students' and teacher's reports, a nice analytical move that allows the data to explore whether the teacher's and students' reports (dis)agree and how this level of (dis)agreement changes over time. Rather than rely on observations or archival or historical records, Pittinsky used a questionnaire to elicit responses. Because the interest was on the whole network (i.e., the class), the entire set of actors, in this case students, was surveyed, not just a sample of them.

Therefore, the Peer Groups network data can be represented as a graph, a common way to represent social networks, consisting of two dimensions: actors (students) sending relations, represented as rows, and receiving actors (also students) represented as columns. Therefore, the network, X, consists of n actors, or in the language of graph theory, nodes. For example, consider the collection of $n = 27$ students in the Peer Groups network data set. We have $N = 27$ (Student 1, Student 2, ... Student 27), a collection of 27 actors, so that each student can be referred by symbol: n_1 = Student 1, n_2 = Student 2 ... n_{27} = Student 27. Figure 3.1 shows how these data are represented in a graph. Each actor can send or receive ties from every other actor.

Graphs such as the one in Figure 3.1 can immediately highlight several important features of overall network structure and provide a good entry point for introducing key

Figure 3.1   Peer Groups Data Network Graph. This graph consists of 27 students, and each directed line indicates that a "best friend" or "friend" nomination has been sent from one student to another. Because these ties are directed, they are referred to as arcs.

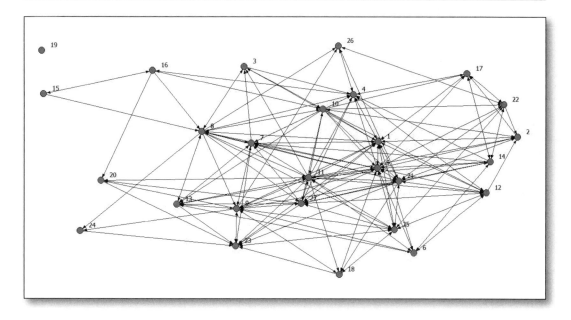

network concepts. Graphs consist of two features: (1) nodes, n, which represent actors, and (2) lines, which represent relations. Each circle represents a student (node), and each line represents whether a student "sent" a friendship nomination to another student (relation); that is, they sent a 1 or 2 to another student ("best friend" or "friend"). Students can be connected by either arcs or edges. Arcs represent those relations that are directed from one student to another, meaning that the friendship nomination has not necessarily been reciprocated. Edges, on the other hand, are those lines that do not have arrowheads (since friendships are directed, there are no edges in Figure 3.1), which are appropriate when the relation is by definition reciprocated (e.g., "studies with"). Therefore, Figure 3.1 is what is referred to as a directed graph. Conversely, an undirected graph would consist exclusively of edges, nondirected relations between nodes.

Looking at the entire graph, there are several properties that become evident, which highlights how a relatively simple graph can immediately suggest some important structural features. Specifically, it is evident that there is an unevenness in the network's pattern of friendship relations; predictably, friendship nominations among these adolescents are distributed unequally. A small number of students receive a large number of nominations, and the overall connectivity across the entire graph is relatively low. In addition, clearly there are some students on the periphery who receive very few nominations.

Individual students occupy different positions in the graph, indicating students are embedded in the network in quite varied ways. For example, Student 1 (middle, Figure 3.1) sends and receives many nominations (13 and 19 nominations, respectively), suggesting that that student gets along with others in ways that are quite different than Student 15 (upper left, Figure 3.1), who sends and receives very few nominations. Also, consider Student 11, who is located between numerous pairs of students. Such a position may enable this student to serve as a broker between two different students or groups of students.

Graphs such as Figure 3.1 can provide useful snapshots by simply representing actors as nodes and relations as lines that are either edges (undirected) or arcs (directed). The book's final chapter proves an extended treatment of network visualization, including an overview of best practices and widely used applications.

GRAPHING ACTORS (NODES) AND RELATIONS (LINES)

Graphs can easily incorporate colors and shapes to convey attributes of each node. Homophily, for example, might suggest that relations among students of the same gender would be more common than relations between students of the opposite gender. Peer influence theory suggests that a division between high- and low-achieving students might influence these friendship patterns.

Figure 3.2 shows how these two attributes can be incorporated into a graph, making it much more informative about the hypotheses of differential friendship patterns among students. Girls are represented as square nodes and boys as circles. Light-colored

Figure 3.2   Peer Groups Data Network Graph with Node Shape and Color Representing Gender and Achievement Level. Girls are represented as square nodes and boys as circles. Light-colored nodes are average achievers and dark nodes are high achievers. Those nodes without color are low achievers. From this graph, there appears to be evidence that friendship nominations are possibly influenced by homophily and peer influence, with high achievers occupying positions in the center of the graph and low achievers on the periphery.

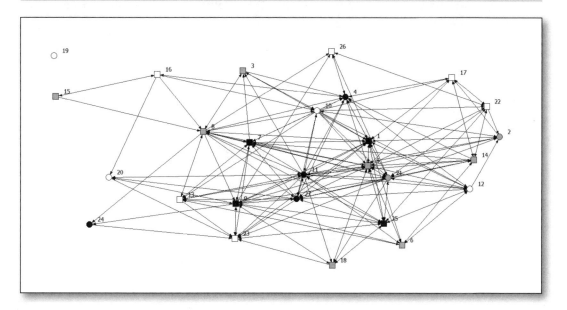

nodes are average achievers and dark nodes are high achievers. Those nodes without color are low achievers. From this graph, there appears to be evidence that friendship nominations are possibly influenced by homophily and peer influence, with high achievers occupying positions in the center of the graph and low achievers on the periphery.

Not only may nodes differ by attribute, they may also vary quantitatively based on their relations with other nodes. In the Peer Groups data, for example, it might be insightful to make each node's size proportional to the number of friendship nominations received (in-degrees) or sent (out-degrees). Or the size or color of the node can be adjusted to reflect the group with which one is affiliated. Figure 3.3 incorporates these two dimensions by first adjusting the size of each node to reflect the number of friendship nominations that node has received. In addition, the graph also shows the different subgroups within the network, with each subgroup representing a *K*-core (this is one approach to identifying subgroups through relational data discussed in Chapter 5). Each shape represents one of nine different subgroups.

This graph demonstrates a few interesting properties. First, students who receive many nominations, most of whom are near the center of the graph, are also members of

Figure 3.3 Peer Groups Data Network Graph With Node Size and Shape Reflecting In-degree and Group Membership. Node size reflects number of friendship nominations received (bigger nodes equal more nominations), and node shape reflects same subgroup membership (K-core). This graph demonstrates a few interesting properties. For example, students who receive many nominations, most of whom are near the center of the graph, are also members of the same subgroup. This subgroup is large (18 members), while the network's remaining nine students are split among eight subgroups that are small (1–2 members).

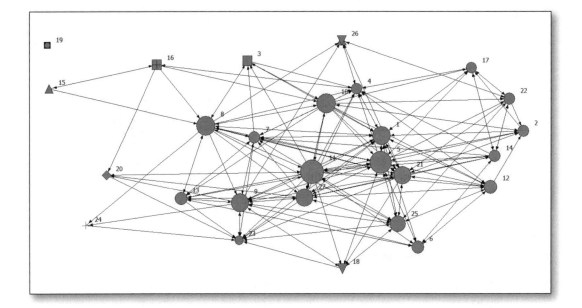

the same subgroup. This subgroup is large (18 members), while the network's remaining nine students are split among eight subgroups that are small (1–2 members). This large subgroup also hints at the network having what is referred to as a core-periphery structure: a group of well-connected actors at the center of the network with a set of actors residing on the periphery whose only connections are typically to those actors affiliated with this core group.

The relations, shown in graphs as either edges (undirected) or arcs (directed), can also be represented in ways that reflect several interesting properties. It can also be very helpful to use color and thickness to indicate a difference in kind and amount among the relations. When ties are measured as a value, as they have been in the original Peer Groups data (values range from 1–6), the strength of the tie can be indicated by using thicker lines to represent stronger ties and vice versa. For example, in Figure 3.4, thicker lines represent "best friend" nominations, originally coded as 1s, and regular

Figure 3.4   Peer Groups Data Network Graph With Line Width Representing Tie Strength. Thick lines represent "best friend" nominations, thinner lines "friends." In addition to altering the lines' thickness, it is possible to use colors and dashes to indicate different kinds of relations (e.g., who studies with whom or seeks advice from whom), allowing what is referred to as multiplex data to be displayed in one graph.

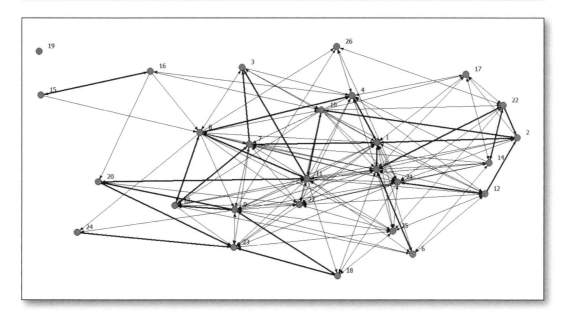

lines "friend," originally coded as 2s. These types of relations, therefore, are referred to as "valued," as opposed to the binary (yes/no) relations shown in Figure 3.1. Colored and dashed lines can also be used to indicate different kinds of relations (e.g., who studies with whom or seeks advice from whom), allowing what is referred to as multiplex data to be displayed in one graph. Multiplex data, discussed later in this chapter, are those network data that measure more than one kind of relation, which most contemporary network studies incorporate.

UNDERSTANDING GRAPHS THROUGH EGO NETWORKS

A helpful way to parse complicated network graphs—and it should be evident from Figures 3.1 through 3.4 that things can become complicated quickly—is to see how they emerge from the immediate ties of individual focal actors (Hanneman & Riddle, 2011a). The network formed by targeting one node, including all other nodes to which that node is connected (friends) and all the other connections among those other nodes (friends of friends), is referred to as the ego network, also called the one-step neighborhood of a node. These neighborhoods can also be extended for two (the friends of friends' friends) or more degrees from ego.

To graph the way in which individual nodes are embedded in the whole network, visual representations of ego networks can be useful. One of the fundamental insights of the social network perspective established in Chapter 1 is that an actor's behaviors and attitudes are influenced by those with whom that actor has relations, and these relations, in turn, are shaped by one's own behaviors and attitudes. Graphing ego-level neighborhoods and comparing them can provide hints into the similarities and differences among the network's actors. For example, using the Peer Groups data, you could ask whether the ego neighborhoods of high-achieving students are bigger than those of low-achieving students or which students have neighborhoods that consist mainly of reciprocated ties.

Questions such as these are descriptive or even exploratory in nature, which, as noted in Chapter 2, reflects a majority of empirical social network studies. Only recently has confirmatory hypothesis testing been employed more regularly in network studies, and this is primarily due to recent advances in inferential statistics that incorporate the nonindependence of observations (see Chapter 8). For small networks such as those represented by the Peer Groups data, graphs can provide an intuitive means through which you can inspect the network's structure and get an intuitive sense of how individual actors are incorporated into its larger structure. Chapters 5 and 6 provide a more formal way of representing these intuitive properties by showing how certain complete and ego network features are precisely calculated.

Social network analysis relies extensively on graphs to represent social structure. As noted by Hanneman and Riddle (2011a), a well-constructed graph can be very useful, perhaps even more useful than words, for communicating a network's properties. Large networks (> 25 actors) , however, are not so easy to study visually. In addition, because social network analysis is often concerned with more then one type of relation among actors, graphs are limited in what they can "do." Therefore, the formal description of network properties and testing hypotheses about them requires that graphs be converted to numbers. This is where we shift from representing networks as graphs and turn toward the uses of sociometry and matrices.

MATRICES AND NETWORK DATA

When there are many actors or many kinds of relations, graphs are not terribly useful. The more common and flexible way of representing networks is through matrices. The advantages of representing network data in this fashion will become clear, but for now, keep in mind that a matrix is simply an array of data. This section briefly reviews the most commonly used matrix representations of social network data. It also introduces some language associated with matrices and matrix operations that differs from the language used when dealing with networks as graphs. This language is important when working with network data. While it is unlikely that you will have to do the math associated with matrix operations, as computers do the bulk of the heavy lifting, the mathematical concepts to be introduced will provide an efficient means through which you can understand the logic of network data and how it is ultimately analyzed (Hanneman & Riddle, 2011a).

When network data are organized in an array, it means that they are in a list. For example, you might call the list of 27 students in the Peer Groups data *X,* as an array is typically denoted with a bold letter. Each element (student) in the array can then be indexed by its place in the list: Student 1, Student 2...Student 27. This obviously is the simplest type of array, but there are several different types that are used—typically in combination with each other—in social network analysis. Following Hanneman and Riddle's (2011a) lead, this section considers the five most often-used matrices in social network analysis, with a special emphasis on how these matrices are both different from and similar to the actor-by-attribute data matrices that constitute most social science research.

Vectors

When a matrix has a single dimension, it is referred to as a vector. For example, the simple list of students' names noted earlier is vector. Row vectors are horizontal lists of elements, and column vectors are vertical. In social network analysis, row and column vectors are most typically used to present information about the attributes of actors, referred to later in this chapter as attribute variables. These are the types of variables with which most are familiar. For example, Table 3.1 shows a column vector that vertically lists the 27 different elements, in this case, students who are part of the Peer Groups data set, and two other columns that include an ordinal measure of achievement (1 = high, 2 = average, 3 = low) and gender (1 = girl, 0 = boy). The first column is an ID column and the second and third columns contain attribute variables. Therefore, this data array can be considered 27-by-2 (the number of rows by number of columns), a rectangular matrix that is sometimes referred to as a "list of lists."

Most social network analyses include arrays of variables that describe attributes of variables, ones that are either categorical (e.g., sex, race, etc.) or continuous in nature (e.g., test scores, number of times absent, etc.). Rather than have a separate vector for each attribute variable, it is more efficient to include all attribute variables in a rectangular array that mimics the actor-by-attribute that is the dominant convention in social science: Rows represent cases, columns represent variables, and cells consist of values on those variables.

Rectangular arrays such as Table 3.1 are used to provide information on each actor. This information can come from a number of sources, including standard survey

Table 3.1 Rectangular Matrix With ID and Attribute (Achievement and Gender) Vectors. This table shows a column vector that vertically lists the 27 different elements, in this case, students, who are part of the Peer Groups data set and two other columns that include a measure of achievement (1 = high, 2 = average, 3 = low), and gender (1 = girl, 0 = boy). The first column is an ID column and the second and third columns contain attribute variables. Therefore, this data array can be considered 27-by-2 (the number of rows by number of columns), a rectangular matrix that is sometimes referred to as a "list of lists."

	1	2
1	1	1
2	2	0
3	2	1
4	1	0
5	2	1
6	2	1
7	1	1
8	2	1
9	1	1
10	3	0
11	1	0
12	3	0
13	3	1
14	2	1
15	2	1
16	3	1
17	3	1
18	2	1
19	3	0
20	3	0
21	2	0
22	3	1

	1	2
23	3	1
24	1	0
25	1	1
26	3	1
27	1	0

instruments or observations (these and other data-collection techniques are discussed at length in the next chapter). Each actor can also be described by a variable that has been derived from that actor's relations with others. Referred to later in this chapter as relational variables, information about these variables can also be included as a vector in a rectangular data matrix. For example, you could imagine a separate vector for the Peer Groups data that includes information about the number of friendship nominations sent or received (out- or in-degree). Another way in which attribute vectors are used is to indicate the "group" to which an actor belongs. Here, groups are not defined by some exogenous attribute such as grade level or sports team affiliation but rather, one's group membership is determined by the relations that have been measured. Recall how Figure 3.3 visually shows each student's membership in a K-core (one of a number of techniques social network analysts employ to identify cohesive groups discussed in Chapter 5). An attribute vector could be created from these groups to indicate the group in which each of the 27 students belongs. This is what is known as a partitioning vector, which can be used to select subsets of actors, reorganize the data, and calculate more advanced summary measures.

Single-Mode (Square) Matrices

While vectors represent an array of variables for a set of elements (most typically attribute and relational variables), square matrices represent how the elements relate to each other on some measured tie—that is, for example, whether n_1 and n_2 are connected. These matrices are square, meaning that the columns and rows consist of the same nodes. The cells, therefore, indicate whether any two nodes share an arc (undirected) or edge (directed). Table 3.2 shows a simple representation of the Peer Groups data in a square matrix.

Table 3.2 is the simplest and most common network data matrix. First, the relationship is binary; if a tie exists, a 1 is entered into the cell, a 0 if there is no tie. As an aside, the Peer Groups data had to be transformed in order for them to be represented in this fashion. Both nodes had to rate the other as either a 1 or 2 (friend or best friend) in order for the cell to be coded as a 1. Square matrices with

Table 3.2 Binary and Undirected Peer Groups Data Network Data in Square Matrix. A 1 indicates an edge between two nodes, which are therefore adjacent to each other. A 0 indicates that there is no friendship tie between two students. For example, Students 1 and 2 are adjacent because they have an edge between them, indicating that they are friends.

	1	2	3	4	5	6	7	8	9	10	11	12	13	14	15	16	17	18	19	20	21	22	23	24	25	26	27
1	0	1	1	1	1	1	1	1	1	1	1	1	0	0	0	0	1	0	0	0	1	0	1	0	1	0	1
2	1	0	0	0	1	0	0	0	1	1	1	0	0	0	0	0	0	0	0	0	0	0	0	0	0	0	0
3	1	0	0	0	0	0	1	0	0	1	1	1	0	0	0	0	1	0	0	0	1	1	0	0	0	0	0
4	1	0	0	0	1	1	1	1	1	1	1	0	0	0	0	0	0	0	0	0	0	0	0	0	0	0	1
5	1	1	1	1	0	1	1	1	1	1	1	1	1	1	0	1	1	0	0	0	1	0	0	0	1	0	1
6	1	0	0	1	0	0	0	1	0	1	1	1	1	1	0	0	0	0	0	0	0	0	0	0	0	0	0
7	1	0	1	1	1	0	0	1	1	1	1	0	1	0	1	0	0	0	0	0	0	0	1	0	0	1	1
8	1	0	0	1	1	1	1	0	1	1	1	1	1	1	1	1	0	0	0	1	0	0	0	1	1	1	1
9	1	1	0	1	1	0	1	1	0	1	1	1	1	1	1	1	1	0	0	0	1	0	0	1	0	1	1
10	1	1	1	1	0	1	0	0	1	0	1	1	1	1	0	0	0	0	0	0	0	0	0	0	0	0	0
11	1	1	1	1	1	1	1	1	1	1	0	1	1	1	1	1	0	0	1	0	0	1	0	1	0	0	1
12	1	0	1	0	1	1	1	0	1	1	1	0	1	0	1	1	1	0	1	0	1	0	1	0	1	0	1
13	0	0	0	1	1	1	1	1	1	1	1	0	0	0	0	0	0	0	0	0	0	0	0	0	0	1	1

	1	2	3	4	5	6	7	8	9	10	11	12	13	14	15	16	17	18	19	20	21	22	23	24	25	26	27
14	0	0	0	1	1	1	1	0	0	0	0	0	0	0	0	0	0	0	0	0	1	1	0	0	0	0	1
15	0	0	0	0	0	0	1	0	0	0	1	0	0	0	0	0	1	0	0	0	0	0	0	0	0	0	0
16	0	0	0	0	0	0	0	1	0	0	0	0	0	0	0	1	0	0	0	0	0	0	0	0	0	0	0
17	1	1	0	1	1	0	0	1	1	1	0	0	0	0	1	0	0	0	0	1	0	0	0	0	0	0	0
18	0	0	0	0	1	0	0	0	0	0	0	0	0	1	0	0	0	0	0	0	0	0	1	0	0	0	0
19	0	0	0	0	0	0	0	0	0	0	1	0	0	0	0	0	0	0	0	0	0	1	0	0	0	0	0
20	0	0	0	0	0	0	0	0	1	0	0	0	0	0	0	0	0	0	0	0	0	0	1	0	0	0	1
21	1	1	1	1	1	1	0	1	1	1	1	1	1	1	0	1	0	1	0	0	0	0	0	0	0	1	1
22	0	1	0	0	0	0	0	0	0	0	1	1	0	1	0	0	0	0	0	0	0	0	1	0	0	0	0
23	1	0	1	0	0	0	0	1	0	0	0	0	0	0	0	0	0	0	0	0	1	1	0	1	1	1	1
24	0	0	0	0	0	0	0	0	1	1	0	0	0	0	0	0	0	0	0	0	0	0	0	0	0	0	0
25	1	0	0	0	0	0	0	1	1	0	0	1	0	0	0	0	0	1	0	0	1	0	1	0	0	0	1
26	0	0	0	1	0	0	0	1	1	1	0	0	0	0	0	0	0	0	0	0	0	0	0	0	0	0	0
27	1	0	0	1	1	1	1	1	1	1	1	1	1	1	0	1	0	0	1	1	1	1	1	1	1	0	0

55

binary relations such as these—all the ties are edges and represented as 1s—are typically the starting point for most social network analyses. This type of matrix is also referred to as an "adjacency matrix" because it represents who is near (adjacent) whom in the social structure. Second, this is also referred to as a "single-mode" matrix, as the rows and columns represent the same set of nodes.

However, matrices can also consist of arcs. Whereas Table 3.2 consists entirely of edges and is therefore considered symmetric, the relational data in Table 3.3 are asymmetric: n_1 could send a tie to n_2, but this tie need not be reciprocated. Convention dictates that in a directed (i.e., asymmetric) matrix consisting of arcs, the sender is the row and the target is the column. The data in Table 3.3 highlight this point. For example, consider Student 3, who "sends" a friendship tie to Students 1, 4, 8, and 10. In return, Student 3 "receives" friendship nominations from Students 7, 8, 10, and 11. Asymmetric ties are not necessarily reciprocated, even though they may very well be (Student 3 has a reciprocated tie with Student 8). Hanneman and Riddle (2011a) note that symmetric matrices typically represent "bonded ties" or "co-membership" of any kind of tie in which, if n_1 is tied to n_2, n_2 must be tied to n_1. In educational research, you might be interested in symmetric relations such as membership in the same class or participation in the same extracurricular activities. However, if the focus is on relations such as "advice," or "support" that are not necessarily reciprocal, it is likely that the data will first be recorded as asymmetric arcs such as the friendship data in Table 3.3. In terms of the language introduced earlier, these lines would be arcs between pairs of actors.

Each single-mode, square matrix reflects a specific relation between all pairs of actors in the network. The quantity in each cell of the matrix indicates the direction (arcs are directed, edges are undirected) and strength (binary or valued) of the tie between any two actors. The strength of relations can be measured a few different ways. In its simplest form, it can be binary (either the relation exists or not) and shown as an adjacency matrix or measured at higher levels, which is discussed in the following chapter, which includes a detailed treatment of measurement issues.

One question arises when representing network data as a single-mode, square matrix: Is it possible for n_1 to send or receive a tie from itself? The question is what to do with the information on the main diagonal, or trace, of the matrix. Oftentimes, the values on this diagonal are meaningless and ignored. In these instances, the values are left blank or filled with 0s, as in Table 3.3. Sometimes, however, the information on this diagonal is important and is included in the matrix. Consider participation patterns in online classrooms. Isn't it possible to send a question, only to eventually answer it yourself? In this case, the diagonal would certainly reveal something interesting about participation patterns and would likely have to be included in the data matrix.

Table 3.3 Binary and Directed Peer Groups Data Network Data in Square Matrix. A 1 indicates an arc between two nodes, which are therefore adjacent to each other. A 0 indicates that there is no arc between two students. For example, Student 3 sends a friendship nomination to Student 1 but does not receive a nomination in return. This relationship is asymmetric.

	1	2	3	4	5	6	7	8	9	10	11	12	13	14	15	16	17	18	19	20	21	22	23	24	25	26	27
1	0	1	0	1	1	1	1	1	1	0	1	0	0	0	0	0	1	0	0	0	1	0	1	0	1	0	1
2	1	0	0	0	1	0	0	0	1	1	0	1	0	0	0	0	1	0	0	0	1	0	0	0	0	0	0
3	1	0	0	1	0	0	0	1	0	1	0	0	0	0	0	0	0	0	0	0	0	0	0	0	0	0	0
4	1	0	0	0	0	0	0	1	0	0	1	0	0	0	0	1	0	0	0	0	0	0	0	0	0	1	0
5	1	1	0	0	0	0	0	0	0	0	1	1	1	1	0	0	1	0	0	0	1	0	1	0	1	0	1
6	1	0	0	1	0	0	0	1	1	1	1	1	1	1	0	0	0	0	0	0	0	0	0	0	0	0	0
7	1	0	0	1	1	0	0	0	1	0	1	1	0	0	0	0	0	0	0	0	0	0	1	0	0	0	0
8	1	0	0	1	1	1	0	1	0	1	1	0	1	0	0	0	0	0	0	0	0	0	0	1	1	0	1
9	1	0	0	0	0	1	1	0	0	0	0	0	0	0	0	0	0	0	1	0	1	0	1	1	1	1	1
10	1	1	0	1	1	1	1	1	0	0	1	1	0	0	0	0	0	1	0	0	1	0	0	0	0	0	1
11	1	1	0	1	1	1	1	1	0	1	0	1	1	0	0	0	1	0	1	0	1	0	1	0	1	0	1
12	1	1	1	0	1	1	1	0	0	0	1	0	0	0	0	0	0	0	0	0	0	0	0	0	1	0	1
13	0	0	0	0	1	1	1	1	1	0	0	0	0	0	0	0	0	0	0	0	0	0	1	0	0	0	1

(Continued)

Table 3.3 (Continued)

	1	2	3	4	5	6	7	8	9	10	11	12	13	14	15	16	17	18	19	20	21	22	23	24	25	26	27
14	0	0	0	1	0	1	1	1	0	0	1	0	0	0	0	0	1	0	0	0	0	1	1	0	0	0	0
15	0	0	0	0	0	0	1	0	0	0	0	0	0	0	0	1	0	0	0	0	0	0	0	0	0	0	0
16	0	0	0	0	0	0	0	1	0	1	0	0	0	0	1	0	0	0	0	1	0	0	0	0	0	0	0
17	1	0	0	1	1	0	0	0	1	0	1	0	0	0	0	0	0	0	0	0	0	1	1	0	0	0	0
18	0	0	0	0	1	0	0	0	1	0	0	0	0	1	0	0	0	0	0	0	0	0	0	1	1	0	0
19	0	0	0	0	0	1	0	0	0	0	1	0	0	0	0	0	0	0	0	0	0	0	0	0	0	0	0
20	0	0	0	0	0	0	0	0	0	0	0	1	0	0	0	0	0	0	0	0	0	0	1	1	0	0	1
21	1	1	1	0	1	0	1	0	1	0	0	0	0	1	1	0	1	1	0	0	0	0	0	0	0	1	1
22	0	1	0	1	0	0	0	0	0	0	0	0	0	1	0	0	0	0	0	0	1	0	0	1	0	1	0
23	1	0	0	0	0	0	0	1	0	0	0	0	0	0	0	0	0	0	0	0	0	0	1	0	1	0	0
24	0	0	0	0	0	0	0	0	0	0	0	0	0	0	0	0	0	1	0	0	0	0	0	0	0	0	0
25	1	0	0	0	1	0	0	0	1	0	1	1	0	0	0	0	0	0	1	0	1	1	1	0	0	0	0
26	0	0	1	0	0	0	0	0	0	1	0	0	0	0	0	0	0	0	1	1	1	0	0	0	0	0	1
27	1	0	1	1	0	1	0	1	1	0	1	1	1	1	0	0	0	0	0	0	0	0	1	0	1	0	0

Multiplex Matrices and Relations

It is true that most network studies across the social sciences and within the field of educational research focus on a single relationship among actors: friendship, support, advice, and the like. However, because social relations are more complex than this and contemporary analytical tools so flexible and efficient, social network analysis is increasingly concerned with a number of different relations among the same set of actors. Students, for example, are connected in many ways other than friendship simultaneously. Students may have emotional ties and exchange relations, co-memberships, and other kinds of connections concurrently. If schools are the actors, they too have multiple relations with other schools, including information exchange, alliances, partnerships, and other connections.

When different kinds of relational data are collected on the same set of actors, this is referred to as multiplex data. Multiplex data consist of a set of matrices, each being a single-mode, square matrix that describes one type of tie. The data in each matrix can either be undirected or directed and either binary or valued. The two matrices in Table 3.4 are two different looks at the Peer Groups data (for the purposes of presentation, only the relations between Students 1–10 are shown). The top panel shows the friendship network from the perspectives of the students themselves in the form of a directed, binary matrix (same as those data in Table 3.3). The matrix in the bottom panel is also directed and binary but includes information on the students' friendship nominations from the teacher's perspective. While the same relation has technically been measured, the fact that the data matrices with the same set of actors (same rows and columns) are generated from two different sources makes these data multiplex in nature. This is a special kind of multiplex data referred to as cognitive social structure (Krackhardt, 1987a). Data such as these illustrate the potentially different ways in which, different actors perceive ties between the same pairs of actors. For example, in Table 3.4, Student 2 sends a friendship tie to Student 1 (as reported by the student, top panel), but the teacher does not perceive that same tie (bottom panel).

Working with multiplex data induces a few analytic choices. You can use all the tools of social network analysis to analyze each data matrix separately. For example, in the Peer Groups data, you may ask whether the subgroups are more distinct in the teacher's report of friendship nominations or if there is more overlap among subgroups in the students' reports? Or does the teacher report greater or fewer friendship ties than the students themselves? But you may also want to combine the information from more than one relation among the same set of actors. This leads to one of two approaches (Hanneman & Riddle, 2011a). The first of these is the reductionist approach, which collapses information about multiple relations among the same set of actors into one single relation that captures the quantity of ties. This could be as simple as "adding" the matrices together and, therefore, the cells of the new matrix represent sums. The combination approach is similar in that the goal is to create a single new matrix derived from multiple

Table 3.4 Binary and Directed Peer Groups Data Network Data in Square Matrix Generated From Students' (top panel) and Teacher's Reports (bottom panel). While the same friendship relation has been measured, the fact that the data matrices with the same set of actors (same rows and columns) are generated from two different sources makes these data multiplex in nature. Only data from Students 1 through 10 are presented.

	1	2	3	4	5	6	7	8	9	10
1	0	1	0	1	1	1	1	1	1	0
2	1	0	0	0	1	0	0	0	0	1
3	1	0	0	1	0	0	0	1	0	1
4	1	0	0	0	0	0	0	0	0	0
5	1	1	0	1	0	1	1	1	1	0
6	1	0	0	0	1	0	0	0	1	0
7	1	0	1	1	0	0	0	0	1	0
8	1	0	1	1	1	0	1	0	1	1
9	1	0	0	0	0	1	1	0	0	0
10	1	1	1	1	1	0	1	1	0	0

	1	2	3	4	5	6	7	8	9	10
1	0	0	0	1	0	0	0	0	0	0
2	0	0	1	0	0	0	0	1	0	1
3	0	1	0	0	0	0	0	1	0	1
4	0	0	0	0	0	0	0	0	0	0
5	1	0	0	0	0	0	0	0	0	0
6	0	0	0	0	0	0	0	0	0	0
7	0	0	0	0	0	0	0	0	0	0
8	0	1	1	0	0	0	0	0	0	1
9	0	0	0	0	0	0	0	0	0	0
10	0	1	1	0	0	0	0	1	0	0

relations, but the focus is on quality, not quantity. The relational algebra behind this transformation is too advanced for this introduction to basic network concepts, but is revisited in the book's final chapter when newer advances such as these are discussed.

Two-Mode (Affiliation) Matrices

Thus far, the discussion on matrices has focused on those relational data sets that consist of the same set of actors. However, an important focus for educational researchers and social scientists in general is one's location in larger social structures such as neighborhoods, professional associations, communities, and other "identity" categories. Social network analysis can be used to examine the relations within and between multiple analytical levels. For example, students affiliate with groups, and groups are linked by their overlapping memberships.

When relational data represent the connections between two different sets of actors, the data is considered "two–mode." In two-mode data, the rows and columns represent different sets of actors. Typically, rows represent individual actors and columns represent events, organizations, or some other identity category. Because the number of rows and columns is likely to differ, these matrices are no longer considered square. In addition, the actors are not considered adjacent but rather affiliated. Hence, these two-mode matrices are known as affiliation networks (Borgatti & Everett, 1997). Affiliation networks reflect the connections of two different sets of actors. Similar to single-mode adjacency matrices, the relational data in two-mode matrices can be binary or valued, with rows sending relations to the columns. Because affiliation data consist of two sets of actors, the techniques used to analyze these data are different and somewhat more complex. The two basic approaches (conversion and direct) to the analysis of affiliation data are also discussed in Chapter 7.

For now, it is important to note that the conversion approach is most frequently employed. In this approach, two-mode data are collapsed into a single-mode adjacency matrix. For example, you might transform an undirected (binary) matrix that displays which students were members of certain school-sponsored extracurricular organizations into a matrix that shows how many times each pair of students happened to be co-members. Or you can transform the same data into a single-mode matrix that shows how many times each pair of organizations was connected by overlapping student memberships. The idea is simple: Convert a two-mode data matrix into one prior to analysis. However, in doing so, much information is "lost," and because of this, the direct approach is gaining traction among social network analysts.

Regardless of whether you rely on graphs or matrices to represent relations, ultimately these representations include variables, most likely many of them. The relations that are measured among actors also determine which analytic methods are ultimately appropriate. Therefore, it is important to consider the different types of variables that can be employed in social network analysis. These variables were briefly noted throughout the previous sections, but it is important to emphasize the distinctions among them as well as the importance of including them in analyses of social networks.

NETWORK VARIABLES

Generally, there are three different types of variables used in the analysis of social networks (Valente, 2010). The first two are derived from the network data themselves, and the third type is the one with which most are familiar. The first type of variable is relational, which is constructed from the respondents' set of direct ties with others. An example of this variable at the ego level would be density, the degree to which an ego actor's alters know one another. So, in the Peer Groups data set, each student could have a measure of his or her ego network density, that is, a variable that captures the degree to which the friends of n_1 are also friends with each other. Examples of other relational variables include connectedness, reach, in-out-degree, constraint, and several others that will be discussed in subsequent chapters.

The second type of variable employed in social network analysis is similar to relational variables in that these, too, are also derived from network data. The difference is that these variables, referred to as structural variables, are constructed from the entire network of connections, that is, they are calculated on N. This distinction, however, is not rigid, since relational and structural measures are often associated (Valente, 2010). Examples of structural variables include centrality and positions. Centrality, measured a number of different ways, generally refers to the degree to which relations are concentrated or dependent on one or more actors. Positional analyses, on the other hand, parse the network's structure by grouping actors based on their (dis)similarity of network ties. Similar to centrality, there are several different ways in which to identify positions within a network and the relations between and within these positions. Both types of structural variables are discussed in Chapter 5, which focuses on these measures as derived from complete networks.

The third type, attribute variables, is increasingly employed in social network analysis and has been the cornerstone of social science research for some time. Also referred to as compositional variables (Wasserman & Faust, 1994), these variables capture properties of individual actors. As such, they are defined at the level of individual actors, n. For example, the Peer Groups data set also includes information about students' race, sex, and achievement test scores. Table 3.1 shows how two attribute variables are recorded as vectors, in this case an ordinal measure for achievement and an indictor (dummy) variable for gender. Similar to conventional social science research, these, too, can be incorporated into the statistical analysis of social networks (introduced in Chapter 8).

SUMMARY

This chapter used the Peer Groups data to show how a pattern of relations among a set of actors (in this case, friendship among students) can be represented in two different formal ways: graphs or matrices. These representations can then be used to define numerous ideas about a network's social structure in precise mathematical terms. Prior to moving on to that task, however, the next chapter addresses the measurement, collection, storage, and manipulation of network data.

CHAPTER FOLLOW-UP

To answer these questions, please refer to the graph in Figure 3.5.

1. Is this graph directed or undirected? Are the lines arcs or edges? Given your responses to these questions, what type of relation might this graph represent? Based on what you see in this graph, is this relation valued or binary?

2. Create a matrix that represents the relational data evident in the graph. How many actors are in this matrix? How many rows and columns are in this matrix? What type of data are in the cells of this matrix? Is this matrix symmetric? Explain the values on the diagonal of the matrix.

3. What attribute data might you want to incorporate into analysis? Create a rectangular data matrix that represents this variable as a vector. Be sure to describe what the values on this variable represent.

Figure 3.5   Example Graph for Follow-Up Questions.

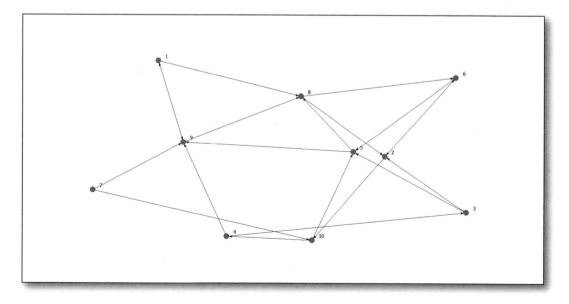

ESSENTIAL READING

Hanneman, R. A., & Riddle, M. (2005). *Introduction to social network methods.* Retrieved from http://faculty.ucr.edu/~hanneman/

Hanneman, R. A., & Riddle, M. (2011). A brief introduction to analyzing social network data. In J. Scott & P. J. Carrington (Eds.), *The Sage handbook of social network analysis* (pp. 331–339). Thousand Oaks, CA: Sage Publications.

Krackhardt, D. (1987). Cognitive social structures. *Social Networks, 9*(2), 109–134.

PART II

Methods and Measures

4

Collecting and Managing Network Data

OBJECTIVES

The previous chapter introduced the two different ways in which network data are represented (graphs and matrices) and the three different types of variables that are included in social network analyses (relational, structural, and attribute). This chapter takes a step back and addresses issues related to the collection and measurement of these network variables and how they can be stored and managed for subsequent analyses. Specifically, this chapter addresses issues related to boundary specification, sampling, measurement, collection, storage, and measurement; methodological issues that are generic across empirical social science disciplines. The key difference is that social network data are derived from relations in context; therefore, the methodological issues inherent to the collection and management of social network data are somewhat unique in several different ways. These issues are critical for a range of analytical decisions, which are addressed in the next three chapters. By the end of this chapter, you will understand how to measure, collect, and manage network data.

To highlight these issues, this chapter will rely on the Daly's Network of District School Leaders data set ("School Leaders" data set). As noted in Chapter 1, these data were collected from school leaders in two districts over 3 consecutive years. In addition to attribute data (e.g., sex, ethnicity, marital status, etc.), multiplex data on 11 different relations were collected, including collaboration, support, and expertise among others.

BOUNDARIES

Chapter 1 noted that social networks can be analyzed at four different levels: ego, dyad, triad, and complete. Analyzing social network data at one or more of these levels, however, requires that you focus on either one of two objects of measurement: egocentric or complete-networks. Egocentric network studies have a more limited goal of describing a focal actor's (ego) social environment relative to one or more others (alters). On the other hand, complete-network studies measure the relations among actors in some bounded social group by collecting data on one or more relations among the group's actors. Complete-network studies can, therefore, subsume the three lower levels of analysis: Complete-network data include egocentric data for each actor as well as information about the network's dyads and triads. Recall, however, that most analyses of social networks are done at either the ego- or complete-network level. Given this information, the School Leaders data set can be considered an example of a complete-network study: one complete network of school leaders from two separate school districts.

BOUNDARY SPECIFICATION

When collecting either ego- or complete-level network data, one of the first decisions you must make is to define the target population and construct a sampling frame that adequately provides access to that population of interest. On one level, this is no different from the standard sampling logic advocated in the quantitative social sciences. In studies of social networks, these decisions about populations and samples are referred to as the "boundary specification problem" (Laumann, Marsden, & Prensky, 1989).

In complete network studies, the issue of boundary specification is somewhat easier to negotiate. Formal or positional criteria typically offer a clear definition of who is a member of the group. Consider the school leaders data set; each leader who held a formal administrative position in the school district was considered to be within the network's boundary. Other examples of how formal criteria can be applied to determine the network's boundary include a classroom of students (Pittinsky & Carolan, 2008) or school staff within the same district (Spillane, Healey, & Kim, 2010).

However, boundaries in complete network studies may not be so clear cut. Delineating the network's boundary for actors that do not share some formal criteria is tricky. Examples of such groups may include students who regularly use the school library, adolescents who often socialize outside of school, or parents who run into each other and discuss school-related issues. Because there is no formal boundary demarcating who is "in" and "out" of the network, social network analysts use a few different ways to construct a bounded sample. These different means are discussed in the following section, but note that they also shape decisions regarding the collection of ego-network data.

Ego-network studies are typically conducted as part of a representative sample survey. Therefore, unlike complete-network studies, the collection of actors in an ego-network study represents some larger target population. As Marsden (2011) notes, the boundary specification of ego-network studies follows the definition of the study's target population. Once a sample of respondents (egos) has been identified, a second boundary-determination issue surfaces. This issue has to do with delimiting the set of alters within any given respondent's egocentric network. Because there is no predetermined network of potential alters as there is in complete network studies, how can social network analysts elicit information about ego's alters? This issue is discussed in the section on collection.

STRATEGIES FOR BOUNDARY SPECIFICATION

Collecting network data for either egocentric or complete-network studies requires you to consider issues related to boundary specification, sampling, and measurement. This section directly addresses the first of these issues in more detail and sets up the subsequent sections on sampling and measurement. Specifying the boundary of a network is analogous to asking: Where do you set the limits when collecting relational data when, in theory, there are no limits (Barnes, 1979; Knoke & Yang, 2008)? There are three generic approaches to addressing this issue: positional, relational, and event-based.

Positional

The first of these approaches, positional, has already been mentioned as the most common way to identify a complete-network population bounded by some common attribute (e.g., all school leaders within a district). But it can also be employed in ego-network studies in which respondents are not all drawn from the same bounded network as in the School Leaders data set, but, rather, they share some common attribute such as grade or achievement level. This positional approach generates a set of actors that occupy a similar position in some social structure. Each actor, however, need not be directly connected to every other actor.

There are a few issues to keep in mind when constructing networks through this positional approach (Knoke & Yang, 2008). First, network structures uncovered through this approach look different from one another. For example, a collaboration network among teachers in a school's English department may look very different from the teachers' collaboration network in the same school's math department. Even in a similar context, in this case the school, the teachers' collaboration networks may not exhibit the same social structure, and, therefore, making an inference from one network to another is unwise. A second issue is that relations among actors in bounded networks, particularly large ones, are likely to be sparse. Most likely there will be pockets of actors lacking connections to each other. While this may expose something interesting, the lack of overall connectivity may provide too little with which to work. A third issue when employing the positional approach is that you are obligated to justify the inclusion or exclusion of certain positions. For example, in the School Leaders data, Daly employed a nominalist criterion that included all administrative personnel in the two districts that have 1 of 14 possible administrative titles. This criterion was justified by the fact that leaders at these levels were charged with devising, implementing, or monitoring an array of school policies.

Relational

The second approach to specifying a network's boundary is relational and is most commonly employed in ego-level network studies (Knoke & Yang, 2008). This approach is either based on your knowledge about relations among a set of actors or relies on the actors themselves to nominate additional actors for inclusion. This approach leads to several different procedures that address the issue of boundary specification in slightly different ways. Five of these are introduced now and discussed in more detail later in this chapter's subsection on sampling: reputational methods, snowball sampling, fixed-list selections, expanding selection, and K-core methods.

The first procedure specifying a network's boundary using a relational approach is through a reputational method. This method is as straightforward as it sounds. You identify the most knowledgeable informants and asks them to list a set of actors for your study. For example, using this approach, you may investigate the national network of charter school advocacy organizations by first compiling a master list of these organizations from archival records. You can then ask respondents—that is, people "in the know" about these organizations —to identify the small number of organizations from that list that are most important. These two steps, first compiling a list of actors and then asking key informants to rate them, can uncover the set of important organizations for future analyses. In addition, these informants can be asked to expand the master list by identifying others based on their inside knowledge.

While the benefits of this reputational approach are obvious, so too are three related shortcomings. First, it relies on key informants whose ability to provide accurate and complete information needs to be questioned. How can you be assured that the respondents can really identify those charter school advocacy organizations that are most important? In addition, there is no standard by which you can evaluate the accuracy of the boundary's specification. Finally, while you are obligated to provide a strong theoretical and empirical justification for choosing certain key informants, there is still the potential for the key informants to produce data that are systematically different than the data collected through other methods.

In particular, the data collected through reputational methods are likely to be much different than the data collected through snowball sampling, the second of the five relational approaches. Useful in finding members of hard-to-reach populations, snowball sampling begins with a small set of actors who are then asked to nominate others with whom they have a certain kind of relation. In turn, these actors nominate others, and the process goes on until few or no new names emerge. The obvious problem with this approach is the ethical concerns it raises, as securing informed consent, protecting anonymity, and assuring confidentiality become difficult as you ask for information about each ego's alters (Borgatti & Molina, 2005). Assuming that you can secure human subjects approval for this sampling strategy, it can be a useful one for educational researchers interested in studying topics such as bullying, cheating, or any behaviors that occur within "hidden" populations.

The third and fourth relational approaches can be distinguished by whether informants provide their own list of actors or you provide that list to them. For example, in fixed-list selection, a respondent is limited to reporting ties between actors that have already been identified by you (e.g., you provide students with a list of all the other students in their high school). On the contrary, in the expanding-selection approach, respondents can list as many actors as they want, which resembles snowball sampling, and therefore with it come the difficulties associated with implementing this strategy in practice (e.g., you ask the students to list the names of a fixed or undefined number of students in their school). The downside to the fixed-list selection approach is that it is subject to nonrandom sampling bias. Because it relies on your knowledge of the network's boundary, the tendency is to include only "central" actors and ignore those on the periphery who, according to your perception, may be less important.

The fifth and final relational approach to boundary specification is used infrequently but is worth noting. The K-core method is useful for finding subsets of connected actors within a much larger and sparser network (e.g., all school district superintendents in a given state). A K-core, discussed in more detail in the next chapter, is a subset of actors that has ties with at least K other actors. You determine the value of K, thereby setting a more (high-K) or less (low-K) restrictive criterion for bounding a network. The recommendation is to first use a low K to establish network boundary and then increase K if you want to focus on a more exclusive subset of the network. This technique has superior potential for empirically locating a network's boundaries and has been made much easier by network analysis software developments. Despite these benefits, it is curious why it is not used more frequently.

Event-Based

The third broad approach to specifying a network's boundary falls under the heading of event-based strategies (Knoke & Yang, 2008). These strategies delineate a network's boundaries by selecting only those actors who participated in an "event" at a specific time and place. For example, you may be interested in observing participants at local board of education meetings, collecting relational and attribute data on only those participants who attended three consecutive meetings in the past 6 months. As opposed to positional or reputational approaches that focus on actors' behaviors, the criterion for inclusion through this approach is an event rooted in time and place.

The success of this approach rests on your ability to select events that specifically address the questions that are motivating the study. For example, you may include an event that is insignificant or have an event (or set of events) that excludes important players. So, while you may be interested in studying how a community's interests are actualized in the context of local school district policies, the local board of education meetings may not be the right event to uncover these relational dynamics. Important players may be absent, or the actual "action" occurs outside the formal setting of the meeting. Therefore, it is unwise to focus on a single event and better practice to observe multiple events (e.g., parent–teacher organization meetings, nonpublic meetings among the district's leaders, collective bargaining sessions between employees and district leaders, etc.) that would produce a more comprehensive network. Every event, therefore, would produce a distinct network whose actors may only partially overlap with those attending other events. It is possible to then collapse participants across all events, thereby producing a more representative network that can address the study's guiding question(s).

NETWORK SAMPLING

In light of these three approaches to specifying a network's boundaries, there are a few things to keep in mind when constructing samples for analysis at either the ego- or complete-network levels. The most significant distinction to be mindful of is whether a study is motivated by an interest in complete or egonetwork-level data. Complete network studies collect attribute and relational data on all actors in a population. As discussed in the previous section, there are few ways to delineate the complete network's boundary, most likely relying on a positional approach that has clear-cut criteria for inclusion. While these types of designs can produce rich accounts of both static and dynamic network properties, they are limited by their ability to make inferences to other populations of actors.

However, ego-level network data can be used to make inferences about larger populations. In these instances, ego-level network data are drawn from a larger target population, often by a sample survey instrument. Ideally, these egocentric-network data are representative of this larger population, thereby permitting statistical inferences to be drawn.

Frank (1981) describes several sampling schemes through which such inferences can be made. One approach relies on drawing a probability sample of actors using, for example, simple random selection. Then only those relationships among this sampled subset of actors are observed. A second means through which ego-level network data can be used to make statistical inferences is by drawing a probabilistic sample of ego actors and then observing all relationships incident on those actors. A final way is through snowball sampling (also known as link tracing). These three different means are most closely aligned with the reputational approach discussed above.

Marsden (2011) notes that different inferences about network properties are available through different sampling designs. Therefore, you must first consider what properties of a network are of interest when designing a social network sampling scheme. Once this decision has been made, you can then move on to issues involving the collection of relational data.

NETWORK DATA COLLECTION

The collection of network data—specifically, relational data on a set of actors—is primarily informed by whether you are interested in a complete–or ego–level of analyses. Because ego-level analyses can be extracted from complete network data, this section first discusses the common strategies and instruments through which complete network data are collected. It then turns more specifically to ego-level data collection, with a special focus on name-generator instruments that produce extensive network data and are most likely shaped by a reputational approach to boundary specification. The section then concludes by briefly discussing a third type of network data collection referred to as partial network data.

In addition, it will be helpful to introduce some new notation that will be used to discuss the different strategies and instruments used for network data collection. Specifically, actors will be denoted as i or j, where $i \neq j$. In the language of graph theory introduced in the previous chapter, i and j represent a pair of nodes in graph $\mathbf{X}$. The relationship between i and j is represented as a_{ij}, meaning that a can take a value ≥ 0. To further simplify this discussion, only single-mode networks, such as the School Leaders data set, are considered, in which the rows and columns of the data matrix consist of the same set of actors.

Complete-Network Data Collection

In complete-network studies, you select the set of actors that serves as the study's bounded population. Informed by either positional or event-based approaches to network boundary specification, these studies typically measure a small number of relations between each pair of the network's actors. There are two primary sources of complete-network data: census and archives. Both, however, require information about the relations between actors within the network's boundary. With archives, these relations can be inferred from the documentary evidence, such as an organizational chart of who reports to whom (see, e.g., Carolan, 2008b). The most popular technique for gathering relational data from a census is doing so through a sociometric survey instrument: a tool that requires respondents to provide information about their relations with others. This section also revisits a special variant of compete network data collection, cognitive social structure (CSS), in which respondents are asked about their perceptions of the relationships among alters.

Network data collection through a census is the simplest manner through which relational data are collected on a well-defined population of interest. This method of data collection consists of gathering relational data from all (or almost all) actors in a population. Actors who either occupy certain positions (e.g., students in a classroom) or participate in certain events (e.g., attendance at student government meetings) represent common frames through which participants are sampled. This type of network data collection is preferred when you can enumerate all actors, i and j, of the network such as teachers within a school, school leaders within a district, or school-aged children in a delineated neighborhood (Valente, 2010). Because of advances in computing power, researchers can now study census networks that consist of thousands and even millions of actors.

Census

Census data collection requires that you obtain a master list of actors bounded by some context and then ask each actor, i, to rate various types of relations with all or some limited number of actors, j. These types of data provide a complete snapshot of the entire network so that it is possible to examine how attitudes or behaviors move across the network, assuming you have collected this information over time. This can be important for studies that seek to understand how network dynamics influence individual outcomes, including students' engagement or resistance.

To elicit complete network data, you may use a nomination (reputational) or roster (positional) method. For example, using the positional method, you may give a student a roster of all students in his or her grade and have the student rate the frequency with which he or she discusses school matters with every other student (this would be a directed and valued relation). Or, using the nomination method, you would ask the student to write down the names of those that the student discusses school matters with.

There are advantages to each method. Valente (2010) identifies six advantages of the nomination method: (1) It is an unassisted recall; (2) it is less demanding on the respondent; (3) the rank order in which a respondent lists alters can be preserved and used as a proxy for tie strength; (4) the number of alters that each respondent can list can be adjusted; (5) data entry and management are easier (discussed later in this chapter); and (6) it is more likely to identify actors outside of the network's imposed boundary. However, there are also advantages of the positional method. Namely, weak and strong ties are measured and the network's boundary is unambiguous, as everyone on the list is in the network. Often, however, researchers combine elements of both approaches. One common way to do this is to use a nomination format but also provide a roster to which respondents can refer. This technique combines the strengths of both methods.

Archives

Complete network data can also be gathered through archival sources (Valente, 2010). The sources of such data are varied and include diaries, public records, email, participation in social networking platforms, and school transcripts. Using these sources, you need not directly ask, or cannot even ask, respondents to report on their network. Rather, the network is reconstructed from these records and a number of different relations can be captured. For example, using the public Facebook profiles of a set of students in the same school, it is possible to construct a network of who bullies whom, so long as you can precisely define how bullying is measured. These critical issues of measurement are discussed later in this chapter.

For example, those who have worked in the field of bibliometrics—the study or measurement of text—have been able to reveal the structure and dynamics of scholarly networks, often by examining reference lists from publications. These efforts construct networks of who has cited whom or who has collaborated with whom. A similar technique was employed by Carolan (2008) is his study of one prominent educational research journal. Using its electronic database, Carolan was able to create a large two-mode network of readers and articles that captured which readers read what articles. This information was then used to partition the network into sets of distinct communities that were surprisingly well–connected. As digital archival sources become more accessible, they represent a wonderful opportunity to yield insights into actors' behaviors and attitudes. For example, with the proliferation of online learning venues, you can easily imagine using the digital archives from these sources to examine an array of relational dynamics among students.

Sociometric Instrument

However, a majority of complete network studies require that you employ some type of sociometric instrument to capture relational data on some clearly delineated population of actors. Unlike network data that are harvested through archival sources, these types of instruments require that each i actor within a network report on some relationship, a, with some set of alters, j. This produces a value of a_{ij}, which represents i's choice or nonchoice of j. Pioneered by Moreno, these sociometric "tests" measure relationships between pairs of actors, including relations such as support, friendship, and collaboration. They can also be adapted to collect two-mode network data in which i and j are not the same; in this case, respondents, i, would be asked to report on memberships or affiliations in or with j. For example, students could be asked to identify the extracurricular activities in which they regularly participate. Sociometric items—that is, items that elicit relational data—are typically administered through a standard survey instrument, either in person or self-administered. More frequently, however, this information is collected through computer-assisted means, which can simplify presentation and ease data-management concerns.

Social network analysts use different criteria to extract information about a respondent's sociometric choices. These criteria are primarily determined by both theoretical interest and the substantive questions they pose to respondents. In the School Leaders data set, Daly asked respondents to report on a number (11) of different relations, thereby inducing what is referred to as multiplex network data. Asking school and district leaders, for example, to state how often they collaborated with other members of the administrative team and the frequency with which they discussed matters of a confidential nature with these other members helped generate Daly's sociometric data.

Most sociometric surveys, like Daly's, supply a list of possible alters in the network for respondents to consult; others, however, permit respondents to freely recall their ties to alters from memory. While both methods are acceptable, there are two reasons why it is recommended that analysts provide respondents with a list of possible alters (Marsden, 2011). First, providing a roster to respondents eases the respondents' reporting burden by reminding them of the network's eligible alters. In addition, a roster minimizes measurement error, as respondents are often prone to forget potential alters. But there are tradeoffs you must consider. For instance, asking a respondent to review and evaluate all the alters on a large roster is tedious and time consuming, even if assisted by a computer interface. Whatever technique you choose, however, the analyst must exercise caution with alters' names. Recall methods must somehow make sure that respondents' alters known by different names (e.g., changes in surnames due to marriage, nicknames, etc.) are correctly matched. Along these lines, rosters that provide respondents with a list of potential alters must use those names by which the alters are actually known.

Researchers have offered conflicting guidance as to how to best construct sociometric data-collection instruments. These different suggestions center on the number of alters that respondents are allowed to choose. Early guidelines suggested that respondents be given the opportunity to make an unlimited number of nominations, while others have suggested that the number of nominations be limited to three or four. Limiting the number of alters is currently the more widely exercised option; when administering a survey, it is simply more practical to specify a sociometric task for respondents and make things as straightforward as possible, which eases the respondents' burden. However, in doing so, you may also be increasing measurement error. Imposing a limit on the number of alters a respondent may nominate potentially induces what Marsden (2011) refers to as a false negative (the respondent's actual number of alters is higher than the imposed limit) or a false positive (the respondent's actual number of alters is lower than the imposed limit). The conclusion to be drawn from this is that, similar to standard survey-based research, bias is generated in many sociometric tasks, and it is your responsibility to mitigate these adverse effects as much as possible. These measurement issues are discussed later in this chapter.

Sociometric tasks capture relational data through a number of different possible response categories or formats. The simplest and one of the most widely used is binary measurement. Respondents identify those alters with whom they have a given relationship by making a separate yes/no (1/0) distinction for each of them. As noted in the previous chapter, binary measures such as this result in a sociomatrix that consists of a_{ij}, which represents i's choice ($a = 1$) or nonchoice of j ($a = 0$). This is the technique used by Penuel, Frank, and Krause (2010), in which teachers were asked to list their closest professional in-school colleagues, and this information was then used to identify subgroups within the network (these techniques to identify subgroups are discussed in the following chapter). Other sociometric tasks, however, require an ordinal response. For example, in the School Leaders data set, Daly asked respondents to select the number of times they engaged in different types of relations from four different response categories: 1 (the least frequent) to 4 (1–2 times a week). Therefore, in the relationship between i and j, represented as a_{ij}, a can take a value of 1, 2, 3, or 4. These values become the cells of the single-mode sociomatrix. Finally, sociometric responses can be also be ranked. Newcomb's Fraternity Data illustrates this technique. Newcomb asked all 17 members of the fraternity to rank all other members from 1 to 16, with 1 representing the first friendship preference, and no ties were allowed. From this, it follows that in the relationship between any two members, represented as a_{ij}, a can take a value of 1, 2, ... 16. The sociomatrix that reflects these relational data consists of cells ranging in value from 1 to 16 and a main diagonal consisting of 0s (one could not rank the relationship with oneself).

Table 4.1, adapted from Marsden (2011), provides several examples of the questions that researchers have asked to elicit sociometric data on complete networks. It is evident from this table that sociometric choices can be generated through many different means, but the means that you choose to employ are dictated by substantive issues in which you are interested. In addition, these questions do not reconcile the outstanding issue as to whether you should provide respondents with a list of possible alters or rely on respondent's free recall.

Table 4.1 Examples of Complete Network Sociometric Questions.

A. Single-criterion recognition question (Pittinsky & Carolan, 2008)

To collect student reports of friendships, students were given a class roster and asked to describe their relationship with each student in the class. Choices included best friend, friend, know-like, know, know-dislike, strongly dislike, and do not know (1–6, with 0 = don't know).

B. Multiple-criteria recognition questions (Moolenaar, Daly, & Sleegers, 2011)

"Whom do you go to for work-related advice?"

"Whom do you go to for guidance on more personal matters?"

A school-specific appendix was attached to each survey, which included the names of all the school's team members and a corresponding letter combination (e.g., Mrs. Erin Smith = AB). Respondents (teachers and principals) could answer the social network questions by indicating the letter combination of the intended colleague(s) (e.g., Mrs. Erin Smith = AB), and they could name all the colleagues with whom they interacted.

C. Free-recall questions (Cairns, Leung, Buchanan, & Cairns, 1995)

The interviewer asked, "Some people have a number of close friends, but others have just one 'best friend,' and still others don't have a best friend. What about you?" Children (in the fourth or seventh grades) were free to nominate any number of friends. No class lists or photographs were provided to assist the children: the method involved the free recall of persons. Similarly, children were free to name persons outside the classroom and outside the school.

D. Cognitive social structure task (Gest, 2006)

The teacher was asked, "Are there some children in your class who hang around together a lot? Please use the boxes below to list the names of the children in each group. For very large groups, you can continue listing names in the next box and indicate you are describing one large group." Nine boxes were provided, with lines for six names within each box. At the bottom of the page, teachers were asked, "Are there any children in your class who do not have a group? If so, please list."

Source: Marsden, P. V. (2011). Survey methods for network data. In J. Scott & P. J. Carrington (Eds.), *The Sage handbook of social network analysis* (pp. 370-388). Thousand Oaks, CA: Sage Publications.

Cognitive Social Structures (CSS)

Researchers (e.g., Krackhardt, 1987a) have long advocated that the role of cognition, as opposed to plain structure, be more strongly considered in social network analysis (de Lima, 2010). While de Lima (2010) considers this a third level of analysis, the fact is that it relies on complete-network data, so it will be treated as such in this section. CSS emphasize that actors' perceptions of relational patterns have implications for their own individual attitudes and actions. These implications outweigh the structural reality in which the actors are embedded. To identify these CSS, researchers rely on self-report data that reflect an actor's perception of who is linked to whom and in what ways. Rather than focus on an actor's self-report of his of her own relations with others, the analytic focus is shifted toward asking respondents about how they perceive the relations between any two alters. In these instances, the respondent acts as an informant about the social ties between pairs of actors. For example, in the Peer Groups data set referred to in the previous chapter, the teacher was asked to rate the friendship between each pair of students on a six-point scale (1 = best friend, 2 = friend, 3 = know-like, 4 = know, 5 = know-dislike, 6 = strongly dislike). While this approach yields interesting insights, the obvious drawback is that it places a significant burden on the respondent. In addition to being time consuming and memory intensive, it is also limited to networks that are relatively small in size, as collecting these data on even moderate-sized networks is not feasible.

Egocentric Network Data Collection

While studies that rely on complete-network data may resonate more clearly with what you may typically think of as social network analysis, many network studies operate at a different analytical level. Egocentric network analysis, also referred to as local network analysis, views a social network as a particular actor's set of connections (de Lima, 2010). Oftentimes these types of data are collected as part of a representative sample survey and are therefore drawn from some target population (Marsden, 2011). There are two advantages associated with working at this analytical level (Butts, 2008). First, the data requirements are fairly modest; you do not need to collect relational data from a complete network, which often results in thorny problems with missing data (discussed below). Second, egocentric data collection can be incorporated into large-scale survey research and potentially be used to make inferences about its target population. Therefore, within this framework, researchers usually examine a sample of egocentric networks within a population. The key assumption, and one that is very reasonable if selected from a large enough population, is that each ego's network is independent from those of other respondents.

While egocentric network data are typically part of large-scale surveys, these types of data differ from the simple attribute data that are elicited through standard survey efforts. Egocentric data-collection instruments collect data on the characteristics of the respondent's (ego) alters. In addition to collecting information on the relationship between the respondent and alters, egocentric network data-collection instruments also sometimes go further by asking respondents to provide information on the relations between alters. Valente (2010) notes that this additional information is often useful in order to examine the relationship between personal network characteristics and the possible influence on one's behavior and attitudes. Marsden (2011) delineates the four different ways in which these egocentric network data are collected, often as part of a standard survey instrument: name generators, position generators, resource generators, and social support scales.

Name Generators

These types of questions are the most common way in which egocentric relational data are elicited. Name generators are questions, most often employed in a free-recall format, that ask respondents themselves to identify members of their network. These types of questions, therefore, require that a "focal" ego generate a list of his or her alters. They are referred to as name generators for the simple reason that they elicit a roster of alters within an egocentric network and, in doing so, establish the ego network's boundaries.

These types of questions share many of the same characteristics as sociometric items used in complete network studies. However, one key difference is that name generators rely exclusively on respondent recall, as a roster of possible alters is typically not made available. Like sociometric items, name-generator questions focus on a particular type of relationship. These relationships can be based on role, relational content, or specific types of exchanges. For example, the name generator used in the Educational Longitudinal Survey of 2002 (ELS: 02; Ingels, Pratt, Rogers, Siegel, & Stutts, 2004) asked respondents (10th-grade students) to identify alters based on role; specifically, the prompt asked respondents to list their three closest friends in school. Other name generators focus on the relational content or resource exchange, asking respondents, for example, to identify those that they turn to for advice or with whom they discuss family, home, and personal issues (e.g., Cole & Weinbaum, 2010).

In addition to specifying a particular type of relationship, there are several other issues you should consider when collecting egocentric data through name generators. One issue is the number of probes you should use in order to induce additional alters. This can substantially increase network size as the respondents list additional alters that may have been previously forgotten. Marsden (2011) recommends that these probes be used judiciously, as respondents may interpret their use as an expectation that they are to name more alters, leading them to bend the definition of the generator's role or relational content. A second issue is whether to use more than one generator to identify an egocentric network. For example, you could ask about different kinds of relational content (e.g., help with schoolwork, frequency of contact, etc.), which could possibly produce different sets of alters and, therefore, different networks (Burt, 1997). In addition, when using multiple name generators, you should be aware of how the ordering of the name-generator questions affects the number of alters given in response. A final issue to keep in mind when collecting egocentric data through name generators is whether to provide a fixed number of possible alters. Whereas the ELS: 02 limited the possible number of alters to three and Cole and Weinbaum (2010) in their study of teachers' attitude formation toward reform limited their number of alters to five, many other egocentric instruments do not impose a limitation.

After a list of alters has been produced through one or more name-generator questions (and possibly probes, too), name interpreters are then used to gather information about those named alters and ego's relations with them. Because of this second step, egocentric data collection must be mindful of respondents' time and efforts, as providing this information asks much of respondents. Marsden (2011) identifies three types of name-interpreter items. The first type of name-interpreter questions ask the respondent to provide information about the alters' attributes, including basic demographic characteristics such as race/ethnicity and gender, or other interesting characteristics such as the importance that the alter attaches to grades in school. A second type of name-interpreter item asks about ego's relations with alters. These types of questions are likely the focus of the study and can include questions about the duration, frequency, or intensity of ego's relationship with each alter. For example, after generating a list of friends through a name generator, a name interpreter could be used to ask the respondent to rate the intensity of his or her friendship with each alter. Or the name interpreter could be used to ask the respondent to state the frequency with which the respondent discusses school-related matters with that alter. The third and final type of name interpreter poses the biggest burden on the respondent but yields valuable information about the egocentric network structure. These types of questions follow the preceding two types and ask about the relationships among the alters themselves. So these questions, for example, would ask the respondent to rate the intensity of the friendship between each pair of alters or the frequency with which the two alters discuss school-related matters.

Egocentric data collected through name generators and interpreters can be done through a variety of means (Marsden, 2011). These means include in-person interviews, telephone interviews, or written questionnaire instruments, the standard means through which quantitative social science data are collected. Because name-generator instruments, especially those with multiple name generators, can become difficult for respondents to follow, one of the more promising avenues of egocentric data collection involves self-administered and adaptive computer interfaces. Whether administered online or on a stand-alone computer (e.g., Maroulis & Gomez, 2008), this technique often results in a more streamlined instrument that is easier for respondents to complete. Because these are likely to be self-administered, this also promotes higher levels of disclosure and data quality. But the absence of an interviewer may also reduce motivation and respondents' attentiveness. However, if opting to employ a self-administered egocentric data-collection instrument through a computer interface, it is critically important to be mindful of the interface's visual design. For instance, something as trivial as the amount of space provided to the respondent will influence the content of the response. Table 4.2, adapted from Marsden (2011), provides examples of both name generators and interpreters.

Table 4.2 Examples of Name Generators and Interpreters Used to Elicit Egocentric Network Data.

A. Single name generators

1. "Please write down the names of your best friends at your present school. Please fill in up to three names. If you have fewer close friends, provide less than three names." Respondents asked to provide first name and last initial of each named friend (from 2002 Educational Longitudinal Study [ELS: 02], Ingels et al., 2004).

   Interpreters (Alter attributes and Ego-Alter ties)

   1. Is this friend male or female?
   2. How important is getting good grades to this friend?
   3. Do you know either or both of this friend's parents?
   4. Does your mother or father know either or both of this friend's parents?

2. In the friendship section of the Add Health in-school questionnaire, the respondent was asked to nominate up to five male and five female friends from the roster of all students enrolled in the respondent's school and in the sister school. Once friends were nominated, the respondent entered each friend's identification number on the questionnaire (from The National Longitudinal Study of Adolescent Health [Add Health], Harris, et al. 2009).

   Interpreters (Ego-Alter ties)

   1. Did you go to this friend's house in the last 7 days?
   2. Did you go with this friend after school to hang out or go somewhere in the last 7 days?
   3. Did you talk with this friend about a problem in the last 7 days?
   4. Did you spend time with this friend last weekend?

B. Multiple name generator (Kogovšek & Ferligoj, 2005)

1. From time to time, people borrow something from other people, for instance, a piece of equipment, or ask for help with small jobs in or around the house. Who are the people you usually ask for this kind of help (material support)?

   From time to time, people ask other people for advice when a major change occurs in their life, for instance, changing jobs or a rather serious accident. Who are the people you usually ask for advice when such a major change occurs in your life (informational support)?

   From time to time, people socialize with other people, for instance, they visit each other, go together on a trip or to a dinner. Who are the people with whom you usually do these things (social companionship)?

Interpreters (Ego-Alter ties)

1. Indicate how frequently you have contact with this person. Frequency of contact is measured in five or six ordered categories, with possible responses ranging from "rarely" to "more than once a week." This is asked for each named alter.

2. Indicate whether each friend named was an acquaintance (coded 1), a good friend (2), or a very close friend (3). This was also asked for each alter.

Source: Marsden, P. V. (2011). Survey methods for network data. In J. Scott & P. J. Carrington (Eds.), *The Sage handbook of social network analysis* (pp. 370-388). Thousand Oaks, CA: Sage Publications.

Position Generators

Another means through which egocentric network data are collected is through position generators (Lin, Fu, & Hsung, 2001), which share several characteristics with the more frequently used name generators. Developed out of the literature on social capital, position generators, however, focus on the collection of relational data about actors' resources by asking ego to report on whether they have contacts (alters) in certain social positions (Knoke & Yang, 2008). Investigating an ego's personal contacts with alters that occupy those positions reveals information about the types of social resources to which they have access and, just as importantly, how they gain access to those resources.

The success of position generators to capture an ego's access to a wide array of social resources is dependent on your choice of positions. For example, the position generator in Table 4.3 asks respondents to indicate whether they have a certain type of relationship with any alter in a specific position. These positions are predetermined by you. This is an important step that should be carefully considered and cover the range of variation within the dimensions that are of interest; for example, if examining relations among actors in certain occupations within a school district, you might consider listing all relevant occupations as they vary by prestige. Ego is then asked a series of follow-up questions on the strength of the relationship with each position with which ego has identified having a relationship.

Position generators have three advantages. First, responses can be collapsed into summary measures that reflect the composition and range of an egocentric network. Common summary measures include extensivity, upper reachability, and range (Lin, Fu, & Hsung, 2001). In addition, the position-generator instrument is efficient, requiring less interview time than the name generators described earlier (Marsden, 2011). However, as the number of positions listed by you increases along with the follow-up questions, the demands on the respondent also increase. The advice offered by

Table 4.3 Examples of Position Generators Used to Elicit Egocentric Network Data. Developed out of the literature on social capital, position generators focus on the collection of relational data about actors' resources by asking each ego to report on whether they have contacts (alters) in certain social positions. This is a promising but underutilized technique that should be considered by educational researchers operating from a social capital framework.

A. Do you know anyone well enough to talk to in each of the occupations?

   1. Physician

   2. Elementary school teacher

   3. Police officer

(etc.)

Twelve occupations were presented to respondents in random order. Two measures of individual social capital were derived from the position generator. Reach is the number of occupations in which participants said they knew someone in the three highest-ranked positions. Diversity is the number of different occupations in which participants said they knew people (Johnson, 2010).

B. Do you know anyone who is a . . .

   1. Hairdresser

   2. Cook

   3. Nurse

(etc.)

Thirty occupations were presented. As a minimum criterion of "knowing" a person who could give access to each of them was asked to imagine that when accidentally met on the street, he or she would know the name of that person, and both could start a conversation with each other. Then the respondent was asked whether he or she knew an acquaintance, a friend, or a family member in that position. Assuming an order of increasing tie strength, answers are coded into four categories: no person at all (0), an acquaintance (1), a friend (2), a family member (3); the interpretation of the distinction between these answer categories to label the relationship was left up to the respondent (Van Der Gaag, & Snijders, 2005).

Source: Marsden, P. V. (2011). Survey methods for network data. In J. Scott & P. J. Carrington (Eds.), *The Sage handbook of social network analysis* (pp. 370–388). Thousand Oaks, CA: Sage Publications.

Van der Gaag, Snijders, and Flap (2004) is to keep the number of positions made available respondents around 15 to 20. The final advantage of position generators is that they capture respondents' access to those occupying different positions and, therefore, their access to varying social resources.

Resource Generators

A third means through which egocentric network data are collected is through resource generators (Van der Gaag & Snijders, 2005). Resource generators attend to a significant shortcoming of position generators. This shortcoming is that ego actors often receive help from alters beyond those in the positions listed by you. Therefore, unlike position generators that ask egos whether they have contact with alters in certain positions, a resource generator asks egos whether they know alters that are useful for any specific purpose. Table 4.4 provides some examples from resource generators. It is evident from these examples that, like the position generator, the resource generator does not list an ego's alters individually or measure egocentric network structure (Marsden, 2011). Rather, the focus is on the resources that comprise one's network.

Social Support Scales

A fourth means through which egocentric network data are collected is social support scales. Marsden (2011) points out that there is a vast literature on social support that

Table 4.4   Examples of Resource Generators Used to Elicit Egocentric Network Data. Resource generators attend to a significant shortcoming of position generators. This shortcoming is that ego actors often receive help from alters beyond those in the positions listed by the researcher. Therefore, unlike position generators that ask egos whether they have contact with alters in certain positions, a resource generator asks egos whether they know alters that are useful for any specific purpose. However, there are few, if any, examples of their use in educational research.

A. "Do you know anyone who . . . "
1. Can repair a car, bike, etc.?
2. Can play an instrument?
3. Is active in a political party?

(etc.)

For each item to which respondents answer "yes," they are asked:

What is his/her relationship to you?
1. Family member
2. Friend
3. Acquaintance

Source: Marsden, P. V. (2011). Survey methods for network data. In J. Scott & P. J. Carrington (Eds.), *The Sage handbook of social network analysis* (pp. 370–388). Thousand Oaks, CA: Sage Publications.

details the different instruments that ask respondents to report on the support perceived to be available or the support actually received. Some of these measures look like name-generator instruments that ask respondents about the support they perceive or receive from named alters. Other measures, however, employ a format similar to resource generators and ask respondents whether they have access to others who could provide support. A final type of social support instrument asks separate questions about the various types of support available from different types of alters, including friends, family, neighbors, etc. Table 4.5 presents these three different examples of social support scales.

Partial Network Data Collection

There are occasions when network data collection cannot be easily classified as being at either the complete– or egocentric– level. In this instance, partial network data

Table 4.5 Examples of Social Support Scales Used to Elicit Egocentric Network Data. In addition to name generators/interpreters, position generators, and resource generators, these types of scales represent a fourth possible means through which egocentric data can be collected.

A. Name generator instrument that associates support with named alters (Burt, 1984)

From time to time, people borrow something from other people, for instance, a small sum of money or a piece of equipment, or ask for help with small jobs in or around the house. Who are the people you usually ask for this kind of help (instrumental support)?

B. Ego access to a given type of support (from The Early Childhood Longitudinal Study of 1999, Kindergarten Class [ECLS-K], Tourangeau, Nord, Lê, Sorongon, & Najarian, 2009)

What adult do you to talk to when you need . . .

Someone to cheer you up?

Help with schoolwork?

Advice about important decisions?

For each type of support, respondents could select one or more of the following: parent, adult relative, adult at school, other adult, or no one.

C. Forms of support available from different classes of alters (Turner & Marino, 1994)

To measure ego's experience or perception of being supported by their spouse/partner, relatives, friends, and coworkers, respondents completed a shortened version of the Provisions of Social Relations Scale. Using subsets of items from this scale, Turner and Marino separately assessed the level of support each respondent experienced from these four different classes of alters.

collection (also referred to as sequenced data) consists of you collecting information from all or some portion of ego's alters (Valente, 2010). This type of relational network collection addresses the boundary specification issue through a relational approach in which a respondent's named alters guide subsequent data-collection efforts. The most common type of partial network data is collected through snowball sampling. While there are several drawbacks to this type of respondent-driven approach (noted earlier in this chapter), it is a cost-effective means of contacting a hard-to-reach population (Salganick & Heckathorn, 2004).

Another way in which partial network data are collected is through a general sequenced approach. In this approach, you take a random sample of those alters that have been nominated by ego (the respondent) and collect data only from that sample. This approach has three advantages over snowball sampling (Klovdahl, et al., 1994): (1) they are less likely to end in a social dead end; (2) they provide more entry points into a community of interest; and (3) they provide better estimates of social structure, which can then be employed in inferential models. In relation to this last point, both egocentric and partial network data-collection techniques can work within a random sampling framework and, therefore, can be used to make population parameter estimates.

QUALITY OF RELATIONAL DATA

Having addressed the twin issues of boundary specification and sampling and various complete, egocentric, and partial data-collection instruments, it is now appropriate to turn to issues regarding the measurement quality of relational data. Recall from the previous chapter that social network analysis can employ three types of variables: attribute, relational, and structural. The first of these will not be discussed here, as the measurement of these types of standard social science variables is discussed widely in introductory research methods texts. In addition, this section will not address structural variables, as they are derived from relational data. Rather, the focus is on the relational variables that are the cornerstone of social network analysis. Similar to standard attribute variables, the quality of relational measures hinges on their reliability, validity, accuracy, and measurement error. Moreover, these concerns cut across the different levels of network analysis. It should be noted, however, that available studies on the quality of network data have not produced a consensus about the quality of network measures (Marsden, 2011). Therefore, the ideas offered below are more suggestive than perscriptive.

Reliability

The first threat to the quality of relational data concerns their reliability, generally defined as the extent to which a particular instrument yields a similar result every time when applied repeatedly to the same participant. Social network researchers can rely on several common reliability measures, including interobserver reliability, internal consistency reliability (which includes split-half reliability and Cronbach's alpha), and test–retest reliability (Knoke & Yang, 2008). The latter, however, is the most commonly used means through which network researchers check informant reliability. Consider the following hypothetical example. A teacher nominates all those other teachers from whom he or she seeks advice about professional matters. The retest repeats the same (or similar) request at a later time. Then a comparison between the two sets of responses reflects the teacher's reliability; a perfect correlation between them indicates high reliability. If the retest, however, yields a different set of alters, then the comparison would indicate little reliability. The important issue for a network researcher to consider is the time between the initial test and retest. Differences between the two may reflect an authentic change in respondents' networks; after all, respondents' relations with others change for a variety of legitimate reasons. Reducing the time between the test and retest, however, can mitigate this turnover. Researchers that have examined test–retest reliability in network studies include Morgan, Neal, and Carder (1997), White and Watkins (2000), and Bignami-VanAssche (2005). The general conclusion from this work is that closer ties tend to be reported more reliably than weaker ones, a point that should be kept in mind when designing a network study.

Numerous studies have examined other issues related to the reliability of relational items that constitute network studies (Marsden, 2011). Focusing on the reciprocity of ties—two different respondents nominate each other—these studies have operated on the wholly reasonable assumption that an undirected tie should be reported by both respondents. For example, Feld and Carter (2002) reported a reciprocation rate of 58% for college students who were asked to report on the issue of with whom they spend time. Gest, Farmer, Cairns, and Xie (2003), in their study of peer relations among elementary school children, report that observed interaction is higher in reciprocated pairs of children. These points lend evidence to the claim that reciprocated relations may, in fact, be more valid.

Validity and Accuracy

Validity is the second issue you must consider when collecting and analyzing relational data, which is often correlated with informant reliability (Romney & Weller, 1984). Validity in the case of network studies refers to the extent to which a measure actually measures what it is intended to measure (Wasserman & Faust, 1994). Often, network researchers assume that they are working with valid measures, an assumption that needs to be checked. For example, in eliciting egocentric network data from students through a name generator that asks, "List the five classmates you regularly study with," you can assume that it has face validity in the sense that this prompt will provide a set of alters related to ego through studying behavior. But the validity of this measure would need to be tested in a rigorous manner. This is what is referred to as construct validity: A concept's measure behaves as expected according to theoretical predictions (Wasserman & Faust, 1994).

Since Wassermann and Faust's (1994, p. 58) contention that "there has been very little research on the construct validity of measures of network concepts," surprisingly few studies have sought to address this issue that was brought to the field's attention by the classic Bernard and Killworth (1977) and Bernard, Killworth, and Sailer studies (1980). The issue is whether a respondent's reported behavior reflects his or her actual behavior. For example, one may list those five classmates with whom one studies, but actual observed behavior may indicate something totally different. These behaviors can also be captured, perhaps more accurately, through diaries, logs, or preferably systematic observation. Survey reports and "behavioral" measures of interaction tend to exhibit moderate, at best, levels of agreement (Marsden, 2011). Therefore, the quality of cognitive reports of social ties obtained through surveys is questionable.

Similar to the standard survey instruments, there are ways in which social network researchers might be able to induce more valid responses. The first way is to focus on more stable relations, as opposed to ones that are time specific (Freeman & Romney, 1987). So asking a respondent to identify who one regularly studies with as opposed to asking who one studied with this past month might be the better option. A second way is to limit the number of alters one can nominate in order to counteract "expansiveness bias," the tendency to under/overreport the number of alters in one's network (Feld & Carter, 2002). The number of options made available to the respondent in this "fixed choice" should be theoretically and empirically justified; that is, if the average size of an adolescent's peer group consists of three to five members, then it only follows that there should be a maximum of five fixed options. A third way is to check respondents' reports (Feld & Carter, 2002). Even where it is entirely impractical to collect information from all the others that a respondent nominates, you might reduce the extent of expansiveness bias merely by explicitly asking respondents to try to answer what the others would say as well as what they themselves think and by telling respondents that some information may be confirmed with others.

Measurement Error

Related to concerns about the reliability and validity of network data is the issue of measurement error. Wasserman and Faust (1994) define this as the difference between the "true" score of a concept and the observed score of that same concept. For example, in the School Leaders data set, respondents were asked to rate the frequency with which they had certain types of relations on a scale of 1 to 4, with 4 being the most frequent (1–2 times per week). The assumption on which researchers rely is that the observed score is equivalent to the "true" score plus error. This measurement error, then, is the difference between the "true" and observed scores. The best way to reduce this error is to design the measurement instrument in ways that are most likely to result in observed scores that most closely approximate the "true" score.

There are three issues that researchers should consider in order to best address measurement error. The first is the debate over how to best elicit respondents' recollections: free-recall versus recognition (roster). The former refers to the technique in which you ask respondents to indicate, by recall, those alters with whom they have a specific kind of relation. The latter, which is the technique employed by Daly to generate the School Leaders data set, relies on a roster that is provided to respondents. While both techniques have advantages and disadvantages, it is recommended whenever possible to use a roster technique, as it helps remind respondents about relations that otherwise would have been forgotten (de Lima, 2010; Ferligoj & Hlebec, 1999). This is especially relevant when the number of actors in a complete network study is large. The obvious tradeoff with the roster technique is that it can become quite large and is only generally useful when there are fewer than 50 possible alters (Butts, 2008).

A second issue related to measurement error is the number of alters respondents can nominate. Fixed-choice designs, those preferred by Feld and Carter (2002), limit the number of alters that a respondent can nominate. Free-choice designs, on the other hand, do not provide respondents with any limits as to how many people they can include. Both designs have strengths and weaknesses that you must carefully consider when designing the instrument. Fixed-choice designs limit the burden on the respondent but may artificially distort the number of alters present in one's network (Holland & Leinhardt, 1973). However, there is little agreement as to which design best minimizes measurement error, so the best advice is to employ a combination of both. For example, the "discuss important matters with" name generator on the General Social Survey does not limit the number of people a respondent can nominate, but it does have a follow-up probe if a respondent lists fewer than five people.

A third issue regarding measurement error involves measuring the intensity of relationships. Here the question is one of ratings versus rankings (de Lima, 2010). Designs that require ratings ask that respondents assign a value to each of their ties with alters. These ratings reflect dimensions such as strength, frequency, or intensity and are often captured through a scale that ranges from low to high values. The School Leaders data set was constructed through an instrument that asked respondents to assess the frequency of different types of relations on a four-point scale. In contrast, ranking designs require that respondents rank order all the other actors in their network. The Peer Groups data set referenced in the previous chapter relied on this method: Students were asked to rank their friendship preference for every other student in the class.

In smaller networks, this may be possible, but rank ordering becomes problematic in larger systems ($n > 20$) where there is a bigger burden on respondents and issues related to missing data become more apparent. In addition, ratings are easier to administer and quicker for respondents to complete. The final and perhaps most important reason is that ratings provide a more precise measure of the relationship, as the score need not be relative to others as in a rank-order design.

While ratings are the generally preferred method for capturing a relationship's intensity, it is also preferable to have scores for this intensity as opposed to a score that reflects the presence or absence of a tie. This is the difference between valued and binary relational data that was introduced in the previous chapter. Binary relational data provide you with the least information; therefore it is recommended that you collect some measure of tie strength (that is, collect "valued" relational data). Valued data, in addition to being more useful, is important, as ties that vary in strength have been shown to perform different expressive and instrumental functions in networks. Finally, when trying to induce a measure of tie strength, it is advisable to provide a clear scale to respondents. For example, rather than provide a four-point scale that simply asks respondents to rate the frequency of ties (with higher scores indicating more frequency), it is best to attach a more precise meaning to each possible value. Therefore, similar to the School Leaders data set, it is best to avoid ambiguity in the interpretation of participants' responses by indicting what a score of 4 means. In this instance, "very frequent" is denoted as 1 to 2 times per week.

Missing Data

In addition to the measurement issues discussed above, another concern about the quality of relational data is that network analysis may be hypersensitive to missing data (Kossinets, 2006). Costenbader and Valente's (2003) study confirms this point. Using social network data from eight studies and 58 different networks, they randomly removed an increasing percentage of actors from each network and calculated, then recalculated, a number of different network measures. They concluded that measures that reflect a network's centrality are most sensitive to missing data, whereas simple measures that capture other characteristics remain fairly stable. Borgatti, Carley, and Krackhardt's (2006) analysis found similar results.

The influence of missing data is dependent on whether you are conducting a complete or egocentric network study. For example, if conducting a complete network study on a school district's teachers who have been identified through a census sample, each teacher contributes $N - 1$ pieces of information, the ties or nonties to other teachers. A response rate of, say, 75 to 85% would be high by most any social scientific standard but might not be good enough to accurately calculate most network measures. Recent studies have further investigated these effects and have concluded that it is possible to estimate networks from just parts of them (Rhodes & Keefe, 2007), but more research is needed to model networks that are robust when faced with missing data (Carley, 2004).

Because, however, egocentric network data are sampled from some larger target population, this threshold is different. Here the important consideration is whether the data are missing at random (MAR) or completely at random (MCAR). If the data are not MAR or MCAR, the problem is likely serious, as there may be some systematic error in data collection that "missed" some part of the target sample. The question you need to consider is whether the exclusion of some set of egos due to missing data affects the representativeness of the sample. Another related problem regarding missing data in egocentric network studies is that respondents do not report ties among their alters, which prevents certain egocentric measures from being calculated. Burt (1987) reports that missing relations among alters in an egocentric network tend to be weak ones, thereby indicating a systemic bias in missing data that may affect one's analyses. The way in which network researchers calculate response rates differs according to whether you are collecting egocentric or complete network data. For a brief review of these calculations, see Knoke and Yang (2008).

Despite one's best efforts, the curse of missing data is likely to affect one's network study. There are, however, several different strategies for dealing with missing data in network studies. The six strategies that de Lima (2010) delineates provide some clues as to how researchers might mitigate the adverse effects of missing data: (1) respecification of the network's boundary; (2) imputation; (3) reconstruction; (4) dichotomization; (5) symmetrization; and (6) triangulation. While none of these can be considered "solutions" to missing data, some combination of these strategies will likely allow the analysis to proceed without inducing a tremendous amount of error into the analysis. Of course, the best solution is to prevent missing data as best as possible. In addition to good sampling techniques and appropriate instrumentation, this requires a combination of persuasion techniques, including personal letters, monetary incentives, and phone contacts. This is no different than what you must go through when implementing a standard survey.

MANAGING RELATIONAL DATA

The management of relational data is determined by the study's analytical level: egocentric versus complete network (Valente, 2010). In other words, how you organize the data in preparation for subsequent analysis is contingent on the study's analytical level. Data that are collected as part of an egocentric network study are typically analyzed using standard statistical packages such as SPSS, SAS, or STATA. The analysis of these relational data requires that the analyst construct various network measures for each case in the data file. These measures, discussed in Chapter 7, include egocentric network properties such as size, density, and centrality. In order to calculate these measures, egocentric data first have to be reshaped so that each tie is treated as a separate case in the data set, thereby creating what is referred to as dyadic data. That is, the data file has to be reshaped from "wide" to "long." For example, a respondent who nominates two alters contributes two new cases to the data file, while someone who nominates four alters contributes four new cases. The analysis then follows the creation of these dyadic cases. Valente (2010) cautions that any statistical inferential tests that are performed using dyadic data must be carefully interpreted, as each dyad is not necessarily independent of the other (a violation of the usual assumption of independence). Fortunately, multilevel models can address this violation, so the analysis of egocentric network data should be done in this framework (Snijders & Bosker, 1999). In addition, each individual and dyad can also have attribute data that can be included in the analysis. Reshaping the data from wide to long is fairly simple in standard statistical software packages, and you can easily consult the application's documentation.

Complete network studies—those types of studies that most closely correspond to what you think of as social network analysis—require that the data be managed in a different manner. In these types of studies, the data can be managed in either a node-list or edge-list format. The node-list format is consistent with typical survey data storage, with each row representing a respondent and the columns representing the alters listed by that respondent. The node-list format, however, does not allow for valued data; that is, the data are binary, with a tie being either absent or present. The edge-list format is slightly different in which each row is the respondent and one alter. Therefore, each row is a dyad, which can also contain other information regarding the strength or duration of the relationship between the two actors constituting the dyad. It follows, therefore, that the number of cases in the edge-list format is equivalent to the number of ties present in the entire network. These complete network data can then be read (or directly entered) into specialized network computer programs and labels can be added to the each node's ID number. Table 4.6 shows the same relational data managed in both the node-list (top panel) and edge-list (bottom panel) formats. The programs used to analyze network data such as these are reviewed in the book's final chapter.

Regardless of whether you manage your data using a node-list or edge-list format, these specialized network programs read these data into a matrix, the data representation discussed in the previous chapter. A matrix simply consists of rows and columns that represent the respondents and alters in a network study. In a directed network study, the rows would be the respondents who send ties and the columns would be the alters that receive ties. You always have the option of entering network data into this matrix format directly, which is advisable if you are to new social network analysis. This is feasible so long as the network has a limited number of actors and you are interested in a small number of relations. Once the data are in this matrix format, the different computer programs

Table 4.6 Example Relational Data in Node-List (Top Panel) and Edge-List (Bottom Panel) Formats. In the node-list format, the first node in each row is ego, and the remaining nodes in that row are the nodes to which ego is connected (alters). So node 1 is tied to nodes 2 and 3. These relations are directed and binary (nonvalued).

1	2	3
2	1	
3	1	
4	1	2	5
5	1	2	

1	2	2
1	3	1
2	1	2
3	1	2
4	1	1
4	2	2
4	5	2
5	1	1
5	2	2

In the above edge-list format (bottom), the fourth line of data says that node 3 is connected to node 1 with a tie-strength of 2. If a dyad is omitted, for example (5, 3), that indicates that there is no relationship between the pair. This format is appropriate when your data are directed and valued.

calculate a variety of network measures and also provide useful graphical displays. Table 4.7 shows how the valued data from the edge-list format in Table 4.6 are represented in an adjacency matrix. Similar to the edge-list format in Table 4.6, this adjacency matrix shows that node 4 is connected to node 1 with a tie-strength of 2.

Table 4.7   Example Valued and Directed Relational Data From Table 4.6 in an Adjacency Matrix Format. Regardless of whether you manage your data using a node-list or edge-list format, specialized network programs read these data into a matrix. Alternatively, you can enter your data directly into a matrix format, which is possible so long as your network is relatively small.

	1	2	3	4	5
1	0	2	1	0	0
2	2	0	0	0	0
3	2	0	0	0	0
4	1	2	0	0	2
5	1	2	0	0	0

SUMMARY

This chapter covered a set of important issues in the preanalytical stages of any network study. In some respect, this chapter can be thought of as unfolding in a series of steps that you should consider in order to successfully design a network study. These steps require that you first decide whether you are interested in an egocentric study drawn from some randomly sampled population or a complete network study that aims to explains structural properties of an entire bounded network. Determining this boundary sets up a number of critical decisions that influence data collection, measurement, and management. There are three general ways in which the network's boundary can be specified (positional, relational, or event-based). These sampling issues influence the instruments through which you can collect relational data. For example, in complete network studies in which the actors have been identified through a census, a sociometric instrument is designed to capture information about the relations among actors that constitute that network. On the other hand, in egocentric studies, you must employ some form of name generator and interpreter to induce information about each ego's network. Regardless of the analytic level and instrument that are used, there are three elements that you must keep in mind in order to ensure the highest-quality network data. Issues of reliability and validity are critically important, just as they are in standard social scientific work that operates from a quantitative framework. However, while missing data are the bane of just about any researcher, this issue is particularly problematic for network researchers, as certain relational properties are very sensitive to missing data. Therefore, every effort should be made to minimize missing data through sound sampling procedures and good instrumentation. Finally, this chapter briefly addressed how you manage relational data after they have been collected. These management issues vary according to the study's analytical level. The following chapter discusses how data collected at the complete level can be analyzed to reveal important structural properties that have historically been of interest to network researchers across various disciplines.

CHAPTER FOLLOW-UP

Select a peer-reviewed empirical research article that employs social network analysis and is related to a topic of interest to you. You may consider searching various education-related databases (e.g., ERIC) or searching directly in a small number of influential journals (e.g., *Social Networks, American Educational Research Journal, Sociology of Education*, among others).

Please use that article to respond to the following questions.

1. Describe whether the study employs a positional, relational, or event-based approach to specify the network's boundary.

2. Were the data collected on the complete, ego, or partial network? Describe the sources of these network data.

3. What relations were measured and what instruments were used to measure them? Evaluate the quality of these relational data in terms of validity, reliability, error, and patterns of missingness.

ESSENTIAL READING

Bernard, H. R., Killworth, P. D., & Sailer, L. (1980). Informant accuracy in social network data IV: A comparison of clique-level structure in behavioral and cognitive network data. *Social Networks, 2*, 191–218.

Feld, S., & Carter, W. C. (2002). Detecting measurement bias in respondent reports of personal networks. *Social Networks, 24*, 365–383.

Kossinets, G. (2006). Effects of missing data in social networks. *Social Networks, 28*, 247–268.

5

Structural Measures for Complete Networks

OBJECTIVES

The primary objective of this chapter is to introduce important concepts and measures that you use to describe static properties of social networks. More specifically, these concepts and measures apply to the analysis of complete networks, those networks for which you have complete relational information on each pair of actors, i and j, that constitute any given network. These measures are derived from relational data that are organized in a matrix whose rows and columns represent actors and whose cell values indicate the presence/strength of a tie. The concepts and measures that are discussed in this chapter reflect a variety of structural properties that have been of interest to network researchers for some time. This chapter allows you to ask a question that has been at the core of most network analyses: What does this network look like?

Understanding these properties will eventually allow you to assess a network's dynamics (Hanneman & Riddle, 2011b). So, if a network of 25 teachers in the same school has few connections (low density), does this structure look the same a year after the introduction of teacher professional communities? To address questions that probe a network's dynamics (i.e., its change over time), it is necessary to first figure out what the network looks like at one point in time, what is commonly referred to as the network's topography. This chapter will provide the conceptual tools and precise measures that are needed to perform this first set of analytical steps.

EXAMPLE DATA

To demonstrate these concepts and measures, this chapter will rely on a fairly simple network data set: Newcomb's Fraternity Data (referred to as Fraternity Data). The original sociometric data collected by Newcomb required each of the 17 actors (all members of the same fraternity) to rank all the others in terms of friendship preferences, ranging from 1 to 16, with 1 indicating first preference. These rankings were done across the entire semester, resulting in 15 separate 17 × 17 single-mode, directed, and valued matrices. However, to better illustrate these concepts and measures, these data have been transformed to keep things a little simpler. In addition, the focus will be on one of these networks at a single point in time (week 0, the beginning of the study). These recoded data have been dichotomized, with friendship rankings ranging from 1 to 3, now coded as 1, 0 otherwise. Therefore, using the terminology introduced in Chapter 4, the recoded data set is now directed (asymmetrical) and binary (nonvalued). This was done simply for purposes of presentation; any manipulation of network data should have some theoretical or empirical basis. Table 5.1 shows the recoded data file in the node-list format, with each row starting with the ID number of the responding student followed by three other ID numbers, the alters

Table 5.1 Transformed Fraternity Data in Node-List Format. These binary and directed data consist of 17 students, numbered 1 through 17 (column 1). The next three columns are the ID numbers of the alters who have "received" a tie. For example, Student 2 has sent a tie to Students 4, 7, and 16.

1	11	13	17
2	4	7	16
3	11	12	17
4	2	7	17
5	11	12	17
6	4	8	13
7	4	12	17
8	6	10	11
9	11	12	17
10	1	17	15
11	9	12	17
12	3	11	17
13	1	6	15
14	7	9	10

15	5	10	11
16	4	9	11
17	4	9	12

that are "receiving" friendship nominations. For example, based on the recoding scheme described above, Student 1 sent a friendship nomination Students 11, 13, and 17.

These data can also be represented as a sociomatrix, the format in which the data are then processed for analysis. There are several excellent software packages that facilitate these analyses. The measures demonstrated in this chapter have been calculated with UCINET (Borgatti, Everett, & Freeman, 2006), one the most popular and intuitive applications for social network analysis (reviewed along with other software applications in Chapter 12). Table 5.2 shows the recoded Fraternity Data in

Table 5.2   Transformed Fraternity Data in Square Adjacency Matrix. These are the same data from Table 5.1, but in the form of an adjacency matrix. For example, Student 3 nominated Students 11, 12, and 17 as friends but received only one nomination in return from Student 12.

	1	2	3	4	5	6	7	8	9	10	11	12	13	14	15	16	17
1	0	0	0	0	0	0	0	0	0	0	1	0	1	0	0	0	1
2	0	0	0	1	0	0	1	0	0	0	0	0	0	0	0	1	0
3	0	0	0	0	0	0	0	0	0	0	1	1	0	0	0	0	1
4	0	1	0	0	0	0	1	0	0	0	0	0	0	0	0	0	1
5	0	0	0	0	0	0	0	0	0	0	1	1	0	0	0	0	1
6	0	0	0	1	0	0	0	1	0	0	0	0	1	0	0	0	0
7	0	0	0	1	0	0	0	0	0	0	0	1	0	0	0	0	1
8	0	0	0	0	0	1	0	0	0	1	1	0	0	0	0	0	0
9	0	0	0	0	0	0	0	0	0	0	1	1	0	0	0	0	1
10	1	0	0	0	0	0	1	0	0	0	0	0	0	0	1	0	0
11	0	0	0	0	0	0	0	0	1	0	0	1	0	0	0	0	1
12	0	0	1	0	0	0	0	0	0	0	1	0	0	0	0	0	1
13	1	0	0	0	0	1	0	0	0	0	0	0	0	0	1	0	0
14	0	0	0	0	0	0	1	0	1	1	0	0	0	0	0	0	0
15	0	0	0	0	1	0	0	0	0	1	1	0	0	0	0	0	0
16	0	0	0	1	0	0	0	0	1	0	1	0	0	0	0	0	0
17	0	0	0	1	0	0	0	0	1	0	0	1	0	0	0	0	0

this matrix format. This matrix shows that, for example, Student 2 sent a friendship nomination to Students 4, 7, and 16 but only received a nomination from Student 4. One can determine this by simply reading the matrix's rows (ties sent) and columns (ties received). These are the very same relational data as seen in the node-list format, Table 5.1.

Before preceding any further, it is helpful to take a look at a directed graph generated from the sociomatrix in Table 5.2. Recall from Chapter 3 that each point on the graph represents a node (student) and each line an arc, that is, a directed tie sent from one node to another. Several striking features of the graph are evident.

When looking from this vantage point at Figure 5.1, it is apparent that the network is fairly small (size) but pretty well connected (one component), with no isolates (the reason for the latter is obvious, as each student had to rank all the others). Few of the friendships, however, are reciprocal (reciprocity), and some parts of the network are "thicker" than others (density). That indicates that there are subgroups within the graph—certain clusters of students who are friends with each other (cliques and clans). There are also a couple of students, Students 11 and 17, for example, who

Figure 5.1   Graph of Transformed Fraternity Data Generated from the Adjacency Matrix in Table 5.2. From this graph, we can tell that the network is fairly small (size) but pretty well connected (one component), with no isolates (the reason for the latter is obvious, as each student had to rank all the others). Few of the friendships, however, are reciprocal (reciprocity), and some parts of the network are "thicker" than others (density).

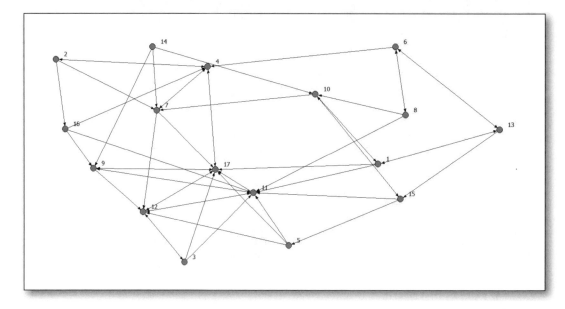

occupy equivalent positions and, consequently, perform the same role in the network (positions and roles).

This chapter introduces the formal algorithms that precisely describe these key features of social networks. Social network and graph theorists have developed an array of indices to characterize these features. These indices rely on some basic—and not-so-basic—mathematical computation. There is no way to avoid this fact without distorting and oversimplifying the advances made by mathematics, specifically graph theory and algebra, to the study of social networks (a point established in Chapter 2). However, an effort is made not to let this fact get in the way of your understanding and application of these concepts and measures. The rest of this chapter introduces the most common ways in which features of complete networks are described, first starting with a set of basic network measures, then, in Chapter 6, moving on to the ways in which subgroups are derived from relational data and, finally, the related ideas of positions and roles.

NETWORK-LEVEL STRUCTURAL MEASURES

Network-level structural measures are those that are calculated from the entire network. Therefore, they provide an excellent snapshot of the network's structure—the pattern of relations among the network's actors. This section introduces seven indicators of network structure. In addition to providing a more global view, these indicators can be used to address questions such as whether the friendship, social support, and advice-seeking networks within the same fraternity, for example, are comparable.

Size

The simplest structural property of a social network is its size, an often ignored but important feature. Size plays an important role in determining what happens in the network—what resources are exchanged among actors, for example. In a network of 17 students, it is not hard to imagine that the pattern of who studies with whom, for example, would look much different than if the network consisted of 200 students. Size affects other network measures, but on a conceptual level, it influences the structure of relations, as actors only have so many resources and capacities for creating and maintaining ties with others. Also, in smaller networks, it is easier for actors to know each other. In formal terms, size is simply a measure of the number of nodes in the network. In the case of the Fraternity Data, it is not a terribly interesting property, as it simply reflects the network's boundary.

Density

Density is intricately linked to network size. Density refers to the number of ties in the network reported as a fraction of the total possible number of ties. Equation 5.1 below shows how a network's density is calculated:

$$D = \frac{L}{N(N-1)} \qquad \text{(Equation 5.1)}$$

where L is the number of lines (directed ties) in the network and N is network size. So, in the Fraternity Data with 17 actors and 51 directed ties, density equals 0.19. The closer this number is to 1.0, the denser the network. A density score of 1.0 indicates that all possible relations are present.

It is also possible to calculate the density of the network's subgroups. For example, you might hypothesize that network density differs by some attribute, GPA, for example. That is, students with denser friendship networks might have access to resources—class notes, information about upcoming assignments, support, and so forth—that may contribute to their academic performance. Density could be calculated on ties among those with GPAs above 3.0 and then compared to those below that threshold.

However, the density of 0.19 reported above is somewhat deceptive, at least in terms of what it means for the Fraternity Data set. This formula needs to be adjusted to account for the limited number of friendship nominations (three) that was imposed when the data were recoded. In a nomination study in which you ask the respondent to list a certain number of alters (or you impose this limit after the data have been collected), it is more sensible to report what is referred to as effective density, which is the number of lines (ties) multiplied by the number of possible alters:

$$D_E = \frac{L}{N(\lambda)} \qquad \text{(Equation 5.2)}$$

where L again is the number of lines (directed ties) in the network, N is network size, and λ is the maximum number of alters requested or permitted. Using this formula, the density of the Fraternity Data is 1.0: All possible relations are present, which is unsurprising given that the original ranked data were recoded ($1 - 3 = 1$, all others $= 0$) and each respondent had the maximum number of three friendship nominations.

Reciprocity

A third network measure that indicates an aspect of the network's social structure is reciprocity, defined as the degree to which actors in a directed network select one another. Stated another way, reciprocity indicates the mutuality of the network's ties (this is why reciprocity is also referred to as mutuality). This property is important because it reveals the direction through which resources such as help, advice, and support flow. It also indicates the network's stability, as reciprocated ties tend to be more stable over time. Finally, networks with high reciprocity may be more "equal," while those with lower reciprocity may be more hierarchical.

While some relations are by definition reciprocal, such as "studied with," others such as friendship are potentially asymmetrical and indicate imbalances in influence, status, or authority.

Borgatti, Everett, and Freeman (2006) provide the following measure of reciprocity:

$$R = \frac{(A_{ij} = 1) \ and \ (A_{ij} = 1)}{(A_{ij} = 1) \ or \ (A_{ij} = 1)} \qquad \text{(Equation 5.3)}$$

where A_{ij} indicates a tie from actor i to j. A high degree of reciprocity means that a network's actors choose one another. It could also mean that while some actors choose one another, they are not choosing others, which results in a high degree of clustering within the network. At the complete network level, reciprocity is reported as the proportion of reciprocated ties in the network. Therefore, values closer to 1.0 indicate higher reciprocity.

Applying Equation 5.3 to the Fraternity Data, reciprocity for the entire network is 0.31, indicating that slightly less than one-third of all ties are mutual. This low value should be considered unsurprising, as this particular network snapshot was taken at the beginning of the study, well before the participants got to know each other. One could reasonably expect that the network's reciprocity, as well as its density, will increase over time, which would be associated with a greater likelihood of engaging in behavior together and sharing similar attitudes. For example, Moolenaar and Sleegers (2010) hypothesize that teacher networks with high reciprocity would be positively associated with teachers' perceptions of their schools' innovative climate and trust. Their analyses, however, do not support this hypothesis. According to their models, dense networks (on two different network relations: "discuss work" and "regard as friend") are significantly related to both a teacher's perceptions of trust and the school's innovative climate, while reciprocity is not. However, despite this null finding, others have shown that networks with high reciprocity are associated problem solving and the exchange of complex knowledge (Uzzi & Spiro, 2005) but are also associated with less desirable outcomes such as risky drug and sexual behaviors (Valente & Vlahov, 2001).

Transitivity

Transitivity is another feature of complete networks that reflects the social structure's tendency toward stability and consistency. Whereas reciprocity focuses on the ties between two actors (dyads), transitivity is based on the triad, any "triple" of actors.

The addition of this third "other" reflects a more authentic character of social life and has been the basis for much theorizing about social networks (Simmel, 1908/1950). Much of this theorizing revolves around a triad's tendency toward transitivity: if Teacher A collaborates with Teacher B and Teacher B collaborates with Teacher C, then Teacher A collaborates with Teacher C. In this instance, the triad is considered transitive because Teachers A and B have the same relationship with C.

Valente (2010) notes that early theorizing about this tendency focused on the concept of balance, first introduced by Heider (1958) to explain a person's observed preference for equilibrium with the people around them. The theory of cognitive dissonance grew out of this work, attempting to explain how people felt when their immediate environment was unbalanced (Festinger, 1954). The argument then extended to postulate that increasing the number of transitive triads of which one is a part could reduce cognitive dissonance. Even Granovetter's strength of weak ties theory (1973) emerged from this work, showing that intransitive triads are relatively rare, resulting in networks with fewer weak ties. The paradox, of course, is that the relative paucity of weak ties is what makes them "strong," as they provide early access to diverse information.

Measuring triadic relations within a network of undirected (symmetric) relations is straightforward (Hanneman & Riddle, 2011b). There are only four possible types of triadic relations: no ties, one tie, two ties, or all three ties. Performing what is called a "triad census" on these data can reveal the extent to which the network can be characterized as consisting of isolates (actors not connected to any other actors), dyads (actors who are only connected to one other actor), structural holes (one actor connected to two others who, in turn, are not connected to each other), and clusters (groups of three actors that are all connected to each other). With undirected data, one can simply count how often each of these four types occurs across all possible triples.

However, things get more interesting when performing a triad census on directed data, such as the transformed Fraternity Data. There are 16 possible types of relations among any three of the network's actors (Holland & Linehardt, 1979). Different forms of relationships can be observed among these groups, including hierarchy, equality, and exclusivity. This is one of the reasons why researchers with an interest in social group relations suggest that the most fundamental forms of social relationships can be observed at the triadic level. A triad census for a network with directed data counts the proportion of triads that fall within each of these 16 categories. These categories are typically called MAN categories, which reflects the number of mutual (M), asymmetric (A), and null (N) ties in each triad. Therefore, a triad with a code of 111 would have one mutual tie, one asymmetric, and one null tie, indicating that one actor serves as a go-between for the triad's other two actors. Of these 16 possible types of directed triads, only four can be classified as transitive (Wasserman & Faust, 1994). In the Fraternity Data there are, for example, five 030 triads (zero mutual, three asymmetric, and zero null ties); these triads are considered transitive because Students 1 and 2 have the same relationship to 3.

Going one step further, a transitivity analysis divides a network's number of transitive triads by the number of triads of all kinds. More formally, the density of transitive triples is the number of triples, which are transitive, divided by the number of paths of length two (i.e., the number of triples that have the potential to be transitive). In the Fraternity Data, this value is 10.70%. This lack of transitivity suggests that there are numerous null ties, indicating a relatively sparse network in which resources will have difficulty flowing from one part of the network to another. This is not too surprising given that these relations were measured at the start of the study (week 1) and, as a result of the data transformation, each actor has three out-degrees (that is, they sent three friendship nominations). Here, too, this can be attributed to a measurement issue. Faust (2008) has shown that fixed-choice survey instruments (recall that these manipulated data "fixed" the number of friendship nominations to three), artificially limit the triad census and the subsequent analysis of transitivity. Regardless, establishing a network's transitivity is important, as it is theoretically connected to actors' tendencies to divide into exclusive subgroups over time, especially relational data that capture positive affect, such as friendship.

Diameter and Distance

Similarly, the next two network-level properties, diameter and distance, also indicate how well resources can move from one part of the network to another. Whereas transitivity focuses on the importance of certain configurations of triads, these two related concepts are more straightforward. A network's diameter refers to the longest path between any two actors. This property is important, as networks that have the same size (equal numbers of actors) and even the same density (equal percentages of ties present) can have different diameters. Consider the network's diameter in Figure 5.1. The length of the longest path between two actors is five. To "get from" Student 15 to 16 in this directed network requires five steps: $15 \rightarrow 5 \rightarrow 17 \rightarrow 4 \rightarrow 2 \rightarrow 16$. This is the only five-step path in the network and is the maximum distance between any two actors.

Related to this is another property that captures how "far" actors are from one another. The average path length measures the mean distance between all pairs of actors in the network. When this value is small, this indicates that there is a cohesive network with minimal clustering. Conversely, when this value is high, the network likely has little cohesion, thereby making it difficult for resources—whether these resources be advice, trust, information, or the like—to move from one part of the network to another. The average path length in the Fraternity Data is 2.18. The interpretation of this is that, on average, all students in the network are slightly more than two steps from everyone else in the network, assuming they could reach one another (an assumption that is incorrect given that there are no paths between some pairs of students). To calculate this, you first have to identify the distances between each pair of actors in the network and then calculate the average of all these pairs.

Both diameter and average path length are important network-level structural properties. Valente (2010) goes as far as to note that you need not know anything else about a network's topography to draw several important conclusions. For example, a network with a large diameter and small average path length suggests a structure in which there are parts of the network that some network actors may be unable to access. This is evident for Student 15 who, in a network with a total of 17 actors, needs five steps to reach another member (Student 16).

Clustering

Another structural network-level property that is of interest to network researchers is a network's clustering. Clustering is a measure of a network's actors' tendency to "group together" into pockets of dense connectivity (Valente, 2010). High clustering indicates that there are numerous pockets in which some actors are connected to each other but not to others. Low clustering, on the other hand, suggests that relations are more evenly distributed across the network with very few pockets of dense connectivity among subsets of actors. The tendency, of course, is for people to interact with a fairly small set of actors who share similar attributes—the "birds of a feather flock together" (homophily) phenomenon. Knowing the degree to which actors cluster says a great deal about the structure of these everyday relations, a structural pattern that may even seem somewhat paradoxical (Watts, 1999). This is related, in part, to what is referred to as the small-world phenomenon.

The small-world phenomenon combines two ideas (Valente, 2010). The first is a network with a short average path length. That is, relatively few steps connect each pair of actors, on average. The second part of this is that "small-world" networks also have a high degree of clustering—groups of actors who interact almost exclusively in their own immediate "neighborhoods." This second part is the network's tendency to form dense local pockets of connectivity: clusters. "Small worlds" are those that paradoxically have a low average path length but high clustering.

Measuring the extent to which a network displays clustering involves two steps. First, one calculates the density of each actor's local neighborhood (the density of each ego's network, which equals the total number of ties present divided by the total number of possible ties). Then, after doing this for all actors in the network, the degree of clustering can be characterized by the average of all the ego neighborhoods in the complete network. For example, the Fraternity Data network has a network-level clustering coefficient of 0.24, which reflects the average neighborhood densities of all 17 actors. This seems pretty low; students are surrounded by local neighborhoods that are sparse. However, this should be considered in light of the network's overall density, which was 0.19 (Equation 5.1). So the average density of these local neighborhoods (clustering) is not much different than the density of the entire network. There is also a weighted version of the measure that accounts for the size of each ego's neighborhood. That is, actors with more alters in their immediate neighborhoods get more "weight" in computing the average density. When computing this weighted version of the Fraternity Data, there is little difference with the nonweighted version.

Centralization

A final structural property of complete networks is centralization. A network that is highly centralized is one in which relations are focused on one or a small set of actors. This is, however, different than a structural property such as density, which measures the presence of relations, not whether they are focused on a small set of actors. In other words, a network can be dense but have low centralization (many relations that are spread evenly across the network's actors) and vice versa (few relations that are concentrated on a small set of actors). Networks that are centralized, regardless of their density, are ones in which only a small and exclusive set of actors hold positions of power and control. Decentralized networks, conversely, are those in which power and control are diffuse and spread over a number of actors.

Centralization can be based on a number of metrics (these are discussed in Chapter 7 when individual ego centrality measures are introduced), with degree being one of the most common (Freeman, 1979). *Degrees* refers to the number of ties an actor either sends (out-degree) or receives (in-degree). Valente (2010) summarizes the calculation of network centralization. Network centralization is calculated by determining the highest individual centrality score (either in-degree or out-degree) and then subtracting it from all the other individual scores in the network. Next, these differences are added and that total is divided by the maximum sum of differences theoretically possible in a network of that size. Freeman's (1979) formula for centralization degree (CD) is:

$$CD = \frac{\Sigma(Max(C_{Di}) - C_{Di})}{n^2 - 3n + 2} \qquad \text{(Equation 5.4)}$$

where $Max(C_{Di})$ is the network's maximum centrality score, C_{Di} indicates individual actors' centrality scores, and n is the network's size. This formula can also be applied to the other types of centrality, including betweenness and closeness, to be discussed in Chapter 7.

Applying Equation 5.4 to the Fraternity Data, the network's (in-degree) centrality score is 33.20%. Figure 5.2 shows this network with a different layout. This circle layout includes three students (numbers 12, 11, and 17), who receive the most friendship nominations (six, eight, and eight in-degrees, respectively), who are at the center of the circle. This layout demonstrates just how "central" these actors are to the network. However, this overall centralization score is not too high, indicating that friendship nominations are spread more or less evenly across the network's actors. Why is this property important?

A network's centralization affects the process through which resources traverse the network. Imagine if Students 12, 11, and 17 have information about what was to be included on an upcoming exam. Their location can either accelerate or prevent the spread of that information to other students. These central actors likely wield a disproportionate amount of influence on the network. Therefore, high centralization provides fewer actors with more power and control.

Figure 5.2 Circle Layout of Fraternity Members Network With Three Central Students. This circle layout includes three students (numbers 12, 11, and 17) who receive the most friendship nominations (six, eight, and eight in-degrees, respectively), who are at the center of the circle. This layout demonstrates just how "central" these actors are to the network.

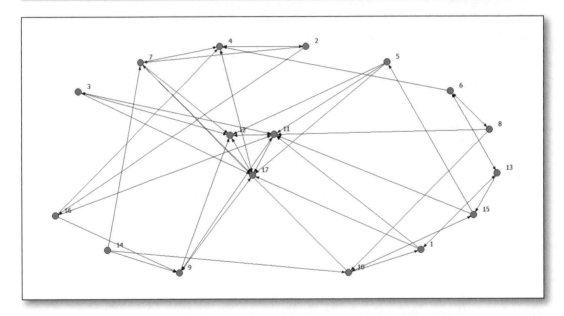

SUMMARY

This chapter introduced structural measures that you can be calculated on complete network data. The introduction of these concepts, definitions, and measures parallels the analytic process that is often employed in network studies. First, you identify the main structural properties of a network, including those related to its size, density, and connectivity. After performing the analyses covered in this chapter, you will typically move on to a group or positional analysis, which is addressed in Chapter 6. Although these structural measures for complete networks are considered a baseline for most analyses, their use should be guided by questions of theoretical interest. Each measure will give you a slightly different perspective on the network's structure, so it is best to use measures that reflect your theoretical interests.

CHAPTER FOLLOW-UP

1. Assume you have complete network-level data on school leaders in a large urban district that is transitioning to a new teacher-evaluation system. You have relational data on the frequency with which ego discusses this new system with each alter (0 = never, 1 = sometimes, 2 = regularly, and 3 = frequently) and whether ego turns to alter for advice regarding general professional matters (1 = yes, 0 = no). Which structural properties of the complete network might be of interest to you? Please explain why these properties might be of interest.

2. Given the same network described above, what would high centralization scores on both relations indicate about this network's ability to successfully transition to a new evaluation system?

3. How might your response to #2 differ if you knew that the networks also had high density scores? Given this new information, what would you predict about the transition to a new evaluation system?

ESSENTIAL READING

Freeman, L. C. (1979). Centrality in social networks. *Social Networks, 1*, 215–239.

Watts, D. (1999). Networks, dynamics, and the small-world phenomenon. *American Journal of Sociology, 105*(2), 493–527.

Wellman, B. (1988). Structural analysis: From method and metaphor to theory and substance. In B. Wellman & S. D. Berkowitz (Eds.), *Social structures: A network approach* (pp. 19–61). New York: Cambridge University Press.

6

Groups and Positions in Complete Networks

OBJECTIVES

The objective of this chapter is to show how a complete network can be analyzed further by using different algorithms to identify its groups and positions. You will also evaluate the difference between the "top-down" and "bottom-up" approaches through which groups are identified. Unlike most social science, the idea is to identify these groups through their relational data, not an exogenous attribute such as grade level, departmental affiliation, or years of experience. After reviewing these different approaches, you will learn how the concept of group differs from position. Positions are also identified through relational data, and you will learn the different ways through which this is done. These different ways are based on contrasting definitions of equivalence, a key concept that you will encounter at the end of the chapter. Finally, once you examine the different ways in which positions are identified, you will then see how relations among different positions can be analyzed and visually represented.

GROUPS

Once you have a handle on the network's topography using some combination of the structural properties covered in Chapter 5, complete-level network analysis typically moves on to an analysis of the network's substructures. It is at this point in the analysis that you seek to identify those larger groupings that give contours to the network's topography. This section follows the lead of Hanneman and Riddle (2011b) by looking at these groups from either the "top-down" or "bottom-up." More specifically, through the bottom-up approach, you can identify groups that are built up from simple dyads and triads that extend into dense clusters that give the network its "clumpiness." Attention in this approach is given to how larger structures are composed of smaller groups of actors. Similar to complete network measures, there are several important properties for which precise definitions and algorithms have been developed, including cliques, clans, plexes, and cores.

"TOP-DOWN" APPROACHES TO GROUP ANALYSES

The "top-down" approach focuses on how larger structures are built from smaller ones (Hanneman & Riddle, 2011b). Therefore, this approach takes the complete network and considers parts of it that are dense and somewhat distinct from the rest of the network. These "parts" can be defined and measured in different ways, including components, bi-components, and factions. However, the approach that you use, whether top-down or bottom-up, will likely yield different groups. The important thing to consider when selecting a method is your definition of what constitutes a meaningful group and then to select the algorithm that best matches this definition.

To illustrate these ideas about groups, this section will again rely on the Fraternity Data, a binary, directed set of complete network data. When permitted by the algorithms, these directed data will be used. However, not all algorithms can handle (or are appropriate for) directed data. Therefore, in these instances, symmetrical data will be used; a friendship tie exists between each pair if either $x_{ij} = 1$ or $x_{ji} = 1$. It should be noted that conceptually, this is suspect; to consider that a friendship exists between two students because one nominates the other is a stretch. But, for the purposes of presentation, those algorithms that require symmetrical data will rely on this transformation. These symmetric data are presented in Table 6.1, which is simply an undirected version of the relational data in the sociomatrix in Table 5.2. If a student either sent or received a friendship nomination, the symmetrical sociomatrix represents this as a reciprocated tie. Using these symmetrical data, this section first reviews the three different definitions of substructures identified through the top-down approach and then moves on to the four ways associated with the bottom-up approach.

Table 6.1 Symmetrized Fraternity Data Sociomatrix. These transformed symmetric data are an undirected version of the relational data in the sociomatrix in Table 5.2. It is sometimes necessary to use undirected data such as these in a group or positional analysis. Transforming these relational data from directed to undirected is typically done through a general social network software package.

	1	2	3	4	5	6	7	8	9	10	11	12	13	14	15	16	17
1	0	0	0	0	0	0	0	0	0	1	1	0	1	0	0	0	1
2	0	0	0	1	0	0	1	0	0	0	0	0	0	0	0	1	0
3	0	0	0	0	0	0	0	0	0	0	1	1	0	0	0	0	1
4	0	1	0	0	0	1	1	0	0	0	0	0	0	0	0	1	1
5	0	0	0	0	0	0	0	0	0	0	1	1	0	0	1	0	1
6	0	0	0	1	0	0	0	1	0	0	0	0	1	0	0	0	0
7	0	1	0	1	0	0	0	0	0	1	0	1	0	1	0	0	1
8	0	0	0	0	0	1	0	0	0	1	1	0	0	0	0	0	0
9	0	0	0	0	0	0	0	0	0	0	1	1	0	1	0	1	1
10	1	0	0	0	0	0	1	1	0	0	0	0	0	1	1	0	0
11	1	0	1	0	1	0	0	1	1	0	0	1	0	0	1	1	1
12	0	0	1	0	1	0	1	0	1	0	1	0	0	0	0	0	1
13	1	0	0	0	0	1	0	0	0	0	0	0	0	0	1	0	0
14	0	0	0	0	0	0	1	0	1	1	0	0	0	0	0	0	0
15	0	0	0	0	1	0	0	0	0	1	1	0	1	0	0	0	0
16	0	1	0	1	0	0	0	0	1	0	1	0	0	0	0	0	0
17	1	0	1	1	1	0	1	0	1	0	1	1	0	0	0	0	0

Components

One of the most basic ways in which network researchers first characterize a network's substructure is to identify its components. It may be helpful to consider this concept in terms of graphs (Chapter 3). A component is a connected subgraph in which there is a path between all pairs of nodes (Wasserman & Faust, 1994); that is, all pairs in the component are reachable. If a graph has one component, the graph is considered connected. If it has more than one component, it is disconnected. Each isolated node (an actor with zero ties) is considered its own component. Directed graphs, such as the graph that constitutes the Fraternity Data, have two different kinds of components: weak and strong. A weak component ignores the direction of a tie; strong components do not. Stated differently, strong components consist of nodes that are connected to one another via both directions along the path that connects them. Weak components consist of a set of nodes that are connected regardless of the direction of the ties. This concept of a component is simple and very useful, especially when analyzing a large network with many components. Typically, researchers extract each component and analyze it as a separate network.

Researchers are also interested in components for a few different reasons. For example, networks can be described in terms of their number of weak and strong components. A network with one component (in this case, the graph is equal in size to its one component) is very different than a network with many components. Components can also be used to define and describe groups within a network. If there is a path connecting two nodes, you can describe them as being part of the same group. This first pass can then be used to further identify groups within each component using different and stricter definitions.

Because the Fraternity Data are directed with friendship relations being sent from one student to another, it makes sense to first analyze the network's strong components. In these data, there are four strong components: two are isolates, one has nine members, and the other has six. However, if you are interested in the network's weak components, thereby ignoring the direction of the tie, the network has one component consisting of all 17 students, which is expected given that each student was initially asked to rank the others. If these data were valued—that is, the cells of the sociomatrix had values ranging from $0 \ldots x$—it would be necessary to define what is known as a cut-off value. A cut-off value is determined by you from valued data to identify whether a relationship between two nodes exists or not. The selection of this value should not, however, be arbitrary. It should be informed by theory (for example, how often does one have to study with another in order to be identified as study partners?) and subject to sensitivity analyses. Continuing to think of the network's substructures in terms of graphs, there are several other ways to define groups within a network.

Bi-Components

Bi-components are an especially useful way of identifying the important "weak" spots in a graph (Hanneman & Riddle, 2011b). This technique allows you to ask what would happen to the network if an actor were removed. Would the network become divided into disconnected segments? Nodes that serve this purpose are referred to as "cutpoints" and are usually important actors; that is, they "keep things together." When a graph is divided in such a manner, it is referred to as bi-component (also called "blocks," which are different than the blocks identified in a positional analysis discussed later this chapter). Applying this idea to the symmetrized Fraternity Data, there is only one bi-component. This parallels the early finding of the network's relatively low centralization (CD) score. No one student is responsible for keeping the network connected.

Factions

Factions are a third means through which a network's substructures can be defined through a top-down approach. In addition, this procedure also indicates the density within the groups that have been identified. However, before describing how this works, consider the following hypothetical example. There is a classroom (graph) in which each student (node) was closely connected to all the others in his or her group (subgraph) and there are no connections between these groups, with each group therefore being its own component. Of course, most classrooms or real social systems do not look like this, but this hypothetical example is a useful frame of reference for assessing a network's factions.

If the students in each faction were then placed (permuted) in their own rows and columns in an adjacency matrix, you could then see a pattern of blocks consisting of either 1s or 0s (referred to as 1-blocks or 0-blocks). All connections within a 1-block would be present and connections between factions (blocks) would be absent. Running this routine on the symmetrized Fraternity Data reveals several interesting structural properties that are reported in the UCINET output, Figure 6.1. The number of "blocks" to enter is up to you, and after working upward from two, it was decided that three was a meaningful number of blocks.

The UCINET output provides results regarding the routine's "goodness of fit," a permuted adjacency matrix, and block densities. The "final proportion correct" can be thought of as a goodness-of-fit measure. This value, 0.79, reflects the sum of the number of 0s within factions (where all the ties in the ideal type are supposed to be present) and the number of 1s in the nondiagonal blocks (ties between members of different factions, which are supposed to be absent in the ideal type) divided by the networks total number of ties (51). This is a pretty good fit. The three factions are identified, with Students 2, 4, 7, 14, and 16, for example, belonging to faction #3. The grouped adjacency matrix shows the permuted solution. On the diagonal of this matrix, it is evident that most of the relations are present (1s), indicating that relations within these groups are dense. The final panel in this output confirms this point by reporting the block densities: the number of ties in the bock as a proportion of all possible ties. For example, within the first block, 80% of relations are present, whereas only 14% are present between the first and second blocks.

Figure 6.1 Output from UCINET's Factions Routine on the Symmetrized Fraternity Data. Three factions have been identified with Students 2, 4, 7, 14, and 16, for example, belonging to faction #3. The grouped adjacency matrix shows the permuted solution. On the diagonal of this matrix, it is evident that most of the relations are present (1s), indicating that relations within these groups are dense. The final panel in this output confirms this point by reporting the block densities: the number of ties in the block as a proportion of all possible ties.

```
FACTIONS
--------------------------------------------------------------

Number of factions: 3
Measure of fit: Hamming
Input dataset: NEWC0LE3-Sym (C:\Program Files\Analytic Technologies\Ucinet 6\
DataFiles\chap 5\NEWC0LE3-Sym)

Initial proportion correct: 0.684

...Badness of fit: 58.000
...Badness of fit: 58.000
...Badness of fit: 58.000

Final proportion correct: 0.787

Group Assignments:

    1:   3 5 9 11 12 17
    2:   1 6 8 10 13 15
    3:   2 4 7 14 16

Grouped Adjacency Matrix

           1     1 1   1     1 1           1 1
         9 2 3 5 1 7   0 6 8 5 3 1   2 4 4 6 7
         ------------------------------------
    9 |   1     1 1 |             |     1 1   |
   12 | 1   1 1 1 1 |             |         1 |
    3 |   1     1 1 |             |           |
    5 |   1     1 1 |     1       |           |
   11 | 1 1 1 1   1 |   1 1     1 |     1     |
   17 | 1 1 1 1 1   |         1 | 1         1 |
         ------------------------------------
```

```
10 |                   |   1 1    1 |     1    1 |
 6 |                   |   1    1   |   1        |
 8 |          1    | 1 1           |            |
15 |        1 1    | 1         1   |            |
13 |               | 1    1    1 |            |
 1 |          1 1 | 1          1   |            |
   -----------------------------------------------
 2 |               |               |    1    1 1 |
 4 |            1 | 1             | 1       1 1 |
14 | 1             | 1             |         1 |
16 | 1        1   |               | 1 1        |
 7 |    1         1 | 1           | 1 1 1      |
   -----------------------------------------------


Density Table

            1     2     3
          ----  ----  ----
      1   0.80  0.14  0.20
      2   0.14  0.47  0.10
      3   0.20  0.10  0.60
```

There are two other relatively recent top-down approaches that identify a network's substructures that deserve a brief mention. While the algorithms behind both approaches are complex, the intuitive logic undermining them is very appealing. The first is the Girvan-Newman (GN) technique (2002; Newman & Girvan, 2004), which emphasizes those ties between actors that, if removed, would partition the network into mutually exclusive groups. In general, GN subgroups are identified by first calculating betweenness centrality (this version of centrality is discussed in Chapter 7) on the ties, and, second, determining if there are any components revealed once ties with the highest betweenness scores are removed. This process is repeated until the number of desired groups is obtained. Similar to the factions routine, you can predetermine the number of groups. Or the analyses can proceed until no groups greater than a certain size are detected. The GN technique, in addition to partitioning the network into some number of mutually exclusive groups, also measures how well the partition characterizes the network. This measure is called modularity (Newman & Girvan, 2004). The equation it provides calculates what is referred to as Q, the percentage of ties in the network that occur within the subgroups found by the GN algorithm. Therefore, a Q of 100% reflects that all the ties are to actors within the groups. There is, however, no current standard for an acceptable Q value. Regardless, the algorithm provides a nice way to divide the network into mutually exclusive subgroups and index how well the partition captures the network's pattern of ties. Therefore, you have the ability to choose among competing partitions derived from this algorithm and select the one that best fits.

A second noteworthy top-down approach is Moody and White's (2003) technique for identifying nested cohesive subgroups. This approach differs significantly from those already discussed in one important way. Whereas routines such as factions and GN partition the network's actors into mutually exclusive groups (i.e., each actor belongs to one group), the algorithm developed by Moody and White identifies hierarchies of nested cohesive groups. In essence, this approach permits actors to be embedded in more than one group simultaneously, which is a closer approximation of what social life looks like. This algorithm is based on the removal of individual nodes and the identification of K-components (maximal K-connected subgraphs, where K equals the number of nodes specified by you). Both the GN subgroups and Moody and White cohesive subgroups, though computationally complex, represent significant advances in identifying a network's subgroups through a top-down approach.

"BOTTOM-UP" APPROACHES TO GROUP ANALYSES

K-Cores

The first of four different ways in which a network's substructures can be identified through a more "bottom-up" approach is through K-cores. Recall that this bottom-up approach starts first with the dyad and extends upward (Hanneman & Riddle, 2011b). The network's overall structure, then, is viewed as emerging from overlaps of the graph's smaller parts. K-cores reflect this logic. Whereas a component consists of all the nodes that have at least one connection, a K-core is a substructure (a subgraph) of the network in which each node within the K-core is connected to at least K other nodes (Valente, 2010). Therefore, a $3K$-core is a substructure, a subset of actors, in which each node is connected to at least three other nodes; a $2K$-core would be a subset in which a node is connected to two others, and so forth. Those nodes that do not meet K, which is defined by you, are dropped from the network. As you increase the value of K, the remaining relations will appear increasingly dense as less-connected others are removed from the network. A technique that is often used is what is called a K-core collapse: what happens to the pattern of nodes as K increases. By charting this process, you are able to identify whether there is a "core" group of actors at the center of the network, while others are on the periphery.

The K-core routine is especially helpful when dealing with larger networks of actors (unlike the Fraternity Data set). It is also intuitively appealing: If an actor is connected to a sufficient number of other actors in the network, they may feel as though they belong to that group even if they are not directly connected to many or even most members. From this perspective, one's membership in a group is based on connections rather than immersion in a subgroup, as is the case with cliques.

N-Cliques

K-cores allow you to identify the network's core group of actors, which may be of empirical interest. However, you might also want to reveal how groups are distributed in the network and which actors belong to which groups. A clique analysis is one way to satisfy these purposes. A clique is a maximally connected subgraph of nodes (> 2) in which all nodes are connected to each other.

Figure 6.2 shows the UCINET output from the clique analysis. In the symmetrized Fraternity Data, there are 11 cliques. There are three cliques that consist of four students, with students in multiple cliques. For example, Student 11 is in six cliques (cliques 1–6). The bottom section of the output shows each student's proximity to each of the 11 cliques (or how "adjacent" they are to the clique). Student 1 is adjacent to half (0.50) of the members of clique 1, and Student 3 is adjacent to more than three-quarters of the members in clique 1 (0.75). There is a fairly high degree of co-clique membership in these data. Again, this can be somewhat expected, as these relations were measured at the beginning of the study. You can reasonably expect that as the semester progresses, this degree of overlap would change.

Figure 6.2   Output from UCINET's Clique Routine on the Symmetrized Fraternity Data. This output shows that there are three cliques that consist of four students, with students in multiple cliques. For example, Student 11 is in six cliques (cliques 1–6). The bottom section of the output shows each student's proximity to each of the 11 cliques (or how "adjacent" the student is to the clique). Student 1 is adjacent to half (0.50) of the members of clique 1, and Student 3 is adjacent to more than three-quarters of the members in clique 1 (0.75).

```
CLIQUES
------------------------------------------------------------------

Minimum Set Size: 3
Input dataset: NEWC0LE3-Sym (C:\Program Files\Analytic Technologies\
Ucinet 6\DataFiles\chap 5\NEWC0LE3-Sym)

11 cliques found.

    1:   9 11 12 17
    2:   5 11 12 17
    3:   3 11 12 17
```

(Continued)

Figure 6.2 (Continued)

```
   4:   1 11 17
   5:   5 11 15
   6:   9 11 16
   7:   2  4  7
   8:   2  4 16
   9:   4  7 17
  10:   7 10 14
  11:   7 12 17

Clique Participation Scores: Prop. of clique members that each node is
adjacent to

          1     2     3     4     5     6     7     8     9    10    11
        ----- ----- ----- ----- ----- ----- ----- ----- ----- ----- -----
   1    0.500 0.500 0.500 1.000 0.333 0.333 0.000 0.000 0.333 0.333 0.333
   2    0.000 0.000 0.000 0.000 0.000 0.333 1.000 1.000 0.667 0.333 0.333
   3    0.750 0.750 1.000 0.667 0.333 0.333 0.000 0.000 0.333 0.000 0.667
   4    0.250 0.250 0.250 0.333 0.000 0.333 1.000 1.000 1.000 0.333 0.667
   5    0.750 1.000 0.750 0.667 1.000 0.333 0.000 0.000 0.333 0.000 0.667
   6    0.000 0.000 0.000 0.000 0.000 0.000 0.333 0.333 0.333 0.000 0.000
   7    0.500 0.500 0.500 0.333 0.000 0.000 1.000 0.667 1.000 1.000 1.000
   8    0.250 0.250 0.250 0.333 0.333 0.333 0.000 0.000 0.000 0.333 0.000
   9    1.000 0.750 0.750 0.667 0.333 1.000 0.000 0.333 0.333 0.333 0.667
  10    0.000 0.000 0.000 0.333 0.333 0.000 0.333 0.000 0.333 1.000 0.333
  11    1.000 1.000 1.000 1.000 1.000 1.000 0.000 0.333 0.333 0.000 0.667
  12    1.000 1.000 1.000 0.667 0.667 0.667 0.333 0.000 0.667 0.333 1.000
  13    0.000 0.000 0.000 0.333 0.333 0.000 0.000 0.000 0.000 0.000 0.000
  14    0.250 0.000 0.000 0.000 0.000 0.333 0.333 0.000 0.333 1.000 0.333
  15    0.250 0.500 0.250 0.333 1.000 0.333 0.000 0.000 0.000 0.333 0.000
  16    0.500 0.250 0.250 0.333 0.333 1.000 0.667 1.000 0.333 0.000 0.000
  17    1.000 1.000 1.000 1.000 0.667 0.667 0.667 0.333 1.000 0.333 1.000
```

The definition for a clique, however, is very strict. Does each member of the clique need to be connected to all others in order for a group to be defined as such? This definition is likely too strong for most purposes and poorly reflects interaction within social groups. Rarely do members of a group have direct ties with each and every member. To relax this definition, researchers often use what is referred to as an *n*-clique, where *n* equals the maximum lengths of paths to all other members. Typically, a path distance of two is used, corresponding to the "friend of a friend" idea (Hanneman & Riddle, 2011b).

Therefore, a 2n-clique is a set of actors connected to each other within two steps. This permits actors to be identified as being part of the same group even if they are not directly tied to each other. You can also increase the value of *n*, but this is not advisable, as it seems odd for actors to be in the same clique if they are three steps from one another. Figure 6.3 reports the 2n-cliques for the symmetrized Fraternity Data. By relaxing the criterion for group membership, the number of cliques has increased from 11 to 20, with Student 1, for example, being a member of 16 cliques.

Figure 6.3 Output from UCINET's 2n-Clique Routine on the Symmetrized Fraternity Data. A 2n-clique is a set of actors connected to each other within two steps. This permits actors to be identified as being part of the same group even if they are not directly tied to each other. By relaxing the criteria for group membership, the number of cliques has increased from 11 to 20, with Student 1, for example, being a member of 16 cliques.

```
N-CLIQUES
----------------------------------------------------------------
Max Distance (n-): 2
Minimum Set Size: 3
Input dataset: NEWC0LE3-Sym (C:\Program Files\Analytic Technologies\
Ucinet 6\DataFiles\chap 5\NEWC0LE3-Sym)

20 2-cliques found.

    1:   1 3 4 5 7 8 9 11 12 16 17
    2:   1 4 5 7 8 9 10 11 12 17
    3:   1 4 7 8 9 10 11 12 14 17
    4:   1 4 7 8 9 11 12 14 16 17
    5:   1 4 6 7 8 10 11 17
    6:   1 4 6 7 8 11 16 17
    7:   2 4 7 9 10 11 12 14 17
    8:   2 4 7 9 11 12 14 16 17
    9:   2 4 6 7 11 16 17
   10:   2 4 6 7 10 11 17
   11:   1 4 6 8 10 11 13 17
   12:   1 4 5 8 10 11 13 17
   13:   1 3 5 7 8 9 11 12 15 16 17
   14:   1 5 7 8 9 10 11 12 15 17
   15:   1 7 8 9 10 11 12 14 15 17
```

(Continued)

Figure 6.3 (Continued)

```
16:    1 7 8 9 11 12 14 15 16 17
17:    1 6 7 8 10 11 15 17
18:    1 6 7 8 11 15 16 17
19:    1 6 8 10 11 13 15 17
20:    1 5 8 10 11 13 15 17


        1   2   3   4   5   6   7   8   9  10  11  12  13  14  15  16  17
       --  --  --  --  --  --  --  --  --  --  --  --  --  --  --  --  --
   1   16   0   2   8   6   6  12  16   8  10  16   8   4   4   8   6  16
   2    0   4   0   4   0   2   4   0   2   2   4   2   0   2   0   2   4
   3    2   0   2   1   2   0   2   2   2   0   2   2   0   0   1   2   2
   4    8   4   1  12   3   5  10   8   6   7  12   6   2   4   0   5  12
   5    6   0   2   3   6   0   4   6   4   4   6   4   2   0   3   2   6
   6    6   2   0   5   0   8   6   6   0   5   8   0   2   0   3   3   8
   7   12   4   2  10   4   6  16  12  10   8  16  10   0   6   6   8  16
   8   16   0   2   8   6   6  12  16   8  10  16   8   4   4   8   6  16
   9    8   2   2   6   4   0  10   8  10   5  10  10   0   6   4   5  10
  10   10   2   0   7   4   5   8  10   5  12  12   5   4   3   5   0  12
  11   16   4   2  12   6   8  16  16  10  12  20  10   4   6   8   8  20
  12    8   2   2   6   4   0  10   8  10   5  10  10   0   6   4   5  10
  13    4   0   0   2   2   2   0   4   0   4   4   0   4   0   2   0   4
  14    4   2   0   4   0   0   6   4   6   3   6   6   0   6   2   3   6
  15    8   0   1   0   3   3   6   8   4   5   8   4   2   2   8   3   8
  16    6   2   2   5   2   3   8   6   5   0   8   5   0   3   3   8   8
  17   16   4   2  12   6   8  16  16  10  12  20  10   4   6   8   8  20
```

N-Clans

The *N*-clan is a second way of relaxing the rigid criterion for clique membership. This third of four bottom-up approaches is based on distance rather than direct connections. This technique for identifying a network's subgroups addresses a shortcoming of *n*-cliques; it is possible for actors associated with a particular *n*-clique to be connected by actors who are not themselves members of the clique (Hanneman & Riddle, 2011b). Actors in the same clan are all connected at *n* distance, *n* (or less), and all actors in between are also members of the same clan. Another way to think about *n*-clans is that they are *n*-cliques in which the distance between nodes *i* and *j* in a subgraph is no greater than *n* for the paths within that subgraph (Wasserman & Faust, 1994). *N*-clans, therefore, are those *n*-cliques that have a diameter less than or equal to *n*. *N*-clans are relatively easy to find by examining n-cliques and then eliminating those with a diameter more than n. However, despite the simplicity of this idea and its availability in social network analysis software packages, this technique is not used often.

K-Plexes

The K-plex is another alternative way of relaxing the rigid criterion for clique membership and is more commonly used than n-clan method. One reason for its use is that it nicely reflects real-life group structures in that it requires actors associated with a group to be connected to most of that group's members and that a connection through a nonclique intermediary does not qualify an actor for group membership (Hanneman & Riddle, 2011b). A K-plex, therefore, can be defined as the set of actors connected to all but K other actors in the group. To find a network's K-plexes, you set the value of K and n to the size of the groups, where the minimum size of n is set to $K - 2$. For example, 3K-plexes with $n =$ 10 will find all of groups with 10 actors in which each actor is connected to at least seven others in the group. If K is increased to four, 4K-plexes, all groups of size 10 in which each actor is connected to at least six others will be reported. Therefore, as the value of K increases, so too does the number of groups identified. Valente (2010) notes that in practice, you set K and finds all the groups as n increases from $K + 2$ to $n - 1$.

Figure 6.4 reports the 2K-plexes in the symmetrized Fraternity Data. It is evident from this output that the image of group structure that results from a K-plex approach is vastly different from that of the 2n-clique approach (Figure 6.3): with $K = 2$ and $n = 4$, the algorithm returns 28 different subgroups. It is also evident that these results demonstrate that actors are embedded in "overlapping social circles," which more closely reflects individuals' interactions with social groups. For example, Student 11 is in 17 different 2K-plexes.

These bottom-up approaches—K-cores, N-cliques, N-clans, and K-plexes—provide different ways to understand the subgroups within a network. Similar to the three top-down approaches (components, bi-components, and factions), these different subgroup identification methods allow you to characterize the network according to patterns of who interacts with whom. Though each procedure will provide you with a different take on the network's substructures, they are all based on the ways in which actors are interconnected. These connections within and between groups influence an array of social processes relevant for educational researchers, including solidarity, shared norms, trust, identity, and collective behavior. Identifying these groups through the different techniques introduced here is a means to an end rather than an end in itself. The ultimate goal of using information about a network's substructures is to test whether attitudes and behaviors differ within and between these groups. This brief introduction merely introduced ways to identify and describe these subgroups. Chapter 9 introduces ways to more formally test whether there is a relationship between these groups and outcomes

Figure 6.4 Output from UCINET's 2K-plexes Routine on the Symmetrized Fraternity Data. The K-plex is an alternative way of relaxing the rigid criterion for clique membership and is more commonly used than the n-clan method. One reason for its use is that it nicely reflects real-life group structures in that it requires actors associated with a group to be connected to most other group members, and a connection through a nonclique intermediary does not qualify an actor for group membership. It is evident from this output that the image of group structure that results from a K-plex approach is vastly different from that of the 2n-clique approach (Figure 6.3): with $K = 2$ and $n = 4$, the algorithm returns 28 different subgroups.

```
K-PLEX

--------------------------------------------------------------

Value of K:                    2 (each member of a K-plex of size N has
N-K ties to other members)
Minimum Set Size =             4
Input dataset:                 NEWC0LE3-Sym (C:\Program Files\Analytic
Technologies\Ucinet 6\DataFiles\chap 5\NEWC0LE3-Sym)

28 k-plexes found.

    1:   1  3 11 17
    2:   1  5 11 17
    3:   1  7 10 17
    4:   1  8 10 11
    5:   1  9 11 17
    6:   1 10 11 15
    7:   1 10 13 15
    8:   1 11 12 17
    9:   1 11 13 15
   10:   2  4  7 16
   11:   2  4  7 17
   12:   3  5 11 12 17
   13:   3  7 12 17
   14:   3  9 11 12 17
   15:   4  7 12 17
   16:   4  9 16 17
   17:   4 11 16 17
   18:   5  7 12 17
   19:   5  9 11 12 17
   20:   5 11 12 15
```

```
21:  5 11 15 17
22:  7  9 12 14
23:  7  9 12 17
24:  7  9 14 17
25:  7 11 12 17
26:  8 10 11 15
27:  9 11 12 16
28:  9 11 16 17
```

```
        1  2  3  4  5  6  7  8  9 10 11 12 13 14 15 16 17
       -- -- -- -- -- -- -- -- -- -- -- -- -- -- -- -- --
    1   9  0  1  0  1  0  1  1  1  4  7  1  2  0  3  0  5
    2   0  2  0  2  0  0  2  0  0  0  0  0  0  0  0  1  1
    3   1  0  4  0  1  0  1  0  1  0  3  3  0  0  0  0  4
    4   0  2  0  5  0  0  3  0  1  0  1  1  0  0  0  3  4
    5   1  0  1  0  6  0  1  0  1  0  5  4  0  0  2  0  5
    6   0  0  0  0  0  0  0  0  0  0  0  0  0  0  0  0  0
    7   1  2  1  3  1  0 10  0  3  1  1  6  0  2  0  1  8
    8   1  0  0  0  0  0  0  2  0  2  2  0  0  0  1  0  0
    9   1  0  1  1  1  0  3  0  9  0  5  5  0  2  0  3  7
   10   4  0  0  0  0  0  1  2  0  5  3  0  1  0  3  0  1
   11   7  0  3  1  5  0  1  2  5  3 17  7  1  0  5  3 11
   12   1  0  3  1  4  0  6  0  5  0  7 12  0  1  1  1  9
   13   2  0  0  0  0  0  0  0  0  1  1  0  2  0  2  0  0
   14   0  0  0  0  0  0  2  0  2  0  0  1  0  2  0  0  1
   15   3  0  0  0  2  0  0  1  0  3  5  1  2  0  6  0  1
   16   0  1  0  3  0  0  1  0  3  0  3  1  0  0  0  5  3
   17   5  1  4  4  5  0  8  0  7  1 11  9  0  1  1  3 19
```

HIERARCHICAL CLUSTERING OF OVERLAP MATRIX

```
              1   1  1 1   1           1 1 1
   Level    6 2 4 8 3 1 0 5 4 6 3 5 7 9 2 1 7
   ------    - - - - - - - - - - - - - - - - -
   11.000    . . . . . . . . . . . . . . . XXX
    8.333    . . . . . . . . . . . . . . XXXXX
    6.000    . . . . . . . . . . . . . XXXXXXX
    5.200    . . . . . . . . . . . . XXXXXXXXX
    4.000    . . . . . XXX . . . . . XXXXXXXXX
```

(Continued)

Figure 6.4 (Continued)

```
3.500    . . . . . XXX . . . . XXXXXXXXXXX
3.000    . . . . . XXXXX XXX . XXXXXXXXXX
2.429    . . . . . XXXXX XXX XXXXXXXXXXXX
1.750    . . . . . XXXXX XXXXXXXXXXXXXXXX
1.733    . . . . XXXXXXX XXXXXXXXXXXXXXXX
1.013    . . . XXXXXXXXX XXXXXXXXXXXXXXXX
0.769    . . . XXXXXXXXXXXXXXXXXXXXXXXXXX
0.528    . . XXXXXXXXXXXXXXXXXXXXXXXXXXX
0.450    . XXXXXXXXXXXXXXXXXXXXXXXXXXXX
0.000    XXXXXXXXXXXXXXXXXXXXXXXXXXXXXX
```

relevant to educational researchers. For example, is a cluster of highly effective teachers within a school more likely to socialize with another cluster of highly effective teachers?

To answer such a question, you must first identify a network's subgroups through one of the techniques introduced above. In exploratory research, it is recommended that you first look for components, then apply K-cores, and then search for complete triads to further subdivide large K-cores, if necessary. The decision tree presented in Figure 6.5 is designed to help you make some of these decisions as you seek to identify the groups within a network. These decisions should also be guided by a form conceptualization of what constitutes a "group." This requires that the analytic decision be theoretically justifiable.

POSITIONS

In addition to examining a complete network's structural properties and the groups within that network, analysts are often interested in identifying the positions in a network and the relationships between these positions. Similar to describing a network's structural properties, a complete network-level positional analysis is performed using mathematical algorithms to find positions and their relationships. Positions, however, differ from groups. Groups, as described above, are collections of actors who share some relation or are connected (degree) to each other at a higher rate (density). A network position, on the other hand, is a set of actors that occupy the same place or have similar patterns of relations with others. So positions consist of actors who share the same place in the network, but they need not be connected to each other, though they very well might be.

Broadly speaking, a position is a set of actors that have the same connections to similar others or types of others. For example, two veteran teachers in the same school

Figure 6.5 Decision Tree for the Analysis of a Network's Groups. In exploratory research, it is recommended that one first look for components, then apply K-cores, and then search for complete triads to further subdivide large K-cores, if necessary. Working from the top down, follow the steps in this decision tree to help you explore a complete network's group structures.

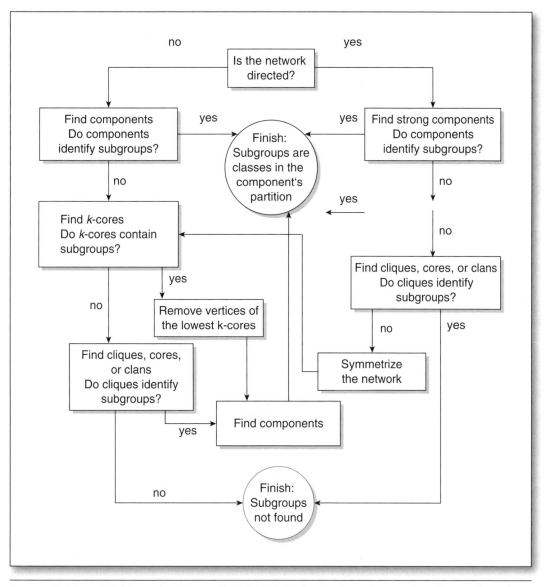

Source: de Nooy, W., Mrvar, A., & Batagelj, V. (2005). *Exploratory social network analysis with Pajek.* New York: Cambridge University Press.

(the school being the network's boundary) share the same position (veteran teacher), but they need not share a relation of any kind. The fact is that they occupy this position because they both report to assistant principals and mentor junior teachers. These two teachers are alike even though they mentor and report to different others. Given the school as a social system, a veteran teacher is a position and the veteran teacher's roles include mentoring younger colleagues, among others. The assistant principal is another position that carries expectations of appropriate leadership conduct toward both veteran and junior teachers. Expectations for teachers and assistant principals—as well as all the other positions in the network—are coupled into a system of roles.

Determining these positions, as well as the relations between them, consists of three general steps (Valente, 2010): (1) using mathematical algorithms to identify unique positions; (2) examining how these positions relate to each other; and (3) determining how these positions influence behaviors and attitudes. This section introduces the idea of blockmodeling, the primary means through which network researchers perform a positional analysis; the difference across these blockmodeling techniques is the way in which the various algorithms identify the positions. Positional analysis was a popular strand of network research up to early 1990s; however, there are few, if any, recent examples of this type of analysis in educational research. Therefore, this discussion on positional analysis will be kept brief.

Equivalence

A positional analysis is grounded in the concept of equivalence. Equivalence, in general, refers to actors who occupy the same position. But, similar to the varied ways in which groups can be defined, there are different ways in which the concept of equivalence is defined. These definitions, in turn, lead to the identification of different positions. The most restrictive of these definitions is structural equivalence: In a directed, binary graph, two actors are structurally equivalent on a specific relation if they have exactly identical patterns of ties sent to and received from all the other actors in the network.

Real network data, however, rarely consist of dyads that meet this rigorous standard for equivalence (identical ties to and from identical others in the same graph). A less restrictive definition, which also applies only to a single graph (network), is automorphic equivalence. Two actors are automorphically equivalent if they are connected to other corresponding positions but not to identical actors. For example, for two high school teachers to occupy a structurally equivalent position, both teachers must teach the same set of students, something that is highly unlikely. But, to hold an automorphically equivalent position, the two teachers need only teach different sets with the same number of students. The students, therefore, occupy a second position that is defined by what they do—receive instruction from teachers. This brings to mind an important point about positional analysis. Positions are established through relational data, not exogenous attributes. Related to this definition of equivalence and often incorrectly interchanged (Borgatti & Everett, 1992a) is isomorphic equivalence, which applies to two networks of actors. In practice, this means that if two actors are connected in one network, then the corresponding actors in the other network must also be connected in the same way.

The least restrictive of these definitions is regular equivalence, which requires neither structural equivalence's ties to identical actors nor automorphic equivalence's indistinguishable positions (Knoke & Yang, 2008). Actors are regularly equivalent if they have identical relations to and from equivalent actors (Wasserman & Faust, 1994). For example, two popular elementary school teachers occupy the same social position, though in different grades, because they are well liked by some children and respected by some parents, but they do not teach the same kids nor are they respected by the same parents. Again, the important point is that their position of "popular teacher" is established by relational data (affinity and respect), not characteristics that are removed from context.

To demonstrate the difference among these three equivalence definitions, Figure 6.6 shows a hypothetical hierarchy of a school district's organizational chart, which consists of three levels linked by supervisory relation. In this figure, there are seven structurally equivalent positions. Recall that two nodes are considered to be structurally equivalent if they have the same relationships to all other nodes. Therefore, because there is no actor who has exactly the same set of ties as actor A, that one actor is in a class by itself. The same is true for actors B, C, and D. Each of these actors has a unique set of ties to others, so they form three classes, each with one member. Actors E and F, however, fall in the same structural equivalence class. Each has a single tie, and that tie is to actor B. Since E and F have exactly the same pattern of ties with all other actors, they are structurally equivalent. Actor G, again, is in a class by itself; its profile of ties with the other nodes in the diagram is unique. Finally, actors H and I fall in the same structural equivalence class—that is, they have exactly the same pattern of ties to all other actors.

However, if the definition of equivalence were to be relaxed, the positions identified in the graph would be different. Consider that even though actors B and D are not structurally equivalent (they do report to the same supervisor but do not supervise the same actors), they do seem to be "equivalent" in a different sense. Actors B and D can switch locations, but the distances among all the network's actors would remain the same. Therefore, actors B and D form an automorphic class. In Figure 6.5, there are actually five automorphic equivalence positions: {A}, {B, D}, {C}, {E, F, H, I}, and {G}. These positions are groupings whose members would remain at the same distance from all other actors if they were switched and members of other classes were also switched.

The definition of equivalence can be further relaxed by identifying those actors that have the same profile of ties with members of other sets of actors. Two principals, for example, are equivalent because each has a certain pattern of ties with a superintendent and teachers. The principals do not necessarily have ties to the same teachers, however.

That is, they are not structurally equivalent. Because two different principals may supervise different numbers of teachers, they will also not be considered automorphically equivalent. But they are similar because they have the same relationships with some member or members of another set of actors. This is an intuitive and attractive idea. Regular equivalence sets describe the "social roles" that are the basic building blocks of all social institutions. Actors that are regularly equivalent do not necessarily fall in the same network positions or locations with respect to other individual actors; rather, they have the same kinds of relationships with some members of other sets of actors. In Figure 6.6, there are three regular equivalence classes. The first is actor A (superintendent); the second is composed of the three actors B, C, and D (principals); the third is composed of the remaining five actors E, F, G, H, and I (teachers). The easiest class to observe consists of the five actors across the bottom of Figure 6.6 (E, F, G, H, and I). These actors are considered regularly equivalent to one another because they have no tie with any actor in the first class, and each has a tie with an actor in the second class (either B or C or D). Each of the five actors, then, has an identical pattern of ties with actors in the other classes.

Taken together, Figure 6.6 shows the restrictiveness of structural equivalence compared to automorphic and regular equivalence, with the latter being the least restrictive and most intuitively appealing. Regular equivalence is, therefore, the most flexible

Figure 6.6   A Visual Comparison of Structural, Automorphic, and Regular Equivalence. Consider this a graph of a hypothetical hierarchy of a school district's organizational chart, which consists of three levels linked by supervisory relation. Depending on your preferred definition of equivalence, different positions will be identified.

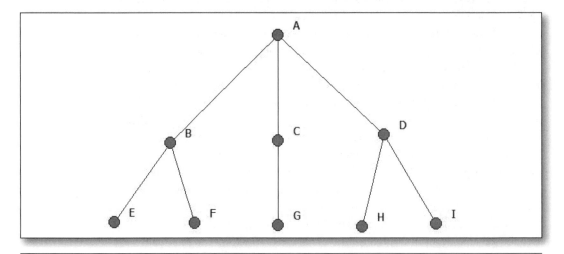

Source: Knoke, D., & Yang, S. (2008). *Social network analysis* (2nd ed.). Thousand Oaks, CA: Sage Publications.

method for identifying positions and social roles in a network. The following section briefly describes the general technique for identifying these equivalent classes of actors.

Blockmodeling

Blockmodeling is the general technique in which the relations among a network's actors can be reduced to a set of positions (blocks) and the relations among these positions also treated as a network (Valente, 2010)—what is often called a reduced-form network. Lorrain and White (1971) were the first to propose that a network could be reduced to a set of blocks and then the relations among these blocks studied; hence the term *blockmodeling*. There are many ways to identify blocks and determine the relations among them (reviewed in Doreian, Batagelj, & Ferligoj, 2005), each varying by how they define equivalent positions. While positional analysis and blockmodeling can quickly get messy and muddled, a short demonstration using the Fraternity Data will illustrate how positions are defined and how such analyses can be useful in educational research.

Recall that the Fraternity Data in Table 5.2 represent a binary and directed friendship network consisting of 17 male students at the start of a semester-long study. Several structural patterns are evident in these data, and it is instructive to reiterate a few of them prior to moving on to the positional analysis. The network has one weak component, and its average path length is slightly more than two, meaning that it takes, on average, about two steps for one student to "reach" any other student. The network is not highly centralized, and fewer than one-third of the ties are reciprocated. As for its substructures, there are 20 $2n$-cliques, suggesting that there is connectivity across different cliques, with several students belonging to more than one $2n$-clique. From this information, you can conclude that (1) actors are not tightly clustered into distinct social groups; (2) influence and/or power are not highly concentrated; and (3) strong, reciprocated relations have yet to emerge. These conclusions provide some clues about what you might expect from a positional analysis of these same data.

CONCOR Example

Are there any distinct positions in these data that reflect these structural patterns? To address this question, a positional algorithm, CONCOR ("convergence of iterated correlations"), was applied to the data. This algorithm is based on structural equivalence and does a good job of identifying positions based on node similarities. While the technical details about this algorithm are available elsewhere (see, e.g., Breiger, Boorman, & Arabie, 1975), suffice it to say that its appeal is rooted in the fact that it provides an unbiased, mathematical partition of the network into positions that requires little theoretical or substantive input from the researcher (Valente, 2010). For a more detailed discussion on blockmodeling, as well as its different applications, see Ferligoj, Doreian, and Batagelj (2011).

Figure 6.7 presents the UCINET output for the blockmodel analysis of the Fraternity Data using the CONCOR algorithm. CONCOR allows you to choose one of the partitions that best conforms to your understanding of the data's underlying structure; hence the need to first investigate the network's overall structure and its substructures (groups). It was decided that the third and final partition best reflected the network's positions. The top panel of the output in Figure 6.6 shows a partition diagram, with Level 3 representing this third partition. From this, you can see that Students 12, 11, and 17 are in one position, and 2, 14, and 16 are in another. There is a total of eight positions, with Students 1 and 6 being sole members of two other positions.

The second panel of the output in Figure 6.7 shows the blocked matrix, which shows ties within and between positions; the second step in a positional analysis. For example, Position 3 (Students 5, 3, and 9) sends nine ties to Position 4 (Students 12, 11, and 17). However, Position 3 only receives three ties in return, indicating that there is an asymmetrical relationship between these two positions. You can easily see from this output if there are ties (1s) within and between positions and blanks representing an absence of ties.

To take this further, the bottom panel in Figure 6.7 reports the density within and between blocks. The general rule is to compare densities within and between blocks

Figure 6.7 Results of the Blockmodel Analysis of the Fraternity Data Using the CONCOR Algorithm. CONCOR allows the researcher to choose one of the partitions that best conforms to the researcher's understanding of the data's underlying structure; hence the need to first investigate the network's overall structure and its substructures (groups). It was decided that the third and final partition best reflected the network's positions. The top panel of the output shows a partition diagram, with Level 3 representing this third partition. From this, one can see that Students 12, 11, and 17 are in one position, and 2, 14, and 16 are in another. There is a total of eight positions, with Students 1 and 6 being sole members of two other positions.

```
CONCOR
---------------------------------------------------------------

Diagonal: Ignore
Max partitions: 3
Input dataset: NEWCOLE3 (C:\Program Files\Analytic Technologies\Ucinet 6\
DataFiles\chap 5\NEWCOLE3)
```

```
PARTITION DIAGRAM


                    1 1 1   1 1     1 1 1
Level   1 4 7 5 3 9 2 1 7 2 4 6 6 8 5 0 3
-----   - - - - - - - - - - - - - - - - -
   3    . XXX XXXXX XXXXX XXXXX . XXX XXX
   2    XXXXX XXXXXXXXXXX XXXXXXX XXXXXXX
   1    XXXXXXXXXXXXXXXXX XXXXXXXXXXXXXXXX
```

```
Relation NEWC0
Blocked Matrix


                    1 1 1     1 1           1   1 1
       1    4 7   5 3 9   2 1 7   2 4 6   6   8 5   0 3
      -------------------------------------------------
   1 |    |    |      |     | 1 1 |       |    |   | 1 |
      -------------------------------------------------
   4 |    |  1 |      |     | 1 | 1     |  |    |    |
   7 |    | 1  |      | 1   |   1 1 |    |  |    |    |
      -------------------------------------------------
   5 |    |    |      | 1 1 1 |      |    |    |    |   |
   3 |    |    |      | 1 1 1 |      |    |    |    |   |
   9 |    |    |      | 1 1 1 |      |    |    |    |   |
      -------------------------------------------------
  12 |    |    |  1   |     | 1 1 |       |    |    |   |
  11 |    |    |    1 | 1   1 |     |     |    |    |   |
  17 |    | 1  |    1 | 1   |       |     |    |    |   |
      -------------------------------------------------
   2 |    | 1 1|      |     |     | 1 |   |    |    |   |
  14 |    |  1 |    1 |     |     |   |   |    | 1  |   |
  16 |    | 1  |    1 | 1   |     |   |   |    |    |   |
      -------------------------------------------------
   6 |    | 1  |      |     |     |   |   | 1  |    | 1 |
      -------------------------------------------------
   8 |    |    |      | 1   |     |   | 1 |    | 1  |   |
  15 |    |    | 1    | 1   |     |   |   |    | 1  |   |
      -------------------------------------------------
```

(Continued)

Figure 6.7 (Continued)

```
10 | 1 |   1 |        |        |       |   | 1 |     |
13 | 1 |     |        |        |   | 1 |   | 1 |     |
     ---------------------------------------------------------


Density Matrix

            1     2     3     4     5     6     7     8
         ----- ----- ----- ----- ----- ----- ----- -----
    1          0.000 0.000 0.667 0.000 0.000 0.000 0.500
    2    0.000 1.000 0.000 0.500 0.167 0.000 0.000 0.000
    3    0.000 0.000 0.000 1.000 0.000 0.000 0.000 0.000
    4    0.000 0.167 0.333 0.833 0.000 0.000 0.000 0.000
    5    0.000 0.667 0.222 0.111 0.167 0.000 0.000 0.167
    6    0.000 0.500 0.000 0.000 0.000       0.500 0.500
    7    0.000 0.000 0.167 0.333 0.000 0.500 0.000 0.500
    8    1.000 0.250 0.000 0.000 0.000 0.500 0.500 0.000

R-squared = 0.517
```

with the density of the whole network (overall density = 0.19, reported earlier). If block densities are larger than or equal to this value, you can conclude that there is a connection between these blocks. When densities are less than this value, the blocks (positions) are not connected. In this example, Position 2 is connected to 4 and 5, because the densities are greater than 0.19. Along these same lines, Position 3 is connected only to 4, and so forth. It should be obvious from this that relations between positions do not need to be reciprocated. For example, Position 4 does not send a tie to Position 3.

Now that all 17 students have been assigned to positions and relations between positions have been established, the more substantive work involved with a positional analysis is to label the positions and interpret the relations among them. Rather than refer to these as positions, they can then be characterized by their attributes and/or their relationships with other positions. Because no attribute data on these students are available (e.g., do "smart" students occupy one position?), these positions will be labeled according to how they perform. Figure 6.8 shows the relations among these eight positions. The nodes in this figure are no longer individual students, but rather the positions into which students have been partitioned through the CONCOR

Figure 6.8   Reduced-Form Network of the Fraternity Data. Positions Identified Through CONCOR. The nodes in this figure are no longer individual students but, rather, the positions into which students have been partitioned through the CONCOR algorithm. From this reduced-form network, it is clear that three positions are vying for control (Positions 2, 4, and 8), with each of those "controlling" access to the periphery positions.

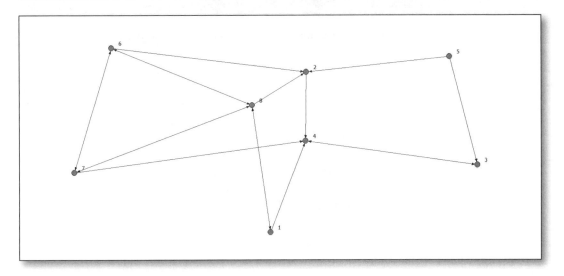

algorithm. From this reduced-form network, it is clear that three positions are vying for control (Positions 2, 4, and 8), with each of those "controlling" access to the periphery positions. These positions and the relations among them conform to other characteristics of the network's structure. For example, Students 11, 12, and 17 (Position 4) were also those students with the most in-degrees (ties received). Student 17 was also a member of all 20 of the network's 2n-cliques. When relations between positions are asymmetrical, this usually indicates a relationship based on control or influence, something that Position 4 seems to possess. Position 3 (Students 5, 3, and 9) has a reciprocated relationship with this position, suggesting that this actor, too, may reap some advantages by having a mutual tie with these actors; no other position receives a tie from them.

While positional analyses such as the simple one described above are not often used in educational research, the concepts of positions and roles are central to much social science research (Ferligoj, Doreian, & Batagelj, 2011). Given the advances made in this area, especially in regard to conceptualization, computation, and visualization, it is likely that positional analysis will become a more prominent area for educational researchers. After all, it is one's position in a social structure that determines expectations for performance, and a great deal of educational research is focused on this (for both teacher and students). Therefore, performance is not something that is solely attributable to one's individual characteristics. Rather, you need to consider how expectations both shape and are shaped by the social structure of which they are part. Positional analyses are a step in this promising direction.

SUMMARY

Once a network's topography has been mapped (Chapter 5), the analysis of a complete network generally proceeds to uncover the substructures within that network. These groups are critical, as they provide individual actors with access to resources such as information, advice, and friendship that influence one's own behavior and attitudes. While there are many different ways to define groups using relational data, most agree that a group consists of at least three members who are connected in a way that is greater than their connections to others in the rest of the network.

After the network's substructures are mapped using one of the "bottom-up" or "top-down" approaches discussed in this chapter, the analysis can then proceed to a positional analysis. This chapter emphasized the important conceptual difference between groups and positions, highlighting the different ways in which equivalent positions are defined and ultimately measured. A positional analysis, while not often used in educational research, typically follows the same procedure as a group analysis. First, the positions are identified (the example in this chapter used the CONCOR algorithm based on structural equivalence. Next, the relationships among these positions are mapped from a reduced-form matrix, in which the nodes are positions. Finally, a positional analysis involves linking these positions to outcomes, a step that was not presented in this chapter but could easily be incorporated if you have relevant data available.

CHAPTER FOLLOW-UP

Once again, select a peer-reviewed empirical research article that employs social network analysis and is related to a topic of your interest. More specifically, locate an article that identifies a network's groups and positions. Use that article to respond to the following questions.

1. How has a group been defined and measured? Were any alternatives considered? Does this definition of a group make sense given the network's actors and relations among them? Is this definition restrictive or flexible?

2. Was a "top-down" or "bottom-up" approach used? Both?

3. How were the network's positions defined and measured? How do these positions differ from the network's groups? Is this difference made evident? What definition of equivalence informed the definition and measurement of the network's positions? Was a reduced-form network presented? What does it indicate about the network's hierarchy?

ESSENTIAL READING

Borgatti, S. P., & Everett, M. G. (1992). Notions of position in social network analysis. *Sociological Methodology, 22,* 1–35.

Lorrain, F. P., & White, H. C. (1971). Structural equivalence of individuals in social networks. *Journal of Mathematical Sociology, 1,* 49–80.

Moody, J., & White, D. R. (2003). Structural cohesion and embeddedness: A hierarchical concept of social groups. *American Sociological Review, 68,* 103–127.

7

Measures for Egocentric Network Analysis

OBJECTIVES

In this chapter, you will learn an array of ways in which properties of ego networks are conceptualized and measured. You will learn about how ego network data differ from complete network data, particularly in terms of data collection, management, and analysis. In addition, you will learn about the types of questions that egocentric analyses can address. A majority of this chapter is dedicated to the different indices that are used to characterize ego networks, with special attention given to the types and sources of data that are needed to calculate these indices. The conceptual and measurement tools in this chapter are essential for performing the more advanced egocentric analyses that are introduced in subsequent chapters.

EGOS AND ALTERS

It is generally agreed that being connected to others matters. Students who can get support from other high-achieving students do better. Teachers who share best practices with others expand their own teaching repertoires. School leaders who can turn to the "right" others for advice are in a better position to make good decisions. Implicit in all three situations is that an individual's (ego) connections with others (alters) provides access to some instrumental (e.g., advice) or expressive (e.g., support) resource that may, in turn, be beneficial. The structure and content of these relations between an ego and a set of alters is the focus of egocentric network analysis. Egocentric analysis shifts the analytical lens onto a sole ego actor and concentrates on the local pattern of relations in which that ego is embedded as well as the types of resources to which those relations provide access.

Purpose

Whereas the previous chapter focused on concepts and measures most appropriate for complete network analysis, this chapter shifts the perspective to the analytical level of a sole focal actor—ego. Here, the emphasis is on an individual (ego) and her or his connections with others (alters). Therefore, egocentric analysis is primarily concerned with describing how individuals are embedded in local social structures and, ultimately, how these individual indices of social structure relate to varied outcomes. For example, ego-level analysis can be used to ask questions such as whether a "well-connected" teacher is more or less likely to be measured as an effective teacher or whether students whose connections are to similar others are at a disadvantage when it comes to learning something new. Unlike the previous chapter, the focus is on an individual actor and that actor's relations—local structures that are referred to as ego-neighborhoods. This chapter introduces the concepts and measures that are used to describe properties related to these neighborhoods. The following chapters go on to demonstrate how these different indices are then used in statistical models that associate these properties with outcomes that are of interest to educational researchers.

WHY STUDY EGO NETWORKS?

The study of ego networks represents the intersection of the social network perspective and its emphasis on the importance of relations and the types of data that have long been preferred by mainstream social science. That is, ego-level analyses can and often do incorporate information about actors' attributes as well as their relations with others. An ego's network is considered a source of an array of important resources, including support, information, normative pressures, influence, and so on. All these different resources shape an individual ego's attitudes and behaviors. For example, as hypothesized by Coleman (1990), if a student's parent is embedded in a dense, redundant ego network with other students' parents (an ego network in which all parents know each other), then these networks with high social closure provide an important source of monitoring that exerts normative pressure on that student's behavior. Or consider

Maroulis and Gomez's (2008) study of students within one small high school. Using ego network data, they concluded that egos with highly dense networks that consist of low-performing peers yield the largest negative effect on student achievement, and highly dense ego networks of high-performing peers yield the largest positive effect on achievement. Both examples are grounded in the broad literature on social capital (Chapter 10 is dedicated to this topic) and demonstrate how theory and sociometric data are used to examine the importance of an ego's immediate alters on ego's behaviors and attitudes.

Generally, there are two instances in which egocentric analyses are warranted. The first instance if is one's research question is about individual entities across different settings (networks). For example, does the size of a student's within-school friendship network influence his or her attachment to school? To address this question, you would need information about the size of each ego's friendship network (the number of alters that the person has nominated as friends) and some composite measure of school attachment likely derived from a set of survey items. Alternately, you would also use an egocentric approach if your research question is about different patterns of interaction within defined groups. An example of this would be a question such as whether a teacher's centrality is related to his or her attitude toward a school reform effort. Theories that frame these types of questions focus on (1) the topography of an ego's network and (2) the composition of that network, including the attributes of the alters to whom ego is connected.

SOURCES OF EGOCENTRIC DATA

The concepts and measures to be discussed in this chapter can be used on complete networks or egocentric data. The difference is that the focal analytical point is the ego and how that ego actor is embedded in some larger social structure. Ego actors can be individual persons, groups, or even some larger entity. Education-related ego network analysis typically focuses on individual actors such as students (Farmer et al. 2011), teachers (Penuel, Riel, Krause, & Frank, 2009), or administrators (Moolenaar, Daly, & Sleegers, 2011).

There are two ways in which ego network data emerge (Hanneman & Riddle, 2011b). First, ego network data can be generated from a sociometric survey administered to some sample of respondents, such as 1,500 children drawn from the population of 3.4 million pre–K through Grade 8 students. Using this example, you could survey all children in the sample and ask them to identify all the others with whom they have some type of relation and then report on the connections among these others. In addition, the survey could capture attributes about these named others, including, for example, gender. Alternatively, you could also employ a snowball approach in which each ego identifies others with whom they have some relation, then these others are asked about their relations with additional others. As the process moves forward, the size of the network increases until all egos of the component originally sampled are included. This latter approach, as noted in Chapter 3, is useful in finding members of hard-to-reach populations. As such, its use in educational research is not widespread. Most egocentric studies in educational research draw a sample from a target population and employ a sociometric instrument to collect relational and attribute data.

Egocentric network data generated in this manner, however, cannot be used to describe the overall embeddedness of the networks in some larger population. On the other hand, they can be used to indicate the prevalence of different kinds of ego networks in even very large samples. Analyses done along these lines result in a data structure that consists of a collection of networks. Because the actors in each network (ego and alters) are likely to be different, each pair of actors (ego and alter) needs to be treated as a separate row in a standard actor-by-attribute data file. This process is described in Chapter 4 under the section "Managing Relational Data."

A second way in which ego network data can be generated is by extracting them from complete network studies. This is the approach that will be used to generate the example data referenced in this chapter. Using this approach, you might, for example, extract all the ego networks from a complete network so that the ego networks of tenured teachers could be compared to the ego networks of untenured teachers; therefore, you can ask a question such as whether tenured teachers have denser ego networks than untenured teachers. However, when generating a sample of ego networks from a complete network, a thorny analytical issue arises: each ego network is not independent of the other; therefore, normal statistical assumptions do not apply. Part III wades into these issues by reviewing the different ways in which properties of complete or ego networks can be statistically analyzed.

It should be noted that, unless sampled from a dense complete network (i.e., one in which ego and alters are well connected), it is unlikely that one's ego network will overlap with another's (Knoke & Yang, 2008). Therefore, the measures discussed in this chapter are based on the attributes of alters associated with unconnected respondents (egos). Of course, this approach contrasts with the concepts and measures discussed in the preceding chapter in which the focus was on all the ties among actors in a network whose boundary was clearly specified (complete network-level analyses).

In addition, most analyses of ego networks use binary data: Two actors are either connected or they are not. This makes the analytical task of defining an ego's "neighborhood" much easier. However, if the relational data between ego and alter is valued—that is, the strength of the tie has been measured—you have to decide the point at which a tie exists. For example, if you have information on the frequency with which ego collaborates with a given alter measured on a four-point frequency scale ranging from 1 (the least frequent) to 4 (1–2 times a week), then a choice has to be made as to whether an alter is considered part of that ego's neighborhood. This is typically done by exploring several different cut-off values and working with the one that makes the most sense given your conceptualization of the relation.

Finally, while most analyses of ego networks use simple graphs—binary data that simply indicate whether an undirected tie is present between two actors—it is possible to incorporate directed relations into ego network analysis. This enables you to define two different types of ego neighborhoods (Hanneman & Riddle, 2011b). The first is an "out neighborhood," which includes all the actors to whom ego sends a tie. Conversely, a directed ego network can be defined as an "in neighborhood," which simply includes all those actors who send ties to ego. Using these two types of neighborhoods, you could also define a neighborhood as consisting only of reciprocated ties. The choice of defining ego neighborhoods is driven by the questions motivating the research.

EXAMPLE DATA

To describe and define these ego-level concepts and measures, this chapter will rely on the School Leaders data set. More specifically, these ego network data have been transformed so that they are nondirected and binary; a tie is either present or absent and is nonvalued. This is the simplest type of ego network data, which makes defining the ego neighborhood a straightforward task. In addition, these ego-level data have been extracted from the complete network; therefore, they have been generated by the second of two means just discussed. Given that the original data set captures 11 relations among 43 actors over 3 years, this chapter will focus on and present a narrower sliver of these rich data.

Recall from Chapter 4 that these multiplex data include ties that have been measured on a four-point frequency scale, with a high score of 4 indicating that ego engaged in that relation 1 to 2 times a week. Therefore, in addition to selecting only one relation on which to focus, the data have been transformed so that a tie between two actors is either present or not (a process referred to as dichotomization). More specifically, the egocentric concepts and measures to be demonstrated through these data will focus on the "information about work-related topics" relation. To generate these relational data, ego was asked, "How often do you turn to each Administrative Team member for information on work-related topics?" The data have been dichotomized so that only those ties that were originally coded a 3 or 4 are now 1s, indicating that there is a relation between ego and alter. Any tie that was originally absent or coded 1 or 2 is now a 0, indicating that a tie does not exist. Furthermore, the relations were symmetrized using a weak criterion: If one actor reported a tie (1), then the relation is considered present. As noted earlier, it is possible to examine directed relations in egocentric network studies, or what are referred to as out- and in-neighborhoods: ties sent or ties received. Finally, since the data were collected once every 3 years, this chapter will focus solely on this one nondirected relation in the third year. These decisions were primarily driven by this chapter's intent of keeping the presentation of egocentric analyses as succinct as possible. Along these lines, seven of the most commonly used concepts and their related measures are presented using these data and analyzed at the ego level.

There are two different ways in which egocentric data extracted from the School Leaders data set can be stored and managed prior to analysis. The first manner is most appropriate when ego network data from some larger population of individuals has been sampled. When collected in this manner, you need to keep track of lots of different information: characteristics of ego, characteristics of ties that ego has with alters, characteristics of alters, and aggregated characteristics of each ego network. Managing all this different information requires that the data be reshaped so that each ego–alter pair, in essence, becomes its own data file. A survey, for example, that captures five different types of relations and up to five alters generates 25 data files. All these dyadic data files can then be read into a few different programs (e.g., R, GAUSS, STATA/MATA) that will then append them into one data file with ego's unique ID, alters' IDs, and any other data needed for the alters. These applications, which employ matrix-level programming language, can then be used to calculate an array of aggregated measures related to ego's networks (discussed in this chapter). This is the format in which ego network data are stored, managed, and processed when collected from a sample of egos drawn from a target population. Managing ego network data in this manner requires you to be fluent and comfortable moving data from one format to another, often across different computer applications. Fortunately, there are several how-to guides that users can consult when doing this type of work using applications such as SAS (Haythornthwaite & Wellman, 1996) and SPSS (Müller, Wellman, & Marin, 1999). There are also some tools available that calculate ego network measures (the same measures to be discussed in this chapter) and export them into these common statistical packages (e.g., Egonet and E-Net, discussed in the book's final chapter).

Egocentric network data can also be stored in a nodelist format, which is an efficient way to store binary ego data that have been extracted from a complete network and is the preferred method for widely used applications designed exclusively for social network analysis. Attribute data can also be stored in this format, which enables these types of variables to be merged with the relational data (this utility is also available in these applications). Because the example egos used in this chapter data have been extracted from a complete network study, this latter nodelist format is preferred. Table 7.1 shows the egocentric network data for three school leaders (Leaders 1, 25, and 35) as well as a separate data file that includes data on two attribute variables (self-efficacy score and gender) in nodelist format for all 17 actors that are included in these ego networks. For example, Leader 1's ego neighborhood consists of Leaders 3, 4, 18, 27, 28, 36, and 38; that is, Leader 1 exchanges information about work-related topics with these seven different alters. The bottom panel in Table 7.1 includes information on two attribute variables for all 17 actors (columns 2 and 3). For example, Leader 1 has a value of 1 under the column labeled gender (1 = Female; 2 = Male) and an efficacy score of 6.05. Once the data are in either format (dyadic or nodelist), it becomes possible to examine an array of characteristics that illustrate an ego's neighborhood.

Table 7.1   Egocentric Network Data for Three School Leaders in Nodelist Format. For example, Leader 1's ego neighborhood consists of Leaders 3, 4, 18, 27, 28, 36, and 38; that is, Leader 1 exchanges information about work-related topics with these seven different alters. The bottom panel in Table 7.1 includes information on two attribute variables for all 17 actors (columns 2 and 3). For example, Leader 1 has a value of 1 under the column labeled gender (1 = Female; 2 = Male) and an efficacy score of 6.05. Once the data are in either format (dyadic or nodelist), it becomes possible to examine an array of characteristics that illustrate an ego's neighborhood.

```
DL
N = 17
FORMAT = NODELIST1 DIAGONAL PRESENT
   1    3    4   18   27   28   36   38
  25    3    4   18   27    8   21   24   32   34   42
  35   21   13

DL
NR = 17, NC = 2
Gender Efficacy

        1           1           6.05
       13           1           8.27
       18           2           5.00
       21           2           7.44
       24           1           5.22
       25           1           6.94
       27           1           5.06
       28           2           7.61
        3           1           7.39
       32           1           5.88
       34           2           5.11
       35           2           7.44
       36           1           7.72
       38           2           7.56
        4           1           4.89
       42           2           8.06
        8           2           7.50
```

EGOCENTRIC MEASURES

Regardless of how they are stored and managed, there are two types of measures that can emerge from egocentric data (Valente, 2010). First, compositional measures are those created by counting or taking the average of egocentric network variables. An example of this type of measure in the School Leaders data set would be the number or proportion of principals in one's ego network. A similar example that focuses on attitudes in one's ego network would be the number or proportion of those alters with high or favorable perceptions of innovation (another attribute that was measured on the survey instrument across all 3 years of data collection). Variance measures, the second type of measure to emerge from egocentric data, are simply those that are derived by calculating the variance or standard deviation of the egocentric network variables. For example, the standard deviation of the "raw" efficacy scores is a variance measure, which would serve as an indication of the amount of variability in efficacy available in one's egocentric network. Another example from an egocentric study of students would be the standard deviation of the grade point average of an ego's alters.

Taken together, egocentric network data are used to describe an individual actor's personal network. Building on the information introduced in Chapter 4, there are seven types of network questions that can be asked to induce information about one's ego networks. Table 7.2 reviews these seven types. Both compositional and variance

Table 7.2 Types of Questions Used to Elicit Egocentric Network Data. Data generated from these types of questions can be used to create compositional and variance measures on each ego's network.

Characteristic	Example
Strength of relationship	Closeness, acquaintance, stranger, how long known
Frequency of interaction	How often talked to, how often sought advice from
Type of relation	Family, friend, colleague
Socio-economic characteristics	Educational attainment, income, occupational title
Demographic characteristics	Race, age, sex
Substantive characteristics	Attend class regularly, perceptions on innovation, support current administration
Content of interaction	Discuss work-related issues, seek advice from, or input on a work decision

Source: Valente, T. W. (2010). *Social networks and health: Models, methods, and applications.* New York: Oxford University Press.

measures can be derived from these questions. These measures can then be related to an individual ego's attitudes and behaviors. There are several standard measures that can be calculated from egocentric network data, including size, strength, diversity, centrality, constraint, and brokerage. In some cases, these measures require relational data and attribute data from both ego and alter. In other cases, the measures simply require relational data.

Size

This first characteristic of an ego's neighborhood, size, is very much related to the same idea for a whole network (the same goes for the next two characteristics: density and distance). This is one of the most straightforward characteristics of an ego network: the number of alters that are directly connected to ego, a calculation that only requires relational data. Here, you simply need relational data about the number of alters with whom ego is connected. Size, therefore, is a count of the number of alters provided in responses to a name generator. The size of ego networks typically ranges from 0 to 6, since a name generator typically limits the number of alters that ego can list. In the School Leaders data set, egos were given a list of potential alters, therefore providing a high upper limit on the number of alters in one's network. As discussed in Chapter 4, you must be mindful of the cognitive burden that any name generator places on the respondent.

Consider Leader 25, row 2 in Table 7.1. This table indicates that the size of that ego's network is 10; ego has 10 others with whom he or she exchanges information on work-related topics. Size matters, as it indicates the amount of potential resources available in one's network. For example, a school leader with a small ego network may be at a disadvantage when it comes finding out information about topics relevant to one's job performance. While this makes sense on some level, this is the type of issue that can be investigated and formally tested using egocentric data. Figure 7.1 provides a graph that illustrates the size of Leader 25's egocentric network. From this figure, it is plainly evident that ego exchanges information about work-related topics with a fairly large number of other school leaders.

Density

A second standard characteristic of an ego's neighborhood is density: the extent to which an ego actor's alters are connected to one another. Similar to density measured at the complete network level, this measure is a percentage calculated from the number of ties present divided by the total number of potential ties. More formally, assuming that relations are nondirected binary (present/absent) ties, the density, D, measure is the

Figure 7.1 Graph of One School Leader's Egocentric Network (Leader 25). School Leader 25 has 10 alters—that is, 10 others with whom he or she exchanges information on work-related topics.

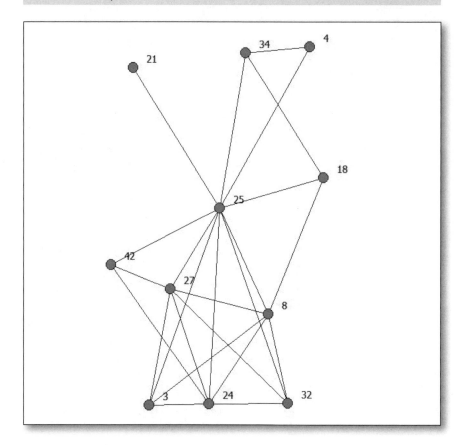

ratio of the number of reported dyadic ties, L, among alters divided by the maximum possible dyadic ties (Knoke & Yang, 2008):

$$D = \frac{L}{C_N^2}$$ [Equation 7.1]

where $C_2^N = \dfrac{N!}{2! \times (N-2)!}$. For example, suppose ego has five alters and reports only three relations among them. Because $C_5^3 = \dfrac{5!}{3! \times (5-3)} = \dfrac{(1 \times 2 \times 3 \times 4 \times 5)}{(1 \times 2 \times 3) \times (1 \times 2)} = \dfrac{120}{12} = 10$, the density is $D = \dfrac{L}{C_N^2} = \dfrac{3}{10} = 0.30$ or 30%. The closer this value is to 1.0, the denser one's ego network. This formula can also be adapted to handle binary directed relations,

valued nondirected relations, and valued directed egocentric data. But, given the transformation of the School Leaders data set, Equation 7.1 is appropriate, as the data are
binary and nondirected; that is, either a mutual relation is present between actors or it
is absent. Applying this equation to School Leader 25, the density of her egocentric network is 0.31, suggesting that slightly less than one-third of potential ties are present in
this ego's network.

Regardless of which density formula you need in order to compute this characteristic, the important piece to keep in mind is that the instrument used to collect
egocentric data must elicit alter-to-alter data. Put another way, in addition to collecting relational data about ego and his or her alters, relational information on each
pair of alters must also be collected. This is automatically done when egocentric
studies are derived from complete networks (as in the School Leaders data). However, when egocentric data are sampled from some target population, the name
interpreter must induce this type of relational data. This is typically done by asking
ego to evaluate the relationship between each pair of alters, a process that puts a
burden on the ego respondent.

Similar to measuring density on a complete network, the measurement of egocentric
density is important for several reasons. Dense local structures exhibit high social closure,
indicating that one's behaviors or attitudes are unlikely to escape the observation or critique of others. Viewed from this perspective, dense networks reinforce prevailing norms
and behaviors and insulate one from outside influences (these can be, however, either
good or bad). Those ego neighborhoods that display little social closure—that is, they are
less dense—may have greater freedom to act or think but have limited access to the
instrumental or expressive resources available in their local neighborhoods. These less
dense networks, often referred to as radial networks, can also be favorable or unfavorable,
depending on the behavior or attitude that you are interesting in studying. In fact, density
is a foundational concept and measure in the literature on social capital. Figure 7.2 shows
two ego networks from the School Leaders data set that are of the same size—meaning
that they have the same number of alters (seven)—yet they vary in terms of their density.
For example, the density for School Leader 1 is 71% versus 33% for School Leader 42.
When comparing these two figures, it is evident there is more connectivity among alters
in School Leader 1's egocentric network than there is 42's.

Distance and Diameter

The next two characteristics of egocentric neighborhoods are closely related. The
measures for these characteristics parallel those for complete networks, the difference
of course being that they are calculated on each ego network separately. The first of
these, average geodesic distance, simply refers to the mean of the shortest path lengths
among all connected pairs of alters in ego's network. If every actor is connected to every

Figure 7.2 Graphs of Two Egocentric Networks with the Same Number of Alters, but Different Densities. The density for School Leader 1 is 71% (bottom) versus 33% for School Leader 42 (top).

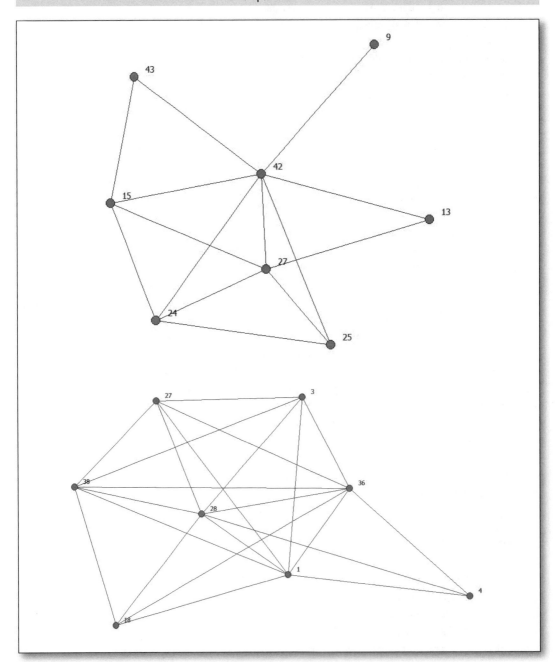

other actor (therefore, density = 100%), the average geodesic distance is one. Second, the diameter of an ego network equals the length of the longest path between connected actors. This translates into the number of "steps" that separate the two most distant actors in an ego's network.

Applying these measures to School Leaders 1, 25, and 35 highlights the differences among these three ego networks. For example, the average geodesic distance for School Leader 1 is 1.29, meaning that, on average, it takes a little more than one "step" for any actor to reach another. This value, however, cannot even be calculated for the other two ego networks because if one or more pairs of alters cannot reach the other except through ego, this measure is undefined and left blank. The diameter of School Leader 1's network, which equals 2.00, is also different from the other two egos. Again, the diameter for these two egos cannot be calculated, as one or more pairs of alters in these ego networks cannot reach the other except through ego, so this measure is also undefined and will be blank.

Figure 7.3 illustrates this point by showing a graph of School Leader 35's ego network. It is obvious that this ego's network size equals 2, and that those two alters are only connected to ego. The average geodesic distance and diameter cannot be calculated, as School Leaders 21 and 13 cannot reach each other except through ego (School Leader 35). Recall that the relation constituting these ego networks is "exchange information on work-related topics." Therefore, School Leader 35's ego network is small (size), with its

Figure 7.3   Egocentric Network of School Leader 35 Showing Distance and Diameter. School Leader 35's ego network is small (size), with its two alters unable to exchange information work-related topics without going "through" ego.

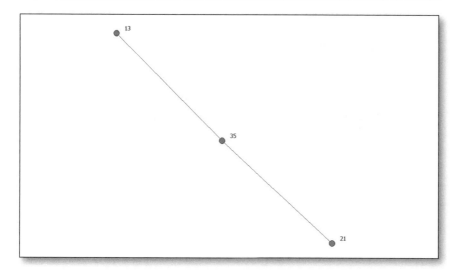

two alters unable to exchange information on work-related topics without going "through" ego. Given these characteristics, you can question whether such an ego network is disadvantageous for School Leader 35, particularly if these characteristics were related to an outcome such as the successful implementation of a schoolwide reform effort. An ego network that is both small and so poorly connected is unlikely to be associated with this particular desired outcome, a hypothesis that can be formally tested, which is discussed in the following chapter.

Tie Strength

Another characteristic of ego networks that may be of interest to educational researchers is tie strength. This characteristic shifts the focus onto the strength of the relationship between ego and each named alter (Valente, 2010). Therefore, unlike the example School Leaders data used through this chapter, the relational data must be "valued," indicating that there are variations in either the strength or frequency of relations between ego and each alter. The example data used in this chapter were transformed so that a relation is either absent or present (dichotomized) and nondirectional (symmetrized). However, the original data were, in fact, valued and directional, allowing tie strength to be incorporated into the analysis.

Tie strength has been a core idea throughout the network field, with weak ties serving as important bridges between different groups and strong ties being influential in behavioral adoption. Generally, weak ties are important for the spread of instrumental resources (e.g., work-related advice), while strong ties are important for expressive resources (e.g., guidance on personal matters) (Lin, 2001a). Stated another way, weak ties are important for transmitting information but less so for transmitting behavioral influence (Valente, 2010). Granovetter's (1973) classic work has laid much of the foundation for much of the work that has focused on the tie strength.

Figure 7.4 shows how tie strength can be incorporated into an egocentric analysis. This graph shows an ego (School Leader 1) and its relations with 11 alters, as well as the valued, nondirectional relations among those 11 alters. Thicker lines indicate that ego and alter exchange information about work-related topics more frequently (3–4 times per week) than thinner lines (not frequently); therefore, thicker lines are "stronger" ties and thinner lines are "weaker" ties.

To calculate a compositional measure of this ego's tie strength, you would simply need to calculate the mean and standard deviation of tie strength between this ego and its 11 alters (this calculation would, therefore, exclude alter-to-alter tie strength). Specifically, the values for these 11 ties are: 3, 2, 1, 1, 4, 1, 3, 4, 1, 4, and 3. The mean for these values equals 2.45 and the standard deviation is 1.29. These compositional measures can be used to explain an individual's behavior or attitudes. For example, it might be hypothesized that school leaders with more high-average tie strength but varied personal

Figure 7.4 Graph of School Leader 1's Two-Step Ego Network. This graph shows how tie strength can be incorporated into an egocentric analysis. This graph shows an ego (School Leader 1) and its relations with 11 alters, as well as the valued, nondirectional relations among those 11 alters. Thicker lines indicate that ego and alter exchange information about work-related topics more frequently (3–4 times per week) than thinner lines (not frequently); therefore, thicker lines are "stronger" ties and thinner lines are "weaker" ties.

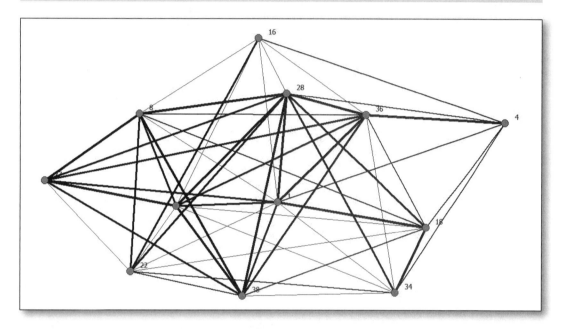

networks (on "exchange information about work-related advice") are more likely to be innovative. These school leaders are probably exposed to more varied perspectives and can therefore draw on these differences to generate fresh ideas. This very idea is at the core of Granovetter's strength-of-weak-ties argument.

Diversity

Another way in which an ego network can be characterized draws on the attributes of those alters to which ego is connected. This is very similar to the previous measure of tie strength, the difference being that diversity can also capture the extent of heterogeneity of social characteristics of the alters in an ego's network (Knoke & Yang, 2008). For example, depending on the level of measurement of alters' characteristics, egocentric diversity can be measured by the standard deviation for continuous variables or by an index of qualitative variation for categorical variables.

Two examples highlight the way in which egocentric diversity can be measured. For instance, you might expect that an ego teacher whose alters have, on average, higher scores on a measure of teacher effectiveness and less variation (therefore a lower standard deviation) would be more likely to be rated as highly effective. When a characteristic such as this (teacher effectiveness) is measured on a continuous level, the standard deviation indicates the variable's diversity within a given ego's network. The formula of this is:

$$^{s}X_{i} = \sqrt{\frac{\sum\limits_{j=1}^{N}(X_{ij} - \overline{X})^2}{N-1}} \qquad \text{[Equation 7.2]}$$

where for the ith ego with N alters, the jth alter's characteristic X_{ij} is a continuous variable. The mean of the standard deviations for all egos reflects the attribute's diversity in a sample of egos. Therefore, to get a sense of the diversity of teacher effectiveness in a sample of egos, you would simply have to average across the standard deviations for each ego.

A second example highlights how egocentric diversity can be captured for a categorical variable. To do so, you would calculate an index of qualitative variation (IQV; Knoke & Yang, 2008). For the ith ego with N alters, where the alters are classified into K (discrete or ordered) categories, the IQV is

$$IQV_i = \frac{1 - \sum\limits_{j=1}^{K} p_j^2}{(K-1)/K} \qquad \text{[Equation 7.3]}$$

where p_j^2 is the percentage of alters in the jth category. The IQV is a standardized measure ranging from 0 to 1, where 0 indicates that all N cases are in one category and 1 indicates that that alters are equally dispersed across the K categories. For example, if a school leader (ego) names four white and one nonwhite alters, the race composition IQV is $\dfrac{1 - [(0.8)^2 + (0.2)^2]}{(2-1)/2} = 0.64$, whereas if a school leader were to name three whites and two nonwhites, there is a race composition IQV of 0.96. Therefore, this latter egocentric network has greater racial diversity.

Centrality

Centrality has been an important concept and measure in social network analysis for some time. Graph theory has been put to use in social network analysis to identify those prominent or important actors at the group (complete network analysis) or individual levels (egocentric analysis). The focus here is on the latter, in which centrality concepts and measures have been used to quantify an ego's prominence or importance in his or her ego neighborhood. Because most centrality indicators require only binary tie measurement (a tie is either present or absent), the concepts and measures rely on the transformed School Leaders data described earlier in this chapter. In addition, the focus will be on nondirected relations, but these measures can handle directed relational data.

Conceptually, centrality captures the extent to which a focal actor occupies an important position of prestige and visibility. Typically, being at the center of things is viewed as a good thing. Consequently, centrality has been an important focus of social network analysts. However, there are numerous ways to measure centrality (Borgatti & Everett, 2006), each emphasizing a slightly different way in which centrality is conceptualized. These varied measures were summarized and further developed by Freeman (1979), in which he introduced three core properties of centrality measures (Valente, 2010):

1. They can be calculated on individuals, referred to as point or node centrality.

2. The point centrality measure should be normalized by the size of the network so that calculations from different networks can be compared.

3. A complete network centralization score can be computed, indicating the degree of centralization derived from a specific measure.

Degree

This is most frequently used centrality measure, and it is directly related to egocentric network size described earlier. *Degree* is the number of ties to and from an ego. Obviously, in a directed egocentric network, *in-degree* is the number of ties received, whereas *out-degree* is the number of ties sent. However, to make this metric more useful, it can be normalized so that ego networks of different sizes can be compared. This requires that the number of ties be divided by the number of maximum number possible, which is $N - 1$. Therefore, normalized degree centrality can vary from 0 to 1, with scores closer to 1 indicating higher centrality. Formally, an ego's degree centralization, C_D, is represented as (Freeman, 1979)

$$C_D = \sum \frac{d_i}{N-1} \qquad \text{[Equation 7.4]}$$

where d_i is the number of ego's ties. This formula can be applied to both in-degrees and out-degrees, assuming one's relational data are directional. However, it cannot be applied to valued data. In addition, this calculation is only appropriate when egocentric data have been derived from a complete network.

For example, to calculate the degree of centrality of School Leader 25 (Figure 7.1), you would first need to identify the number of degrees in this ego's network (degrees = 10) and the total size of the network since, theoretically, an actor in the School Leaders data set can be nominated by everyone else in the network ($N - 1 = 42$). Therefore, the normalized degree centrality for School Leader 25 is $10/42 = 0.24$ or, 24% after multiplying by 100. Normalized degree centrality can serve as a useful indicator for personal attributes and can be correlated with a number of other individual-level education outcomes. Spillane, Healey, and Kim (2010), for example, use an individual's in-degree centrality to define whether a school staff member was an advice giver (those with in-degrees greater than two were considered as such).

Closeness

Degree centrality is a local measure because it can be calculated without needing information about the overall pattern of relations among ego and alters. Therefore, a shortcoming of this measure is that it does not take into account indirect ties among all the alters in an ego's network. The second centrality measure, *closeness*, does this by requiring information on the pattern of ties in an ego's network; that is, it requires data about the relation between each pair of ego's named alters (two-step ego neighborhoods—"friends of friends"). Therefore, this and the next centrality measure (betweenness centrality) are most easily calculated when you are examining ego networks derived from a complete network, as is the case with egocentric analyses derived from the School Leaders data set. This centrality measure is intuitively appealing in that being "close" to others may provide an advantage by, for example, giving you early access to new information. Closeness can also be used to indicate how quickly an actor can exchange something with others, for example, by communicating directly or through very few intermediaries (Knoke & Yang, 2008).

Closeness centrality captures the average distance an actor is from all other actors in the network and is a function of an actor's geodesic distance to others, which equals the length of shortest path connecting a pair of actors. Actor closeness centrality is calculated as the inverse of the sum of the geodesic distances between actor i and the $g - 1$ actors in the network. The formula for this measure is:

$$C_c(N_i) = \frac{1}{[\sum_{j=1}^{g} d(N_i, N_j)]} \ (i \neq j) \qquad \text{[Equation 7.4]}$$

This measure, of course, requires an actor to have at least one tie to another actor. Therefore, it cannot be calculated for isolated actors, those without any connections to others. When an actor is close to others, $C_C = 1/(g-1)$. This, however, varies with the network's overall size. Therefore, to control for the size of the network, this formula can be standardized, which then allows for meaningful comparisons across networks. Closeness centrality is standardized by simply multiplying it by $(g - 1)$, where g equals the number of actors in one's egocentric network.

For example, the normalized closeness centrality for School Leader 1 is 0.50. This was calculated by summing the geodesic distances between School Leader 1 and the other 42 actors in the network, dividing this by 1, and then multiplying it by 42, $(g - 1)$. The higher an actor's centrality score (1.0 is the maximum value), the closer it is to others in the sense that the actor can reach other actors through shorter distances (Knoke & Yang, 2008).

Moolenaar, Daly, and Sleegers (2010) employ a measure of closeness centrality in their investigation of the relationship between transformational leadership and schools' innovative climates, hypothesizing that a principal's closeness centrality mediates this relationship. According to their conceptualization, closeness centrality indicates how "close" a principal is to the team members, or how quickly a principal can reach all team members through the social network. Closeness centrality is thus interpreted as a measure of "reachability" by the principal. The higher a principal's closeness centrality, the quicker information dispensed by the principal will reach all team members. In contrast to degree centrality, closeness centrality includes principals' indirect relationships to all team members. Uzzi (1996) suggests that not only direct but also indirect connections are important, as these relationships may dampen or enhance leaders' effectiveness.

Moolenaar, Daly, and Sleegers (2010) go on to argue that, by occupying a more central position, a leader is more often sought for resources (friendship, expertise, etc.) and has easier access to resources, information, or support from the social network (Adler & Kwon, 2002). Moreover, having more relationships increases a leader's opportunities to access novel information (Balkundi & Kilduff, 2006; Krackhardt, 1996). This access to diverse resources provides a central leader with the possibility to guide the flow of information and resources within the team (Burt, 2004). A leader may use the power and status attained through occupying a central position to direct certain knowledge and information to the right people who might need it most. Therefore, they hypothesize (and ultimately confirm) that principals who hold more central positions, as assessed by higher degree centrality and closeness centrality, are associated with schools that are characterized by more innovative climates.

Betweenness

This third centrality measure captures how actors control or mediate the relations between pairs of actors that are not directly connected. Suppose, for example, that a principal wants to exchange resources with another principal in the same school district, but in order to get these resources, he has to go through one or more intermediaries. This gives those intermediaries who are positioned "between" the principals more power and influence. To the extent that the principal can pursue multiple pathways to reach these others, the dependency on any single intermediary is reduced (Hanneman & Riddle, 2011b). Therefore, betweenness centrality measures the degree to which other actors lie on the shortest geodesic path between pairs of actors in the network. Therefore, this measure is an important indicator of control over information exchange or resource flows within a network (Knoke & Yang, 2008). The more any given actor is located on the path between numerous dyads, the higher that actor's potential to control network interactions. If principals in the school district contact one other principal to facilitate the exchange of resources among all principals, this second principal serves as an important conduit through which transactions occur. This concept and its associated measure is very appealing, as it captures the degree to which an actor occupies a strategically important position.

Like closeness centrality, you can calculate a point measure for betweenness as well as a normalized version. Point betweenness is calculated by counting the number of times an actor lies on the shortest paths connecting all other actors in the network. The normalized version, which again enables a comparison across networks, is calculated as (Freeman, 1979):

$$C_b = \frac{\dfrac{g_{ij}p_k}{g_{ij}}}{n^2 - 3n + 2} \qquad \text{[Equation 7.5]}$$

where $g_{ij}p_k$ counts the number of times point k lies on the geodesic (shortest path) connecting all other actors (i and j) and g_{ij} is the total number of geodesics in the network. Betweenness is, therefore, the frequency with which an actor lies on the shortest path connecting other actors in the network. The maximum value that the numerator can have is $n^2 - 3n + 2$, which is the normalization factor. When an actor's normalized betweenness is 1, that actor falls on the geodesic (shortest) path of every pair of actors among the remaining $g - 1$ actors. Therefore, the closer an actor's standardized betweenness centrality is to 1, the more that actor controls the flow of resources across the network.

Betweenness centrality has been employed in a number of education-related studies. For example, in Spillane, Healey, and Kim's (2010) study on the relations between schools' formal and informal organization and how this relates to managing and leading instruction in schools, they examine both an individual's in-degree centrality and the normalized betweenness scores. This allows them to capture how "central" a school's staff member is in the flow of information from two slightly different conceptualizations. Combining these individual measures with subgroup and school levels of analyses, they conclude that those formally designated as school leaders were more likely than their colleagues without this designation to connect staff members who weren't otherwise connected. They conclude that this finding suggests that these formal leaders serve as key intermediaries among school staff.

Intuitively, these three different centrality measures (degree, closeness, and betweenness) are similar, leading you to conclude that they are correlated. However, this correlation is far from 1 (Valente, 2010), as they each capture a different view or purpose of centrality. Degree, for example, is a more localized measure, capturing the degree to which an actor is connected to other actors regardless of how those other actors are related to each other. Closeness centrality, on the other hand, captures a communication role such that actors with high closeness scores can exchange something with many others relatively quickly. Finally, betweenness centrality measures a gatekeeping function—if a school leader, for example, with a high betweenness score dislikes an idea, its spread to other actors in the network might be hindered. Conversely, if the leader likes the idea, the idea may move more freely to other parts of the network.

Because of these slight but important differences, these three measures often identify different actors as being central. For example, consider Figure 7.5, which shows the complete network of School Leaders on the "information about work-related topics" relation. Three different centrality scores (degree, closeness, and betweenness) were calculated for each of the 43 actors in this network. Table 7.3 reports these scores. For example, School Leaders 28 and 38 have the highest degree centrality scores, as well as the highest closeness centrality scores. Finally, these same two leaders also have the highest betweenness centrality scores. This is confirmed by the graph in Figure 7.5, in which it is evident that these leaders are central to the network. This finding, however, is the exception; often these three measures will yield different results (Costenbader & Valente, 2003). Costenbader and Valente (2003) report that the overall average correlation

Figure 7.5   Graph of School Leaders "Information About Work-Related Topics" Complete Network (*N* = 43). Using relational information from this complete network, it is possible to calculate different centrality scores for each ego, specifically, degree, closeness, and betweenness centrality.

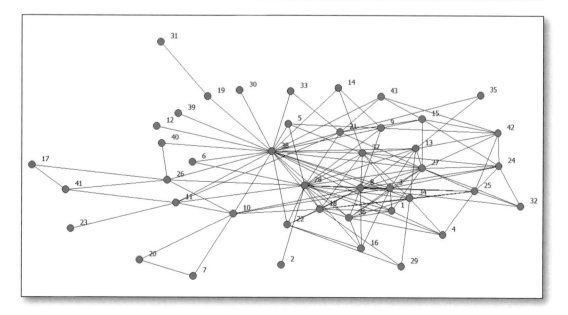

Table 7.3 Three Different Normalized Centrality Scores for School Leaders' "Information About Work-Related Topics" Network.

	Degree	Closeness	Betweenness
1	0.17	0.50	0.00
2	0.02	0.38	0.00
3	0.29	0.54	0.03
4	0.12	0.42	0.00
5	0.10	0.46	0.00
6	0.05	0.44	0.00
7	0.05	0.34	0.00
8	0.36	0.57	0.06
9	0.14	0.48	0.01
10	0.19	0.51	0.10
11	0.14	0.50	0.08
12	0.02	0.42	0.00
13	0.21	0.51	0.03
14	0.07	0.44	0.00
15	0.14	0.47	0.01
16	0.12	0.43	0.00
17	0.05	0.33	0.00
18	0.26	0.53	0.03
19	0.05	0.43	0.05
20	0.05	0.34	0.00
21	0.19	0.51	0.04
22	0.14	0.48	0.01
23	0.02	0.33	0.00
24	0.19	0.42	0.01

	Degree	Closeness	Betweenness
25	0.24	0.45	0.02
26	0.14	0.48	0.07
27	0.31	0.53	0.04
28	0.50	0.62	0.16
29	0.07	0.37	0.00
30	0.02	0.42	0.00
31	0.02	0.30	0.00
32	0.10	0.40	0.00
33	0.05	0.44	0.00
34	0.21	0.51	0.02
35	0.05	0.37	0.00
36	0.24	0.51	0.01
37	0.26	0.53	0.02
38	0.64	0.73	0.47
39	0.02	0.42	0.00
40	0.07	0.44	0.00
41	0.10	0.35	0.00
42	0.19	0.40	0.01
43	0.10	0.46	0.00

among these and other centrality measures is slightly more than 0.50, a moderately strong relationship. They conclude that these centrality measures represent a consistent concept, but there is some distinctiveness to each individual measure.

All three centrality measures can also be adapted and applied to complete network-level data analysis, measuring the degree to which a given centrality measure varies across the network's actors. Employing these and other centrality measures at this level would require you to shift analytical focus from the egocentric to the complete network level. For a review of how these measures can be adapted and applied to the analysis of complete networks, see Wasserman and Faust (1994) or Freeman (1979).

In addition to these three common centrality measures, at least seven others have been developed, most of which require that egos be examined as part of a larger complete network. These alternative centrality measures include eigenvector centrality (Bonacich, 1972), entropy (Tutzauer, 2007), power (Bonacich, 1987), Katz centrality (1953), and random-walk centrality introduced by Noh and Rieger (2004). These different centrality measures can be calculated in most common social network-analysis software applications. But, before deciding which measure or combinations of measures to employ, you must have an understanding of the strengths and purposes of each measure. For example, link centrality, which enables you to determine which relations are most central to a network, is very useful if you want to identify which relationships are most central. Removing a "central" tie would therefore interrupt the flow of resources more than would the removal of any other tie. On the other hand, a centrality measure such as power centrality is useful because you are able to vary the degree to which the centrality of ego's neighbors is included in the calculation (Valente, 2010). One way, of course, to identify the most appropriate centrality measures given your research interest is to use the precedent established by those working in similar topical areas.

Constraint

Another measure of egocentric networks, constraint, extends the egocentric network density measure to include more information about the structural pattern of relations among ego's alters. Therefore, similar to density, this measure requires that you have not only relational data on ego and his or her alters but also relational data on each pair of named alters. This is fairly straightforward if you extract egocentric data from a complete network study, but it poses of larger burden on the respondent if these type of data are collected from a sample of egos drawn from some larger population.

Constraint can be demonstrated through the following example from Hanneman and Riddle (2011b). Consider a network of three students: A, B, and C. Each student is connected to the two others. Suppose Student A wanted to influence or exchange resources with another student. Assume that both Students B and C may also have some interest in engaging in some interaction or exchange. Student A is not in a strong position because both of A's potential exchange partners (Students B and C) have alternatives to interacting with A. For example, they could choose to isolate A and then only interact or exchange with each other.

The example they offer then asks that you now imagine a "structural hole" (Burt, 1992) between Students B and C. That is, a relation is absent, preventing B and C from interacting or exchanging. This could happen because B and C do not know each other, dislike each other, or there are high transaction "costs" involved in forming a relation. In this situation, Student A is at an advantage because she or he has two possible interaction partners, whereas B and C have only one choice (Student A). Student A can be considered to be in a more powerful position since she or he is not constrained by the possibility of being excluded from the possible interaction.

Burt (1992) developed a number of measures related to this concept of structural holes, most of which are computed on binary relational data that can be either directed or nondirected (valued data can also be used, but the interpretation becomes much more difficult). The most common measure of structural holes is constraint. Others include efficiency, hierarchy, and effective size. Constraint can be considered the degree to which an ego's alters are connected to each other; therefore, ego's behaviors and attitudes are more likely "controlled" by his or her personal network. In an ego network with low constraint, one's alters are not connected to one another, which may prevent alters from colluding to keep information from ego. This measure is calculated as follows (Burt, 1992, p. 55, Equation 2):

$$C_i = \left(p_{ij} + \sum_q p_{iq} p_{qi} \right)^2, \; q \neq i, j$$

Admittedly, while the logic of the measure is pretty simple, its calculation is not. In short, what the calculation does is add the degree to which each of the alters is connected to the others in the focal ego's network. This may seem similar to density, but the difference is that constraint uses more information from the ego network (Valente, 2010). Low constraint scores (closer to 0) indicate that the ego occupies a position of structural holes in which they can access different parts of the network more effectively. In addition, if an ego has low constraint and high betweenness centrality scores, this ego is likely to serve as "bridge" to other parts of the network, a key position in a network's social structure. Drawing from a population of business managers, Burt (2004) has amassed an impressive body of evidence showing that low constraint is associated with an array of favorable outcomes, including early promotion, greater compensation, and higher levels of innovation. Egos with high constraint, on the other hand, may lose freedom of action and may be not have access to diverse streams of information.

Figure 7.6 shows the ego networks of three different ego actors extracted from the School Leaders data set on the "exchange information about work-related topics" relation, which is a binary, undirected relation. These graphs illustrate the different levels of constraint across three ego networks. For example, School Leader 8, with a network size of 15, has a constraint score of 0.24, indicating that this leader occupies a position in which he or she has a large number of alternative exchange partners. Contrast this with the ego network of School Leader 17, whose network is small (2), dense (1.0), and highly constrained (1.13). It is very likely that this leader may be at a serious disadvantage when it comes to acquiring new or diverse streams of information about work-related topics. School Leader 14 has a constraint score of 0.84, a moderate level of constraint. Given these scores, you can hypothesize and test whether leaders who occupy structural holes are more likely to innovate. This type of inferential analysis is introduced in the following chapter.

Figure 7.6 Graphs of Three Ego Networks (School Leaders 8, 14, and 17) With Different Levels of Constraint. These graphs illustrate the different levels of constraint across three ego networks. For example, School Leader 8 (bottom), with a network size of 15, has a constraint score of 0.24, indicating that this leader occupies a position in which he or she has a large number of alternative exchange partners. Contrast this with the ego network of School Leader 17 (top), whose network is small (2), dense (1.0), and highly constrained (1.13).

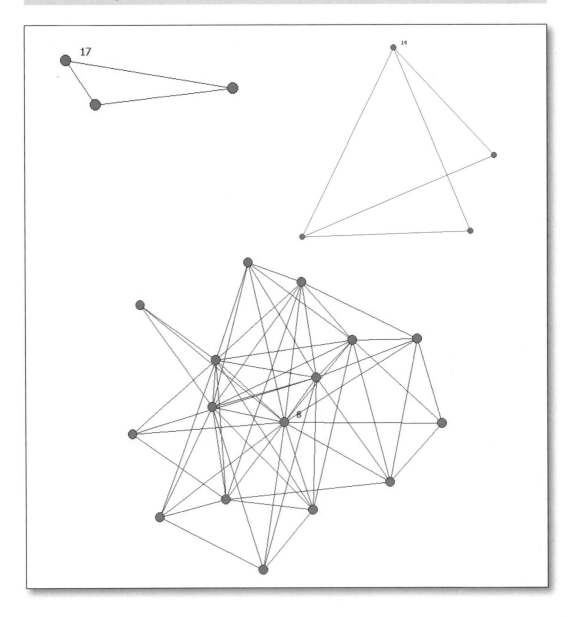

Brokerage

A final concept and measure that describes an ego's local social structure is broker-age. Here, the egocentric network must be part of a larger, complete network. Brokerage can be thought of as an extension of betweenness centrality and structural holes analy-ses in that it, too, focuses on the extent to which a focal ego is located "between" two alters. Gould and Fernandez (1989) extend this idea in an attractive way that accounts for the possibility that egos and their alters might also be affiliated with social groups (Hanneman & Riddle, 2011b). Fernandez and Gould also examined the ways in which actors' embedding might constrain their behavior. However, they took a quite different approach; they focused on the roles that ego plays in connecting groups. That is, this notion of "brokerage" examines ego's relations with its neighborhood from the perspec-tive of ego acting as an "agent" in relations across groups (though, as a practical matter, the groups in brokerage analysis can be individuals).

To examine an actor's brokerage, you find every instance in which that actor lies on the directed path between two others. Each actor, therefore, has numerous opportuni-ties to act as a broker. Each time an ego acts as a broker, the types of actors that ego is between are examined. To do so, the group memberships of all three actors must also be incorporated into the analysis, requiring that attribute data be collected along with the relational data. There are five possible combinations of brokerage roles, which are dis-played at the top of the output in Figure 7.7.

Consider the following example, which illustrates these roles using a focal actor, ego (Hanneman & Riddle, 2011b). If ego falls on a directed path between two members of the same category as itself (e.g., an English teacher falling between two other English teachers in a path), ego is referred to as a *coordinator*. If ego falls on the path between two members of a group of which it is not a part, the ego is called a *consultant* (e.g., an English teacher falling on the path from one math teacher to another). If ego falls on the path from a member of another group to a member of its own group, the ego is called a *gatekeeper*. Such a situation may arise when, for example, an English teacher falls on the path from a math teacher to another English teacher. If ego falls on the path from a member of its own group to a member of another group, ego is considered a *representa-tive* (e.g., the English teacher falls on the path from English teacher to math teacher). Finally, if ego falls on a path from a member of one group to another but is not a member of either group, ego is a *liaison* (e.g., the English teacher falls on the path from science teacher to math teacher).

The first two brokerage roles involve mediation between members of one group. In the first role, coordinator, the mediator is also part of the group. In the second role (con-sultant), two members of a group use a mediator from the outside. The other three bro-kerage roles describe mediation between members of different groups. The gatekeeper regulates the flow of resources *to* his or her groups, while the representative regulates the flow *from* his or her group. The liaison mediates between members of different groups but does not belong to either group. These five roles were initially conceived for directed networks, namely transaction networks (de Nooy, Mrvar, & Batagelj, 2005). However, the directionality is only needed to differentiate between the representative and gatekeeper roles. The other three roles are also apparent in undirected relations, so they can be applied to undirected networks if you do not distinguish between representatives and gatekeepers (in an undirected network, there is no difference between roles).

To further illustrate these different roles, consider the ego networks for School Leaders 1, 2, 3, 21, and 5. These networks consist of directional (nonvalued) data on the "turn to for information on work-related topics" relation and attribute data on school leaders' gender (group 1 = female). As an aside, the attribute data can also be a vector of categorical demographic data (e.g., gender) or a vector that identifies the group affiliation of an actor that has been assigned through one of the means (e.g., cliques) introduced in the previous chapter. Figure 7.7, for the sake of presentation, shows the partial UCINET output of a basic analysis of brokerage roles for these leaders. The actors have

Figure 7.7 Partial UCINET Output of a Basic Analysis of Brokerage Roles for School Leaders 1, 2, 3, 21, 5, and 7. From this output, it is evident that School Leaders 3 and 21 are key levers of connectivity between females and males.

```
GOULD & FERNANDEZ BROKERAGE MEASURES

Unnormalized Brokerage Scores

                  1         2         3         4         5         6
          Coordinat Gatekeepe Represent Consultan   Liaison     Total
        -----------------------------------------------------------------
     1 |        2         6         2         1         0        11 |
     2 |        0         0         0         0         0         0 |
     3 |       20         8        14         2         0        44 |

    21 |        9         8         5         3         0        25 |
     5 |        0         0         1         0         0         1 |
     7 |        0         0         0         0         0         0 |
        -----------------------------------------------------------------

Legend: (given flow 1-->2-->3, where 2 is the broker)
       Coordinator:  A-->A-->A  (all nodes belong to same group)
        Gatekeeper:  B-->A-->A  (source belongs to different group)
    Representative:  A-->A-->B  (recipient belongs to different group)
        Consultant:  B-->A-->B  (broker belongs to different group)
           Liaison:  B-->A-->C  (all nodes belong to different groups)
```

been grouped together by a vector (partition) for gender: Leaders 1, 2, and 3, for example, are female and the other three are male. Each row in this condensed output counts the "raw" (unnormalized) number of times each of the six school leaders plays each of the five brokerage roles in the whole ($N = 43$) graph. This calculation, rather than using the complete network, can also be restricted to each ego's one-step neighborhood. From this output, it is evident that School Leaders 3 and 21 are key levers of connectivity between females and males. School Leaders 2 and 3, one female and one male, have zero incidents of overall brokerage. None of the six leaders acts as liaison, which is not surprising given that there are only two groups (males and females) and acting in this role requires that egos be affiliated with one of at least three groups. Finally, there are few incidents of leaders serving as consultants, which is also to be expected given that it would be odd for two leaders to bring in a mediator of the opposite gender in order to broker an exchange of work-related topics. It would not, however, be so odd if the partition vector were an attribute such as whether one was a senior or junior school leader (in terms of seniority). In this instance, it would make more sense if a junior leader were to turn to a senior leader (ego) in order to facilitate an exchange with a junior colleague. Therefore, the choice of partition vector (i.e., the group to which one belongs) should make sense given one's topical focus.

SUMMARY

This chapter introduced several of the most common concepts and measures related to analysis of egocentric networks. What distinguishes analyses that operate at this level, as opposed to complete-level network analyses, is that the focus is a sole ego actor's pattern of relations with those alters that constitute his or her own ego neighborhood. Egocentric data can be collected by asking individuals to name those with whom they share a relation (name generator) and then asking that they evaluate the relations among those that have been named (name interpreter). When sampled and collected in this manner, egocentric data can be used to characterize the personal networks of populations. Egocentric data can also be extracted from a complete network study. The School Leaders data cited throughout this chapter relied on egocentric data collected through this manner.

Once the egocentric data have been collected and organized, a number of different measures can be calculated to reveal different properties. These properties are related to connectivity (size and density), centrality (degree and betweenness centrality), structural holes (constraint), and brokerage (coordinator, gatekeeper). These different measures describe the content and contours of an ego's neighborhood. Researchers have used these and other measures to test whether they are associated with an array of outcomes relevant to educational researchers. The following chapter gently introduces the ways in which these indices, as well as those measured at the complete level, can be used to more formally make predictions, test hypotheses, and even generalize to larger populations.

CHAPTER FOLLOW-UP

1. Locate an egocentric network study that addresses something related to educational research. What makes this an egocentric network study? How were the egocentric network data collected? What measures of egos' networks were included in the analysis?

2. Assume you wanted to examine whether a student's popularity was associated with her or his attachment to school. How could you use a measure introduced in this chapter to capture "popularity"? Why did you select this measure over any others? Would you simply need ego-to-alter data or also alter-to-alter data?

3. If you wanted to examine the process through which a school reform initiative spreads throughout a school district, which egocentric concepts and measures would you employ?

CRITICAL QUESTIONS TO ASK ABOUT STUDIES THAT EMPLOY EGOCENTRIC NETWORK ANALYSIS

1. How were the ego network data collected? Were they randomly sampled from a population, or were they collected as part of a complete network study?

2. What questions were asked in order to identify ego's alters? Or was the respondent provided a list of potential alters?

3. What other information about the alters was collected?

4. What egocentric measures were calculated? Did these measures make use of any information about tie strength or any other alter attributes?

5. If a measure of centrality was calculated, why was one measure chosen over the other possible options?

ESSENTIAL READING

Burt, R. S. (2004). Structural holes and good ideas. *American Journal of Sociology, 110*(2), 349–399.

Freeman, L. C. (1979). Centrality in social networks. *Social Networks, 1*, 215–239.

Granovetter, M. (1973). The strength of weak ties. *American Journal of Sociology, 81*, 1287–1303.

PART III

Applications and Examples

8

An Introduction to Statistical Inference With Network Data

OBJECTIVES

In this chapter, you will learn about the difference between the mathematical and statistical approaches to social network analysis. In Part II, many social network measures for concepts related to both complete and ego networks were presented. These measures reflect a mathematical approach that focuses on what a network of actors "looks like." This approach does not, however, consider whether a certain configuration is predictable and normal, how one relation is associated with another relation among the same set of actors, or whether one network structure could be thought of as "better" than another. To attend to these important issues, in this chapter, you will learn about the ways in which statistical inference has evolved in order to move social network analysis beyond the social scientific goal of description and closer to explanation and ultimately prediction. It is assumed that you have a basic understanding of probability and statistical inference.

MAKING AND TESTING PREDICTIONS

Is there a relationship between the frequency of collaboration between school leaders and how often they turn to each other to discuss issues of a confidential nature? Do school leaders prefer to collaborate with those with whom they have collaborated in the past, or is there some other reason? Could it be that gender or some other individual attribute predicts confidential exchanges between school leaders, or does some previous relation have a stronger effect? Does collaboration between leaders explain one's level of trust in one's administrative colleagues? Can we distinguish among different groups of school leaders based on how frequently they collaborate, and if so, are these groupings related to the level at which they work (school versus district)?

The chapters in Part II focused on ways in which different algorithms can be used to describe properties related to ego or complete networks. This chapter moves beyond these static snapshots and provides an introduction to the ways in which recent advances in inferential statistics can be used to make predictions from social network data and address the questions in the previous paragraph. Other introductions to statistical network models can be found in Wasserman and Faust (1994), Scott (2000), and Goldenberg, Zheng, Fienberg, and Airoldi (2009). Unlike these other introductions, the ideas to be presented in this chapter are intentionally presented in a nontechnical manner, avoiding the use of formulas and focusing on a conceptual understanding rather than calculation. The primary aim of this chapter is to convey the importance of statistical models and how they can be used to test whether some network features were expected and normal or whether one network configuration could be thought of as "better" than another.

This chapter begins by describing the critical differences between mathematical and statistical approaches to social network analysis and how these approaches reflect the important analytic difference between description and prediction. While recognizing that most social network analysis is descriptive and, therefore, implicitly relies on the mathematical approach, this chapter lays the foundation for some of the newer and exciting ways in which statistics can be applied to the study of social networks in and around education. The goal of this chapter is not to provide a comprehensive overview of the logic and mechanics of statistical inference with network data but rather introduce you to how statistics have been adapted to further strengthen the inferential claims emanating from social network studies. Consequently, as a result of these techniques, social network analysis has moved beyond description and toward prediction, a direction in which most network analyses in education are headed.

The development of these statistical tools and their application to social network analysis can be traced to two general dissatisfactions with earlier social network studies. First, the measures presented throughout Part II were merely descriptive, with networks being described by creating indicators for their structure (e.g., density, reciprocity, etc.)

and the members of networks characterized by their position (e.g., centrality). These measures convey the image of a fixed network with attitudes or behaviors passing through it, much like airplanes flying to and from different airports. In reality, unlike airports, networks change, and in some instances quickly. Teachers confer with new colleagues and no longer do so with old ones. Some students seek extra help for the first time, while others quit after receiving that help for some time. Relationships may change because of the behavior change, while in other cases people change behaviors or attitudes because those closest to them have changed theirs (Valente, 2010). For example, if a teacher favors a certain instructional approach, he or she may form friendships with other teachers who prefer that same approach. Alternatively, a teacher may adopt an instructional approach because his or her friend has adopted it. Consequently, we need a way to simultaneously analyze changes in networks and behaviors. These issues surrounding the co-evolution of behavior and social networks have been addressed through the development of statistical models that estimate the likelihood that two actors form ties in a network based on their existing relationships and behaviors (Valente, 2010).

In addition to earlier studies not accounting for network dynamics, thereby limiting the types of questions that could be asked, they also did not account for the dependencies between a network's actors. For example, associations among network exposure (e.g., attitudes of one's peers), network indicators (e.g., size, transitivity), and individual attributes are nonindependent—a critical assumption that provides the foundation for most conventional statistical tests. For example, let's say a statistical analysis reveals that two high-achieving students are more likely than low achievers to have high-achieving friends. This association, however, may be the result of both the focal student and the network alters being connected to a third student who is also a high achiever. Therefore, a different statistical approach was needed that did not assume the independence of a network's actors. Because of these two issues, there has been a marked shift toward a statistical approach that can test propositions about network-related properties rather than simply relying on descriptive statements. This statistical approach not only avoids the assumption of independence but also provides ways to model a network's change over time and test hypotheses related to these changes.

MATHEMATICAL VERSUS STATISTICAL APPROACHES

Social network analysis is more a branch of "mathematical" social science than of "statistical or quantitative analysis," though social network analysts often reflect both approaches (Hanneman & Riddle, 2005). The distinction between the two, however, is not clear cut. Mathematical approaches tend to regard the measured relationships and their strengths as accurately reflecting the "real," "final," or "equilibrium" status of the network. In addition to this deterministic thinking, the mathematical approach also assumes that the observations are not a "sample" of some larger population of possible observations; rather, as is the case with complete network studies, the observations are usually regarded as *the* population of interest. That is, the sample in these instances is the same as the population.

Statistical analysts, on the other hand, tend to regard the particular scores on relationship strengths as stochastic or probabilistic realizations of an underlying true tendency or probability distribution of relationship strengths. Statistical analysts also tend to think of a particular set of network data as sampled from some larger class or population of such networks or network elements. The concern of the statistical approach, therefore, is on the reproducibility in a subsequent study of similar samples (Hanneman & Riddle, 2005).

It should be evident that the chapters in Part II were concerned with the mathematical rather than the statistical side of network analysis. Before moving on to the statistical analysis of social networks, there are a few main points about the relationship between the material in this chapter and the main statistical approaches employed in educational research.

In one way, there is little apparent difference between conventional statistical approaches and network approaches (Hanneman & Riddle, 2005). Univariate, bivariate, and even many multivariate descriptive statistical tools are commonly used in describing, exploring, and modeling social network data. Social network data are, as pointed out in Chapter 3, easily represented as arrays of numbers—just like other types of actor-by-attribute data. As a result, the same kinds of operations can be performed on network data as on other types of data. Algorithms from statistics are commonly used to describe characteristics of individual observations (e.g. the mean tie strength of Student A with all other alters in his or network) and the network as a whole (e.g. the mean of all tie strengths among all students in the network). Statistical algorithms are often used in assessing the degree of similarity among actors and in finding patterns in network data (e.g., factor analysis, cluster analysis, multidimensional scaling). Even the tools of predictive modeling are commonly applied to network data (e.g. correlation and regression).

Inferences With Network Data

Descriptive statistical tools such as those in Part II are really just algorithms—some, admittedly, complicated—for summarizing characteristics of the distributions of scores. That is, they are mathematical operations. Where statistics really become "statistical" is on the inferential side, that is, when attention turns to assessing the reproducibility or likelihood of an observed pattern. Inferential statistics can be and are applied to the analysis of network data. Hanneman and Riddle (2005) note that there are several important differences between the flavors of inferential statistics used with network data and those that are most commonly taught in basic courses in statistics courses.

Probably the most common emphasis in the application of inferential statistics to social science data is to answer questions about the stability, reproducibility, or generalizability of results observed in a single sample (Hanneman & Riddle, 2005). According to this emphasis, the main question asked is: If a study is repeated on a different sample (drawn by the same method), how likely is it that you would get the same answer about what is going on in the whole population from which both samples have been drawn? This is a really important question because it helps you evaluate the confidence (or lack of it) that you should have in assessing theories and giving advice. This use of inferential statistics represents a majority of the quantitative work done in contemporary educational research.

To the extent the observations used in a network analysis are drawn by probability sampling methods from some identifiable population of actors and/or ties, the same kind of question about the generalizability of sample results applies. Often, however, this type of inferential question is of little interest to social network researchers. In many cases, network analysts are studying a particular network or set of networks and have no interest in generalizing to a larger population of such networks (either because there isn't any such population or because they simply do not care about generalizing to it in any probabilistic way). For example, how attitudes about a new school reform initiative diffuse through one school's faculty and staff doesn't mean the process plays out in the same way at another school. In some other cases, however, there may be an interest in generalizing, but samples are typically not drawn through probability methods. Network analysis often relies on artifacts, direct observation, laboratory experiments, and documents as data sources, and usually there are no plausible ways of identifying populations and drawing samples by probability methods.

The other major use of inferential statistics in educational research is for testing hypotheses. In many cases, the same or closely related tools are used for questions of assessing generalizability and for hypothesis testing. The underlying logic of hypothesis testing is to compare an observed result in a sample to some null hypothesis value relative to the sampling variability of the result under the assumption that the null hypothesis is true. If the sample result differs greatly from what was likely to have been observed under the assumption that the null hypothesis is true, then the null hypothesis can confidently be rejected.

The key link in the inferential chain of hypothesis testing is the estimation of the standard errors of statistics—that is, estimating the expected amount that the value a statistic would "jump around" from one sample to the next simply as a result of accidents of sampling (Hanneman & Riddle, 2005). Rarely, of course, can standard errors be directly observed or calculated because there are no replications. Instead, information from a sample is used to estimate the sampling variability.

Hanneman and Riddle (2005) go on to note that with many common statistical procedures, it is possible to estimate standard errors through validated approximations (e.g., the standard error of a mean is usually estimated by the sample standard deviation divided by the square root of the sample size). These approximations, however, only hold when the observations are drawn through independent random sampling. Network observations are almost always by definition nonindependent (except, of course, ego-level network studies from which egos have been randomly drawn from some target population). Consequently, conventional inferential formulas do not apply to network data (though formulas developed for other types of dependent sampling may apply). It is particularly erroneous to assume that such formulas do apply, because the nonindependence of network observations will often underestimate the true sampling variability and result in having too much confidence in your results.

Permutations Tests for Network Data

The approach of most network analysts interested in statistical inference for testing hypotheses about network properties is to work out the probability distributions for statistics directly. This approach is used because (1) no one has developed approximations for the sampling distributions of most of the descriptive statistics used by network analysts and (2) interest often focuses on the probability of an estimate relative to some theoretical baseline (usually randomness) rather than on the probability that a given network is typical of the population of all networks. So, how does this actually work?

Network analysts make use of a form of nonparametric tests referred to as permutations (there are others, too). This is just a fancy way that mathematicians refer to a reordering of numbers. Prell (2012) offers the following example, which shows the permutations of the numbers 1 through 5:

{1, 2, 3, 4, 5}

{1, 3, 4, 5, 2}

{2, 3, 1, 5, 4}

{3, 2, 5, 1, 4}

{4, 5, 3, 1, 2}

In this example, each permutation that follows the original ordering has the same numbers but in a different order. Of course, there any many more permutations possible (5! = 120 total permutations). Contrasted with mathematicians, statisticians use the term *permutation* to refer to rearrangements of data. The connection to social networks is that the data that are rearranged are matrices. These matrices are rearranged over and over again, providing a distribution against which the observed data can be measured. These permutations—hundreds and even thousands of them—are used for testing levels of significance, or the likelihood of an observed network property occurring by chance.

So, let's say you are interested in the number of collaborative exchanges that occur between teachers from two different grade levels in a complete network of teachers within one elementary school. First, you count the number of times these types of exchanges occur in the observed network and then permute these relational data lots and lots of times. With each permutation, you calculate the number of times this type of tie (collaborative exchanges between teachers from two different grade levels) occurs and compare this result to the original observed network. After this process of permuting and comparing, you can see how often the results of these permutations are the same as the original observed results: The more often the results of the permutations are the same as your observed data, the more likely that the pattern of exchanges in the observed data was due to chance. If, however, the results from the observed data are so unlikely when compared to the results of the permutations, then you are to conclude that your results are not the byproduct of chance. Therefore, this result would be considered statistically significant.

Here is a second example of how this works. Suppose you were interested in the proportion of seventh-grade students in a middle school who were members of cliques (or any other network-derived group structure). Recall that the notion of a clique implies a rigid structure—nonrandom connections among students. Assume you have relational data from all 100 students in the seventh-grade class, in which there are 60 symmetric ties among students (i.e., Student A nominates Student B and vice versa), and it is observed that there are 15 cliques containing at least four students. The inferential question might be posed as: How likely is it, if ties among students were purely random events, that a network composed of 100 students and 60 symmetric ties would display 15 cliques of size four or more? If it turns out that cliques of size four or more in random networks of this size and degree are quite common, you would be very cautious in concluding that you have uncovered a "real structure" or nonrandomness. If it turns out that such cliques (or more numerous or more inclusive ones) are very unlikely under the assumption that ties are purely random, then it is very plausible to reach the conclusion that there is a "true" social structure present.

EXPONENTIAL RANDOM GRAPH MODELS

But how can you determine this probability? The method used is one of simulation. Like most simulation, a lot of computer resources and (maybe) some programming skills are often necessary. In the current case, you might use a table of random numbers to distribute 60 ties among 100 actors and then search the resulting network for cliques of size four or more. If no clique is found, a 0 for the trial is recorded; if a clique is found, a 1 is recoded. The rest is simple. Just repeat the simulation several thousand times and add up what proportion of the "trials" result in "successes." The probability of a success across these simulations is a good estimator of the likelihood that you might find a network of this size and density to have a clique of this size "just by accident" when the nonrandom causal mechanisms that you think cause cliques are not, in fact, operating.

Valente (2010) notes that the big development in the use of simulations in network studies—that is, the probability that a network measure would occur by chance—was the use of exponential random graph models (ERGMs). These models were first developed (Frank & Strauss, 1986; Holland & Leinhardt, 1981) in order to provide a way to determine whether network properties (e.g., reciprocity) occur by chance as a result of other network properties (e.g., density) or whether the observed properties are unlikely given other parameters in the network (Valente, 2010). In addition to providing a probability distribution against which an observed network parameter can be compared, ERGMs have matured in such a way that they also permit actor attributes to be incorporated into model estimation. So, not only did the use of ERGMs allow hypothesis testing, they also evolved in ways that permitted formal statistical tests that included actor-level covariates such as those related to individuals' demographic (e.g., gender) or behavioral (e.g., class attendance) characteristics.

This development may sound odd, and it is certainly a lot of work (most of which, thankfully, is done by social network applications). But, in fact, it is not really that different from the logic of hypothesis testing with nonnetwork data. Social network data tend to differ from more "conventional" actor-by-attribute survey data in some key ways: Network data are often not drawn from probability samples, and the observations of individual actors are not independent. These differences are important for the generalization of findings and for the mechanics of hypothesis testing. There is, however, nothing fundamentally different about the logic of the use of descriptive and inferential statistics with social network data.

The application of statistics to relational data can be quite complicated and is one that is currently at the forefront of social network analysis. Despite these complications, there are several reasons why it is desirable and often necessary to move beyond the mathematical approach and its emphasis on description and toward the statistical approach and its emphases on explanation and inference (Robins, Pattison, Kalish, & Yusher, 2007). For example, statistical models allow you to understand the uncertainty associated with observed outcomes and more accurately reflect the complexity of social processes. In addition, statistical models allow inferences about whether certain network substructures (e.g., groups of teachers within a school) are more commonly observed in the network than might be expected by chance. Hypotheses about the social processes that might produce these structural properties can then be formally tested. Finally, different social processes may make similar qualitative predictions about network structures, and it is only through careful quantitative modeling that the differences in predictions can be evaluated. For example, clustering in networks might emerge from endogenous (self-organizing) structural effects (e.g., structural balance), or through node-level effects (e.g., homophily).

ERGMs are the primary building blocks of statistically testing network structural effects. Increasingly, researchers are not only interested in describing an ego or complete network but rather in whether an observed network property is significant. ERGMs generate (random) networks derived from features of the observed network, which provide a way to compare the observed and simulated networks. Statistical analysis is then conducted to test whether the ties in the simulated network match those generated by the simulations.

Here is how an ERGM generally works. Suppose an empirical network consists of 100 teachers and 1,000 ties among them, for a density value of 10%. We might be interested in examining whether there is a tendency for reciprocity: If Teacher A nominated B, was B more likely to nominate A? To figure out whether there is a tendency toward reciprocal relations, hundreds or perhaps even thousands of networks are generated with the same number of actors and ties as in the empirical network—100 actors and 1,000 ties. The average of the simulated distribution of reciprocal ties is calculated and then compared to the value in the empirical (observed) network. Then, if the reciprocity in the empirical network differs from the average reciprocity in the simulated networks more than it would be expected to by chance, we can conclude that there is indeed a tendency towards reciprocity. One feature that makes newer ERGMs even more powerful is that they are even flexible enough to allow you to elect which structural parameters (reciprocity, density, transitivity, K-star configurations, among others) to include in the simulation, but these choices should be made with great caution.

In addition to ERGMs, many models in the network literature are important tools for simulation, hypothesis generation, and "thought experiments." However, since this text focuses on more basic and commonplace uses of network analysis in educational research, the following chapter provides a brief and succinct introduction to some of these ideas—many of which have a logic similar to that of ERGMs—with an emphasis on how certain research questions can be addressed through statistical inference without getting mired in technical details.

ERGM Example: Friendship Formation in School

To further demonstrate the logic and utility of ERGMs, consider the example provided by Goodreau, Kitts, and Morris (2009), who used this approach to identify the determinants of friendship formation that lead to pervasive regularities in friendship structure among adolescent students. Or, stated more succinctly, why do similar types of students always seem to become friends? Data were drawn from the first wave of National Longitudinal Survey of Adolescent Health (Add Health). The "in-school" questionnaire asked students to identify their five best male and five best female friends in order of closeness. From this, they focus solely on mutual friendships, those dyads in which students nominate each other. Because they are reciprocated, mutual friendships are cross-validated and thus more likely to be stronger than one-way friendship nominations. In addition, the Add Health survey also collected substantial information on students' sociodemographic attributes and behaviors.

Goodreau, Kitts, and Morris used ERGMs to identify the mechanisms that lead to the formation of these within-school friendships. Specifically, they consider students' overall propensity to make friends (sociality), as well as their propensity to make friends based on their own attributes (selective mixing) and based on their friends' choice of friends (triad closure). ERGMs allow them to tease out which of these three mechanisms or combination of mechanisms is most closely associated with friendship formation and how these mechanisms vary across students with different sociodemographic backgrounds. A common model was applied to all 59 schools and estimates, (and their standard errors) were aggregated to determine whether the effects generalize across schools (Snijders & Baeveldt, 2003). This enabled them to examine whether there were any idiosyncratic variations within schools as well as make comparisons across all sampled schools.

A number of interesting results are reported. First, there is evidence that both selective mixing (associating with same-attribute others) and triad closure (a friend's friends are more likely to become friends) operate across a wide range of sociodemographic settings to structure the process of mutual friendship formation. These processes interact, generating a complex set of effects. The attributes of grade and sex always generate both strong assortative mixing and within-category triad closure. The effects of students' race vary: white, black, and Asian students typically exhibit assortative mixing and within-category triad closure, representing structural cohesion within their subpopulations, but other categories are more complicated. Hispanic students (by far the most numerous of remaining categories) can display random (i.e., unbiased) or even disassortative mixing. Even when Hispanics exhibit assortative mixing, it is often coupled with a relative lack of within-category triad closure, reducing their higher-order cohesion.

In addition, they also find that the higher-order processes governing friendship formation can depend on the school's overall demographic profile. For example, the extent of Hispanic cohesion appears to be partly shaped by the homogeneity of the school's non–Hispanic population: the more homogeneous the non–Hispanic population, the more cohesive the Hispanic friendships. Similarly, the strength of assortative mixing for whites is inversely related to their relative share of the student body: The more they are in the minority, the more segregated their friendships become. This relation does not hold for blacks: Assortative mixing is strongest for blacks when they compose an intermediate proportion of the population. Perhaps blacks are less assortative than whites when they are a small minority because this status is familiar to them.

The modeling goal of Goodreau, Kitts, and Morris (2009) was to move beyond network description to uncover the generative processes that underlie network tie formation. Generative processes refer to those micro-level mechanisms that produce a higher-level network structure: interaction between two actors that leads to a bigger pattern among a larger set of actors. The ERGM framework offers a general set of tools to aid in this goal, and the Add Health survey (with 59 replicate schools) has a unique structure for exploiting these new capabilities. By focusing on personal attributes (race, sex, and grade), they were able to identify some of the demographic correlates of friendship formation and rule out the kind of endogenous feedback processes between friendship choices and personal attributes found in other contexts. By estimating all models within the relatively small units of schools, they were able to get closer to ensuring that all pairs of students are equally able to form friendships, so their choices are less confounded by gross heterogeneities in opportunity. In addition, by simultaneously estimating effects at the individual, dyadic, and triadic levels, they were able to disentangle the effects of each level from the others. This modeling strategy moves the field closer to quantitatively comparing the strength of effects within and across the levels on which student friendship preferences operate.

Two notes of caution about these permutation-based tests are warranted (Prell, 2012). Fortunately, these permutation-based tests of statistical significance, such as ERGMs, are available through both general and specialized social-network software packages and programs (reviewed in Chapter 12). But, depending on the size of your network, these tests can be very demanding of your computer's computational capabilities. If the data require many permutations, it might take quite some time for your computer to calculate a test statistic. Second, while many permutation-based tests can be used to derive probability values, they do not work so well for calculating confidence intervals.

SUMMARY

Like most quantitative social science, we are often interested in making an inference about some sample estimate to a larger population. The process through which this is typically done is predicated on two assumptions: first, the sampling distribution—the distribution of estimates from many samples—is normal and; second, observations within and between samples are independent. This nonindependence of observations often underestimates the true sampling variability and results in inflated standard errors that give you too much confidence in your results. Therefore, you would be more likely to commit what is often referred to as Type I error: rejecting a null hypothesis when it is actually true.

To address the inherent way in which network data violate the assumption of independence, network researchers have developed means to test the likelihood of a network property that do not rely on this assumption of normality. The key has been the development of simulation. These simulated networks provide the basis for comparing an observed network property against what would happen by chance. Some of the first network models to make use of simulation were of exponential random graph models (ERGMs). Used only for cross-sectional data, these models can be used to determine whether an observed network is a function of properties based on the algorithms covered in Part II, including density, reciprocity, transitivity, and so on. ERGMs can help determine whether properties occur by chance as a result of other network properties or whether the observed properties are unlikely given other network parameters.

This chapter ended with an example of how ERGMs were used to examine friendship formation in adolescents within schools. In addition to demonstrating the logic of simulation and its application to estimating the likelihood of a friendship tie between two students, this example also showed how individual attributes (e.g., race and grade level) can be incorporated into model estimation. In general, these models provide a basis for statistical inference and hypothesis testing, but, more specifically, they can (1) describe a network in terms of its structural properties; (2) determine if individual attributes are associated with network structural properties; and (3) determine if individual attributes are associated with behaviors and attitudes while controlling both 1 and 2. For example, an ERGM can be used to estimate whether help-seeking behavior between teachers is likely to be reciprocated if that reciprocation is greater than expected by chance and if it is associated with the grade level that one is assigned to teach (same grade-level teachers are more likely to give and receive help). We can include a behavior or attitude in the model to determine if, for example, teachers with high job satisfaction are more likely to seek and receive help, controlling for grade level and reciprocity.

ERGMs are one class of models that have been developed by network analysts to make inferences from network data and are considered the "building blocks" of statistical estimation with network data (Valente, 2010). The next chapter builds on this introduction and surveys a number of other different modeling approaches that have been developed to account for the inherent dependency of relational data. While these approaches are varied and perhaps even complicated, the key is that they are predicated on the idea of comparing an observed network property to a whole bunch of simulated networks. The earliest variations of these simulated networks (e.g., Bernoulli graphs and Markov random graphs) are based on simple rules and may not result in satisfactory simulated network distributions. Recent developments have resulted in programs that generate better and, therefore, more realistic simulated networks that provide a more reasonable basis for comparison. While these developments are exciting, they are beyond the scope of this introduction. Suffice it to say, the critical idea in this chapter is that simulations permit inferences and hypothesis testing using network data that are by definition nonindependent observations. The next chapter introduces several of these different approaches, all of which have evolved from this idea of using simulations to generate the distributions against which observed properties are tested.

CHAPTER FOLLOW-UP

1. Why are these simulations necessary in order to make probabilistic inferences with network data?

2. Explain in plain language how simulations are used to create a probability distribution that enables you to make a statistical inference with network data.

3. Contrast the aims of the mathematical and statistical approaches to social network analysis. For what reasons would educational researchers prefer one approach versus the other?

CRITICAL QUESTIONS TO ASK ABOUT NETWORK STUDIES THAT MAKE STATISTICAL INFERENCES

1. How were the simulated networks, also known as the dependence graphs, generated?

2. Did these simulations properly and adequately account for the nonindependence of the data?

3. How many simulated networks were generated?

4. What hypotheses were being tested?

5. Is the difference between the observed and simulated networks statistically significant? If so, what does this mean?

ESSENTIAL READING

Goldenberg, A., Zheng, A., Fienberg, S., & Airoldi, E. (2009). A survey of statistical network models. *Foundations and Trends in Machine Learning, 2*(2), 129–233.

Goodreau, S. M., Kitts, J. M., & Morris, M. (2009). Birds of a feather, or friend of a friend? Using exponential random graph models to investigate adolescent social networks. *Demography, 46*(1), 103–125.

Scott, J. (2000). *Social network analysis: A handbook* (2nd ed.). Thousand Oaks, CA: Sage Publications.

9

Network Data and
Statistical Models

OBJECTIVES

In this chapter you will learn about the different techniques that make use of simulations when statistically modeling network data. You will understand that these techniques vary according to the types of questions that are asked and whether the focus is on ties between actors in complete networks, individual attributes, or relations within and between groups. These models are important, as they enable you to employ social network analysis in ways that move beyond description toward explanation, an important goal of social science. Without getting into the technical aspects of each modeling strategy, you will begin to appreciate the ways in which statistical models can be used with network data to address questions that more completely reflect the complexity of educational phenomena. In addition, you will be introduced to a number of studies in the field of education that make use of these models.

CONNECTING QUESTIONS TO STATISTICAL MODELS

To address the types of questions asked at the beginning of the previous chapter, we need models that combine network (relational) data and individual attribute data and/or dyadic attributes. The statistical underpinnings of these advanced models were introduced in the previous chapter, and the models presented in this one reflect the most sophisticated and interesting strands of contemporary social network analyses. Following the lead of van Duijn and Huisman (2011), these models are categorized by the questions they are designed to address. Three different analytical emphases are presented: (1) relationship-level models that focus on the ties between actors in complete networks, (2) models that predict individual actors' attributes, and (3) actor-level models that emphasize the differences within and among groups of actors within a complete network.

The first three questions used to introduce the previous chapter can be answered with models that explain and predict the presence or value of a network's ties. To do so, these models require additional information on the network's relationships or actors, if available. The fourth question predicts an individual outcome (trust) from network data. The fifth and final question is answered with models that identify groups of actors who have the same probability distribution of ties to other actors (known as "stochastically" equivalent actors). Many of these models can—and often do—make use of additional covariate information. These different modeling approaches can be thought of as analyses that make use of the same relational data, but with a different emphasis. In the first (models for ties), the focal variable is the observed relationship between any two of the network's actors, which may be explained by attributes. In the third, for example, the focal variable is the actor's group membership expressed as an unobserved, latent variable whose value is the result of the observed ties among actors (i.e., a group assignment derived from one of the algorithms discussed in Chapter 5) and any other actor characteristics.

After briefly introducing the data to be used in this chapter and revisiting the modeling strategy used to analyze egocentric network data, this chapter's next three sections introduce some of the more cutting-edge approaches to the statistical analysis of social network data and show how these models can be used to address the five questions asked at the start of the previous chapter. First, the statistical analysis of ties within complete networks will be discussed, with a focus on how dyadic ties within a complete relational network can be modeled from both structural and attribute variables. Second, the chapter examines how actors' individual attributes (e.g., trust) can be modeled from both attribute (e.g., efficacy) and relational data (e.g., collaboration). Third, the chapter turns to a set of procedures that are used to model ties between and within groups of actors. The chapter ends with a brief review of recent advances in the statistical modeling of two-mode networks (bipartite graphs, which are networks in which the rows and columns consist of different actors) and an introduction to a handful of advanced approaches, including agent-based modeling and actor-oriented models.

DESCRIPTION OF SCHOOL LEADERS EXAMPLE DATA

These ideas and tools will be demonstrated using a portion of the School Leaders data set, particularly observations in years 1 and 3 of the "collaboration" and "confidential help" networks. Collaboration is a directed valued network measured on five-point scale ranging from 0 to 4, with higher values indicating more frequent collaborations (1–2 times/ week). Similarly, the confidential help network is a directed, valued network measured on the same scale. Complete network data are available on all 43 school leaders drawn from two large school districts. In addition to these relational data, the survey instrument in year 1 captured attribute data, including composite scores from a set of items related to efficacy (19 items) and trust (8 items), as well as information about leaders' gender and whether they worked at the district or school level.

These data are summarized in Table 9.1. For most of the analyses that follow, the collaboration and confidential help network data were dichotomized, with values originally coded as a 3 and 4 recoded as 1s, indicating the presence of a directed tie for both relations, zero otherwise. These dichotomized relations are reported in Table 9.1. A few of the analyses that follow rely on the original ordinal scores that range from 0 to 4. Measures are calculated on the complete network (Table 9.1, total column) and on the two subnetworks, defined by whether a leader works at the school or district level.

For the collaboration networks, the mean number of ties sent and received in year 1 is 1.72 and increases to 8.65 in year 3. This pattern is the same whether you work at the school or district level. For example, district-level leaders send and receive 2.00 and 2.06 collaboration ties in year 1, and these numbers increase to 12.72 and 9.78, respectively. Compared to leaders at the school level, district-level leaders send and receive, on average, more collaboration ties; for example, the average number of collaboration ties received (in-degree) by school-level leaders in year 3, nearly 2.00 ties less than district-level leaders. In addition, in year 3, district-level leaders have a higher standard deviation, suggesting that several leaders send or receive either very few or very many collaboration ties.

A similar pattern is evident for the confidential-exchange networks. On average, leaders send and receive less than 1.00 tie in year 1. Two years after the reform initiative, however, these same leaders send and receive, on average, 3.58 ties. While the average numbers of confidential ties sent and received by school- and district-level leaders are similar in year 1, district-level leaders send and receive about 2.00 more confidential ties than school-level leaders in year 3. This suggests that the reform initiative is related to the frequency with which leaders exchange confidential information and that this relation is especially salient for those working at the district level.

The bottom rows of Table 9.1 report on three attributes collected on 43 leaders in year 1. The trust scores are a composite derived from a set of eight items originally scored on a seven-point Likert scale modified from Tschannen-Moran and Hoy's (2003) instrument. Higher scores reflect high levels of trust in the leaders' schools and districts. School- and district-level leaders report similar levels of trust (4.90 versus 4.60), with school-level leaders having slightly more variation as evidenced by a higher standard deviation. The efficacy scores, derived from a set of 18 items from Tschannen-Moran and Gareis' Principal Efficacy Scale (2004), show that school-level leaders, on average, have scores that are about one standard unit higher than district-level leaders. Finally, 48% of the 25 school-level leaders are male compared to 39% of the 18 district-level leaders.

Table 9.1 Summary Statistics of the School Leaders' Collaboration and Confidential Exchanges Networks (Years 1 and 3) and Attribute Data.

	School-level M (SD)	District-level M (SD)	Total M (SD)
Collaboration year 1			
Out-degree	1.52 (0.94)	2.00 (0.94)	1.72 (0.98)
In-degree	1.48 (1.09)	2.06 (1.73)	1.72 (1.40)
Collaboration year 3			
Out-degree	5.72 (5.93)	12.72 (11.84)	8.65 (9.44)
In-degree	7.84 (1.63)	9.78 (4.21)	8.65 (3.10)
Confidential exchanges year 1			
Out-degree	0.60 (0.71)	0.56 (0.78)	0.58 (.073)
In-degree	0.44 (0.58)	0.78 (1.17)	0.58 (0.88)
Confidential exchanges year 3			
Out-degree	2.72 (3.08)	4.61 (5.59)	3.51 (4.35)
In-degree	2.64 (1.68)	4.72 (2.16)	3.51 (2.14)
Trust	4.90 (0.72)	4.60 (0.67)	4.77 (0.71)
Efficacy	7.01 (0.96)	6.12 (1.11)	6.64 (1.11)
Male	.48	.39	.44
N	25	18	43

Note: SD not reported for the male indicator variable.

The directed and dichotomous collaboration network in year 3 is shown in Figure 9.1. Each directed line represents a collaboration tie. At the center of the graph are four male district-level leaders that send and receive a large number of ties. Given that males constitute 44% of the sample, this "central" location is noteworthy. To confirm what this graph is showing, you could easily calculate one of the centrality measures presented in Chapter 5. The right side of the graph consists mainly of school-level leaders (colored nodes) that primarily, but not exclusively, collaborate among themselves, while the left

Figure 9.1   Directed and Dichotomized Graph of the School Leaders Collaboration Network Year 3. Square nodes are males and clear nodes are district-level leaders. The right side of the graph consists mainly of school-level leaders (colored nodes) that primarily, but not exclusively, collaborate among themselves, while the left side of the graph shows a similar pattern among district-level leaders.

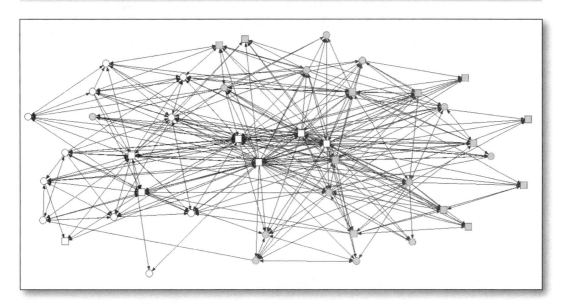

side of the graph shows a similar pattern among district-level leaders. Not one of the leaders is isolated, indicating that the entire graph constitutes one weak component. This is a different picture from the same network in year 1, where there were three isolates (not presented). Using the information presented in Table 9.1 and shown in Figure 9.1, we can ask a number of questions that consider, for example, whether a certain configuration is expected and "normal," how one relation is associated with another among this same set of actors, or whether one network structure could be thought of as "better" than another. The rest of this chapter is dedicated to showing how a statistical approach can be used to address the issues.

STATISTICAL MODELS USING EGOCENTRIC NETWORK DATA

Before turning to these issues, it is worth reiterating a couple important points when using egocentric network data to make a statistical inference. First, recall that egocentric network data can be collected as part of a complete network study (as is often the case) or (ideally) drawn from a random sample of egos from some larger target population. Regardless of how they are sampled and collected, egocentric network data reflect a focal ego actor's (usually the respondent's) network from the perspective of ego. When drawn from samples, egocentric network data have to be transformed prior to analysis. The key is to transform egocentric network data into a dyadic format, in which each observation (case) in the data file consists of ego and one network alter, as was described in the previous chapter. Therefore, there will be one row in the data file for each one of ego's named alters. This transformation is done solely to facilitate statistical analysis.

Second, once the data are converted into this dyadic format, you can create various network measures that capture, for example, the size and diversity in one's ego network. However, the statistical analysis of these data requires that you control for the non-independence of the observations. Having the data in this dyadic format facilitates this. One of the foundational assumptions of statistical analysis is that observations are independent. By definition, network data violate this assumption, with each ego nested in one or more dyads. Another level of clustering could be introduced if the design is longitudinal. Addressing these issues is simple enough if researchers employ hierarchical linear models or random effects models that adjust for the nonindependence of the data. However, such multilevel models (discussed at the end of this chapter) can become quite complex, and you should not employ these models without being familiar with multilevel regression techniques in general.

MODELING TIES IN COMPLETE NETWORKS

An interesting question for the School Leaders data presented in Table 9.1 concerns whether collaboration among the school leaders increased or decreased from years 1 to 3, after taking into account each leader's overall trust in their administrative colleagues and whether they worked at the school or district level. Such a question implies modeling one complete network (collaboration at year 3) as well as attributes of each leader (trust and district/school level). There are several types of statistical models for modeling these complete network data with two distinctions among them: (1) the measurement level of the relational variable (binary or valued) and (2) and the statistical modeling tradition used to make the inference.

This section reviews a few methods used to address questions such as the one above. The first is QAP (quadratic assignment procedure), which is based on regression models and permutation tests for valued (i.e., continuous) relational variables (see Dekker, Krackhardt, & Snijders, 2007 for a review of its development). Second is a set of related models (p_1 and p^*) that predict dichotomous (nonvalued) dyadic relations among actors in a directed graph. These models focus on the ties between each possible dyad within a network, predicting its four possible outcomes (null, mutual, and two asymmetric states). In addition to these there are several other procedures that can be used to model ties in complete networks (see van Duijn & Huisman, 2011 for a review).

QAP/MR-QAP

When examining the relationship between two (or more) complete networks, you have to consider the dependence inherent in the data due to the fact that actors send and receive multiple ties. This results in the observed outcomes of the relational variable being nonindependent. You could use standard ordinary least square regression/correlation models to estimate the relationship between networks, with an implicit (and incorrect) assumption that there is independence within and between each of the network's dyads. As noted earlier, this would result in coefficients with grossly underestimated standard errors (and, consequently, artificially high test statistics). The quadratic assignment procedure developed by Hubert (1987) and Krackhardt (1987b) tests the null hypothesis of no correlation between the two networks and adjusts for this dependence between networks by repeatedly permuting the order of rows and columns of one of the networks while keeping the other network intact. The resulting sample of product–moment correlations provides the distribution of the correlation coefficient under the null hypothesis to which the actual observed correlation can be compared. This is similar to the idea discussed above of using repeated simulations—thousands of them—to determine probability. This procedure can be extended to examine the relationship between two networks, X and Y, while controlling for a third, Z. However, this becomes more complex because of the dependency of the two networks, X and Z, which is similar to the idea of multicollinearity in multiple regression. These procedures are referred to as MR-QAP (reviewed in Dekker, Krackhardt, & Snijders, 2007).

How can this procedure be applied to the School Leaders data? It is useful, for example, in determining whether there is a relationship between collaboration among school leaders in year 1 and how often they engage in confidential exchanges in year 3. Or you could examine the relationship between how frequently school leaders turn to each other to discuss issues of a confidential nature in year 1 and collaboration in year 3. The results of the QAP correlations between these four social networks with ordinal variables (recall that the ties between leaders originally range from 0–4) are presented in Table 9.2. These coefficients can be interpreted like your standard Pearson's product–moment correlations, with absolute values closer to 1 indicating stronger relations.

This correlation matrix reveals a few interesting relationships, two of which are relevant given the above questions. For example, the correlations are highest for the collaboration and confidential-exchange networks in year 1 ($r = 0.56, p < .001$) and collaboration and confidential-exchange networks in year 3 ($r = 0.66, p < .001$). Both of these relationships are somewhat predictable. Those who engage in one type of favorable exchange are also likely to engage in another at a similar point in time. On the other hand, what is interesting is that having one type of tie in year 1 is only weakly related to the same tie in year 3. For example, the correlation between collaboration networks in

Table 9.2 QAP Correlations for the School Leaders Network Data. Based on 5,000 permutations. The QAP correlations are highest for the collaboration and confidential exchange networks in year 1 ($r = .56$, $p < .001$) and collaboration and confidential exchange networks in year 3 ($r = .66$, $p < .001$).

	1	2	3	4
1. Collaboration year 1	–	.14*	.56*	.19*
2. Collaboration year 3		–	.12*	.66*
3. Confidential exchanges year 1			–	.18*
4. Confidential exchanges year 3				–

* = $p < .001$

years 1 and 3 is 0.14, ($p < .001$). This type of analysis, while interesting in and of itself, is most useful when it informs multivariate models that include covariates that are not too strongly correlated.

Therefore, this analysis can be extended in order to predict collaboration in year 3 from the collaboration and confidential-exchange networks in year 1 networks. The question, therefore, is whether school leaders prefer to collaborate with those with whom they have collaborated in the past or with those that they have turned to discuss confidential issues. This is analogous to having two independent variables, with the obvious catch that these predictor variables are complete networks. Therefore, this would require a MR-QAP procedure that controls for the effect of the model's second predictor.

In Table 9.3, the results of an MR-QAP analysis are presented with the collaboration network in year 3 as the outcome variable. Model 1 starts with collaboration in year 1 as the sole predictor, and then Model 2 incorporates confidential exchanges year 1 as an additional predictor. Model 2, therefore, shows which of the two predictors has the stronger relationship with the collaboration network in year 3. When confidential exchanges in year 1 are added to the model, the relationship between collaboration in years 1 and 3 is reduced and no longer significant. The relationship of confidential exchanges in year 1 to the outcome is strong, as is demonstrated by the large increase in adjusted-R^2, the proportion of variance explained by the model. Therefore, while collaboration in year 1 does not significantly predict collaboration in year 3, confidential exchanges in year 1 does. From these results, you can intuit that collaboration among school leaders provides an important foundation for more sensitive, perhaps even deeper, relations (e.g., confidential exchanges) at a later point in time.

Table 9.3   MR-QAP Analyses Predicting School Leaders' Collaboration Network Year 3. Based on 2,000 permutations.

	Model 1	Model 2
Intercept	1.40	.90
Collaboration year 1	.24* (.71)	.02 (.41)
Confidential exchanges year 1		.77* (.57)
R^2 adjusted	.20	.43

* $p < .05$. Standard errors in parentheses.

P_1 and P^* (P-Star)

The next two procedures also model ties in complete networks but do so in a manner that explains the presence (or absence) of dyadic ties as a function of individual- and/or network-level characteristics. So, while QAP and MR-QAP procedures control for network structure through permutations, these next two models attempt to explain it. For example, these models can address questions such as whether gender or some other individual attribute predicts confidential exchanges between school leaders, or does some previous relation have a stronger effect? Both procedures focus on the four different possible outcomes of a dyad in a directed and binary network (therefore, the relational data are nonvalued, 1s or 0s). In this respect, these models are closely related to logistic regression in that they analyze a dichotomous dependent variable (1/0) that is assumed to follow a binomial distribution. While both seek to predict the dyadic relations among actor pairs, the p^* model is able to do so while using relational attributes of each actor and of the network as a whole.

The key difference between them rests with the assumptions of the dependence graphs that are used in the simulations. The dependence graph is the simulated network that is used as the basis for comparison and specifically indicates the nonindependence that exists between a network's actors (Valente, 2010). Technical discussions of this distinction are available in Wasserman and Robins (2005) and Wasserman and Faust (1994). Briefly, the structure of the p_1 dependence graph assumes that all dyads are statistically independent (Holland & Leinhardt, 1981), whereas the p^* model operates from a more realistic assumption that dyads are conditionally dependent. It is for this latter reason that p^* models are preferred. In addition, the p^* model can also include additional global features of the graph such as tendencies toward transitivity and the variance across actors in the propensity to send and receive ties. Both models are some of the first to make use of the ERGM (Chapter 8), which provides the basis for comparing whether a network's observed structural properties occur more frequently than you could expect from chance alone.

While the technical aspects of estimating the p_1 and p^* models are complicated, the interpretation of its individual estimates is fairly straightforward. The basic idea of the p_1 model is to understand relations between pairs of actors as functions of an individual's relational attributes (actor's tendencies to send ties and to receive them) as well as key features of the graph (complete network) in which the two actors are embedded (e.g., the overall density and overall tendency toward reciprocity; Hanneman & Riddle, 2005). Similarly, the basic idea of the p^* is to understand these same relations but to include actor-level and network-level attributes in the model (Pattison & Wasserman, 1999).

How might these models be used make inferences about the social processes at work in the School Leaders data? Using directed and dichotomized relational data, a p_1 model can be used, for example, to test whether school leaders tend to reciprocate relationship choices. In other words, if one school leader turns to another to discuss something confidential, is the latter likely to reciprocate? P^* models are often employed to take this further by including actor- and network-level covariates. In the School Leaders data, these would include an actor attribute variable such as male and a network-level attribute such as transitivity. Therefore, the latter, p^*, can test whether a leader's gender, efficacy score, and other complete graph properties predict a confidential exchange between two leaders. Table 9.4 presents the results of both models, derived from UCINET and PNet, respectively (both applications are reviewed in Chapter 12). The book's companion website also provides a step-by-step guide that helps you perform your own analysis using the p^* model.

The results of these models suggest several interesting social processes that may explain confidential exchanges between school leaders in year 3. The analysis of the School Leaders data with the p_1 (Model 1, Table 9.4) results in a negative estimate for density, implying that the probability of a confidential exchange tie in year 3 is much smaller than 0.50. The reciprocity parameter, on the other hand, is 4.11, slightly larger in absolute value than the density parameter. When the reciprocity value is positive and large, as is the case here, this indicates a strong tendency for mutual ties (Wasserman & Faust, 1994). If this parameter estimate were negative, it would indicate that there are many nonreciprocated confidential exchanges in year 3.

Models 2 and 3 (Table 9.4) go further by including two covariates, one binary measure for male (1 = yes, 0 = no) and one continuous efficacy measure. Parameter and standard errors are provided. Those estimates that are noted as significant are those that are approximately twice its standard error in absolute value. The two significant estimates in both models are structural parameters; that is, they are directly calculated from the network itself. For example, in Model 2, it is evident that there is

Table 9.4   Results of P_1 and P^* Analyses for the Dichotomized and Directed School Leaders Confidential Exchanges Network Year 3.

	P_1	P^*	
	Model 1	Model 2	Model 3
Density	−3.68		
Reciprocity	4.11	3.02*	2.95*
		(0.30)	(0.33)
Arc		−3.27*	−2.72*
		(0.17)	(0.51)
Transitivity		0.13	0.10
		(0.12)	(0.11)
Sender male		−0.01	0.09
		(0.22)	(0.19)
Receiver male		−0.07	0.03
		(0.21)	(0.20)
Sender efficacy			−0.22*
			(0.05)
Receiver efficacy			0.13*
			(0.07)

Notes: Standard errors are in parentheses. A * indicates that an estimate is more than twice the standard error in absolute value.

a strong tendency for confidential-exchange ties to be reciprocated indicating an absence of hierarchy among the school leaders. That same model shows that there is little tendency toward transitivity, which is unsurprising given that a confidential exchange is likely to occur between two people, not among three. Model 2 also shows that being a male is not significantly related to either sending or receiving a tie. Model 3 adds a second attribute, efficacy, which is significantly related to sending or receiving a tie. This suggests that school leaders who believe that they have the capacity to have an effect are more likely to send and receive confidential exchange ties. This last finding speaks to a larger point regarding the importance of efficacy, in general.

The development of both the p_1 and p^* models, especially the latter, reflects an important shift in the analysis of social networks. These were some of the first models to move from the representation and description of social networks toward a statistical approach that emphasized the explanation of relational ties between actors. P^* models explicitly model the influence of relational ties on network and individual characteristics, and because of this, they present an array of opportunities for educational researchers to analyze numerous issues. However, this potential has yet to be fully appreciated, as there are few examples of these models being used in educational research. This is likely due to the absence of didactic texts with substantive illustrations (Knoke & Yang, 2008), which fall outside the scope of this cursory introduction. One of the first and still most accessible primers on p^* models is provided by Anderson, Wasserman, and Crouch (1999), in which they employ this model to predict friendship choices within one fourth-grade classroom and then extend the analysis across a set of three classes and incorporate a covariate for students' gender. While showing a strong tendency for dyads to exhibit mutuality, they also clearly outline the strengths and potentials of this still-underutilized modeling approach. Two other and equally accessible primers are provided by Robins (2011), who demonstrates these models in a step-by-step manner using a new application, PNet, designed explicitly for p^* models, and Prell (2012, Chapter 10), who discusses various aspects of these models, including their probability distributions, the role of network configurations, and parameter estimation.

MODELING ACTORS' ATTRIBUTES

The previous section described models and methods for testing the likelihood of a relation between any two actors in a given network using both local (micro) and global (macro) network properties. This section shifts the analytical lens to predict an individual actor's outcome, whether it is an attribute variable (e.g., a student's test score) or a structural variable (e.g., a teacher's betweenness centrality score), using relational data. For example: does a teacher's gender predict his or her influence (as measured by degree centrality)? This question relates an attribute (gender) to a measure of the actor's location in a network (degree centrality). We might be interested in the relationship between two (or more) aspects of actors' locations. For example: How much of the variation in teachers' degree centrality can be explained by their network's size and the number of cliques that they belong to? We might even be interested in the relationship between two individual attributes among a set of actors who are connected in a network. For example, in a school classroom, is there an association between students' engagement and their academic achievement?

Each of these questions focuses on variables that describe individual actors. These variables may be either nonrelational attributes (e.g., efficacy or gender) or variables that describe some aspect of an individual's relational position or affiliation (e.g., betweenness or clique membership). In most cases, standard statistical tools for the analysis of variables can be applied to describe differences and associations. But, as noted by

Hanneman and Riddle (2005), standard statistical tools for the analysis of these variables cannot be applied to inferential questions—hypothesis or significance tests—because the actors are not independent observations randomly drawn from some large population. Instead of applying the normal formulas (i.e., those built into statistical software packages and discussed in most introductory statistics texts), we need to use other methods to get more correct estimates of the reliability and stability of estimates (i.e., standard errors). The "boot-strapping" approach (estimating the variation of estimates of the parameter of interest from large numbers of random subsamples of actors) can be applied in some cases; in other cases, the idea of random permutation can be applied to generate correct standard errors. Fortunately, these approaches to calculating standard errors are incorporated into specialized programs that analyze social networks. There are three common techniques that are typically part of these programs and can be used to model individual actor attributes that are nonindependent (as is the case with social network data).

T-tests

Suppose we thought that school leaders who worked at the district level were less likely to collaborate with colleagues than those leaders who worked at the school level (year 1). This hypothesis can be tested by comparing the average out-degree (number of dichotomized collaboration ties sent) of district- and school-level leaders. Since each individual leader is an observation, the data are located in a column (or, sometimes, a row) of one or more files: one column indicates whether the leader works at the district or school level and the other column indicates each leader's ego network size (as measured by out-degree). For this test, 10,000 trials (this researcher can choose the number of trials) are used to create the permutation-based sampling distribution of the difference between the two means (comparing the mean out-degree between district- and school-level leaders). For each of these trials, the scores on network size are randomly permuted (that is, randomly assigned to district- or school-level leaders, proportional to the number of each type.) The standard deviation of this distribution based on random trials becomes the estimated standard error for our test. Figure 9.2 shows the results generated by UCINET.

The output in Figure 9.2 first reports basic descriptive statistics for each group. The group numbers are assigned according to the order of the cases in the file containing the independent variable. In this example, the first actor was a district-level leader, so that became Group 1 and school-level leaders became Group 2. From this output, you can see that the average number of collaboration ties by sent by district-level leaders ($M = 2.00$, $SD = 0.94$) is only 0.48 units higher than the average number of collaboration ties sent by school-level leaders ($M = 1.52$, $SD = 0.94$). This would seem to support the hypothesis that district-level leaders are more likely to send collaboration ties than school-level leaders. But tests of statistical significance suggest that this conclusion is unwarranted.

Figure 9.2 UCINET Output of *T*-test Between School- and District-Level Leaders and the Number of Collaboration Ties (Out-Degree) Year 1. From this output, you can see that the average number of collaboration ties by sent by district-level leaders ($M = 2.00$, $SD = 0.94$) is only 0.48 units higher than the average number of collaboration ties sent by school-level leaders ($M = 1.52$, $SD = 0.94$). This difference in means is not statistically significant.

```
TOOLS>STATISTICS>T-TEST
------------------------------------------------------------------

Dependent variable: col 6
Independent variable: col 4
# of permutations: 10000
Random seed: 481




Basic statistics on each group.

                         1       2
                     Group   Group
                     ------  ------
     1       Mean    2.000   1.520
     2    Std Dev    0.943   0.943
     3        Sum   36.000  38.000
     4   Variance    0.889   0.890
     5        SSQ   88.000  80.000
     6      MCSSQ   16.000  22.240
     7   Euc Norm    9.381   8.944
     8    Minimum    0.000   0.000
     9    Maximum    3.000   3.000
    10   N of Obs   18.000  25.000
    11  N Missing   25.000  18.000




SIGNIFICANCE TESTS


      Difference       ...One-Tailed Tests...    Two-Tailed
      in Means      Group 1 > 2    Group 2 > 1      Test
  =============== =============== =============== ===============
        0.480           0.078           0.959          0.1199
```

Differences as large as 0.48 in favor of district-level leaders happen about 8% of the time in random trials. So you would be taking an unacceptable risk of being wrong if you concluded that the data were consistent with the research hypothesis. Therefore, the null hypothesis cannot be rejected.

ANOVA

A similar procedure can be employed to test hypotheses about the means of three or more groups with one-way analysis of variance (ANOVA). Suppose we divided the school leaders into three groups based on each leader's composite trust score: low, medium, and high. Those assigned to the low category have trust scores equal to one standard deviation below the mean, and those in the high category have scores that equal one standard deviation above the mean. Membership in one of these three categories is a column vector, with each leader coded as a 1, 2, or 3 (low, medium, and high). Using the same column vector that reports the number of the school leader's collaboration ties sent, we can ask the following: Do a leader's collaboration ties vary by their level of trust? Figure 9.3 shows the results of a one-way analysis of variance using these two column vectors.

Figure 9.3   UCINET Output of ANOVA Between the School Leaders' Level of Trust (Three Groups) and the Number of Collaboration Ties (Out-Degree) Year 1. The overall differences among these means is not significant ($F_{(2, 40)} = 0.94$ and $p = .42$).

```
TOOLS>STATISTICS>ANOVA
------------------------------------------------------------------------

Dependent variable: Col 6
Independent variable: Col 5
# of permutations: 5000
Random seed: 21934


          ANALYSIS OF VARIANCE

          Source              DF              SSQ      F-Statistic    Significance
    =============== =============== =============== =============== ==============
        Treatment             2             1.83          0.9423           0.4179
            Error            40            38.82
            Total            42            40.65

R-Square/Eta-Square: 0.045
```

The differences among these means are not significant ($F_{(2, 40)} = 0.94$ and $p = .42$). In addition, the output also shows that the differences among group means accounts for only about 5% of the total variance in collaboration ties sent in year 1 among the leaders. Therefore, we cannot reject that null hypothesis that the number of collaboration ties sent in year 1 does not vary by the level of leaders' trust.

REGRESSION

Where the attributes of actors that we are interested in explaining or predicting are measured at the interval level and one or more of our predictors are also at the interval level, multiple linear regression is a common approach. This approach computes basic linear multiple regression statistics by ordinary least squares (OLS) and estimates standard errors and significance using the random permutations method for constructing sampling distributions of R-squared and slope coefficients. Using this method, we can ask the following question: How well does a leader's perceived level of trust in his or her colleagues predict the number of alters to whom the person sent a collaboration tie in year 1, controlling for gender and the level at which the person works (district vs. school)? This question requires three vectors of independent variables (trust score, an indicator for gender, and an indicator for level) and one dependent variable vector (collaboration year 1 out-degree).

The results of this regression are shown in Figure 9.4. The top portion of the output shows the model R^2, 0.09, indicating that slightly less than 10% of the variance in the number of collaboration ties sent in year 1 is explained by these three covariates; that is, how much change in the outcome is explained by this set of covariates. In addition, based on permutation tests, this model's R^2 is nonsignificant ($p = 0.27$, one-tailed). Turning to the model's covariates, trust has a positive but nonsignificant relationship to the outcome ($b = 0.17$, $p = 0.22$), as does the indicator for male ($b = 0.26$, $p = 0.20$). The indicator for whether one works at the school level is negative and also nonsignificant ($b = -0.55$, $p = 0.96$). Therefore, controlling for gender and the level at which they work, a leader's level of trust in colleagues does not significantly predict the number of alters to whom that leader sent a collaboration tie in year 1. The interpretation of this multiple regression is the same as if you were running a multiple regression with non-network data. The coefficients are generated by standard ordinary least squares linear modeling techniques and are based on comparing scores on independent and dependent attributes of individual actors. What differs here is the recognition that the actors, in this case school leaders, are not independent, so that estimation of standard errors by simulation rather than by standard formula is necessary (Hanneman & Riddle, 2005), a point emphasized in Chapter 8.

The t-test, ANOVA, and regression approaches discussed in this section are all calculated at the micro or individual-actor level. Variables that are analyzed as independent

Figure 9.4   UCINET Output of Regression Analysis Predicting the Number of Collaboration Ties (Out-Degree) Year 1. These results show that controlling for gender and the level at which a leader work (district-level is the intercept), a leader's level of trust in his or her colleagues does not significantly predict the number of alters to whom the leader sent a collaboration tie in year 1.

```
REGRESSION
--------------------------------------------------------------------------

Dependent variable: (column 6)
Independent variables: (columns 2 3 4)
# of permutations: 1000
Random seed: 982


NOTE: All probabilities based on randomization tests.


MODEL FIT

        Adjusted                   One-Tailed
R-square R-square     F Value     Probability
---------------       -------     -----------

  0.092    0.002       1.323          0.271


REGRESSION COEFFICIENTS

               Un-st'dized   St'dized   Proportion  Proportion  Proportion
  Independent   Coefficient  Coefficient As Large    As Small    As Extreme
  -----------  -----------   ----------- ----------- ----------- -----------
    Intercept     1.095301    0.000000      1.000       0.000       1.000
        TRUST     0.173922    0.126004      0.221       0.779       0.446
         MALE     0.263656    0.134663      0.196       0.804       0.376
       SCHOOL    -0.554212   -0.281197      0.959       0.041       0.085
```

and dependent may be either relational or nonrelational. That is, we could be interested in predicting and testing hypotheses about actors' nonrelational attributes (e.g., trust) using a mix of relational (e.g., ego network size) and nonrelational (e.g., gender) attributes. We could also be interested in predicting a relational attribute of actors (e.g., centrality) using a mix of relational and nonrelational independent variables.

The examples using the School Leaders data illustrate how relational and nonrelational attributes of actors can be analyzed using common statistical techniques. The key thing to remember, though, is that the observations are not independent (since all the actors are members of the same network). Because of this, direct estimation of the sampling distributions and resulting inferential statistics is needed—standard, basic statistical software (e.g., SPSS, Stata, or SAS) will not give correct estimates.

MODELING GROUPS OF ACTORS

The final set of models and methods can be used to test whether groups of actors cluster together in ways that are consistent with one's expectations or can be understood given some other observed information. For example, to answer whether you can distinguish different groups of school leaders based on how often they collaborate, and if so, whether these groupings are related to the level at which they work (school versus district) requires you to evaluate whether the groupings are stochastically equivalent (i.e., they have the same probability distribution of ties to other actors in their grouping). The focus of these methods and models, therefore, is on groups of actors. Whereas the previous two sections focused on predicting dyadic ties between a network's actors or individual outcomes in complete networks, here the emphasis shifts to groups of actors and whether the actors in these groups share one or more attributes in common. Therefore, these models can be used to test hypotheses about the relations between and/or within groups of actors.

Among the several different ways in which groups of actors are modeled in a probabilistic manner, three are especially noteworthy and are labeled by the software in which they are implemented (van Duijn & Huisman, 2011). First among these is KliqueFinder (Frank, 1995, 1996, 2009), which focuses on identifying groups of actors within a network that have a higher probability of interacting with each other than with members of other groups. KliqueFinder identifies groups based on a simple idea: cohesion. Actors identified as members of the same group should have a higher probability to interact with each other than with actors from other groups. It is based on a model that is very similar to a p_1 but goes further by incorporating a categorical actor covariate (group) in the form of a similarity index. No information other than the observed network is necessary, and the algorithm makes no distinction between the directions of ties.

Kliquefinder works in the following manner. Using iterative partitioning, actors are preassigned to a group, specifically a clique of three actors, and this assignment iteratively changes until the objective function does not improve. The objective function is defined to maximize the likelihood of within-group ties. You can also decide to preassign actors to different groups. Kliquefinder generates a graphical representation of the groups and the actors within them. This representation is obtained by using multidimensional scaling (MDS) on distances between actors and groups defined by the density of ties between them. KliqueFinder has been used widely used in educational research to identify groups of students, including by McFarland (2001), Crosnoe, Riegle-Crumb, Frank, Field, and Muller (2008), and Plank (2000). A useful and appropriate application of the KliqueFinder algorithm to the School Leaders data would allow you to ask whether groups of school leaders can be distinguished based on how frequently they collaborate and if these groups are related to whether one works at the school or district level, or some other nonrelational dimension.

A second model, ULTRAS, uses a different process to address questions of a similar nature (Schweinberger & Snijders, 2003). Like KliqueFinder, ULTRAS finds groupings of actors that have a higher density, but these groupings are nested, with higher-density groups nested in groups with lower density. These nested groupings are represented in a visual that resembles a geographic map with contour lines. The lines, of course, demarcate different groupings. The ULTRAS model can handle valued (continuous) or nonvalued (dichotomous) tie variables, but the data matrix must be symmetric.

ULTRAS is a model based on two assumptions. First, the observed network is generated by hierarchically nested latent transitive structures, expressed by ultrametrics. Second, the expected tie strength decreases with ultrametric distance. The distance between actors is measured by an ultrametric (latent) space defined for each pair relative to their distance to third actors, which implies a transitive structure. Ultrametric structures can be regarded as a mathematical expression of Mazur's proposition (1971, p. 308) that "friends are likely to agree and unlikely to disagree; close friends are very likely to agree and very unlikely to disagree." A larger distance between actors translates into a lower probability of a tie. Like KliqueFinder, the computation behind this process is very complex; fortunately, the ULTRAS software that makes use of this model does all of the computation. Schweinberger and Snijders (2003) demonstrate how this algorithm works and the image it generates by performing a secondary analysis of the data gathered by Bernard, Killworth, and Sailer (1980), who studied the interactions among 58 students living in a fraternity at a West Virginia college for at least 3 months.

A third model, Latentnet, is the most flexible in that it can include actor and dyadic covariates when trying to find the optimal number of positions within a network. It can also handle directed data, a drawback of the previous two models. Using the School Leaders data, this model can be used to assess, for example, whether the level at which a school leader works (school versus district) influences the groups within which the leader most frequently collaborates. The covariate indicating level at which one works can be used either to help generate the clusters or after the fact to assess the clustering.

A didactic example of this model's application is provided by Handcock, Raftery, and Tantrum (2007), who demonstrate its utility on friendship data from 69 students in one school (Grades 7–12). Using these data, which were extracted from the National Longitudinal Study of Adolescent Health (Harris et al., 2009), Handcock, Raftery, and Tantrum apply the Latentnet model to demonstrate a strong tendency for students to form ties with others in their own grade, as the clusters line up well but not perfectly with the grades. In addition, they also reveal a subtle tendency for the within-grade cohesion to weaken as students move up from one grade to another in the school, from the tightly linked seventh graders to the more loosely tied students in the top three grades who associate more easily with students in grades other than their own. Like the other two models just presented, it also estimates the cluster to which each actor belongs. These estimates are probabilistic and estimate the likelihood of each student belonging to each cluster. Finally, Latentnet is an *R* package, which is an extensive suite of open-sourced statistical software.

KliqueFinder, ULTRAS, and Latentnet are just three of the ways in which groups of actors are modeled. This section focused on a few basic ways in which groups of actors can be identified and compared against a simulated distribution, which enables you to assess the likelihood (the "fit") of an observed group structure. Because these three models define differently what it means to be stochastically equivalent (actors that have the same probability distribution of ties to the other actors), they will more than likely return varied solutions. Therefore, you must choose a model that best matches what you think constitutes group membership given the empirical data with which you are working. A more thorough treatment of these different models and the choices you must make as an analyst can be found in Wasserman and Faust (1994) and Scott (2000).

The next two sections on (1) models for two-mode networks and (2) other advanced models provide a brief and nontechnical introduction to several areas in which the statistical approach to social network analysis has made rapid advances in ways that will surely influence network studies in and around education. Given the complexity of these topics, the aim of this introduction is to communicate the importance of these advances in relation to the type of research questions they can address.

MODELING TWO-MODE NETWORKS

Chapter 3 introduced a special kind of matrix, one in which the rows and columns represented different entities. These networks are referred to as having two modes and typically reflect the relationship between actors and events, that is, whether there is a relationship between two actors that share the same affiliation or whether there is a relationship between two events because they share the same actors. For example, two students are affiliated because they are in the same class, or two classes are affiliated because they share similar students. Whether the analytical focus is ultimately on actors or events, these types of data are first organized in a matrix in which the rows (typically) represent actors and the columns represent events.

The most common way to analyze these data is to convert them so the two-mode data are collapsed into a single-mode adjacency matrix. This means that if Student A and Student B are in the same math class, then Student A and B are adjacent (where students [actors] are one mode and math classes [events] are another mode). This is what is typically done with most affiliation networks (e.g., see Carolan, 2008a), a transformation that is easily done through general social network software applications. But recent advances have sought to preserve the duality of actors and events and directly analyze the two-mode network (in graph theoretic terms, these are referred to as "bipartite graphs") without converting it to a single-mode adjacency matrix. The key to understanding the concept of duality is that links between units of the same mode (either actors or events) must pass through units in the other mode (Breiger, 1974). The consequence of this duality is that important structural features of the relations between the elements of one mode can only be completely understood if you simultaneously consider the way in which these same elements form relations among the elements of the other mode (Field, Frank, Schiller, Riegle-Crumb, & Muller, 2006). For example, the relationships between courses (events) that students (actors) take can only be fully understood in terms of the specific students that take those courses. Therefore, when collapsing an affiliation network into an adjacency matrix, you "lose" information that is essential to understanding how people intersect with various social collectivities.

A number of techniques have been developed that retain this duality and do not require the data to be converted into a single-mode graph prior to analysis. These techniques, however, are not "statistical" in the sense that they generally do not make use of simulations for the purposes of hypothesis testing and inferences. Rather, they reflect advances in mathematical approach that take into account that the observed network is not just two mode (bipartite) by happenstance but is so by design (Borgatti & Halgin, 2011). In practice, this requires that measures designed for adjacency matrices be adjusted by applying a *post hoc* normalization. This is the strategy used when applying typical centrality measures to affiliation data (e.g., degree, closeness, betweenness, and eigenvector).

In other cases, however, a totally different approach must be constructed. For example, when trying to find cohesive subgroups in a two-mode network, the bi-clique measure has been developed, which is essentially what a clique is to an ordinary single-mode network but adapted for a two-mode network (Borgatti & Everett, 1997). When conducting a positional analysis on a two-mode network, algorithms have been developed to account for the bipartite nature of the graph (reviewed in Borgatti & Everett, 1992b) and identify similar actors or events based on either regular or structural equivalence. Finally, Field and colleagues (2006) have adapted Frank's Kliquefinder routine (1995) to identify positions of similar actors and events. This algorithm also incorporates Monte Carlo simulations—a popular class of computational algorithms that rely on repeated random sampling to compute their results—to evaluate the internal validity of identified positions and then apply this same algorithm to simulated data with optimal positions to evaluate to what extent and under what circumstances the algorithm recovers the optimal positions. Thus, this last technique combines a number of advances in the mathematical and statistical modeling of two-mode social network data.

ADVANCED MODELS

Most of the recent advances in the statistical analysis of network data address hypothesis-driven research questions about how networks emerge and change and what effects they have on varied outcomes. It should be evident from this chapter that things get statistically complex very quickly, as the nonindependence of observation requires that probability distributions be constructed through simulations (e.g., ERGMs). While complex, these simulations are increasingly necessary, as they permit inferences to be drawn and uncertainty to be modeled. In addition to the methods and measures described thus far, there are three other areas in which computational and statistical advances have allowed researchers to employ the network perspective in ways that were not possible a short time ago (Daly, 2010).

Agent-Based Models (ABMs)

The first of these recent advances relies on simulation to explore systemic implications of rules for behavior and interaction assigned to a set of actors (Frank, Kim, & Belman, 2010). Based on utility functions, these computational agent-based models (ABMs) are becoming important tools for understanding human–environment interactions. Maroulis and colleagues (2010) argue that this modeling process can help educational researchers show how individual actions aggregate into macro-level outcomes, an approach that can help integrate insights from different types of research and better inform educational policy. Such an approach, they continue, can establish not only what works but also how and why it works.

For example, why would one teacher help another teacher? To address this question, a computational agent-based model would work like this. You preselect rules for behavior and interaction among a set of nodes, which, in this instance, are the teachers. These rules (e.g., who interacts with whom) are then modified to examine how patterns of behavior and interactions emerge over multiple iterations. The results of these iterations are then compared against or used to predict what goes on in a social system (Daly, 2010). For example, consider school choice reform. Empirical research on programs that give households more choice is inconclusive, with methodological concerns arising for both observational and experimental studies (Goldhaber & Eide, 2003). To address these concerns, economists have used agent-based simulations to identify features likely to minimize "cream skimming" of top students by private schools in systems in which government-issued vouchers are used to pay for private schooling (Epple & Romano, 2008). In addition, researchers such as Frank, Kim, and Belman (2010) have used agent-based models to examine how teachers respond to external demands for change within the social organization of their schools.

Multilevel Models

Does collaboration between teachers vary by grade level? Such questions rely on relational and attribute data that are nested—pairs of teachers within grade levels within schools—that, by definition, violate the assumption of nonindependence. Therefore, they require a multilevel modeling strategy, which permits network analysts to examine relational data through a regression framework that properly adjusts for the dependency inherent to social network data as well as the "nestedness" of the dyads in higher levels (grade levels and schools). Therefore, these models also allow researchers to simultaneously examine micro and macro perspectives and decompose the variance attributed to these different levels.

These types of models were first developed and employed (Bryk & Raudenbush, 1992) to address the disparity between what theory suggests and what empirical reality shows (McFarland, Diehl, & Rawlings, 2011). Standard linear models, as noted earlier, assume independence among actors, but this clearly is not the case when, for example, studying students who are nested in classrooms, which, in turn, are nested in schools. By allowing variance to be measured at multiple levels, multilevel modeling presents a method more in line with our understanding of how schools are actually structured. Similarly, these models can also take into account the dependencies among related actors. Such models are pervasive in egocentric network studies. In these types of studies, each ego contributes to multiple rows in the data set (dyadic data in which there is one row for each ego/pair). Therefore, multilevel models are necessary to cope with this nonindependence. In addition, these models can also incorporate more than two levels; for example, students who are nested in dyads and dyads that, in turn, are nested in classrooms. This is an example of a three-level model, which can also employ both fixed and random effects at each level. The important conceptual point to keep in mind is that these models properly adjust for the inherent dependencies in the data.

An exemplary education-related example of social network analysis that employs multilevel modeling is Penuel, Frank, Sun, Kim, and Singleton's (2013) study on the normative influences of reading policy on teaching practice in the early 2000s. Drawing on relational and attribute data collected over four time points from 131 teachers with direct responsibilities for reading instruction in 11 schools, this study reached two conclusions. First, teachers' practices did not conform exclusively to the new normative regime but rather depended on exposure to external professional development in reading instruction and on local norms of practice in their schools and collegial subgroups. Second, over time, subgroups' practices diverged with respect to teachers' implementation of skills-based reading instructional practices. To reach these conclusions, they employ a multilevel framework, with teachers (level 1) nested within subgroups (level 2), which, in turn, are nested within schools (level 3). To identify subgroups, they rely on the Kliquefinder algorithm discussed earlier in this chapter. Not only does this multilevel analytic strategy account for the dependencies among observations, it also enables them to decompose the variance in teachers' practices among schools, subgroups, and individuals. This last point ultimately permits them to examine how much change in the outcome is attributed to each analytic level and examine this change over time. This is an excellent example of using social network data in a multilevel framework.

Actor-Oriented Models

A third developing area of network research that makes use of advanced statistical tools focuses on the examination of network change over time. These models show how networks evolve and whether there are actor-level characteristics associated with this evolution. These models are increasingly important, as it is obvious—or, at least it should be—that social networks are dynamic by nature. Ties are established between actors, they may flourish and perhaps evolve into close relationships, and they can also dissolve quietly or suddenly (Snijders, van de Bunt, & Steglich, 2010). These relational changes may be considered the result of the structural positions of the actors within the network—for example, when friends of friends become friends—characteristics of the actors (actor covariates such as gender), characteristics of pairs of actors (dyadic covariates such as whether there is a tie), and residual random influences representing unexplained influences.

Snijders, van de Bunt, and Steglich (2010) give a tutorial introduction to these types of models. They refer to them as *stochastic actor-based models for network dynamics*, a family of models that have the purpose of representing network dynamics on the basis of observed longitudinal data, and evaluate these according to the paradigm of statistical inference. Whereas ABMs rely exclusively on simulation, actor-oriented models make use of observed longitudinal data collected at least two points in time on at least 20 actors with (ideally) complete network information. Current software programs (e.g., SIENA, STATNET, and PNET) require you to specify the parameters that they think govern how the network evolves from one time point to another and then generate a simulation of networks to determine whether imposing those rules will generate networks (dis)similar to the observed network at a later point in time (Valente, 2010). The challenge in creating these models is for you to specify the network's objective functions—the network's assumed behavioral and structural tendencies. The theoretical model that is being tested should guide these objective functions. These stochastic actor-based models allow users to test hypotheses about these tendencies toward reciprocity, homophily, and transitivity and to estimate parameters expressing their strengths while controlling for other tendencies ("confounders").

These models are relatively new and are more complicated than many other statistical models. But there are several interesting examples that show the exciting potential of these models, two of which are noteworthy. First, using four waves of friendship data collected from 26 students in one Dutch classroom, Snijders, van de Bunt, and Steglich (2010) show how this model can be used to examine whether network influence processes play a role in the spread of delinquency among students. They find that there is evidence for delinquency-based friendship selection, expressed most clearly by their delinquency similarity measure, and for influence from pupils on the delinquent behavior of their friends, expressed best by the average similarity measure. The delinquent behavior does not seem to be influenced by sex.

Second, Daly and Finnigan (2010) used this modeling approach to examine three different relational networks (advice, knowledge, and innovation) among 49 school leaders in a district that was in the middle of a reform effort. Their results show that the district's leaders became more connected to one other over time around reform-related knowledge and advice relations, but these connections were still infrequent. On the other hand, the ties associated with innovation became even less frequent over time. This finding suggests that while leaders increased their infrequent interactions around the reform, they interacted less frequently around innovative practices. Furthermore, those that engaged in frequent, stable interactions around knowledge, advice, and innovation demonstrated little change over time. Both the Snijders, van de Bunt, and Steglich (2010) and Daly and Finnigan (2010) examples show how these cutting-edge models can be used to test the hypothesized mechanisms involved in the formation, maintenance, and dissolution of social ties.

SUMMARY

Chapter 8 distinguished between the mathematical and statistical approaches to the study of social networks. The central difference between these two is that the mathematical approach is useful in describing properties of both egocentric and complete networks, whereas the statistical approach emphasizes the generalizability and reproducibility of analytical results. In addition, recent advances in the statistical approach have been extended to include models that change over time and evaluate the likelihood of one network configuration versus another. In many ways, these "new" statistical approaches are similar to the use of statistical inference with the standard actor-by-attribute data through which quantitative data are typically collected and analyzed. Likewise, the statistical approach to the study of social network is primarily concerned with the probability of generating a similar result in a different sample drawn from the same population. The catch is that the statistical approaches discussed in this chapter calculate this probability primarily through simulations, which construct a probability distribution against which the observed result can be compared. This provides the basis for significance testing using relational data that do not conform to your typical inferential assumption of independence. The development of ERGMs was a major breakthrough and provides the basis for most statistical approaches of network data.

This chapter extended the foundation established in Chapter 8 by presenting several procedures that examine 1) ties in complete networks; 2) individual actor attributes, or 3) groups of actors. Therefore, these various techniques can be used to address questions that are especially relevant for educational researchers. Relational and attribute data from the School Leaders data set were used to illustrate how these techniques can be used to answer questions that attend to these three areas. Following an introduction of these varied techniques, the chapter focused on advances that have been made in the analysis of two-mode data, with an emphasis on retaining the duality of actors and events. Finally, this chapter discussed three areas that are especially promising, as they combine several recent computational and statistical advances. These areas were discussed in light of how they have been applied to the study of education-related phenomena. While a complete discussion of these areas is beyond the scope of this introductory text, it is important to have an awareness of the new and exciting ways in which the conceptual and analytical tools associated with the social network perspective are being applied to important topics in and around education.

CHAPTER FOLLOW-UP

1. Using one of the studies mentioned throughout this chapter, identify the statistical model that was employed and evaluate whether this was the appropriate modeling choice.

2. If this same study were to use standard statistical models that assume independence among observations, how would this influence the study's results?

3. Assume you had network data from an entire high school student body ($N = 250$) and were interested in predicting a student's number of friends from covariates such as sex, grade level, and academic performance. What model would be most appropriate to test these relationships?

CRITICAL QUESTIONS TO ASK ABOUT STUDIES THAT USE NETWORK DATA AND STATISTICAL MODELS

1. What is being modeled: ties in complete networks, individual actor attributes, or groups of actors?

2. What procedure was used and what, if any, covariates were included in the models? At what level were these covariates measured: continuous (ratio or interval) or categorical?

3. Did the modeling strategy measure a network's change over time?

4. How were simulations used to create a probability distribution against which observed network parameters were compared?

5. What does it mean when the result from a statistical model using network data is reported as being "statistically significant"? How does this relate to the implied null hypothesis?

ESSENTIAL READING

Daly, A., & Finnigan, K. S. (2010). The ebb and flow of social network ties between district leaders under high-stakes accountability. *American Educational Research Journal, 48*(1), 39–79.

Pittinsky, M., & Carolan, B. V. (2008). Behavioral vs. cognitive classroom friendship networks: Do teacher perceptions agree with student reports? *Social Psychology of Education, 11*, 133–147.

van Duijn, M. A. J., & Huisman, M. (2011). Statistical models for ties and actors. In J. Scott & P. J. Carrington (Eds.), *The Sage handbook of social network analysis* (pp. 459–483). Los Angeles: Sage Publications Ltd.

10

Social Capital

OBJECTIVES

In this chapter, you will learn about the concept of social capital and how it has been defined, measured, and modeled in the context of educational research. Social capital is an important research tradition in the literature on students' outcomes, but it has also been used to map and frame a number of different education-related studies. You will learn about social capital theory and the two different models (social closure vs. structural holes) that have evolved from this framework. This chapter will then evaluate how these competing models have been employed in the context of two different studies, with an emphasis on the ways in which network data have been used to address important questions for educational researchers interested in the relationship between social capital and students' outcomes, particularly achievement. This chapter will demonstrate a number of the ideas introduced in Part II, including those related to network data collection, management, and analysis. This chapter will help you understand what social capital is (and isn't) and how the conceptual and methodological tools associated with social network analysis are essential to testing and refining this rich theory.

EXPLAINING DROPOUT AMONG MEXICAN AMERICAN AND NON–LATINO WHITE STUDENTS

A large body of research has been undertaken to understand how and why students drop out of school. This research has identified numerous factors that contribute to students' early departure from school, including the demographic characteristics of students and their families (Alexander, Entwisle, & Kabbani, 2001), parenting practices (McNeal, 1999), and residential and educational mobility (Ream & Stanton-Salazar, 2007), among others. Recently, attention has been paid to how friendship networks serve as a proximal factor on the path to dropout. Some research has even suggested that the role of peers in the process of school completion and dropout may vary among racial/ethnic groups, especially nonimmigrant Latino and African American students who are more likely to be exposed to an oppositional peer culture (Ream & Rumberger, 2008).

Much of this work has been couched in the framework of social capital, since resources that can be found within peer networks, specifically within friendship networks, are often accumulated and exchanged in a manner that influences educational processes and subsequent outcomes (e.g., Crosnoe & Needham, 2004). This framework emphasizes the importance of others in shaping social processes, in this case, dropout among certain types of students. According to this line of thinking, the resources embedded in the relations that one has with others may be converted to other forms of capital, including material capital (Bourdieu, 1986), human capital (Coleman, 1988), and civic participation (Putnam, 2000). If social capital is indeed important, what role does it play in generating higher levels of dropout among Mexican American and nonwhite Latino students?

Ream and Rumberger (2008) help us answer this question. It turns out that in contrast to the tendency of academically disengaged students to develop "street-oriented friendships," students who are involved in school tend to befriend others who also make schooling a priority. Thus, student engagement influences competing friendship networks in a manner that contributes to the completion of school. Furthermore, engagement behaviors and school-oriented friendship networks have the potential to reduce dropout rates. To their social and educational detriment, however, Mexican American students appear to be less engaged in unorganized academic endeavors and formally sponsored extracurricular activities than are white students. Consequently, these students do not reap the benefits of social capital's upside.

By articulating the social processes that contribute to dropout among a subset of disadvantaged students, Ream and Rumberger (2008) draw our attention to the relations that are thought to serve as the "pipes" through which valued resources flow from one student to another (e.g., an orientation toward the value of school). Their study makes use of a broad theoretical frame—social capital—that has been widely used by educational researchers since Coleman's initial conceptualization. Social capital is an important concept in educational research, as it places theoretical and analytical emphasis on the quality and quantity of resources available in one's network (Lin, 2001a). It also emphasizes how these resources get mobilized to ultimately shape an individual's access and outcomes. What Ream and Rumberger (2008) show is something most of us intuitively know: Whom you know and what you do with them matters. If Mexican American students associate with others who participate in out-of-classroom learning activities (homework, arts, sports, etc.), they will be less likely to drop out. While this result and its underlying logic are appealing, the measurement and modeling of social capital is anything but straightforward.

In this chapter, you will be introduced to the various ways in which this concept has been defined, measured, and modeled. After identifying two competing models of social capital (social closure vs. structural holes) and demonstrating the important similarities between them, this chapter will review two studies that have operated from this framework. These two studies will be presented in light of much of the material discussed thus far, especially the material related to the theory, measurement, and modeling of network-related phenomena. While critiquing the various ways in which social capital can be employed in educational research, this chapter will provide you with suggestions as you construct you own network studies that make use of this framework and the tools introduced throughout the book.

DEFINING SOCIAL CAPITAL

You are at home doing your homework and have no idea how to solve a math problem. But you can call a classmate and ask that they help you work through the answer. It was worth being nice to that classmate even though you do not particularly like him. Do you have to return the favor? Maybe he can grab a ride with you the next time your sibling gives you a ride home from school. Maybe the value of his help was minor enough that you feel little need to reciprocate. Now, however, you need help preparing for a big math exam. Your classmate has made a digital copy of the notes that the teacher prepared for the whole class that you left in your locker. But there is really nothing to return except for the goodwill, because although he passes on this digital copy, your classmate still has it. Another classmate that you have never spoken with has heard from this first classmate that you are real good at writing computer code and asks you to help him. You are busy but feel obligated to at least try and help because you are all in the same math class. Someday you may even have to ask that classmate, maybe even a different one, for help in fixing that computer. What goes around comes around. In fact, you may be in a bad mood because you got that homework question wrong, failed the math exam, and your computer is busted. Someone with whom you have been friends for years and do not see often calls you and makes you feel much better.

The concept of social capital is said to address all of these situations (Kadushin, 2004). You do not have to get help on that math homework just because your classmate can provide it. You may be able to return the favor but through a means other than giving him a ride home. You did "invest" in that relationship by being nice to him in the past. Your other classmate who needed your help in doing some computer programming counted on you even though you have never spoken to him and the only thing you have in common is that you are in the same math class. You wound up helping him because you believe that someone may eventually help you if your computer needed to be fixed. This is a group of students that is rich in resources—from math assistance to rides home to knowledge of computer programming to fixing computer hard drives. Not only do you have what is often referred to as "social capital," but so does the class collectively. Finally, social capital does not have to be associated solely through physical proximity or mutual group affiliation. You also received some social support from the friend who does not attend your school and called you.

These kinds of situations give rise to an array of important, basic questions that confront educational researchers. On the dyadic level, why does one student help another? What are the consequences of this interaction? If all of your classmates have the same answer, should you try and reach out to others not in your class who may give you a better alternative answer? What are the costs associated with getting help on that exam? Suppose you kept asking for help on subsequent exams; is your relationship established enough to do so? There is also the matter of beliefs and norms. Some schools and classrooms may have a strong culture of reciprocity, with individuals looking out for each other, whereas others are more individually oriented. That, of course, would make a difference in asking for and offering resources if the school or classroom has but a few, that is, a small number of students who even are capable of providing that help. These are the very kinds of issues that the concept of social capital attempts to explain. Because these issues are so varied, the definition and measurement of social capital has been much contested.

Before turning to the different ways in which social capital has been defined, it is helpful to first think about what is meant by the term *capital*, which obviously has its roots in economic theory. Marx (1933/1849) was one of the first to use the term *capital*, referring specifically to the surplus value captured by those who controlled the means of production (the capitalists or bourgeoisie). Accordingly, this classical theory of capital consists of two distinct elements: value that is generated and pocketed by the capitalists *and* investment on the part of capitalists with expected returns in the marketplace. Therefore, capital is a surplus value and represents an investment in expected returns (Lin, 2001a). More recent theories of capital focus less on competition between two entities and more on stratified and fluid contests among several entities. Foremost among these neocapital theories is human capital theory (Becker, 1964/1993), which extends this thinking by conceiving capital as an investment (e.g., in education) with certain future expected returns (e.g., earnings). Individuals acquire skills and knowledge in order to maximize what they can get for payment of their labor/skill. Bourdieu's concept of cultural capital (1990) represents investments on the part of members of the upper class in reproducing symbols and meanings that are internalized as their own. Cultural capital theory emphasizes how schools are then used to encourage the internalization of these products' value, thereby "indoctrinating" the masses and helping the upper class retain their advantage through intergenerational transmissions. What does social capital have to do with these different theories of capital?

Rather than focusing on an investment in education or the acquisition of highbrow cultural products, as is the case with theories of human capital or cultural capital, social capital focuses on the investment in social relations. Like all investments, one also expects to receive some return. Students, teachers, and parents engage in interactions and networking in order to produce "profits." Of course, the term *profits* as used here does not simply refer to monetary gains. These interactions may facilitate the flow of information, exert influence over others, enhance one's social credentials, or reinforce one's identity. These, in turn, are the "profits" of investing in social capital and are not accounted for by other forms of personal capital such as economic capital or human capital. These returns, it should be noted, may not always be socially desirable. A high school student can invest in relations with students who have little attachment to school, therefore increasing his own chances of dropping out. So, while that student may get a "return" such as friendship or support from this group of students, this return on the investment may be costly to his success in the long run. This is what is referred to as the "dark side" of social capital (e.g., Portes, 1998).

This idea that there is value in relations undermines the different ways in which the term *social capital* has been defined by a number of prominent theorists, who in the 1980s independently explored the concept in some detail (Lin, 2001a). These definitions sought to bring some clarity to the different situations in which social relations are thought to generate some return. For example, Bourdieu (1986) viewed social capital alongside economic and cultural capital. According to him, social capital consists of one's social obligations and connections. These obligations and connections aggregate actual or potential resources, creating a durable network of relationships of mutual acquaintance or recognition. This network provides its members with collectively owned capital that can be accessed only by those belonging to the group. Capital, in this form, is represented both by the size of the group and the volume and quality of the capital possessed by the group's members. Put simply, according to Bourdieu, social capital depends on the size of one's connections and the volume and quality of capital possessed by these connections. Social capital is thus conceptualized as a collective asset shared by members of a clearly defined, bounded group, with obligations of exchange and mutual recognition. However, this strict vision of class society provides little room for any explanation of social mobility.

Like Bourdieu, Coleman emphasizes the collective nature of social capital and how it facilitates actions. Coleman offers an even more functional definition: "Social capital is defined by its function. It is not a single entity, but a variety of different entities having two characteristics in common: They all consist of some aspect of social structure, and they facilitate certain actions of the individuals who are within the structure" (Coleman, 1990, p. 302). Various aspects of networks and feelings of trust that give a collectivity a sense of being a community and thus enable individuals to draw upon community resources are offered as examples. Specifically, he describes how parent–teacher associations and other social organizations allow individual parents and students to attain personal goals but also offer resources to the school and to all administrators, teachers, students, and parents affiliated with the school. These dense or closed networks around the school community provide a valuable source of norm-reinforcement that is thought to benefit students. In fact, it is these types of networks that were thought to explain what was then known as the "Catholic school advantage" (Coleman & Hoffer, 1987). Coleman's definition is therefore attitudinal (desirable norms that are aligned with those of the school) and structural (dense or closed networks).

Lin (2001a) describes how Putnam's work (2000) strongly reflects the use of this perspective and its focus on the group level. His work on participation in voluntary organizations in democratic societies focuses on how this participation promotes and enhances collective norms and trust. Both of these, he argues, are essential for the production and maintenance of collective well-being. Similar to Coleman, Putnam offers little insight into the specific relational mechanisms through which norms and trust flow within the group from one person to another. In some respects, his conceptualization is even more vague than Coleman's. He goes on to state that social capital emphasizes not just desirable feelings—camaraderie, feelings of belonging, and the like—but a wide variety of quite specific benefits that flow from the trust, reciprocity, information, and cooperation associated with social networks. Additionally, he claims social capital creates value for the people who are connected and—at least sometimes—for unconnected bystanders as well. The major contribution of this conceptualization is that it recognizes that one need not individually possess capital in order to benefit directly from it.

Burt's use of the term shifts its definition in a different direction, one that is less overtly functional and one that offers greater specificity in terms of how it can be measured and modeled (2001/2004). Moving beyond social capital as a metaphor or anecdote, Burt emphasizes connections among actors but focuses more intently on an individual's location in a social structure. Pushing the concept more toward measurement, and rather than conceiving social capital a group-level attribute that is the byproduct of dense, closed networks, Burt views social capital as a function of brokerage opportunities. Brokerage opportunities are those in which an individual is located in a position in which he or she can broker the flow of information between people and control the tasks that bring different people together (Burt, 2001). So, according to this definition, one has social capital when one is in a position to connect two otherwise unconnected parts of the network. For example, the principal that can serve as a conduit between two groups of disconnected teachers, thereby bridging what Burt refers to as a structural hole, possesses social capital. Here the emphasis is not on the returns associated with dense networks but on the returns of being in a structural location between two cohesive parts of the network. By focusing on one's structural location, Burt argues that network location is the key element in identifying social capital.

There are two commonalities across these definitions. First, they all share the understanding that social capital consists of resources embedded in social relations and social structure, which can be activated when one wants to increase the probability of some desired outcome (Lin, 2001b). Similar to human capital, the individual actor invests in order to increase the likelihood of success. However, unlike human capital in which one makes an investment to acquire skills, knowledge, and certifications, social capital is an investment in relationships through which an individual can access or borrow resources possessed by others. While Bourdieu, Coleman, Putnam, and Burt have applied the concept to a wide range of actions (e.g., members of the dominant class engage in mutual recognition to so as to reproduce the group's advantaged position; see Bourdieu, 1986), there is a second implicit commonality across conceptual definitions: Social capital as a theory-generating concept is best conceived in the social network perspective (Lin, 2001b). These definitions recognize that resources are embedded in relations, not just individuals, and that the access and use of these resources reside with individuals.

CONFUSION ACROSS DEFINITIONS

Despite these two commonalities across these different conceptual definitions, it should also be evident that there is some theoretical or measurement confusion across these definitions, which has inhibited the development of a more coherent theory of social capital (Lin, 2001b). One of these confusions is whether social capital is considered an individual or collective good (Portes, 1998), specifically in light of the conceptualizations offered by Coleman and Putnam. Stated differently, is social capital something a student or school has? Can an isolated student still benefit from being in a well-connected school?

Consider this scenario. You are a high school student who prefers to keep to yourself. All your good friends attend other schools in neighboring districts and are much different from your classmates. The school you attend has a student body that, on average, does very well academically and is active in formal extracurricular activities, including sports and special-interest clubs. You are a decent student but do not participate in any of these activities. Unlike other students, you do not consult with teachers outside of class, nor do your parents. According to Coleman, your school possesses social capital in the form of a collective good (a strong achievement norm, for example).

The problem with this is that you do not have any meaningful interactions with anyone in the school. The major shortcoming of conceptualizing social capital as a collective schoolwide good is that is draws attention away from the relational mechanisms through which possible returns are generated. When used in this vein, social capital is stripped from its roots in individual interactions within and across networks, and it becomes a vague term used in the context of promoting social integration and solidarity. Social capital becomes synonymous with trust, cohesion, and norms. Therefore, formulating causal propositions becomes difficult.

Related to this point, a second confusion across these varied definitions of social capital is that the concept is considered both a cause and an effect. Social capital, particularly according to Coleman and Putnam's functional view, is identified when and if it "works." For example, Coleman claims that social capital is any "social-structural resource" that generates returns for someone in a specific action. Accordingly, social capital can be captured only by its effect; whether it is an investment depends on the

Table 10.1   Social Capital Definitions and Confusions.

Theorist	Definition	Confusion
Bourdieu	The aggregate of the actual or potential resources that are linked to possession of a durable network of more or less institutionalized relationships of mutual acquaintance and recognition—or, in other words, to membership in a group, which provides each of its members with the backing of the collectivity-owned capital, a "credential" that entitles them to credit, in the various senses of the word (1986).	Emphasizes class structure and an absence of mobility
Coleman	Defined by its function. It is not a single entity, but a variety of different entities having two characteristics in common: They all consist of some aspect of social structure, and they facilitate certain actions of the individuals who are within the structure (1990).	A tautology in which the cause is determined by the effect and vice versa.
Putnam	The collective value of all social networks and the inclinations that arise from these networks to do things for each other (2000).	Confounded with norms and trust
Burt	Function of brokerage opportunities across structural holes (2001).	Emphasizes social capital as an individual as opposed to a collective good

Source: Lin, N. (2001a). Building a network theory of social capital. In N. Lin, K. Cook, & R. S. Burt (Eds.), *Social capital: A theory of social structure in action.* New York: Cambridge University Press.

return to a specific individual in a specific action (Lin, 2001b). Obviously, it is impossible to theorize social capital when its causes and effects are folded into a single function.

A final confusion is whether relations among a network's actors need to exhibit closure or density in order to generate social capital. This is the fundamental distinction between Bourdieu's and Coleman's definitions of social capital and their emphases on closed, functional networks, and Burt's definition, which emphasizes access to diverse streams of information. More recent efforts to define and measure social capital have connected these preferred structures to outcomes of interest. For preserving or maintaining resources, denser networks may be advantageous, whereas for searching for and obtaining resources, accessing bridges in the network may be more helpful. For example, a teacher in need of socioemotional support after a particularly ugly confrontation with a parent may benefit from a closed network that gives that teacher access to a number of different sources of comfort. On the other hand, that same teacher may be able to rely on a connection to a previous school in which she worked in order to get information to a current colleague who has a new student that transferred from that school. In this instance, the teacher is serving as a bridge between two otherwise disconnected parts of a network. This focus on the outcomes of interest has helped address some of the confusion across these different conceptual definitions.

A CONVERGING CONCEPTUALIZATION OF SOCIAL CAPITAL

Despite these varied definitions and the confusions surrounding them, they all emphasize to one degree or another (1) the resources embedded in relations one can directly or indirectly access and (2) one's location in this network of relations. These two elements are most clearly reflected in Lin's conceptualization, which has informed much of the work in the area of social capital for the past decade or so. Social capital, according to Lin, is *an investment in social relations by individuals through which they gain access to embedded resources to enhance expected returns of instrumental or expressive actions* (2001b).

This definition has three important core elements. First, similar to other theories of capital, social capital involves an investment. Second, this definition emphasizes both access to and mobilization of social capital. This second element draws attention to one's location in a social structure—a set of actors bound by rule-based relations—through which individuals can access differential amounts of valued resources. Third, it specifies two types of returns that one can expect as outcomes. Instrumental action is taken to obtain resources not possessed by ego—for example, consulting a colleague to get some advice as to how to handle a disruptive student. For expressive action, social capital is a means through which individuals seek to consolidate resources. For example, social capital may enhance the amount of trust that one teacher has in his or her colleagues or reinforce the norms among these teachers that shape their everyday professional behaviors. In this instance, social capital pools and shares an embedded resource (trust or norms) in order to provide a collective good. These three elements—investment in relations, network locations, and embedded resources—are sprinkled throughout the different definitions just reviewed; Lin's contribution was bringing these elements together in a useful framework that has guided much scholarship in the area of social capital, especially as it pertains to educational research. For example, Ream and Rumberger's (2008) study on dropout among Mexican American and nonwhite Latino students reflects all three elements.

However, regardless of how it is conceptualized, the analytical models needed to examine its relationship to other variables (e.g., dropout or achievement) must account for the dependencies among observations; two individuals linked together in some social structure are nonindependent (unless, of course, you are dealing with independent ego networks that have been randomly sampled from some larger target population). Therefore, the material discussed in the previous two chapters becomes even more relevant. Applications discussed later in this chapter illustrate this point.

SOCIAL CAPITAL AND THE NETWORK FLOW MODEL

Other network theories, including small-world theory (e.g., Watts & Strogatz, 1998) and strength-of-weak-ties theory (Granovetter, 1973), have also grappled with fundamental conceptual issues. But recent advances in network theorizing have shown that these theories, as well as social capital theory, are all elaborations of the same theory, referred to as the network flow model (Borgatti & Lopez-Kidwell, 2011). According to this recently developed model, social capital is part of broader theory that underlies much contemporary network thinking. Because it has only been developed recently, examples of its application in educational research, and other empirical settings for that matter, are scant. But, as this theory matures, it is likely that educational researchers will no longer think in terms of social capital but in terms of network flow. Therefore, it is worth noting a few core components of this exciting theoretical model.

Borgatti and Lopez-Kidwell (2011) posit that the network flow model consists of three layers. The first layer of the network flow model defines the basic rule of how social systems work: Essentially, they are networks through which resources flow from actor to actor along paths of ties interlocked through shared endpoints. At this point in the text, this basic idea should be familiar to you and provides a foundation for theorizing about networks.

The middle layer in the network flow model consists of the different theorems that can be derived from the first layer. Because all of the elements of the theorem are drawn from the network flow model, the theorem can be tested mathematically or explored further through simulation (i.e., agent-based models). At this level, theory consists of taking constructs defined on the underlying model (e.g., density) and associating them with outcomes such as the similarity of actors on key attributes (e.g., normative beliefs about achievement).

The third surface layer is where the theory interfaces with the variables drawn from the immediate empirical context. For example, Coleman enhances the theory by associating network density to resource flows (e.g., norms and trust) and ultimately to students' achievement in Catholic schools. The density theorem is just one of the many that can be derived from the underlying network flow model. Another example is the idea that an actor positioned along the only or shortest path between two other actors may be able to benefit by limiting, filtering, or even controlling the flow of resources along the path. At this third surface level, Spillane, Healey, and Kim (2010) add whether a teacher is characterized as a formal or informal leader to how this characterization shapes her ability to influence the flow of advice between other teachers and groups of teachers. In addition to these two examples, there are many other basic propositions that can be derived from the network flow model.

The effort to integrate these different propositions into one coherent network theory is a novel and important attempt to extract their underlying principles and the mechanisms they propose. By doing so, the ultimate aim of the network flow model is to identify commonalities across different research efforts and smooth over the inconsistencies that have inhibited the usefulness of social capital and other strands of network theory as they relate to the study of educational phenomena. As the effort to integrate different network theories into a unified theoretical framework moves forward, two models of social capital continue to dominate how we think about and measure social networks in educational research. Both models can be viewed as answering one basic research question: Why do some actors or groups do better (or worse) than others?

MEASURING SOCIAL CAPITAL

To answer this question, the concept of social capital has to be operationalized into an observable measure. Because the conceptual definitions have been so varied, so too has its measurement. The different measures that have been used reflect different aspects of the definitions that were reviewed earlier. Typically, to measure social capital, researchers have emphasized network locations and embedded resources. These two conceptual elements are evident in all the definitions discussed thus far but are made most explicit in Lin's definition. These two elements of social capital—network location and embedded resources—are also reflected in the principle approaches that have been used to measure social capital across an array of empirical contexts in education.

Network Locations

The first measurement strategy focuses on network locations as measurements of social capital (Lin , 2001a). One take on this is that bridges or access to bridges facilitates returns on one's investment, thereby indicating social capital. This was elaborated on and formalized by Burt (1992/2004) in his notions of structural holes and constraints. Other measures also reflect this emphasis on network location, including the different measures for ego-level centrality and betweenness discussed in Part II. In fact, Balkundi, Kilduff, and Harrison (2011) use degree centrality to answer the following question: Does social capital affect a small team's performance because subordinates come to see the leader as charismatic? Using degree centrality as a measure of social capital, they conclude that formal leaders who were central within team advice networks were seen as charismatic by subordinates, and this charisma was associated with high team performance. They are many other measures—size, density, cohesion, closeness—that are potential indicators for social capital. However, the selection of any one of these measures must be grounded in a clear theoretical argument.

Embedded Resources

In addition to network locations, measures of social capital have also emphasized the measurement of embedded resources (Lin, 2001a), a second key element of Lin's definition. Therefore, measurements of these assets typically emphasize the valued resources (e.g., advice, information, and status) of others (alters) that are accessible by an ego actor through their networks and ties. These varied measurements are relative to two frameworks: (1) network resources and (2) contact resources. Network resources refer to those that the individual ego can access through direct or indirect with alters. Measures that capture network resources focus on the range, quality, variety, and/or composition of these resources. Contact resources are slightly different in that they refer to the valued resources possessed by alters (e.g., power) and applied in specific ego actions, such as bullying, choosing a college, or finding a teaching job. When the focus is on embedded resources, this is typically referred to as network content, whereas social capital as measured through network location is referred to as network structure (e.g., Carolan, 2012). While Croninger and Lee (2001) do not focus on network location in their study of the relationship between social capital and dropout among high-risk students, they do employ two measures of social capital that reflect this emphasis on embedded resources. The first is a composite variable that captures how much a student trusts his or her teacher, and the second is a variable that measures how frequently the student and teacher communicate outside of class. Both measures are examples of what Lin would conceptualize as network resources. Table 10.2 depicts the two core elements of social capital (network location and embedded resources) and the different indicators used to represent these assets.

Table 10.2   Measuring Social Capital: Network Location and Embedded Resources. Measures of social capital should ideally include both types of assets: embedded resources and network locations.

Assets	Measurements	Indicators
Embedded resources	Network resources	Range of resources, best resource, diversity of resources, average resources
	Contact resources	Alter's occupation, status, sector
Network locations	Brokerage	Constraint, brokerage, betweenness, centrality
	Closure	Density
	Tie strength	Intimacy, intensity, reciprocity

Source: Lin, N. (2001a). Building a network theory of social capital. In N. Lin, K. Cook, & R. S. Burt (Eds.), *Social capital: A theory of social structure in action. New York: Cambridge University Press.*

SAMPLING METHODS

Whether the focus is on network location, embedded resources, or both, these varied measures are employed along with one of three sampling techniques (Lin, 2001a), which were introduced in Chapter 4. This section briefly revisits these techniques in light of their application to studies that have measured social capital. The first of these techniques is the saturation sampling technique, which is most appropriate when a network's boundaries are clearly specified. In such complete networks, relational data from all actors are collected, and from these data, measurements of network locations (centrality, betweenness, etc.) are calculated. The obvious advantage of this technique is that you are able to get a complete and detailed account of each actor's network location as well as the embedded resources of each actor, especially if attribute data are collected in addition to relational data. However, this strategy is only useful if you are investigating social capital within an organization or small set of organizations. This is because a saturation sampling strategy requires that the network have a defined and manageable boundary (Lin, 2001a). Examples of this strategy include Ahn's (2010) study of nearly 60 college mentors in a college access program and Frank, Zhao, and Borman's (2004) study of the implementation of computer technology in six schools. In both of these studies, there was a near-complete mapping of the network and its actors.

This is a distinctly different strategy than the one that is used to study larger networks that are not as easily defined. In these types of studies, the focus is not on the complete network but rather on the individual egos; therefore, ego-network sampling techniques are used. Most prominent among these is the name generator, which elicits a list of alters from the respondent (ego) and identifies how ego is tied to each alter (referred to as "name interpreters"). Ideally, relational data on how alters are tied to each other are also collected. From these data, you can calculate an ego's location within her or his network of alters. In addition to measuring social capital as location, data on network resources can also be obtained. Derived from attribute or relational variables, a variety of different network resource measures can be calculated, including: composition (standard resource characteristics such as the mean grade point average in students' ego networks), heterogeneity (the diversity of resources such as the standard deviation of number of years teaching in teachers' ego networks), and upper reachability (the most popular student in students' ego networks). There are two advantages to using a name generator and interpreter. First, this strategy can identify specific content areas relative to the actions under investigation. For example, in Carolan's (2012) study of the relationship among high school size, social capital, and adolescents' math achievement, the name generator asks that respondents identify their three closest friends in school and then evaluate, for each named alter, how important it is for them to get good grades. The ability to capture alters' normative beliefs about school performance is relevant given the study's focus on the embedded resources to which students have access. Second, collecting data through this technique also allows one to map locations and characteristics, in addition to the resources embedded in or available through one's alters.

This technique, however, is not without its shortcomings, two of which are noteworthy. First, name generators tend to elicit stronger ties to the exclusion of weaker ones. When a respondent is asked to list those names that first come to mind, the tendency is to provide those names with which ego is more intimate, interacts with more frequently, or exchanges more intensively with. This bias may not be so problematic if the return or outcome concern is expressive, such as quality of life, health, or trust, as these returns are likely influenced by stronger ties. However, if the returns are more instrumental, such as searching for a teaching vacancy, information on weaker ties would be necessary and likely not captured through the name generator. A second shortcoming is that name generators identify individual alters and not their social positions. To address this latter shortcoming, the position generator technique has been developed, which asks respondents to indicate if they know anyone in a specific job or position. From these prompts and their responses, it is possible to construct network resource measures including extensity (number of positions accessed), range (the "distance" between the highest and lowest positions), and upper reachability (highest position accessed). This technique has not yet been applied in educational research; however, there are examples of its use in the literature on social capital in diverse empirical contexts such as social movement mobilization (Tindall, Cormier, & Diani, 2012) and parenthood status (Song, 2012).

TWO COMPETING MODELS?

These different measures and sampling methods have been employed in models that have examined the relationship between social capital and various educational outcomes. The general theory of network flow encompasses two different models of social capital, both of which emphasize network location: Burt's structural holes argument and Coleman's closure theory of social capital. These two different models, which emanate from two different ways in which social capital is defined, reflect a contradiction that remains unresolved in the literature on social capital, especially as this literature pertains to education. For example, does a child benefit from having parents, teachers, neighborhood adults, and so on communicate with each other, or do these relations constrain that child? The contradiction between these two models, then, is that in one, dense and redundant connections among a system's actors are good, and in the other, they are bad. This contradiction parallels one of the confusions noted earlier. In addition, it also speaks to the issue of whether the "benefit," or what was referred to as the "return on one's investment," is instrumental or expressive. This distinction becomes even more important when we consider the influences of these two models on students' achievement later this chapter.

Figure 10.1 presents a straightforward sociogram that will be used to describe these two models. This sociogram consists of 20 high school students and relationships among them as lines—the thicker the line, the stronger the relationship. Each line represents a symmetric tie, in this case, the frequency with which two students discuss issues related to their coursework. Thicker lines indicate that the dyad discusses coursework issues more frequently. The figure shows three clusters of students, each represented by a different shape (circles, squares, and triangles), and a density table below the figure shows the density of within- and between-group relations. This table shows that relationships within groups are stronger than between groups, which reflects the general tendency that resources circulate more within than it does between groups. For example, the within-group density of the cluster on the left (Group 1, circles) is 1.33, while its between-group density with the cluster on the right (Group 2, squares) is 0.00, indicating that there are no direct ties between these two groups. Note that density here is calculated as the proportion of ties divided by the average tie strength (tie strength is ordinal: 0, 1, or 2). Because there are no relations between these two clusters, the students in these two groups are not simultaneously aware of opportunities or resources in all groups. Even if a resource is valuable (e.g., information about what is on an upcoming exam) and eventually reaches everyone, the fact that diffusion occurs over time means that some students will know before others, therefore giving them an advantage.

Figure 10.1 Structural Holes Versus Network Closure. This hypothetical sociogram consists of 20 high school students and relationships among them represented as lines—the thicker the line, the stronger the relationship. Each line represents a symmetric tie, in this case, the frequency with which two students discuss issues related to their coursework. Thicker lines indicate that the dyad discusses coursework issues more frequently. The figure shows three clusters of students, each represented by a different shape (circles, squares, and triangles), and a density table below the figure shows the density of within- and between-group relations. This table shows that relationships within groups are stronger than those between groups, which reflects the general tendency that resources circulate more within than they do between groups.

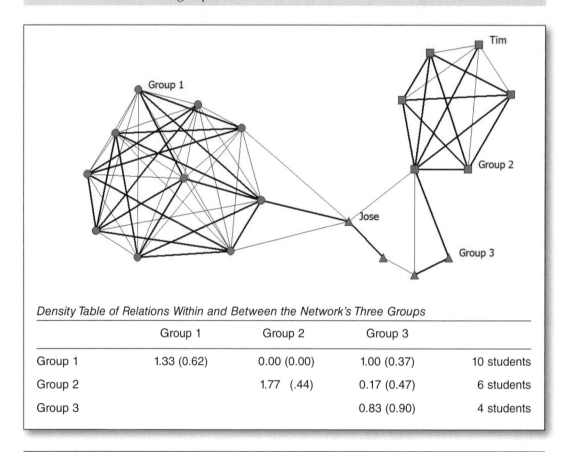

Density Table of Relations Within and Between the Network's Three Groups

	Group 1	Group 2	Group 3	
Group 1	1.33 (0.62)	0.00 (0.00)	1.00 (0.37)	10 students
Group 2		1.77 (.44)	0.17 (0.47)	6 students
Group 3			0.83 (0.90)	4 students

Note: Density = Proportion of ties / Average tie strength. *SD* in parentheses.

Source: Adapted from Burt, R. S. (2001). Structural holes versus network closure as social capital. In N. Lin, K. Cook, & R. S. Burt (Eds.), *Social capital: Theory and research* (pp. 31–56). New York: Walter de Gruyter.

Structural Holes as Social Capital

This logic undermines the structural holes as social capital argument and reflects an emphasis on network location in both its definition and measurement (Burt, 2001). This argument describes and measures social capital as a function of brokerage opportunities and draws on several classic strands of network studies during the 1970s, including Granovetter (1973) on the strength of weak ties, Freeman (1977) on betweenness centrality, and Cook and Emerson (1978) on the benefits of having exclusive exchange partners. To elaborate the core elements of the structural holes as social capital argument, let's revisit Figure 10.1.

The sparser connections between groups in Figure 10.1 are holes in the network's social structure. These holes, what Burt calls "structural holes," create a competitive advantage for those individual students whose relationships span those holes. The structural hole between any two groups does not mean that the students within those groups are unaware of each other; it only means that those students are more likely focused on the behaviors and attitudes within their own groups and do not attend to those of students in other groups. Students on either side of the structural hole circulate in different flows of resources. These structural holes, therefore, provide a potential opportunity for one student to broker the flow of resources between two others and control the types of activities that bring students together from opposite sides of the hole. In addition, these holes separate nonredundant collections of resources; that is; students in one group exchange resources that may be distinctly different from resources exchanged within another group.

Jose and Tim in Figure 10.1 have the same number of ties: five. But Jose has something more. Tim is only directly connected to students within Group 2 via four weak ties and one strong tie. So he only discusses issues about his coursework with members of the same group. Jose also only has one strong within-group tie, but, in addition, he has ties to students in Groups 1 and 2, which serves as a conduit for information between Groups 1 and 2. The connections that Jose has to these other groups are a network bridge in that the relationship is his—and his group's—only path to the information available in these other two groups. Break that relationship and there is no connection between Groups 1 and 2. More generally, Jose can be considered a broker in this network of 20 students. Network constraint, introduced in Part II, is an index that measures the extent to which a person's contacts are redundant, that is, resources flow among the same set of students. Tim has a constraint score that is 30 percentage points higher than Jose: 0.71 versus 0.41. Betweenness, also introduced in Part II (Freeman, 1977) is an index that measures the extent to which a person brokers indirect connections between all others in the network. In the dichotomized network, Jose's normalized betweenness score (Freeman, 1977) is 70.00, compared to Tim's score of 0.00, indicating that Jose is located on a path connecting two students much more frequently, whereas resources do not at all have to flow through Tim in order to reach other students in his ego network.

Normalized betweenness is equal to the number of times that any actor needs a given actor to reach any actor by the shortest path divided by its maximum value.

Jose's bridge connections to Groups 1 and 2, according to the structural holes as social capital argument, give him an advantage with respect to information about his coursework. He reaches a higher volume of information because he reaches more students indirectly. Furthermore, the diversity of his alters across the three groups means that the higher volume of information contains less redundancy: resources within groups are likely to be different than between groups. In addition, Jose is positioned at an intersection of social organization, so he is early to learn about information circulated in all three groups. His diverse contacts mean that he is also more likely to be a candidate for inclusion in new opportunities. These benefits are compounded by the fact that having a network that yields such benefits makes Jose more attractive to other students as a contact in their own networks. Finally, there is a control advantage in which Jose is able to bring together otherwise disconnected students (e.g., those from Groups 1 and 3), giving him a disproportionate say in whose interests are served when the other students eventually come together. In fact, this is a reflection of Simmel's (1908/1950) classic sociological concept, *tertius gaudens*, literally "the third who benefits."

In sum, students like Jose are those that know about, have a hand in, and exercise control over potentially rewarding opportunities. This benefit is primarily derived from his advantageous location, reflecting an emphasis on network location, which is a core element of Lin's definition. The structural-holes-as-social-capital argument is that in comparison between otherwise similar actors like Jose and Tim in Figure 10.1, it is Jose who has more social capital. His network across structural holes gives him broad, early access to and control over resources.

Network Closure as Social Capital

On the contrary, Coleman's network-closure-as-social-capital argument emphasizes the risks associated with being a broker like Jose and the benefits of closed, redundant networks for students like Tim. This is known as the network closure argument, which has influenced much educational research that has employed a social capital framework. The idea is that networks with closure are a source of social capital. These are networks in which everyone is connected in such a way that no one can escape the observation of others. In operational terms, this usually means a dense network.

Network closure does two things (Burt, 2001). First, according to Coleman (1990), it influences access to information. For example, if Tim in Figure 10.1 is not interested in what goes in class but is interested in doing well on an upcoming exam, he can save the effort required to pay attention in class if he can get the information he wants from a friend in Group 2 who pays attention to such matters. The idea is that networks that consist of more direct connections improve the flow of resources from one actor to another. Second, and emphasized by Coleman in his explanation for why Catholic schools produce more learning than public schools, network closure facilitates sanctions that make it less risky for people in the network to trust one another. According to Coleman, students in Catholic schools benefit from larger endowments of social capital generated, in part, by greater intergenerational closure: dense network connections among students' parents. In such networks, parents establish ties with the parents of their children's school friends, which enable them to more effectively monitor the out-of-school behavior of their children and exchange information about school-related activities (Morgan & Sørensen, 1999). In addition to making it less risky to trust others, network closure in and around schools also promotes a system of norms that support and provide effective rewards for high achievement.

The network-closure-as-social-capital prediction, then, is that in comparison between otherwise similar people like Tim and Jose in Figure 10.1, it is Tim who has more social capital. Dense, strong relations among his alters give him more reliable, trustworthy communication channels. The network closure argument reflects Lin's emphasis on network location by positing that those in dense, redundant networks are at an advantage. In addition, network closure protects students like Tim from exploitation because he and his alters are more able to act in concert against someone who violates their norms, for example, if a student from Group 1 were to be caught cheating.

EMPIRICAL EXAMPLES

However, this hypothesized connection between network closure and structural holes and the utility of social capital is too shortsighted. To simply argue that closure or density is a prerequisite for social capital is to deny the importance of bridges, brokers, and structural holes. As noted earlier, whether a closed or dense network is advantageous lies, rather, in certain outcomes of interest (Lin, 2001a). When it comes to the preservation or maintenance of resources (expressive actions such as mobilizing others with shared interests), denser networks with high closure may be more preferable. Therefore, it might be better for a parent to opt that her child attend a small, private school with a cohesive community of like-minded parents so that the child's well-being can be assured. On the other hand, when it comes to searching for and obtaining resources that one doesn't possess, such as finding out about college opportunities or getting help with your homework, accessing and extending bridges in the network may be more preferable. Rather than claim that a closed network or one with structural holes is required in order for social capital to be generated, it is more sensible to (1) conceptualize what outcomes and under what conditions a denser or more sparse network might generate a better return and (2) put forward deductive hypotheses for empirical investigation: for example, Tim in Figure 10.1 would be more likely to share information about coursework, which, in turn, upholds his peers' expectations for their appropriate behavior. The two empirical examples presented in this next section accomplish both of these aims.

The different emphases of these competing models of social capital are evident in the research literature that has used a social capital framework to examine the relationship between social capital and students' achievement. In addition to demonstrating how social capital has been used to provide a theoretical frame for both studies, this section also demonstrates how this network-based theory has shaped the way in which both studies collect, measure, and model their relational data. Therefore, this section brings together much of what was covered in Part II, connects it to a rich body of network-based theory, and makes explicit the fact that it is impossible in social network research to distinguish where theory ends and methodology begins. Both examples discussed below also share a focus on (1) relations, not attributes; (2) networks, not groups; and (3) relations in a broader relational context. These three assumptions help both studies describe and explain their focal phenomena.

"Connectedness" and Students' Achievement in a Small High School

Maroulis and Gomez (2008) use a social capital framework to gain insight into how social relations give rise to relative advantage within a group of students at a large, urban public high school engaged in small-school reform. More specifically, they ask three questions using relational and attribute data derived from a complete network of 85 10th-grade students: First, to what extent is academic performance "contagious" among peers? Second, after accounting for individual characteristics, is a student's location in a social network, as indicated by network density, associated with academic performance? If so, are high-density or low-density ego networks primarily responsible for this association? Third, is there a joint effect of peer achievement and network density on academic performance?

To address these questions, they construct measures of network location and embedded resources, reflecting both elements of Lin's definition of social capital, from two sources. Their measure of network location, density, comes from a web-based social network survey that asked students to cite those with whom they interact in several academic and social contexts. This instrument asked four name-generating questions to elicit discussion partners. Each question asked students to type in the first and last name of up to seven people (1) with whom they discuss schoolwork the most, (2) with whom they discuss personal and private concerns or worries the most, (3) with whom they hang out the most, and (4) whom they try to avoid. For each contact, students were also asked to indicate the frequency of interaction with that person. As a final question, students were asked about the frequency of communication between the names they cited—that is, their perception of how often the people they listed spoke to each other.

These network data were collapsed and transformed into a symmetric matrix of relations, with each cell in the matrix representing whether a relation between two students exists. The rows and columns of the network matrix include the network survey respondents as well as other students in the small school they cited for whom they had data. With the exception of the question about avoidance, discussion partners cited with a frequency of "at least once a month" or more on any of the name-generating questions were included as relations. In cases in which relationship information between students was missing because a student in the matrix was not a respondent of the survey, the answers to the final question about frequency of communication between people cited were used. From these network data, a measure of egocentric network density was calculated—a respondent-specific density measure that takes into account the actual and possible ties only between direct contacts of a respondent. This is an instance in which egocentric data were extracted from a complete network. Specifically, egocentric network density was calculated as the total number of ties that exist between the first-order contacts of a respondent (within the small school) divided by the number of all possible ties that could exist between those contacts, multiplied by 100, with higher scores reflecting ego networks with higher density.

In addition to this measure of network location, they also include a measure of each ego network's embedded resources, what they refer to as network composition. For this, they use administrative data to create a measure of each student's peers' achievement. Using the matrix of relations to define a set of peers for each student, lagged peer achievement was calculated as the weighted average of the grade point averages of a respondent's peers before the start of the semester of interest for this analysis. The weights assigned to each cited student are proportional to the amount of interaction between the students. For the calculation of peer achievement, they focus only on students one step away in the network and do not consider second-order contacts (i.e., friends of friends get a weight of zero unless they are also directly a friend of the respondent). These two measures—network density and lagged peer achievement—are employed in models along with a set of control variables (8th-grade reading test score, gender, race, and absences) that predict a students' GPA. This dependent variable was measured at the same time they collected the network data but is different from the GPA that was used to construct the measure of lagged peer achievement, which relied on the students' GPA as measured earlier in the school year.

The measures derived from the network data (density and peer achievement) were combined with student-level performance and background data to estimate regression models of student academic performance, as measured by GPA. The estimates from these models were also checked using different indices for robustness, mainly to offset concerns about omitted variables. These models show that the resources embedded in students' networks (as measured by lagged peer achievement) and network location (as measured the density of ties between a student's peers) have no average association with student performance after accounting for individual-level characteristics. However, when interacting network composition and network structure, they find a significant joint effect. This implies that the advantages and disadvantages arising from a student's social relations are context dependent and, moreover, suggests that in order to diagnose the impact of building stronger community in schools, it is necessary to consider the network structure of students' relationships when examining the influence of peers. Specifically, students with highly dense ego networks of low-performing peers are associated with the largest negative effect on student achievement, and highly dense ego networks of high-performing peers are associated with the largest positive effect on achievement. This finding is important for a number of reasons, including the fact that school reform efforts that focus on "connectedness" (network location) without attending to network composition (embedded resources) are unlikely to achieve the desired result. For example, to the extent that the student population that is the target of a reform contains a large population of low achievers, this finding leads to the counterintuitive conclusion that it may not be beneficial to encourage a student social environment in which "everyone knows everyone else." Here, ego networks with high density are only advantageous is they are composed of high-achieving peers.

Social Closure and the Catholic School Effect on Learning

Morgan and Todd (2008) provide a second empirical example that demonstrates how the concept of social capital has been conceptualized, measured, and employed to explain students' achievement. Rather than focus on students' ego networks in the context of one school's transition through a small-school reform effort as in Maroulis and Gomez example, Morgan and Todd revisit Coleman's network closure argument in the context of the school sector debate (Catholic vs. non–Catholic schools) that first motivated Coleman's original theorizing on social capital. Coleman hypothesized that the advantage of Catholic schools was attributable to their ability to generate higher levels of intergenerational closure among students' parents—that is, students do better when their parents know the parents of their friends, thus creating a dense, redundant network structure. Despite numerous investigations on the effects of intergenerational closure on students' outcomes, no consensus has emerged. Some support for the closure hypothesis is provided by Bankston and Zhou (2002) and McNulty and Bellair (2003), whereas others have been critical of the closure hypothesis (see, e.g., Horvat, Weininger, & Lareau, 2003; John, 2005; Sandefur, Meier, & Campbell, 2006).

Morgan and Todd (2008) revisit this controversy and analyze more recent data from the 2002 and 2004 waves of the Education Longitudinal Study (ELS). The question motivating their analysis is: What is the relationship between parental social closure and students' math achievement and how does this relationship vary between students in Catholic and public schools? The characteristics of students' and parents' social networks are derived from the base-year sophomore survey. On the student questionnaire, the name generator asked each respondent to list up to three friends in school. Then, for each friend listed, they were asked questions about each nominated friend (name interpreter), including friends' race, importance they attached to grades, and whether their parents knew each listed friends' parents. The primary explanatory variable, *parents know parents*, is a student's mean response to whether their parents knew their nominated friends' parents (up to three friends could be nominated). This partly reflects Lin's social capital asset of network location but indicates little about a student's location in a social structure, as the respondent (ego) provides information about his or her friends (alters), with no alter-to-alter data collected (as would be the case if these ego-level data were sampled as part of a complete network study). The only network structure variable they include is the *number of friends nominated,* as well sex and grade level of these friends. The first of these is a simple count, equal to the size of each ego's network. Interestingly, they employ this variable at two analytical levels: the student level and school level, with the latter being equal to the mean scores on these variables within schools. This decision reflects the idea that social capital may be conceptualized as both an individual- and group-level phenomenon.

The ELS employed a stratified random sample design in which schools with a 10th grade were sampled first within strata; then 10th-grade students within those schools were sampled. This generated a nationally representative sample of 10th-grade students in 2002. Therefore, because students are nested within schools, a multilevel strategy is needed to account for this dependency. The results from these multilevel models produce two interesting results. First, across Catholic schools, parental closure has a substantial association with math achievement in the 10th and 12th grades and with the gains in math achievement between the 10th and 12th grades. Second, though this support within the Catholic-school sector is qualified as additional covariates that weaken the relationship, Morgan and Todd's results suggest a different set of relationships across public schools. Here, associations between parental closure and math achievement are easily accounted for in the 10th-grade models by student network structure and differences in family background without resort to any of the variables that may be argued to be genuine confounds. Taken together, Morgan and Todd's findings suggest that parental closure in its form observed in the ELS data is mostly ineffective in the residential communities that surround public schools but may be effective in the functional communities that surround Catholic schools. Considered in light of Figure 10.1, these results suggest that Tim's social structure would be beneficial in a Catholic school but largely ineffective if he attended a public school. One speculative reason for this difference is that Catholic schools have close ties to a major norm-reinforcing institution (the Church) that has no clear counterpart in the public sector.

Both the Morgan and Todd (2008) and Maroulis and Gomez (2008) studies are exemplary for a number of reasons, including an implicit argument that causation is

Table 10.3 Comparison Between Two Empirical Examples.

	Maroulis & Gomez (2008)	Morgan & Todd (2008)
Network location	Ego-level density	Ego-level network size (number of friends listed)
Embedded resources	Composition (mean) of named alters' grade point averages	Range of resources, including whether the ego's parent knows each alter's parent
Source of network data	Ego-level data derived from near-complete network data of entire class	Egos randomly sampled
Social capital as an individual or group property	Individual	Individual and group (student and school levels)
Analytic strategy	Network measures and covariates used in OLS regression models	Multilevel models that account for the nesting of students in schools with relevant control variables

located in the social structure of the school and its students; an appreciation for the variation in group structure with a recognition that cohesion varies from group to group; and an accounting for how relations between any two students are embedded in and shaped by larger patterns in the schools' social structure. These favorable characteristics aside, both studies confront a number of challenges that reflect subtle—and not-so-subtle—differences in the conceptualization, measurement, and modeling of social capital. Five of these differences are noteworthy: (1) how network location has been measured; (2) social capital conceptualized as a group versus individual attribute; (3) measurement that focuses on network location versus embedded resources; (4) the source of ego-level network data; and (5) an analytic strategy that accounts for the dependencies among observations. Table 10.3 highlights these differences.

SUMMARY

This chapter discussed the concept of social capital and how it has evolved and been applied to an array of educational phenomena. Social capital has a rich tradition in the general literature on social networks. This tradition involves a number of ways social capital has been conceptualized, defined, and measured. In the last 10 years, a consensus has emerged around a definition that emphasizes both network location and embedded assets. This definition has recently been folded into a broader network theory referred to as the network flow model, a promising model that unites several strands of network theorizing. This chapter then discussed the ways in which network location and embedded resources have been measured in empirical examples and the different ways in which sampling strategies have been used to collected data on these measures. Finally, this chapter presented two empirical examples that reflect the various ways in which social capital has been used as a predictor of students' outcomes (GPA and math achievement, respectively).

CHAPTER FOLLOW-UP

1. Find an empirical, peer-reviewed article that examines social capital. Describe how the concept has been defined and measured.

2. Describe a personal situation in which serving as a broker led to some instrumental return for you. Do the same for a situation in which being part of a network with high closure led to some expressive return.

3. You are a school superintendent who is charged with implementing a district-wide reform effort that is unpopular among a small set of vocal, veteran teachers, with the rest of the faculty expressing no opinion on it whatsoever. How would you use your knowledge of social capital in order to design a program that promotes buy-in of this reform effort?

CRITICAL QUESTIONS TO ASK ABOUT STUDIES THAT INVESTIGATE SOCIAL CAPITAL

1. How has social capital been defined?

2. How has it been measured? Does this measure include information on network location and/or embedded resources?

3. Is social capital conceptualized and measured as an individual or collective good?

4. Is social capital treated as an independent or dependent variable? If the former, is it used to predict an expressive or instrumental return?

5. Does the measurement of social capital emphasize structural holes or network closure?

ESSENTIAL READINGS

Lin, N. (2001). Building a network theory of social capital. In N. Lin, K. Cook, & R. S. Burt (Eds.), *Social capital: Theory and research* (pp. 3–30). New York: Walter de Gruyter.

Maroulis, S., & Gomez, L. M. (2008). Does "connectedness" matter? Evidence from a social network analysis within a small-school reform. *Teachers College Record, 110*(9), 1901–1929.

Morgan, S. L., & Todd, J. J. (2008). Intergenerational closure and academic achievement in high school: A new evaluation of Coleman's conjecture. *Sociology of Education, 82*, 267–286.

11

Diffusion

OBJECTIVES

The primary objective of this chapter is to look more closely at a second rich area in which social network analysis has been used to describe and explain an array of different processes and outcomes of interest to educational researchers. In this chapter, you will learn about diffusion theory and the major models used to understand how diffusion through networks occurs. Unlike the previous chapter, which for the purposes of presentation focused on social capital and students' achievement, this chapter focuses on the applicability of diffusion theory to varied education-related phenomena—specifically, how it can been used to explain how influence spreads within and between networks of actors. First, you will learn about diffusion theory, its five basic characteristics, and how it is intertwined with social network analysis. After reviewing a basic homogenous mixing model, we will then turn to four different network-based diffusion models (integration/opinion leadership, structural models, critical levels, and dynamic) that have been used to illuminate processes through which resources flow from one part of the network to another. You will then evaluate how these models have been employed in two empirical examples that focus on (1) dating and drinking in adolescents' peer networks within schools and (2) charter school policy across the United States. Similar to the previous chapter, these two examples will bring together much of what was covered in Part II, emphasizing how network data were collected, measured, and modeled. At the end of this chapter, you will understand the importance of diffusion theory and how it uses social network analysis as a major causal mechanism.

WHY DO CERTAIN TEACHERS USE TECHNOLOGY AND OTHERS DON'T?

One of the most troublesome problems within schools is how to encourage teachers to think and act differently when it comes to the use of computers: Why do some teachers have a positive view of computers in classrooms and make extensive use of them, whereas others are, at best, ambivalent? Frank, Zhao, Penuel, Ellefson, and Porter (2011) help answer this question by focusing on the interplay of formal professional-development opportunities and social experiences as they affect teachers' implementation of innovations, in this case the number of times a teacher indicated her or his students used computers for the core tasks of teaching. As anyone who has spent some time in schools knows, the implementation of technology, like many reforms, has proven a thorny issue for both reformers and organizational theorists (Elmore, Peterson, & McCarthey 1996; Tyack & Cuban, 1995).

Previous research on the diffusion of computers in schools has generally focused on the effects of four sets of factors on the adoption of computers (Frank et al., 2011). First, hardware and software and technical support affect implementation by making the technology more reliable (Zhao, Pugh, Sheldon, & Byers 2002). Second, organizational factors, such as scheduling and types of school leadership, can facilitate conditions affecting teachers' use of computers (Cuban, 2001). Third, aspects of professional development can support the implementation of innovations (e.g., Berends, 2000). Technology uses that require teachers to adopt more constructivist methods, which increase the cognitive demands on students, present particularly significant professional-development needs, since they require teachers to adopt both new pedagogies and technology tools (Windschitl & Sahl, 2002). Fourth, and perhaps most frequently cited, characteristics of individual teachers, including the willingness and ability to use technology and pedagogical style, as well as teacher preparation, affect implementation (Smith et al., 2007).

While recognizing the importance of these factors, Frank and colleagues (2011) shift our attention to the complexity of teaching and the knowledge necessary to perform myriad tasks. More specifically, they frame their investigation around what they call general and local knowledge. General knowledge, for example, is the content of a specific math unit that can be conveyed to same-grade teachers across the district, whereas local knowledge might consist of how one individual teacher adapts that content for his or her particular set of students. They contend that teachers' use of technology is shaped by professional development opportunities and social interactions within schools that transform and activate general knowledge into local knowledge. Therefore, this is an issue of how knowledge flows and is transformed between actors (teachers) through different kinds of interactions (formal vs. informal) bounded by an organizational context (school)—a "problem" that is firmly grounded in the diffusion of innovations literature.

Using data from three different sources (survey of all staff, interviews with key informants in focus schools, and observations of professional development) collected from 25 schools in 10 districts at two points during the school year, Frank and colleagues (2011) test three specific hypotheses related to how the effects of different sources of knowledge depend on the location of an innovation in the diffusion trajectory relative to the organizational boundary. Among their findings, they conclude that (1) teachers at low levels of technology implementation (at time 1) who engaged in technology-based professional development that focused on student learning significantly increased their use of computers; (2) teachers at intermediate levels of technology implementation (at time 1) who had opportunities to experiment with technology significantly increased their use of computers—for each day exploring or experimenting with computers, teachers in this group increased about 1.0 units of computer use; and (3) the estimated effect on teachers' computer use of access to knowledge through interactions with others (friends) was statistically significant for teachers at high levels of implementation at time 1.

The importance of this work—aside from developing an exciting theory of how knowledge flows into schools and then diffuses from teacher to teacher within schools (what they refer to as "focus, fiddle, and friends" theory, corresponding with the three findings noted above)—is that it calls attention to how diffusion processes are shaped by individual and organizational characteristics, including teachers' level of implementation, the focus of professional-development activities, and opportunities to experiment, among others. Figure 11.1 illustrates this process. Most importantly, their results confirm that teachers need to have interaction in order to first adopt and then sustain high levels of implementation. The implication is that when implementation of an innovation is concentrated in dense but disconnected pockets, so too will be sustained implementation of the innovation. This unevenness in implementation is a direct result of the social structure through which the teachers interact. This work focuses theoretical and empirical attention on the interpersonal contacts within and across organizational boundaries through which new ideas and practices spread. Because of this focus, diffusion theory is inextricably linked with social network analysis.

DIFFUSION THEORY

Diffusion theory attempts to explain how new ideas and practices—such as teachers' use of computers—spread within and between groups. As this is a fundamental social process, it has deep roots in a number of social science disciplines, including anthropology, sociology, and epidemiology, among others (see Rogers, 1962/2003, for a review). Its core premise is that one's social network influences whether and when an individual acquires a trait. These traits can be attitudes such as whether one likes the new principal or behaviors such as whether one uses technology as part of his or her instruction.

Figure 11.1 Transformation of Knowledge Through Diffusion Processes (Frank et al., 2011). They infer that the more a teacher at the lowest initial levels of implementing an innovation is exposed to professional development focused on student learning, the more she increases her level of implementation (focus); the more a teacher at an intermediate initial level of implementation has opportunities to experiment and explore, the more she sustains her level of implementation (fiddle); and the more a teacher at a high initial level of implementation accesses the knowledge of others, the more she increases her level of implementation (friends).

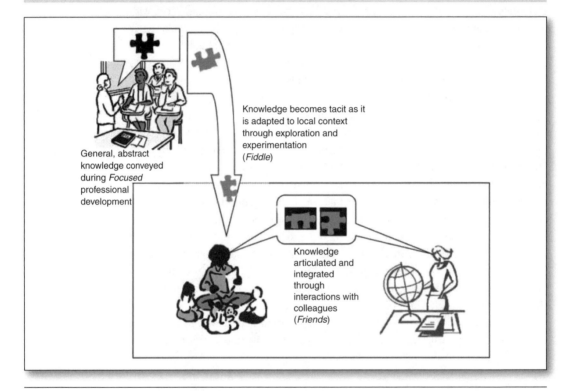

Source: Frank, K. A., Zhao, Y., Penuel, W. R., Ellefson, N., & Porter, S. (2011). Focus, fiddle, and friends: Experiences that transform knowledge for the implementation of innovations. *Sociology of Education, 84*(2), 137–156.

Regardless of the outcome of interest, the causal mechanisms are related to micro-level relations between an ego and alters and the macro-level social structure in which these dyadic relations are embedded.

This seems simple enough in theory, but it wasn't until Ryan and Gross's (1943) classic study on the adoption of hybrid seed corn that the foundation for the diffusion paradigm was laid. Ryan and Gross were interested in why some farmers purchased hybrid corn immediately once it became available while others waited to purchase it until it was almost gone. Similarly, Coleman, Katz, and Menzel (1966) wanted to know why some doctors prescribed tetracycline quickly after it became available, while others waited until a majority of doctors prescribed it before they were willing to do so. The first of these two classic studies is especially noteworthy, as it demonstrated the importance of social factors rather than economic ones as critical influences on adoption (Valente & Rogers, 1995). Studies such as these proliferated in the 1960s across an array of empirical contexts. While diffusion research peaked at this time, it has recently been reinvigorated by the use of sophisticated network models and data-collection technologies. Like the example provided by Frank and colleagues (2011), these more recent developments in diffusion research explicitly recognize that diffusion is a social process, with a new idea or practice being spread through interpersonal contact networks.

Basic Diffusion Model

These early breakthroughs in the 1950s and early 1960s led to the development of a basic diffusion model, which still exerts influence on current diffusion studies. The elements of this diffusion model were popularized by Rogers (1962/2003), whose classic work was responsible for making the case that diffusion is a social process by which an innovation is communicated through certain channels over time among the members of a social system. Synthesizing empirical results from hundreds of studies, Rogers created a theoretical model of diffusion that emphasized that: (1) the perceived characteristics of the innovation affect its rate of adoption; (2) diffusion occurs over time so that the adoption rate often generates a cumulate adoption S-shaped pattern, with individuals being categorized as early or late adopters; (3) individuals move across stages—innovators, early adopters, early majority, late majority, and laggards—during the adoption process; (4) individuals can modify the innovation and even discontinue its use; and (5) mathematical models can be developed to measure the character and rate of diffusion curves (Valente, 1993). These five elements are listed in Table 11.1 and are clearly evident in the example provided by Frank and colleagues (2011).

These five elements are straightforward, but diffusion generally takes time—an often-overlooked aspect of diffusion. For example, facsimile technology was available in 1843 and the first wire photo service in 1925, but fax machines remained a niche product until their use exploded in the 1980s. Similarly, in the Ryan and Gross (1943) study, there were 14 years between the earliest and latest adopters, even though the use of hybrid corn was clearly advantageous early on. This pattern is also evident in the Frank and colleagues (2011) study, as those teachers with the lowest level of initial implementation increased their computer usage between time 1 and time 2 about 4.5 uses. Though statistically significant, this is only about 7% of one standard deviation unit, and this increase was observed over approximately 1 calendar year (for most schools in the

Table 11.1 Five Elements of Diffusion Theory (Rogers, 1962/2003).

1. The perceived characteristics of the innovation affect its rate of adoption.

2. Diffusion occurs over time so that the adoption rate often generates a cumulate adoption S-shaped pattern, with individuals being categorized as early or late adopters.

3. Individuals move across stages—innovators, early adopters, early majority, late majority, and laggards—during the adoption process.

4. Individuals can modify the innovation and even discontinue its use.

5. Mathematical models can de developed to measure the character and rate of diffusion curves.

sample). This slowness with which an innovation diffuses can be attributed, in part, to the social network structure that links individuals. However, there are other factors that influence the speed at which something diffuses, including the prevalence of social media, which has certainly accelerated the spread of information and the adoption of new technologies and products. For example, Twitter spread from a smattering of users to more than 500 million in 2012 in the span of 6 years (Bercovici, 2012).

A second point to consider is that people pass through stages in the adoption process, the third element in Rogers' diffusion model. In order to standardize the usage of adopter categories in diffusion research, Rogers (1962/2003) suggested a total of five categories of adopters. Of course, a teacher doesn't simply attend a professional-development workshop on computer usage in the classroom and integrate it into his or her everyday practice. Rather, the teacher is likely to pass through stages—knowledge, persuasion, decision, implementation, and confirmation (Table 11.2). And, as one passes through these stages, one interacts with others who shape that progression. What Frank and colleagues (2011) encourage us to consider is how the match between the characteristics of the adoptee (in this instance, the teacher and his or her initial use of technology implementation), the types of interactions the person has with others in different settings (focused, fiddle, and friends), and how this (mis)match influences the person's progression through the stages of adoption. Diffusion is studied in many different disciplines (e.g., epidemiology, sociology, etc.) and empirical settings, but the focus for the rest of the chapter emphasizes how social networks influence adoption and diffusion, with a special nod to discussing these models as they relate to educational phenomena. More specifically, much of the remainder of this chapter chronicles the development of specific network-based diffusion models. The mathematical underpinnings of these models can get complex, so every effort is made to focus on a conceptual understanding and practical application of these models while drawing your attention to the primary sources in which these different models are referenced.

Table 11.2   Rogers' Five Stages of an Individual's Adoption Process (1962/2003). An important point to consider is that passing through these stages takes time and is influenced by the social network that links individuals.

1. Knowledge
2. Persuasion
3. Decision
4. Implementation
5. Confirmation

HOMOGENOUS MIXING

A basic mathematical model of diffusion assumes homogenous mixing—that is, where transmission between each pair of prior and potential adopters is equally likely. The shortcomings of this model will be made evident, but it is a useful starting point prior to considering more elaborate network-based diffusion models. Consider Figure 11.1, adapted from Valente (2010, Chapter 10), which demonstrates homogenous mixing with a simple spreadsheet example. This figure and the data on which it is based assume a hypothetical population of 100 school district superintendents at time 1 (year 1, for example) and 99 superintendents who choose not to adopt a scripted curriculum (column 3, nonadopters). The first superintendent to adopt the scripted curriculum may have done so because he or she was swayed by a fancy marketing campaign or simply more willing to try something new. This initial adopter has random interactions with the 99 superintendents who have yet to adopt the curriculum and persuades them to adopt at a rate of 1%. The product of $1 \times 99 \times .01$ yields less than one new adopter (0.99) at the end of year 1. At the start of year 2, there are about 2 new adopters $(1 + 0.99)$ interacting randomly with the 98 superintendents who have yet to adopt the curriculum, and they persuade them to adopt at a rate of 1%, leading to 1.95 new adopters for a total of 3.94 total adopters.

Figure 11.1 illustrates the incidence and prevalence graphs for this hypothetical scenario among 100 school district superintendents. Two points on the classic S-shaped diffusion curve are notable. First, the initial growth in adopting the curriculum occurs gradually and then accelerates around year 5, the middle of the diffusion process. Second, growth decelerates as the number of nonadopters decreases. This basic model assumes that (1) no superintendent quits using the curriculum and (2) the conversion rate of 1% stays consistent throughout the diffusion process (you can change this conversation rate to generate different curves). The model also serves as a useful starting point for considering how something diffuses through a population.

But this model of homogenous mixing presents diffusion as too simple a process (Valente, 2010, Chapter 10). Three points about this model's simplicity are especially salient. First, the model is predicated on the assumption that people randomly interact. For example, one superintendent does not exchange information about a curriculum in a random manner; rather, he or she likely exchanges with those who are similar (homophily) or those with whom they have had a past exchange (reciprocity). Second, conversion rates are not consistent across all people. Some superintendents may be more hesitant to adopt a new scripted curriculum, while others are less so. Finally, there are other externalities (Watts, 2003) that shape a person's decision to adopt something. Another charismatic superintendent may more easily sway one superintendent, whereas the publisher's aggressive marketing tactics may have turned another off.

Because of the shortcomings associated with the homogenous mixing model, social scientists across disciplines have developed other classes of models that have, to varying degrees, accounted for the roles of networks and social structure in the diffusion processes—those social factors that influence one's decision to adopt something new. Four of these models will be covered: integration/opinion leadership, structural, critical levels, and dynamic. All four can be considered approaches that address the weaknesses inherent in the homogenous mixing model.

Figure 11.2 Example of Homogenous Mixing Generated from Hypothetical Data of 100 School District Superintendents. At time 1 there were 99 superintendents (column 4) who chose not to adopt a scripted curriculum and 1 who has chosen to adopt (column 2). At time 10, nearly all of them have adopted the curriculum. Adapted from Valente (2010, p. 176).

Time	Adopters	Adoption Rate	Nonadopters	New Adopters
1	1.00	0.01	99.00	0.99
2	1.99	0.01	98.01	1.95
3	3.94	0.01	96.06	3.79
4	7.73	0.01	92.27	7.13
5	14.85	0.01	85.15	12.65
6	27.50	0.01	72.50	19.94
7	47.44	0.01	52.56	24.93
8	72.37	0.01	27.63	19.99
9	92.37	0.01	7.63	7.05
10	99.42	0.01	0.58	0.58

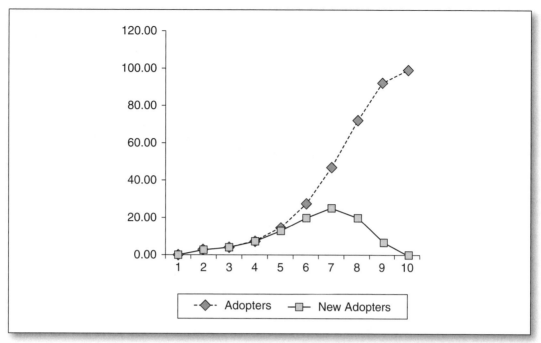

Source: Valente, T. W. (2010). *Social networks and health: Models, methods, and applications.* New York: Oxford University Press.

NETWORK-BASED DIFFUSION MODELS

There are four main classes of diffusion models (Valente, 2010, Chapter 10). All four explicitly explain diffusion but reflect differences in their mathematical rigor and complexity. The commonality across these four models is that they directly account for the role of social networks in the diffusion process.

Integration/Opinion Leadership

Are those who are "better" integrated into a community more likely to adopt new behaviors earlier than others? Early diffusion studies, such as Coleman, Katz, and Menzel's (1966) study of network influences on the adoption of a new drug, emphasized how the number of connections one had influenced diffusion, whereas other early studies (e.g., Rogers & Kincaid, 1981) focused not on the number of connections one had but rather on their level of integration. One idea emerging from this early work was (1) that opinion leaders were early but not the earliest adopters and (2) they significantly influenced the speed at which an idea or practice diffused through a community. The core idea in this first network-based model of diffusion is that well-connected actors, however defined and measured, are key levers in the diffusion process (Valente, 2010, Chapter 10).

Opinion leaders are not always the earliest adopters because they cannot deviate too far from what is acceptable within their community, as they need to represent and uphold their community's norms. Therefore, opinion leaders can lead, but not too far ahead. Good opinion leaders are those who are savvy scanners of their environments, connected to many others with an ability to translate an innovation for the rest of their community only after the innovation has been adopted by someone on the community's margins. Translating is a valued skill that reinforces their leadership status. Once opinion leaders embrace an innovation, diffusion can accelerate due to their connections with many others. These leaders, therefore, reflect a shift from adoption on the network's fringes to its center and accelerate the adoption process. Early research on opinion leaders (Feick & Price, 1987), who Gladwell (2000) popularly referred to as "mavens," consistently demonstrated an overlap of early adoption and opinion leadership (Baumgarten, 1975; Feldman & Armstrong, 1975; Summers, 1970).

These early insights, as well as more recent ones (e.g., Cross & Parker, 2004), have informed a number of network interventions—behavior-change programs that use social network data to identify specific people or groups to deliver/receive the behavior change program (Valente & Pumpuang, 2007). The idea behind interventions that make use of opinion leaders and network data is intuitively appealing: By definition, opinion leaders should have a strong influence on a program's success. Opinion leaders can be identified a number of different ways (three ways are clearly social network methods: snowball, sample sociometric, and sociometric), but once identified, they are used as change agents to advance the intervention's purposes and goals. For example, Story, Lytle, Birnbaum, and Perry (2002) recruited and trained 272 peer leaders from a sample of 1,000 middle school students from schools in Minneapolis/St. Paul, Minnesota, in a school-based nutrition education intervention. After sociometric methods determined the peer leaders, extensive training sessions with these leaders were conducted. Peer leaders then assisted teachers in activities related to a nutrition intervention. Results from peer leader and classroom feedback, direct classroom observation, and teacher ratings and interviews reveal that this peer-led intervention successfully promoted healthy eating among adolescents. Other examples of programs from diverse contexts that have used opinion leaders include community-based promotion of mammography screening (Earp et al., 2002), tobacco prevention in schools (Perry et al., 2003), physician practices (Lomas et al., 1991), HIV/STD risk reduction (Sikkema et al., 2000), and many others (e.g., Gates & Kennedy, 1989). The general conclusion from these studies is that network intervention programs that use peer opinion leaders have been shown to be more effective than those that do not.

Though the opinion leader model is both intuitive and logistically simple, its potential use in a network-based intervention is hampered by three factors (Valente, 2010, Chapter 10). First, there are issues surrounding the amount of training that an opinion leader needs in order to effectively carry out the program's components. One oft-cited suggestion is that leadership training should constitute about 10 to 15% of the total time of the behavior-change program, though more research is needed to inform this rule of thumb. Second, there is little consensus regarding how leaders should contact others. Should the intervention program rely on spontaneous interaction or intentionally create venues through which interaction can be induced? Finally, leaders may be limited in their ability to persuade others, or the leaders themselves may resist the innovation or not completely embrace the behavior being promoted by the program. Despite these implementation issues, network interventions based on the opinion-leader model are a promising area in which diffusion theory is being applied in exciting ways.

Structural Models

While being a prominent or integrated member of a community (however defined and measured) shapes one's adoption of something new, there are other network positions that affect diffusion at a more macro level. Connecting to the material in the previous chapter on social capital, structural models emphasize the position of those occupying structural holes, which enables them to influence how resources flow to disparate parts of the network. This idea is predicated on the tendency for networks to display homophily—people associate with similar others—and triads' tendency toward social closure. Granovetter's (1973) key insight was that because of these tendencies, only some will have networks that are open and able to connect to different groups. As noted when reviewing Burt's ideas on structural holes and constraint, the friends of your friends, for example, typically know the same people you know and have access to the same resources. Therefore, resources received from your close personal networks tend to be redundant. New resources, on the other hand, come from weak ties, those few people you see on occasion or who are connected weakly through distant alters. Burt was able to take these insights further by developing operational measures of structural holes and constraint, mainly employed in the social capital tradition. He also articulated the idea that weak ties were those that were more likely to span a network's structural holes. According to this model, the key lever in the diffusion process is that structural position in which a weak tie connects two otherwise disconnected part of the network.

In addition to Granovetter's (1973) and Burt's (1992) insights on the structural basis of diffusion, Watts and Strogatz (1998) in their analysis of the small-world phenomenon introduced a measure that also captured a network's "clumpiness"—those dense pockets of interconnectivity that are separated by what Valente (2010) refers to as the "white" space in a sociogram. Watts and Strogatz introduced what they called a clustering coefficient (CC), which indicates whether an actor's alters are tied to one another. The CC is defined as:

$$CC = \frac{2T_i}{k_i(k_1 - 1)} \qquad \text{[Equation 11.1]}$$

where T_i equals the number of connections between the direct ties of each actor, and $k_i(k_i - 1)$ is the maximum number of potential connections between each actor's direct ties. Values closer to 1 indicate that an actor's alters are likely to be tied to one another, whereas a value closer to 0 indicates that a given actor's alters are unlikely to be tied. This value can be calculated for each ego in a network and averaged across all egos to provide the overall clustering in the network. But what does clustering have to do with diffusion processes?

As it turns out, quite a lot. Clustering provides a measure of a network's structure that is conceptually and empirically distinct from network size, density, and centralization. Take as a starting point a random network, which will look somewhat uniform (e.g., a network of 100 superintendents with each having five ties to five random others). A clustered network, on the other hand, will have sections of dense interconnectivity, with some ties spanning these visually distinct "clumps." Networks that are clustered are those that give rise to the small-world phenomenon: It takes only a couple of "steps" to reach what may seem like a distant part of the network. Clustering increases the likelihood that two actors who meet will share a mutual friend. For example, if the hypothetical network of 100 superintendents (Figure 11.2) had a high clustering coefficient, it is likely that the adoption of the scripted curriculum would spread more quickly than what the homogenous model and it assumption of randomness predicts. So, in addition to Burt's (1992) constraint measure, the CC developed by Watts and Strogatz (1998) also provides structural measure that is used to explain diffusion processes.

Critical Levels

A third network-based diffusion model focuses on the micro (individual) or macro (system or community) levels and its inflection points—that is, the point at which the adoption curve rapidly accelerates or decelerates (Valente, 2010, Chapter 10). Commonly referred to as "tipping points" (Gladwell, 2000; Schelling, 1978), identifying these critical values at either analytic level provides an understanding for how diffusion occurs. A tipping point can be thought of as the point at which a certain level of behavior has been reached in which the momentum that kept it going is too hard to reverse. Back to the hypothetical population of 100 superintendents, once a macro-level tipping point has been reached, it is likely that the adoption of the scripted curriculum will rapidly accelerate across the remaining nonadopters. Once a critical mass has been reached, the costs of not adopting become too large for one to continue to hold out.

A number of researchers have employed models of diffusion that emphasize both the micro and macro levels in varied educational phenomena. For example, using a comprehensive content analysis, Powell, Bernhard, and Graf (2012) emphasize the importance of macro-level critical values in their study on the diffusion of a newer European model of higher education that combines the ideals and goals of vocational education training and higher education. Suárez, Ramirez, and Koo (2009), on the other hand, emphasize the micro level in their analysis of the likelihood of a country adopting a UNESCO school. This work emphasizes individual (micro-level) tipping points—referred to as thresholds—that help identify different types of adopters (low- versus high-threshold ones) who might have different motivations to adopt. Specifically, they find that a country's likelihood of joining the UNESCO Associated Schools Project is increased by the joining behavior of other countries, by the worldwide increase in international organizations, and by having stronger links to the world environment. Identifying the factors that shape adoption behavior at the micro and macro levels provides insight into how diffusion occurs. While the elements of this model have reached popular consciousness, its popularity has given way to a fourth network-based diffusion model that accounts for what happens at the micro level at each point in time throughout the entire (macro) diffusion process.

Dynamic Models

The fourth class of network-based diffusion models is the most elaborate in that it models what happens at the individual level throughout the diffusion process. These also happen to be the most mathematically and statistically complex. This complexity is partly attributable to the fact that these models treat time explicitly. Two of these models are noteworthy. First is what is considered to be the basic building block for much diffusion research: network exposure (Burt, 1987; Marsden & Freidkin, 1993). The equation for network exposure, also referred to as the nonrandom mixing model is:

$$E_i = \frac{\Sigma W_{ij} y_j}{\Sigma w_i} \qquad \text{[Equation 11.2]}$$

where W is the social network weight matrix and y is a vector of adoptions (see Valente, 2010, Chapter 10). For example, for an ego connected to three alters, E_i is the proportion of those alters who have adopted a behavior. To calculate E_i, the network, W, is multiplied by y_j, which is a vector of behavior scores, typically an indicator for whether one adopted the behavior.

Consider this example using one ego from our hypothetical complete network of 100 superintendents. If y_j represents whether one has adopted the scripted curriculum, the numerator is a calculation of the number of ego's alters who have also adopted it. To adjust for the number of alters named, we divide the numerator by the number of alters to get a percentage. Network exposure, then, is simply the proportion of one's alters who have adopted the curriculum. Figure 11.3 shows three different levels of network exposure for one superintendent with four direct alters. This figure shows how E_i is simply the proportion of an ego's personal network that has adopted the curriculum. The ego network on the (top) left of the Figure 11.3 shows a personal network exposure value of 25%, where the one on the (bottom) left shows a value of 100%, indicating that all four of that ego's direct alters have adopted the curriculum.

It should be noted that W can represent something other than the number of an ego's direct alters (Valente, 2005). It can also represent different kinds of network properties or weights, including other social influence processes. For example, W can be transformed to

Figure 11.3 Illustration of Three Levels of Network Exposure from Four Direct Alters. This figure shows how E_i is simply the proportion of an ego's personal network that has adopted the curriculum. The ego network on the (top) left of the Figure 11.3 shows a personal network exposure value of 25%, where the one on the (bottom) left shows a value of 100%, indicating that all four of that ego's direct alters have adopted the curriculum. Adapted from Valente (2010, p. 186).

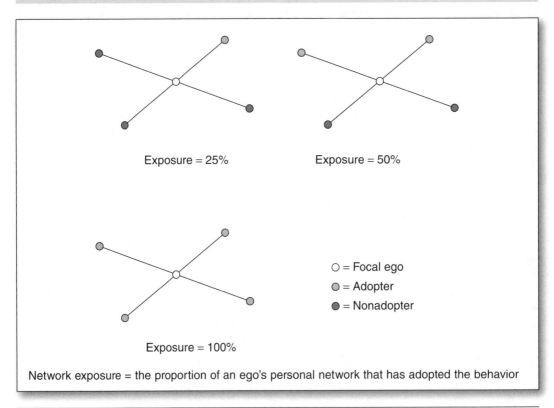

Exposure = 25%   Exposure = 50%

Exposure = 100%

○ = Focal ego
◑ = Adopter
● = Nonadopter

Network exposure = the proportion of an ego's personal network that has adopted the behavior

Source: Valente, T. W. (2010). Social networks and health: Models, methods, and applications. New York: Oxford University Press.

represent the degree of structural equivalence (similarity in network position) among actors in a network. When used in this manner, E_i captures social influence conveyed through comparison to equivalent others by social comparison or competition (Burt, 1987). Properties such as centrality can also be used as a weight in order to reflect social influence by those identified as opinion leaders. Along these same lines, W can be weighted based on social distance: Different weights can be assigned to direct and indirect ties. These different weighting schemes can get complex and should be considered only in light of the different social-influence processes that you are interested in modeling and comparing.

The second of two prominent dynamic network-based diffusion models is the event-history model, which can incorporate the network exposure measure as an additional covariate (Valente, 2005). This model calculates an ego's adoption status at each time period in which there is a recoded observation. There are two slightly different types of event-history models. The first type is discrete time in which the outcome of interest at a given time point is binary (whether one adopts the curriculum; 1= yes, 0 = no), and the second is continuous time, in which the outcome is time to an event (e.g., number of days to adoption). It should be evident that in both types, there is an explicit time dimension. These outcomes can be influenced by both time-varying and time-constant factors. Event-history models generally require that the data be reshaped from simple observations (each person is its own row in a data file) to a person-time format, so that each row in the data file represents an individual at each time period up to and including that person's time of adoption (this is because the ego is the level of analysis). For example, a hypothetical study of 100 superintendents with an average adoption time of 5 years translates into 500 person-time observations (standard software packages assist with the transformation of these data, converting each person-time observation into its own row). Each person-time case (row) has a variable for network exposure at that time period, and both time-varying and time-constant variables can also be included in each case, as well as a binary indicator for whether one adopted.

Valente's (2005) formula for the event history model is:

$$\log \frac{\mathrm{pr}(y_t=1)}{1-\mathrm{pr}(y_t=1)} = \alpha + \Sigma B_j X_j + \Sigma B_{kt} X_{kt} + \Sigma B_{(k+1)} w y_t \quad \text{[Equation 11.3]}$$

where y is a binary indicator of whether one has adopted the behavior, α is the intercept, β_j are parameter estimates for vectors of J socio-demographic characteristics (X_j), β_{kt} are parameter estimates for the matrix of time-varying socio-demographic characteristics (X_{kt}), w represents the social network weight matrix, and t a time indicator. Admittedly, this equation appears intimidating. But standard statistical packages make it fairly simple to carry out this calculation, which tests the probability (the left side of Equation 11.3) of adopting a behavior while accounting for time-constant and time-varying covariates that have been measured at more than one point in time, including social network characteristics, w, including, for example, a measure of personal network exposure. Because observations are nested within persons over time, a multilevel modeling strategy is needed to account for the nonindependence of observations. After reformatting the data into person-time format, maximum likelihood estimation can be used to test the relationship between the independent variables and the binary dependent variable (whether one adopts; 1= yes, 0 = no). While uses of this model have confirmed popular intuition that there is an association between adoption behavior and network exposure, there remain concerns about whether the effect of network exposure is indeed causal. The biggest barriers to demonstrating this effect have been challenges relating to data collection (individual and relational data need to be collected over time, ideally over at least three time points) and statistical methodology (Valente, 2005).

To address these issues, agent-based models (ABMs, discussed earlier in Part III) have been used to model network effects on adoption behavior. This relatively new technique investigates theoretical issues via computer simulation, thereby reducing concerns about data collection. ABMs typically begin with a hypothetical community that consists of actors and a set of rules that dictate actor behavior in the model. You then modify these rules and then the computer simulation runs though the model's various configurations to understand how the macro-level system behaves as these hypothetical conditions change. In addition to dampening concerns about data collection, ABMs are useful in studying the dynamics of diffusion because they allow you to articulate the rules, variables, and models that are of theoretical interest. Of course, the downside to using ABMs to study diffusion dynamics is that their results are only as good as the assumptions that guide the model. If these assumptions do not match real-world situations, then its results are pretty much useless. Despite this concern, ABMs represent an exciting area in which diffusion dynamics can be studied without the cost and time associated with data collection.

The four network-based diffusion models all account for the role of networks and social structure in diffusion processes. The empirical examples presented in the following section demonstrate how two of these models have been applied to two distinct education-related empirical settings. However, while the models implicit in these examples are different, both are concerned with how a new idea or practice spreads within and between groups of actors.

EMPIRICAL EXAMPLES

Dating and Drinking in Adolescent Peer Networks

This first of two empirical examples provides a clear example of the structural model of diffusion. Recall that this model emphasizes how the structural pattern of relations shapes how a resource flows from one part of the network to another. Rather than focus on an actor's (micro) or the complete network's (macro) clustering, Kreager and Haynie (2011) focus on the role of weak ties, those ties that serve as network bridges that promote the spread of a behavior across networks. They examine the influence of these ties in the context of the diffusion of drinking behavior in school-based friendship networks. By focusing on these ties, they sharpen their empirical attention on the social structural pattern of relations in which an adolescent forms friendships, meets romantic partners, and is introduced to substance use (in this case, drinking). Social network analysis provides one of the most promising avenues for understanding how substance abuse diffuses across adolescent networks (Valente, Gallaher, & Mouttapa, 2004). To advance this understanding, they ask two questions: (1) Do romantic partners serve as bridges to new friendship groups? and (2) Do these bridges influence an adolescent's alcohol use? The first question addresses whether a certain type of social structure is present, while the second addresses whether that social structural trait serves as a conduit through which a behavior (drinking) diffuses from one adolescent to another.

To address these questions, they use two waves of data from the National Longitudinal Study of Adolescent Health (Harris et al., 2009). Their data exist at three analytical levels: individual, individual-partner (dyad), and school level. The final sample consists of 449 couples (133 reciprocated) and 898 respondents embedded in 94 secondary schools. Of special interest are the data at the individual-partner level (449 couples); these are the relational data on which several measures of alcohol consumption are calculated. The primary independent variables measure partners', friends', friends-of-partners', and self-reported prior alcohol consumption (the latter is obviously an individual-level measure). All of these variables are based on an item of problem drinking asked in the in-school survey: "During the past 12 months, how often did you get drunk?" Responses are on a seven-point Likert scale ranging from 0, never, to 6, nearly every day. To calculate friends' and friends-of-partners' drinking variables, they averaged peer-reported responses across all friends in respondents' or partners' send-or-receive (i.e., all reciprocated and unreciprocated ties) friendship networks. In addition to these individual-partner covariates, they include a number of others related to the individual or the school. Because of the dependency within dyads, as well the dependencies within schools, they estimate a three-level Actor–Partner Interdependence Model (APIM), which takes the dyad as the unit of analysis and allows for simultaneous estimation of actor and partner effects while adjusting for the nonindependence of dyadic data. The specifics of this model can get quite complex; the important point to bear in mind is that the use of a multilevel modeling strategy such as this addresses the fact that observations within dyads and schools are not independent; therefore, it is important to parse the variance at three distinct analytic levels.

The results of these models find strong support for a structural model of diffusion in which weak ties serve as a liaison—that is, these ties act as conduits for behavioral diffusion between groups of otherwise disconnected peers. Specifically, they draw five conclusions. Among these five, one is particularly salient for this liaison hypothesis. Their findings indicate that friends-of-partner's drinking has a large independent association with an adolescent's individual drinking. These indirect ties to drinking peers through a romantic partner are associated with significantly higher future drinking than is the drinking of more proximal friends or romantic partners. They go on to suggest that this pattern illustrates that romantic partners are critical for changes (positive and negative) in adolescent substance use, because they provide bridges to potentially novel friendship groups and contexts. The empirical example offered by Kreager and Haynie (2011) demonstrates how a network-based structural model of diffusion can be used to explain how a behavior (drinking) spreads through networks with an emphasis on the role of weak ties in fostering peer influence.

Charter School Policy and Diffusion Across States

Rather than operating from a structural model, this second example demonstrates the utility of a dynamic diffusion model, specifically one that employs event history analysis. Renzulli and Roscigno (2005) use this technique to examine how interstate dynamics and intrastate attributes affect the adoption of legislation on and the creation of charter schools within states. In the face of skepticism by many educators and little in the way of evidence to suggest that such schools and arguably the competition they would breed would be beneficial to learning, the United States has witnessed not only a significant wave of legislative adoptions across states during the 1990s and 2000s but also a proliferation of charter schools themselves. Figure 11.4 shows the pattern of legislative adoption throughout the 1990s. The imagery conveyed in Figure 11.4 motivates two questions: (1) What factors have influenced the adoption of this legislation *across* states? and (2) What factors have influenced the creation of charter schools *within* states? These are questions best addressed through a diffusion framework.

Central to understanding the passage and implementation of policy, including that pertaining to charter schools, is attention to the spatial proximity of units (in this case, states), their structural similarity, and thus the likelihood that they will mimic one another. The diffusion framework employed by Renzulli and Roscigno (2005) does so by including a measure for spatial proximity, which was constructed from an adjacency matrix in which they identified each state that shares a border with another. Along with this proximity measure, which taps into diffusion processes, they used indicators pertaining to the internal features of states. Particularly central in this regard are states' politics, teachers' opposition, and racial composition. These measures are used in event-history analysis models that assess probability of adoption of charter school legislation over time (1= yes, 0 = no). The models they employ consist of two levels: interstate and intrastate. The key covariate at the interstate level that detects spatial diffusion is *proximate states with strong laws*, a continuous measure that captures the number of states adjacent to a state that has strong charter school legislation prior to the state-year (recall that event-history models require that the data be transformed in person-time format, which in this case is state-year). This measure was calculated by multiplying the adjacency matrix (two states are adjacent if they share a border) by the number of border states that had adopted strong charter school laws. This is a time-varying characteristic across each state-year observation.

Figure 11.4 States' Adoption of Charter School Legislation Throughout the 1990s (Renzulli & Roscigno, 2005). This figure shows the spread of charter legislation, first starting in Minnesota in 1991 and diffusing to all but 12 states by the end of the decade.

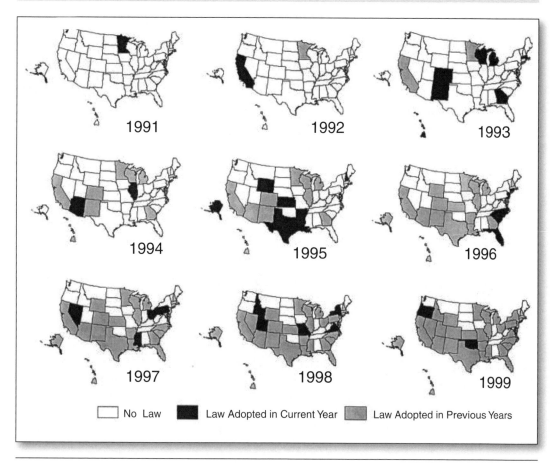

Source: Renzulli, L. A., & Roscigno, V. J. (2005). Charter school policy, implementation, and diffusion across the United States. *Sociology of Education, 78,* 344–366.

Using this measure, along with a number of others in two different event-history models, they draw several conclusions. For one, they conclude that states that are adjacent to other states with strong charter school laws are significantly more likely to adopt charter school legislation themselves (about 98% more likely in the full model). One reason strong legislation in neighboring states affects the adoption of charter school laws may be that strong laws result in more actual charter schools and, thus, greater visibility. Visibility, they argue, increases the infectious nature of the policy across states and time. Diffusion of policy innovation across state lines is clearly supported by the results: States that are adjacent to adopters of strong laws are nearly twice as likely to become adopters themselves, controlling for internal state attributes. Their results go further by showing that internal attributes of states also matter. For example, as the percentage of nonwhite students increases, the likelihood of a state adopting charter school legislation increases 7%. These conclusions reflect the important fact that diffusion is a process best captured through longitudinal data that include measures of individuals' (in this case, states) time-varying (e.g., an indicator for whether the state has a Republican governor) and time-constant (e.g., state urbancity) covariates. Aside from the important theoretical and empirical contributions of this work, it draws our attention to the challenges related to collecting data for dynamic network-based models. Renzulli and Roscigno (2005) relied on multiple sources of publicly available administrative records (e.g., U.S. Census, Common Core of Data) to piece together their longitudinal data. Using these data, then constructing a network-based measure for proximity and employing this and other measures in event-history models, Renzulli and Roscigno (2005) provide an excellent example of how a network-based diffusion model can be used to show how educational policy spreads from one state to another.

LIMITATIONS TO DIFFUSION THEORY

Diffusion theory as applied in varied empirical contexts has shown that it has impressive explanatory power. However, there are two important limitations to diffusion theory to keep in mind as you consider its application to educational research (Valente, 2010, Chapter 10). First, as evident in the empirical examples reviewed in the previous section, the data requirements for adequately testing diffusion processes are tough to meet. Not only must data be collected over time and include information on adoption at each time point, but the data must also include information on the social network contacts for each analytical unit. This, of course, is made even more challenging as most innovations diffuse over long periods of time.

Another limitation is that most diffusion research has emphasized macro-level properties, giving less attention to studies that seek to understand individual decision making. For example, are teachers in dense networks less likely to incorporate computers into their teaching practice? It is sensible to hypothesize that diffusion occurs more rapidly in dense networks, but it is unclear as how this social structural property (density) shapes—and is shaped by—an individual's attitudes and behaviors.

SUMMARY

This chapter reviewed diffusion theory and its applicability to an array of educational phenomena, including teachers' adoption of computers in the classroom, the implementation of school reform practices and the spread of information necessary for school improvement. These varied phenomena can be explained through diffusions of innovation theory. This chapter reviewed the five core elements of diffusion theory (Figure 11.1) and the five categories of adoption initially articulated by Rogers (1962/2003). After noting the shortcomings of a basic homogenous mixing model, the chapter presented four main classes of network-based diffusion models: (1) integration/peer leadership, (2) structural, (3) critical levels, and (4) dynamic.

While these models vary in terms of their complexity and emphases, all four account for the role of social networks in the diffusion process. Two of these four models were then discussed in light of two empirical examples that highlighted how diffusion processes can be conceptualized, modeled, and measured. Both examples reflect the importance of social influences on whether an individual adopts or implements a new behavior or policy. The chapter closed with a brief discussion on the limits and future directions of diffusion theory.

CHAPTER FOLLOW-UP

1. Find an empirical, peer-reviewed article that uses a network-based model of diffusion to explain how an innovation spreads. What data did they use when testing this model? Were these data longitudinal? Were time-varying and time-constant characteristics considered?

2. Suppose you wanted to study how a certain system of teacher evaluation spread from one school district to another over a certain time period. What time-varying and time-constant data would you need in order to test the appropriate network-based model of diffusion? At what analytical levels would these data need to be collected and modeled?

3. How would you design a network-based intervention whose goal was to have teachers adopt a more student-centered instructional approach? How might you nominate opinion leaders to implement key components of this intervention? How could you design a study that examined whether this network-based approach was successful?

CRITICAL QUESTIONS TO ASK ABOUT DIFFUSION MODELS IN EDUCATIONAL RESEARCH

1. In what ways does the study employ a network-based diffusion model? What makes this a network-based diffusion model?

2. Which of the four network-based diffusion models is most evident in the study's design and analysis?

3. Is this study more concerned with micro- or macro-level processes or outcomes?

4. How does the study's diffusion model account for time? Is it explicitly modeled? What is the study's time span? How many data-collection points were there within this span?

5. In addition to social network data, were there any other time-varying or time-constant data collected and included in their models?

ESSENTIAL READING

Frank, K. A., Zhao, Y., Penuel, W. R., Ellefson, N., & Porter, S. (2011). Focus, fiddle, and friends: Experiences that transform knowledge for the implementation of innovations. *Sociology of Education, 84*(2), 137–156.

Kreager, D. A., & Haynie, D. L. (2011). Dangerous liaisons? Dating and drinking diffusion in adolescent peer networks. *American Sociological Review, 76*, 737–763.

Renzulli, L. A., & Roscigno, V. J. (2005). Charter school policy, implementation, and diffusion across the United States. *Sociology of Education, 78*, 344–366.

12

Looking Back, Looking Ahead

OBJECTIVES

This book has introduced the theories, methods, and applications that constitute the interdisciplinary field of social network analysis and its potential uses in educational research. The purpose of this chapter is to succinctly summarize these ideas, reiterate its limitations, and ultimately prod you to start thinking about and doing social network analysis in educational research. After reviewing the main themes across this book's chapters, this final chapter provides you with a concise series of steps that provide a blueprint to conduct your own social network analysis study. The chapter also provides a summary of the different software tools that are available to assist with these studies. These different applications are presented as either general packages that perform an array of routine and advanced analyses or specialized packages that are intended to conduct specific, more advanced analyses. Next, the chapter revisits some of the ethical challenges of conducting social network analysis in and around educational settings and offers practical guidance when proposing a social network analysis to your institutional review board. Finally, in this chapter, you will learn about some of the areas in which social network analysis is likely to lead to new insights that are of interest to educational researchers.

CHAPTER SUMMARIES

This book has introduced an assortment of theories, procedures, techniques, methods, measures, and applications of social network analysis to topics related to education. In Part I, Chapter 1, you learned about the social network perspective and the importance it places on how relationships influence a person's behavior above and beyond the influence of one's individual characteristics. To help develop this perspective, this chapter also introduced you to several foundational concepts, including actor, ties, groups, relation, and social network. These concepts provided the vocabulary that was used throughout the text. Once these concepts were defined, this chapter argued that social network analysis is a powerful tool for empirically studying the dynamic and fluid view of schooling that is at the core of contemporary educational theory. After introducing a few exciting areas in which social network analysis has generated insights, this chapter closed by delineating between the different analytical levels at which social network analysis operates.

Chapter 2 provided a concise summary of the interdisciplinary origins of social network analysis. From its early ideas and practices to its contemporary applications that emphasize the mathematical modeling and visualization of social networks, social network analysis has sought to integrate theory with method. This is the core idea developed in Chapter 2: Social network analysis goes beyond methodology to inform a new theoretical paradigm that emphasizes that the elemental unit of social life is the social relation. Oddly enough, social relations were often de-emphasized throughout much of the history of educational research. After speculating on reasons why this has been the case, Chapter 2 offers three specific ways in which social network analysis can further advance educational research: (1) bridge theory and data; (2) develop and employ advanced statistical techniques; and (3) refine and reconceptualize varied phenomena. This chapter also briefly discussed some of the ethical challenges that educational researchers encounter when conducting social network analysis.

The final chapter in Part I, Chapter 3, introduced basic network concepts and surveyed the means through which network data and their characteristics at either the ego or complete network level are represented. Furthermore, this chapter provided an overview of additional foundational ideas and concepts. For example, in this chapter, you learned about how network data can be represented as a graph or matrix and the ways in which these data differ from traditional actor-by-attribute data that dominates most social science. Additionally, you learned the difference between one-mode and two-mode matrices and multiplex matrices. This chapter ended with a discussion of the three types of variables that are often used in network studies: relational, structural, and attribute. As you become more proficient, it is likely that your own network-based research will ultimately incorporate all three kinds.

Part II of this book consisted of Chapters 4 through 7 and focused on the methods and measures associated with ego-level or complete network data. Chapter 4 focused on the collection and management of network data. Key ideas were introduced in this chapter, including boundary specification, sampling, measurement, collection, storage, and measurement. While these ideas are germane to any research endeavor, Chapter 4 addressed specific issues that you need to consider when collecting and working with network data. This chapter began with a discussion of the importance of specifying the network's boundary and the three strategies through which this can be done: positional, relational, or event-based. The chapter then went on to discuss the ways in which you can collect or generate relational data for complete and ego-centric network analyses, including archives, sociometric instruments, and name generators/interpreters. This chapter also discussed important issues related to the quality of network data, including validity, reliability, measurement error, and patterns of missingness.

Chapters 5 through 7 introduced an array of different ways in which the static properties of egocentric or complete networks can be mathematically modeled. Using Newcomb's Fraternity Data, Chapter 5 specifically focused on structural measures that are calculated on the complete network. These measures include size, density, and reciprocity, among others. This chapter then went on to identify the ways in which groups (substructures) of actors can be identified in complete networks using relational data. These approaches were presented as either "bottom-up" (e.g., *K*-cores and *N*-cliques) or "top-down" (e.g., components and bi-components).

Chapter 6 continued addressing the analysis of complete network data but turned toward the issues of identifying positions and the relations among positions. Here, the key distinction between groups and positions is that a network position is a set of actors that occupy the same place or have similar patterns of relations with others. That is, positions consist of actors who share the same place in the network, but they need not be connected to each other (like actors in groups), though they very well might be. This is what distinguishes a position from a group. A number of different techniques to conduct a positional analysis were introduced, each based on a different definition of equivalence.

The final chapter in Part II, Chapter 7, shifted your attention to egocentric network measures. The point was made that ego-level network analysis can be done using ego data that are collected as part of a complete network study or (ideally) randomly selected from some target population. Regardless of the method through which the ego data are collected, most egocentric indices require information on an ego's alters and preferably information on each alter-alter pair (this is much easier when the ego data are collected as part of a complete network study). Once the egocentric data have been collected and organized, a number of different measures can be calculated to reveal different properties. These properties are related to connectivity (size and density), centrality (degree and betweenness centrality), structural holes (constraint), and brokerage (coordinator and gatekeeper). These different measures were used to describe the content and contours of an ego's local neighborhood.

Part III represented an effort to bring together much of what was covered in the book's previous chapters. The overarching goal of this section was to show you how the different conceptual and methodological tools you have learned can be applied to educational research. The first chapter in this section, Chapter 8, differentiated between the mathematical and statistical approaches to social network analysis. Whereas much of the material in Part II focused on calculating indices that reflected what a complete or ego network "looks like," this brief chapter introduced you to the logic of statistical inference with network data. While most applications of social network analysis in education continue to be descriptive, educational research is poised and pressured to adopt some of the exciting inferential techniques that allow you to assess the likelihood of a certain network configuration, or whether a certain configuration is expected and "normal." The use of these relatively new classes of inferential techniques, which are based on simulations, will allow you to make and test predictions using network data and move beyond techniques that describe static network properties. Using ERGMs as an example, the goal of this chapter was to not get mired in the technical aspects of this and other related techniques, but rather to sell you on the idea that the use of the inferential modeling techniques facilitates an important shift from description to explanation.

Chapter 9 extended this discussion by demonstrating a number of different techniques that make use of simulations when statistically modeling network data. These techniques were introduced according to the types of questions that are asked and whether the focus is on (1) ties between actors in complete networks; (2) individual attributes; or (3) relations within and between groups. Results of these different analytical techniques, including QAP, p_1, and p^* on data from Daly's School Leaders data set, were presented.

Chapter 10 reflected an effort to connect the methods, measures, and techniques presented in the previous five chapters to a rich theoretical area—social capital—to which educational researchers have made important contributions. This chapter reviewed the different ways in which social capital is defined and measured and the implications these differences have on the study of educational outcomes, particularly students' achievement. Using a number of empirical examples drawn from the educational research literature, the goal of this chapter was to help you understand what social capital is (and isn't) and how the conceptual and methodological tools associated with social network analysis are essential to testing and refining this rich theory. This chapter also revisited some ego-level indices (e.g., constraint and density), first introduced in Chapter 7, that are often employed in studies that operate from a social capital framework.

Similar to the previous chapter, Chapter 11 revisited the methods, measures, and techniques presented in earlier chapters but connects these to a second rich theoretical area—diffusion—that is very relevant to a range of educational processes. Chapter 11 outlined the core elements of diffusion theory and the major models used to understand how diffusion through networks occurs. After introducing four network-based diffusion models (integrated/opinion leaders, structural, critical values, and dynamic), two empirical examples were used to highlight the ways in which network data were collected, measured, and modeled to explain diffusion processes. Caution regarding the data requirements for such diffusion studies was urged and the potential of ABMs was introduced as a way to alleviate some of these concerns in order to study diffusion processes.

As this summary suggests, social network analysis is a broad field that is rapidly expanding, as theoretical insights and methodological techniques and tools from diverse academic disciplines seem to percolate almost daily. Coupled with this is the fact that the last several decades have witnessed an explosion of awareness about networks, not only within these various academic disciplines but within the larger cultural consciousness as well. It is now common to regularly speak of one's social network because of the ubiquitous use of networking platforms (e.g., Facebook) as well as the range of social media affixed to mobile phones (McFarland, Diehl, & Rawlings, 2011). This awareness and popularity are understandable, but they do not translate into making things any easier for you as a researcher. Like any research endeavor, selecting the appropriate methodology for your research questions is a big, important challenge. Social network analysis, in fact, may compound this problem by providing a theoretical perspective and methodology that is, at least on the surface (1) intuitively appealing; (2) appropriate for many empirical settings and questions; and (3) seemingly easy to do. After all, if interested in peer relations in a diverse elementary school classroom, you simply need to ask students in the class to name their closest friends. With this information, you then have access to a bunch of standard measures that help unpack that classroom's hierarchy, groups, positions, and so forth. If you also collect information on students' attributes like gender, for example, you can examine whether there is a tendency for ties to be reciprocated among those who share the same gender. While on the one hand, this seems straightforward, on the other hand, such a study can lead to a dizzying amount of complexity.

LOOKING AHEAD

So where do you begin? Integrating much of the material covered throughout this text, I have adapted Prell's (2012) suggested process, which walks you through the nine steps—from theory to design—that are necessary to conduct your own social network study. These steps confront basic issues such as: How do I design a social network analysis? How do I gather data? In what ways can I address some of the ethical, validity, and reliability issues of social network analysis? Once I gather my data, then what?

These are critical questions to ask and relevant for just about any research that you may conduct. However, within the context of social network analysis, concerns surrounding these issues are handled slightly differently. This section revisits some of the tools covered throughout this text that will help you address these issues. While the steps outlined below can be followed in any order, especially depending on "where" you enter the research process, I recommend that they be followed in as a linear manner as possible, regardless of your level of experience or familiarity. Table 12.1 lists these steps in this recommended order.

Table 12.1 Nine-Step Process for Conducting a Social Network Analysis. Adapted from Prell (2012).

1. Consult the literature
Your search for relevant empirical literature on your topic of interest should also include journals and databases that are not solely focused on education.

2. Develop a theoretical frame
What is the logical explanation that proposes a causal process or mechanism that produces an outcome of interest? What this means is that you as a researcher should have a fairly clear idea of the causal explanation you would like to test through the collection and analysis of social network data. This frame will be informed by your review of the literature.

3. Draft research questions or hypotheses
When constructing research questions or hypotheses pertaining to the study of social networks, the key in this process is to think about how a network variable (either relational or structural; Chapter 3), relates to, affects, or is affected by another set of variables.

4. Select a sample
Whom or what do you plan to study? In making this decision, you will have to consider issues of boundary specification, sampling, and populations (Chapter 4). There is another important issue to consider, one that will affect the five remaining steps: Will you examine ego networks or complete networks?

5. Collect data
With a clear question of hypothesis, you can develop a better image of the type of data you are interested in gathering. These data should reflect your variables of interest and include relational data on how actors are connected to one another.

6. Data considerations
Will you collect directed or undirected relational data? Will these network data be valued or binary? How valid and reliable are the network data? In what ways will you address the issue of missing data?

7. Input and manage data.

There are several options for inputting and structuring your data (reviewed in the second half of Chapter 3). The most common method is your basic network data matrix, also known as an adjacency matrix. Remember that each relation has its own matrix, and attribute data are stored in a separate rectangular matrix with the rows in the same order as the adjacency matrix.

8. Visualize network

So long as the network isn't too large and dense, visualizing a network will give you an intuitive feel for the network's topography.

9. Further descriptive or inferential analyses

Your analysis depends on your questions. But chances are these questions will require you to perform tests of statistical significance to examine the likelihood of (1) ties between actors in complete networks; (2) certain individual attributes predicted from relational data; or (3) relations within and between groups.

Source: Prell, C. (2012). *Social network analysis: History, theory, and methodology*. Thousand Oaks, CA: Sage Publications Inc.

Step 1: Consult the Literature

This first step sounds silly, but I am often taken aback by how often novice and senior researchers ignore—or give little attention to—this first step. You will first need to become familiar with the social network studies conducted on a topical interest similar to your own. This should happen even before you start formulating your own research questions. Of course, all the standard tricks for searching the empirical literature apply, such as using "social networks" or "social network analysis" as your key words. While you should expand your search to include journals that specialize in social network analysis (e.g., *Social Networks* and *Social Network Analysis and Mining*), you should also consider searching journals that are more closely aligned with a specific discipline (e.g., *American Journal of Sociology* and *American Sociological Review*) or are more broad in scope in that they may address issues related to children and schools (*Journal of Research on Adolescence* and *Youth and Society*, e.g.). The point I am making is that your search for relevant empirical literature should also include journals and databases that are not solely focused on education. You will be somewhat surprised how expanding your search in these ways will yield a bigger, better, and deeper pool of literature that can be used to inform your research questions and design. Of course, this first step will help you refine your ideas before you move forward, but you will also find useful concrete examples of how previous researchers have formulated their research questions, collected data, and analyzed those data.

Step 2: Develop a Theoretical Frame

Many of the early examples of social network analysis presented in Chapter 2 were inductive; that is, there was an interest in inducing theoretical concepts and frameworks based on the network data they had collected and analyzed through early mathematical and algebraic models. More commonly, however, social network analysis studies adopt a deductive, theory-driven approach. Remler and Van Ryzin (2010) define theory as a logical explanation that proposes a causal process or mechanism that produces an outcome of interest. What this means is that you as a researcher should have a fairly clear idea of the causal explanation you would like to test through the collection and analysis of social network data. Part III introduced two of these theoretical areas (social capital and diffusion of innovation), but there are many others. These others include network exchange theory (Blau, 1964; Cook, Emerson, Gilmore, & Yamagishi, 1983), which focuses on how a network's structure influences whom in the network emerges as powerful, and social influence theory (e.g., Friedkin, 1998), which considers how actors influence one another's thoughts. Before considering how you might test propositions derived from these theories, it is critical that you immerse yourself in the relevant literature that has developed and tested various components related to these and other network-based theories.

Step 3: Draft Research Questions or Hypotheses

Research questions or hypotheses flow directly from your preferred theoretical framework—assuming, of course, you are operating in a deductive manner. First, start with an initial topic of interest and then turn this topic into a question. The third and final step is to identify the problem your selected question helps resolve—its significance (Booth, Colomb, & Williams, 2008). When constructing research questions pertaining to the study of social networks, the key in this process is to think about how a network variable (either relational or structural, Chapter 3), relates to, affects, or is affected by another set of variables. It is this step in the process that will align your work with the social network perspective and important subsequent data considerations. Putting these pieces together, you have the following framework for focusing your research question and clarifying its significance:

General topic: Adolescent peer influences

Question: How do the characteristics of an adolescent's closest friends shape that student's attachment to school?

Problem (significance): Schools can more effectively and explicitly design learning environments that mitigate the negative effects of peers while also leveraging their positive effects.

When asked in this manner, the implied causal mechanism is the adolescent's friendship network, requiring your data to include a variable that measures the size, structure, and/or content of that local network. This question implicates social networks as affecting variables (e.g. attachment to school), yet this order could easily also be reversed. That is, you could ask how an adolescent's level of school attachment influences the likelihood of forming friendship ties.

Regardless of whether your questions treat the relational or structural variables derived from network data as predictor, outcomes, or both, they require information about an ego and his or her alters. Questions can also be framed in terms of hypotheses, a predictive statement about how you envision the relationship between variables (positive/negative or weak/strong, for example). Using the question posed above, we could test the following hypothesis: If an adolescent's closest friends' parents are involved in school, then that adolescent will demonstrate higher levels of school attachment. This hypothesis has further specified the characteristics on which you will be focusing and makes a prediction about the relationship. Good hypotheses also have several other characteristics—they are declarative, firmly grounded in theory, brief, and testable (falsifiable). Again, consulting the relevant empirical literature (Step 1) will provide some useful clues as to how to best craft these questions and hypotheses pertaining to the study of social networks.

Step 4: Select a Sample

So far in the design process, you have done some background reading and developed questions/hypotheses that examine an issue derived from a larger theoretical perspective. In this next step, you will determine whom you plan to study. In making this decision, you will have to consider issues of boundary specification, sampling, and populations (Chapter 4). There is another important issue to consider, one that will affect the five remaining steps—will you examine ego networks or complete networks? With ego networks, issues related to populations and samples are fairly straightforward. As with standard survey methods, you randomly sample a certain number of egos from a given population. Once you have a sample of egos, you gather your network data for each of your responding egos. Because these network data are on an ego's immediate, local neighborhood, they are likely to include ego-alter information and perhaps even information on alter-alter pairs. Thus, you will be able to calculate a few of the indices presented in Chapter 7, including size, density, and distance. If, however, you perform an ego-level analysis using data derived from complete network study, you have more options to calculate ego-level indices.

Issues related to sampling and populations for complete network data, on the other hand, are negotiated differently. Recall that a network's boundary refers to the set of actors that you consider to be a complete set of actors for the network study. Where do you set the limits when collecting complete network data when, in theory, there are no limits (Barnes, 1979; Knoke & Yang, 2008)? There are three generic approaches to addressing this issue: positional, relational, and event-based. The first of these approaches, positional, demarcates a network's boundary by including those actors bound together by some common attribute (e.g., teachers within school district). The relational approach is based on your knowledge about relations among a set of actors or relies on the actors themselves to nominate additional actors for inclusion. For example, you may specify the boundary of a network of parents within a school district by relying on a small number of influential parents—key informants—to identify those for inclusion in a study on the influence of parent networks on local educational policy decisions. This relational strategy relies on what is referred to as a reputational method, but relational strategies also include fixed lists, expanding selection approaches, and snowball samples. The third approach you may employ to address the boundary specification problem is event based. In this approach, your network would include only those actors who participated in an "event" at a specific time and place. For example, in a study on the relationship between parent networks and local educational policy decisions, your network could choose to include only those parents who physically attended a local board of education meeting within the past 12 months.

Step 5: Collect Data

Now that your network's boundary has been specified, you are ready to collect your data. These data should reflect your variables of interest and include relational data on how actors are connected to one another. Here, your research questions/hypotheses are of critical importance. Are you interested in how collaboration ties affect some behavior; for example, the likelihood of whether a teacher adopts a more student-centered instructional approach? Or are you interested in seeing how actors acquire various types of resources through different kinds of ties to others? For example, are students with more diverse ties likely to get more assistance outside of class from their peers? With a clear question, you can develop a better image of the type of data you are interested in gathering.

As this imagery comes into sharper focus, you will increase your likelihood of creating measurement instruments and a methodological approach that will result in the collection of high-quality network data that address your specific research questions or hypotheses. Chapter 4 describes these different data sources for either egocentric or complete network studies. These sources include census, archives, sociometric instruments, name generators, position generators, and resource generators, with these latter three being most relevant for egocentric studies. Network data can also be gathered through observations, interviews, or extracted from the back end of electronic databases. Qualitative work could also serve as a useful complement and helpful precedent to designing a quantitative social network study (see Hollstein, 2011, for a review of these strategies). Special attention should be given to issues of validity, reliability, and accuracy, which are also discussed in Chapter 4.

Step 6: Data Considerations

This next step is integrated with issues surrounding the collection of network data. In addition to issues of validity, reliability, accuracy, and patterns of missingness, there are two other important issues to consider. The first of these is whether you will collect directed or undirected relational data. If you are observing faculty members in a teachers' lounge, are you interested in who speaks with whom, or are you also interested in who initiated the conversation? Who initiated the conversation and who responded might be more interesting than just recording the pairs of teachers who engaged in conversations. This scenario reflects the difference between directed (arcs) and undirected relational data (edges) data—a point that was emphasized in Chapter 3. Therefore, directed network data includes who sought professional advice from a colleague or who trusts whom. Directed data such as these are typically preferable because more information is held within directed data, as you not only have information on the tie being present/absent but also on the direction of that tie. Directed data also have the benefit of being able to be transformed into to undirected data. For example, if two actors nominate each other as friends (a reciprocal relationship), this can be transformed into an undirected tie in which the actors are coded as friends (the top and bottom halves of the sociomatrix would therefore look the same). However, the reverse is not true; undirected data cannot be used to retroactively attempt to discern the senders and receivers of ties.

A second related issue to consider is whether your network data will be valued or binary. The distinction, also elaborated in Chapter 3, has important implications for how you collect and record your network data. With binary data, your concern is recording the presence or absence of ties (represented as 1/0). For example, you may ask and record whether a teacher discusses nonschool issues with another teacher (of course, this can also be directed or undirected). For many analyses, binary data are sufficient for unmasking many network properties; in fact, many network measures require that the data be in binary form. However, it is often preferable and desirable to get a deeper look into the relation by measuring the strength of the tie. This requires that you collected valued network data. Valued data reflect the relative strength, frequency, or duration of a relationship between a pair of actors. Different options for gathering valued network data include the use of Likert-type scales that assess the frequency with which one engages in a behavior with someone else: 1, 2, 3, or 4; 1 = never, 4 = frequently. This is similar to the ways which relations were measured in Daly's School Leaders data set. Another option for gathering valued network data is to rank actors. This is the method employed in the Newcomb Fraternity data set in which fraternity members were asked to rank all other members in terms of friendship preferences. Another slight twist is that in both of these data sets, data on these relations were measured at more than one point in time, which allows you to best address questions that deal with network dynamics. One last point about valued data is that they can always be transformed into binary data; however, the reverse is not true.

Step 7: Input and Manage Data

Once your egocentric or complete network data are gathered, they are ready to be organized in a manner that is suitable for analysis. There are several options for inputting and structuring your data (reviewed in the second half of Chapter 3). I'll briefly focus on one method that—with a little processing—is readable by most general social network software packages (reviewed later). This method is your basic network data matrix. In this section, I will gently walk you through the creation of a network data matrix.

Table 12.2 presents a hypothetical example of a questionnaire that gathers relational and data for each teacher in a complete network. This questionnaire can also

Table 12.2   Sample Sociometric Questionnaire. This is an example of a questionnaire that can be used to elicit sociometric data from a complete network of five teachers. Each row represents the network's actors (Teachers A, B, C, D, and E). The columns represent the three types of ties on which relational data are being collected. The values in the cells are selected by respondents, which generate valued and directed relational data on each pair of actors.

Teacher	I consider this person my friend.				This person is someone with whom I enjoy collaborating.				I could turn to this person to get professional advice.			
A	1	2	3	4	1	2	3	4	1	2	3	4
B	1	2	3	4	1	2	3	4	1	2	3	4
C	1	2	3	4	1	2	3	4	1	2	3	4
D	1	2	3	4	1	2	3	4	1	2	3	4
E	1	2	3	4	1	2	3	4	1	2	3	4

Please rate on a 4-point scale the extent to which you agree of disagree with each statement for each and every teacher listed (excluding yourself). Please circle a number for each teacher where 1 = strongly disagree; 4 = strongly agree.

Source: Prell, C. (2012). *Social network analysis: History, theory, and methodology.* Thousand Oaks, CA: Sage Publications Inc.

include items that elicit standard attribute data, including, for example, years of experience and whether the teacher has a master's degree (these are not shown on Table 12.2). The sociometric component of the questionnaire gathers data on three different relations: friendship, collaboration, and professional advice. It asks teachers to rate on a four-point scale the extent to which they agree or disagree with each statement for each and every teacher that is listed (excluding themselves) where 1 = strongly disagree; 5 = strongly agree. In addition to these data being directed, they are also valued, providing an indicator of strength of this tie.

The next step is to represent these data in the form of an adjacency matrix, the most common network data matrix in which two actors are considered adjacent if they are structurally "near" each other. When constructing an adjacency matrix, which can be done in any spreadsheet program, you first enter actors' names in both the rows and columns (referred to as a single-mode matrix, Chapter 3). Table 12.3 shows what an adjacency matrix looks like using those same teachers listed on the sociometric questionnaire in Table 12.2. Rows represent senders while columns represent receivers of ties. An important point to reinforce is that each relationship has its own matrix. So, given that the questionnaire measured three types of ties, each would require its own matrix. In this example, there would be three separate matrices on the same set of five teachers: A, B, C, D, and E.

Working with only one of these ties (friendship), you next enter the nominations of each respondent, starting with the row representing that respondent and then inserting a value under the column representing that respondent's choice. For example, Table 12.4

Table 12.3   Example Adjacency Matrix. This one-mode adjacency matrix consists of five actors (teachers). The rows of the matrix "send" ties, and the columns "receive" ties. These data can also be recorded in an edge-list format, which is appropriate for valued and directed network data such as these (described in Chapter 4).

Teacher	A	B	C	D	E
A					
B					
C					
D					
E					

Source: Prell, C. (2012). *Social network analysis: History, theory, and methodology*. Thousand Oaks, CA: Sage Publications Inc.

Table 12.4 First Row of the Example Adjacency Matrix With Valued and Directed Data on Friendship Ties. This row shows the friendship ties "sent" by Teacher A to the four other teachers in the complete network. For example, Teacher A strongly disagrees with the statement that "I consider this person my friend" for Teacher B (strongly disagree = 1). Conversely, Teacher A strongly agrees with the statement that "I consider this person my friend" for Teacher D (strongly agree = 4). The 0 in this row indicates that self-nominations, in this instance, are illogical; that is, Teacher A cannot evaluate friendship with him/herself.

Teacher	A	B	C	D	E
A	0	1	1	4	4

Source: Prell, C. (2012). *Social network analysis: History, theory, and methodology*. Thousand Oaks, CA: Sage Publications Inc.

shows that Teacher A nominated Teachers D and E as friends and "sent" each of them a 4. Teacher A did not consider Teachers B and C as friends; thus, a 1 is recorded in those cells. Of course, self-nominations in this instance make little sense, so a 0 is recorded in the appropriate cell. In most instances, in fact, the diagonal of the matrix is of little interest and is ignored or filled with zeros. The next step is to do this for each respondent in the network until you have a complete adjacency matrix in which all cells (those not on the diagonal) are filled with a 1, 2, 3, or 4, indicating the strength of the tie that has been sent by each row and received by each column.

In addition, you can record your attribute data in a matrix that consists of three vectors (columns). The first vector is the respondent's ID, the second is a vector for the variable "years of experience," and the third is a vector for the binary variable indicating whether they have a master's degree. Table 12.5 shows how these attribute data are structured in matrix format. The complete data files for this hypothetical study, therefore, consist of four matrices: three adjacency matrices containing valued and directed relational data and one rectangular matrix with three vectors containing information on two attributes for each of the five teachers in the network.

A quick note about inputting and managing egocentric network data. The above example focused on the collection of complete network data. If collecting ego-level network data, each ego would have its own data matrix and attribute file. Then, local network properties can be calculated for each ego and exported into a standard statistical software package (with some savvy programming skills, you can even calculate some of these properties directly in standard statistical software) and merged with the attribute data file for each ego. In addition, as mentioned in Chapter 4, after the data file has been converted to a long format, the statistical analysis of egocentric data likely has to be done in a multilevel framework in order to account for the nonindependence of observations.

Table 12.5   Data Matrix with Three Vectors: Actor's ID, Years of Experience, and Master's Degree (1 = yes, 0 = no). These attribute data would need to be collected as part of the sociometric questionnaire, or gathered from existing data sources (school personnel records, for example). These data are stored in a matrix that is separate from the relational data. The important point for subsequent analyses is that the rows of this data matrix are in the same order as those of the adjacency matrices that contain the relational data. For example, Teacher A has 5 years of experience and a master's degree.

Teacher	Years of Experience	Master's Degree
A	5	1
B	14	1
C	2	0
D	21	1
E	7	0

Step 8: Visualize the Network

As you get started, however, I will keep things simple and focus on complete network data, specifically our complete network of five teachers. Before calculating any of the measures mentioned in Chapters 5 and 6, it is very helpful to visualize the network as a graph, which gives you an initial peek at what the network looks like. So long as the network isn't too large and dense, visualizing a network will give you an intuitive feel for the network's topography. Some guidelines for creating useful visualizations from network data are discussed later in this chapter.

For example, using our hypothetical network of five teachers and the valued and directed matrix that measures friendship ties, we can visually discern a few interesting features. Figure 12.1 represents this network as a graph. This graph only shows strong friendship ties between teachers (only those originally coded as a 4 in the adjacency matrix). First, the network consists of one weak component in which a number of the friendship ties are not reciprocated. For example, Teacher A nominated Teacher D, but not vice versa. Second, Teachers B and D have a reciprocal relationship, as they have both nominated each other. They are also the most experienced teachers in the network, suggesting that this mutual friendship may have something to do with their similar lengths of experience. Finally, this network is not very dense (density = 45%), suggesting that this is not a very cohesive network of teachers. Before calculating any descriptive

Figure 12.1 Graph of Teachers' Friendship Network. Each directed line represents a friendship tie that has been sent from one teacher to another. A friendship tie is considered present only if the respondent selected a 4 on the sociometric questionnaire (Table 12.2). The size of each node reflects the attribute "number of years teaching," with bigger nodes equaling higher values on this attribute.

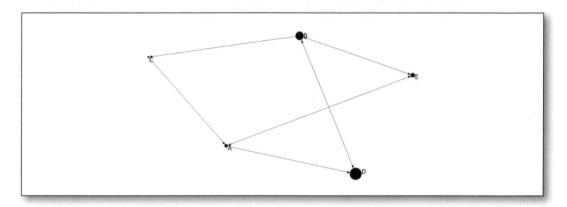

network properties or performing any inferential analyses, visualizing your network in the form of a graph provides some hints as to whether your motivating research questions or hypotheses are worth pursuing or in need of revision.

Step 9: Further Descriptive or Inferential Analyses

This last phase involves analyzing the networks in light of your research questions/ hypotheses. The first phase of your analysis will focus on the descriptive properties of the networks. These properties reflect the network's structure, groups, and positions (Chapters 5 and 6). Depending on your questions, this type of descriptive analysis may be more than adequate. However, your research questions may be nudging in an inferential direction in which you'll want to perform tests of statistical significance to examine the likelihood of (1) ties between actors in complete networks; (2) certain individual attributes predicted from relational data; or (3) relations within and between groups. To do these types of analyses, you should have a firm handle on the material in Chapters 8 and 9.

A final word on getting started. While the above section outlines a series of steps to get you started in your own network study, an alternative may be to directly work with the data files that are available to you at the book's companion website, available at http://www.sagepub.com/carolan. These are some of the same files that have been used to perform the analyses cited throughout this text. These files can be downloaded and copied into UCINET or imported into your preferred software package (described below). These files, which include both relational and attribute data in matrix format, can be used to understand and explore network data. In addition, the companion website also provides instructions for how to get stated with UCINET, conduct a p^* analysis with PNet, and detect and visualize groups in NetMiner.

SOFTWARE SAMPLER

Fortunately all the mathematics, statistics, and visualization associated with social network analysis—especially relevant in regard to Steps 7 through 9 above—are built into a number of general software applications that have been explicitly designed and marketed to social network analysts. In addition to performing these functions without needing to know any programming whatsoever, most applications come with a suite of powerful visualization tools that effectively communicate the static and even dynamic properties of social networks. This section reviews three of these general packages, which can be regarded as the major general packages with respect to functionality and provide both novice and advanced users with more than sufficient capability to perform both routine and advanced analyses. Then this section covers a small number of specialized programs that perform specific types of analyses. Finally, this section introduces two applications designed for network data collection. These programs are not presented in a manner that compares or ranks them, as this depends very much on your purposes and preferences. A more detailed treatment on these applications can be found in Huisman and van Duijn (2011).

General Packages

In this section, I review three of the most widely used general social network analysis software packages. By general, I mean that they posses ample capabilities for general exploration and analysis of network data. These three have been selected from approximately 15 others that are also considered general packages (e.g., InFlow, Network Workbench, Blue Spider). I focus on these three because they (1) have been available for many years; (2) have been extensively reviewed by others; and (3) are updated on a regular basis.

UCINET

UCINET 6 (Borgatti, Everett, & Freeman, 2006) is the most popular, comprehensive package for the analysis of one-mode or two-mode social network data. In fact, most of the analyses presented throughout this book were performed with this application. This menu-driven Windows-based program has a number of strengths.

First, it can handle fairly large networks. Second, through its easy-to-use menu, you can access a number of social network analysis methods, including routines for identifying subgroups, equivalence, and ego-level properties. Additionally, the program has excellent matrix routines that allow you to easily manipulate and transform data. Although its statistical techniques are limited, it does have strong permutation-based testing procedures, including QAP and MR-QAP. Also built into UCINET is NetDraw, a visualization tool that has advanced graphic properties. For these and other reasons, UCINET is an excellent choice, especially for someone new to network analysis.

NetMiner

A second excellent option for someone new to social network analysis is NetMiner (Cyram, 2009). In part, this is an excellent option due to its user friendliness, which is complemented by good user support and documentation. This application allows you to interactively explore network data in a way that integrates analysis with visualization methods. Data can be entered directly through a spreadsheet editor or by opening data sets in different formats, including NetMiner NTF files, Excel spreadsheets, or UCINET data sets. Able to handle large data sets, it contains a number of procedures for investigating a network's connectivity and local neighborhood structure, subgraph configurations, cohesion, and centrality. Like UCINET, it has advanced graphical features (and goes further by supporting 3D visualizations), but it also supports a larger number of statistical procedures. These procedures include correlation and regression analysis and even more complex p_1 and p^* models. These and other features make this package appropriate for both novice and advanced users. It is also available in a free trial version.

MultiNet

A third general and popular package for social network analysis is MultiNet (Richards & Seary, 2009). Designed for the analysis of large networks (like Pajek, another general package), MultiNet is a good choice when the interest is in exploratory network data analysis. Like UCINET and NetMiner, it supports the analysis of ego-level and complete network data. In addition to handling large networks, it can also handle a large number of variables that can be easily recoded, transformed, or manipulated in other ways. Foremost among its strengths is that it combines attribute and relational data into one model to perform a context analysis: It integrates data that describe people with data that describe relationships between people into a single analytic model. In addition, results are presented textually and visually, which will assist you in interpreting the results. It also recently integrated other programs such as PSPAR, which fits p^* models (Chapter 9), and NEGOPY, a program that finds cohesive subgroups (Chapter 6). One drawback for more advanced users is that its statistical procedures on network ties are limited. However, the package supports the user to an unusual extent, providing excellent online help and extensive documentation.

As you consider the package that best suits your needs, consult Huisman and van Duijn's (2011) excellent comparison of these three (and numerous others) different programs on nine criteria: (1) data manipulation; (2) network visualization; (3) network descriptives; (4) procedure-based methods; (5) statistical methods; (6) network dynamics; (7) availability of documentation; (8) online help; and (9) user friendliness. They use a + to denote that it is good, and ++ indicates that it has been scored as very good. In addition, a − indicates that the program has shortcomings in that area, a 0 indicating that the aspect under consideration is absent, and a +− indicating that the issue is undecided (having a mix of both positive and negative). Table 12.6 recaps Huisman and van Duijn's (2011) comparison of the three packages reviewed above. This can be used to help you select the one that is most appropriate for your analytical needs.

A quick note on network visualization. All three general packages also incorporate tools for visualizing networks. While the graphical representations of network data are easier to produce than ever before with the assistance of these embedded tools, the quick dissemination of these technologies has resulted in network images that do not adhere to any consensual set of basic principles (Krempel, 2011). However, as you explore your data through these visualization tools, it is useful to consider the following principles, which will result in better, more useful visualizations. First, the location of nodes and the distance between them should represent similarities and distances based on statistical procedures. Most visualization packages address this placement problem by employing various kinds of spring embedders (e.g., Kamada & Kawai, 1989), which ultimately provide information about local connections, that is, who is connected with whom and the strength of this connection. Closer nodes are typically placed close to one another. Second, shapes and colors should be used to communicate different classes or groups of nodes. Lines can also have different sizes and colors, which help delineate different types and strengths of relations. Altering the visual layers of these network attributes (attributes related to nodes and/or their relations) permits you to convey several pieces of numerical information simultaneously, providing a more complete multivariate view. Finally, extremely large networks with thousands of nodes should be filtered, which reduces the networks to the most connected nodes or most dominant lines. Keeping these principles in mind, the potential of network visualizations is that they are able to identify local combinations of external attributes that are connected to emerging social processes. In addition, network visualizations hint at where additional information is needed and direct our attention to areas of the network that need further theorizing and empirical investigation. Mapping networks is an important early step in the research process for all sorts of inquiries.

Table 12.6 Review of Three General Social Network Software Packages. Adapted from Huisman and van Duijn (2011). A + is used to denote that it is good, and ++ indicates that it has been scored as very good. In addition, a – indicates that the program has shortcomings in that area, a 0 that the aspect under consideration is absent, and a +– that is undecided (having a mix of both positive and negative).

	Functionality					Support		
	Data Visualization	Descriptives	Procedure-based Methods	Statistical Methods	Network Dynamics	Documentation	Online Help	User Friendliness
UCINET	++	++	++	+	0	++	+	+
NetMiner	++	++	++	+–	+–	+	+	++
MultiNet	+–	+	+	–	0	+	++	+

Source: Huisman, M., & van Duijn, M. A. J. (2011). A reader's guide to SNA software. In J. Scott & P. J. Carrington (Eds.), *The Sage handbook of social network analysis* (pp. 578–600). Thousand Oaks, CA: Sage Publications Inc.

Specialized Programs

Chapter 9 noted that the field of statistical methods is one in which major advances in social network analysis have occurred within the last 10 years. These advances have given way to a big increase in statistical routines and specialized packages needed carry them out. These specialized routines, for the most part, were developed to perform a small number of relatively advanced descriptive and statistical procedures, including p^* models (ERGMs), the analysis of longitudinal network data (actor-oriented models), and various measures of ego networks. Therefore, by *specialized*, I mean that they contain a few distinctive procedures for network analysis or a limited range of analytical procedures to perform a specific type of analysis.

PNet

PNet (Wang, Robins, & Pattison, 2008) is a specialized program that is used exclusively for the simulation and estimation of ERGMs, or p^*. It has three major functionalities: (1) simulating network distributions with specified model parameter values; (2) estimating specified ERGM parameters for a given network; and (3) testing the goodness of fit of a specified model to a given network with a particular set of parameters. This free, Windows-based software is a good first option to get started with your own ERGMs, as its supporting documentation is very helpful. It is available at http://www.sna.unimelb.edu.au/pnet/pnet.html.

RSiena

RSiena (Ripley & Snijders, 2010) is a specialized program that evolved from Siena, which was one of the first applications to analyze longitudinal network data and was originally implemented within the StOCNET package. Specifically, this program analyzes the co-evolution of networks and behaviors, that is, how behavior and network ties mutually influence each other. Siena methods are now available in RSiena, which is a package of the statistical system R. This replaced the older Windows-based Siena version 3, which still is available but no longer maintained. RSiena can be executed on all platforms for which R is available: Windows, Mac, and Unix/Linux. R, a free software environment for statistical computing and graphics, can be downloaded from http://cran.r-project.org, and RSiena can be loaded as one of the packages in R. In fact, the number of packages for social network analysis in R has grown tremendously. But using these R packages requires that you be very familiar with the R environment.

E-Net and EgoNet

Whereas the two aforementioned specialized programs focus on specific statistical methods, these final two specialized programs provide a suite of routines tailored specifically to measure various aspects of ego networks. Made by the developers of UCINET, E-Net (Borgatti, 2006) uses attribute data of ego and alters, as well as ties among alters. Measures of the network's composition, heterogeneity, homophily, and structural holes are calculated on all selected egos, and ego networks can also be visualized. Because ego networks more readily meet the independence assumption required for OLS models, analyses using these ego-level measures can be done using statistical packages like SPSS, Stata, SAS, and so forth. One useful feature of E-Net is that it facilitates the process of performing these analyses by getting the data into a format that is readable by these statistical packages.

EgoNet (McCarty, 2003) also provides these same analytical functions, but it also contains helpful routines that assist with questionnaire development and data collection. These questionnaires can incorporate name generators and interpreters and provide a very helpful framework to configure and perform a survey interview. Once the data are collected, it calculates general ego network measures as a first step in data exploration. Another nice feature is that the data can be easily exported in formats that are readable by other general (e.g., Excel) or network software packages (e.g., UCINET).

Programs for Network Data Collection

These general and specialized programs for analyzing network data have made significant advances in recent years. In addition to these improvements in analytical capabilities, there have been developments in the tools needed to collect relational data. In addition to the data-collection capabilities of EgoNet, two other programs developed specifically for network data collection through surveys are noteworthy (Huisman & van Duijn, 2011). First is Network Genie, a web-based application that facilitates the design and management of social network survey projects (Hansen & Reese, 2008). With this package, you can create online survey questionnaires that collect network data on egocentric or complete networks. Either type of survey can include social network items (questions about people in the network) or person-centered items (questions about the person who is completing the survey). Once these different types of data are collected, the program also allows formatted data to be exported to the social network analysis programs of your choice.

Second is the Organization Network Analysis (ONA) survey tool (Optimice, 2012), which was first designed to help organizations gather information about people within and across formal organizational boundaries. Similar to Network Genie, this application can create web-based network surveys and process these data prior to analysis. The surveys designed with ONA can either be (1) person centric, consisting of a number of questions about each respondent, or (2) question centric to evaluate the relationship for each question. In addition, the sampling approach can be bounded, measuring relations within a predefined group, or snowball, where an initial group of respondents is asked to nominate alters, who are then asked to nominate even more alters. Conveniently, this application also has export functions that prepare data for analysis in other applications. The interfaces of these other applications have significantly altered the amount and quality of network data that can be collected. It is strongly advised that network data be collected through means such as these because they reduce respondents' burden and errors in data entry.

FUTURE DIRECTIONS IN EDUCATIONAL APPLICATIONS

While advances in software—both for network data collection and analysis—will certainly influence the number of educational applications that employ social network analysis, the growth of social network analysis will be influenced by even more substantive reasons. Specifically, as emphasized in Chapter 2, social network analysis has the potential to become an increasingly central part of educational research, as it facilitates a paradigm shift from methodological individualism to methodological transactionalism, in which dynamic networks and communication processes are the primary focus of data collection (McFarland, Diehl, & Rawlings, 2011). This shift can be seen in diverse empirical examples, ranging from teacher professional communities (Penuel et al., 2009), school redesign networks (Daly & Finnigan, 2010), and cyber-bullying (Kowalski & Limber, 2007) to the integration of technology into schools (Frank et al., 2004). The growth of network thinking in educational research will continue, as social network analysis offers educational researchers a means for better capturing complex interdependencies and fluid dynamics than many other current and more utilized methods. As this potential becomes realized, what does the future hold for social network analysis and educational research? McFarland, Diehl, and Rawlings (2011) offer the following two hints.

The Collection and Analysis of Large-Scale Dynamic Behavioral Data

One of the most important developments in recent years is simply that there is more and significantly richer behavioral and communication data for researchers across all fields to work with. Most obviously, this refers to the familiar assortment of streaming and interconnected information that is readily available on the Internet in the form of information including text, images, videos, communication, and organizational records that can be rendered into network relations. Even beyond this, already-available data are the technological advancements that are making the collection of streaming behavioral more feasible. One well-known example of this kind of work comes from the Reality Mining project at MIT (Eagle & Pentland, 2006). As part of this project, research participants were given cell phones that continuously recorded their location, the presence of other participants, and all phone calls and text messages. Using these data, researchers could directly model the network of interaction between participants and study its contents in terms of communicative features like expressions of sentiment in text usage and voicing qualities. You could easily imagine extensions that would also allow, for example, the collection of biophysical data from students in classrooms, including physiological change and shifts in body position during interactions.

Longitudinal Analyses

A second future direction identified by McFarland, Diehl, and Rawlings (2011) for social network analysis in education is in the use of longitudinal network models, which help distinguish selection versus influence processes in tie formation. The misattribution of selection effects to social influence, or vice versa, has often led educational researchers to the wrong conclusions about potential causal mechanisms. The longitudinal analysis of social networks, the Holy Grail for network researchers (Wasserman & Robins, 2005, p. 6), has been made possible in the last few years since the development and availability of accessible methods for longitudinal network analysis. The most popular of these methods are the actor-oriented models developed by Tom Snijders and his colleagues available in the statistical package RSiena (reviewed above). These models, first introduced at the end of Chapter 10, are essentially longitudinal ERGMs that combine regular panel data (e.g., individual attitudes) with network panel data (i.e., relational measures collected at separate time points). Importantly, even though network data in this work are generally measured at discrete intervals, the methodological assumption is that relationships are (potentially) evolving states that may change between observations.

The empirical work utilizing longitudinal network methods is just in its earliest stages, but early work on adolescent friendship networks is already beginning to tease apart selection and influence processes related to issues relevant to adolescents, such as drug use (Pearson, Steglich, & Snijders, 2006) and smoking (Mercken et al., 2009). In both cases, the authors find that over time, there is a process of both selection and influence as peers both seek out other "deviants" as well as influence each other's behavior. It is easy to imagine how such models could be employed to examine networks' influences on students' achievement, attitudes toward school, and degree attainment, among others. Existing work outside of the network tradition has already argued for this reciprocal relationship between selection and influence, but utilizing dynamic network analysis allows educational researchers to better specify the mechanisms at work and understand how they shape each other through time.

LIMITATIONS

As social network analysis becomes more prevalent in educational research and advances in these directions, it will still be inhibited by a number of limitations that will shape both how it is practiced and the degree with which it is accepted. Valente (2010) encourages you to consider three of these as you design your network studies. First, most complete network studies are performed on populations in settings with clearly demarcated boundaries (students in a classroom, for example). This lacks the inferential abilities of random sample designs, as each of these settings is unique, thereby questioning whether even inferential results are generalizable to other populations. Second, many educational researchers are understandably uncomfortable with the tendency of social network analysis to quantify—in essence, reducing to a number—the complexity of interpersonal relations. Finally, despite the impressive advances in statistical tests involving nonindependent network data, there are lingering concerns regarding their appropriateness and value.

A SECOND NOTE ON RESEARCH ETHICS

In addition to these limitations, there are still a number of ethical concerns surrounding the collection of primary data and social network analysis. Chapter 2 noted that conducting social network analysis poses some ethical challenges for both researchers and institutional review boards. It is worth reiterating a few key points about the ethical issues related to social network analysis, especially when working with children in classrooms and schools. As with all social research, your primary concern must be on the potential harm to your study's participants. One potential harm is that it is more likely than not that a participant will know who else is participating in the study. Here, the process of informed consent is critical (Prell, 2012). Be sure to clearly explain to your participants how you plan on using the data and that the data will be treated as anonymous once they have been collected and processed. Also be sure to guarantee confidentiality—you will not share information gained from one respondent with another. In addition, as it becomes easier to mine electronic data for use on social network studies (for example, digital exchanges between a school's teachers and parents), the issue of privacy becomes critically important. These data cannot be collected without the consent of the entity that "owns" them, which in this instance can be the district, individual teacher, or even media platform through which these exchanges occur. It is advisable to work with your institutional review board as you design your study.

FINAL THOUGHTS

There is an increasing recognition and appreciation among educational researchers that relationships are key antecedents and determinants of individual behaviors and attitudes. The social network approach presented throughout this text gives you a rigorous and flexible means through which the importance and influence of these relations can be studied in a variety of empirical settings. This focus on relationships, as opposed to attributes, will foster your ability to develop a more complete, rich understanding of the ways in which networks and people are connected and evolve. To that end, I hope this book has given you the insight and tools needed to answer the question posed at the end of Chapter 1: *How does an understanding of social networks help you make sense of educational opportunities and outcomes at the individual and aggregate levels?*

REFERENCES

Abbott, A. (1988). Transcending general linear reality. *Sociological Theory, 6*(2), 169–186.

Adler, P. S., & Kwon, S.-W. (2002). Social capital: Prospects for a new concept. *Academy of Management Review, 27*(1), 17–40.

Ahn, J. (2010). The role of social network locations in the college access mentoring of urban youth. *Education and Urban Society, 42*(7), 839–859.

Alexander, K., Entwisle, D., & Kabbani, N. (2001). The dropout process in life course perspective: Early risk factors at home and school. *Teachers College Record, 103*, 760–882.

Anderson, C. J., Wasserman, S., & Crouch, B. (1999). A p primer: Logit models for social networks. *Social Networks, 21*(1), 37–66.

Atteberry, A., & Bryk, A. S. (2010). Centrality, connection, and commitment: The role of social networks in a school-based literacy initiative. In A. Daly (Ed.), *Social network theory and educational change* (pp. 51–76). Cambridge, MA: Harvard Education Press.

Balkundi, P., & Kilduff, M. (2006). The ties that lead: A social network approach to leadership. *Leadership Quarterly, 17*, 419–439.

Balkundi, P., Kilduff, M., & Harrison, D. A. (2011). Centrality and charisma: Comparing how leader networks and attributions affect team performance. *Journal of Applied Psychology, 96*(6), 1209–1222.

Bankston, C. L., & Zhou, M. (2002). Social capital as process: The meanings and problems of a theoretical metaphor. *Sociological Inquiry, 72*, 285–317.

Barnes, J. A. (1979). Network analysis: Orienting notion, rigorous technique or substantive field of study. In P. W. Holland & S. Leinhardt (Eds.), *Perspectives on social network analysis* (pp. 403–423). New York: Academic Press.

Barnhouse-Walters, P., Lareau, A., & Ranis, S. (Eds.). (2009). *Education research on trial: Policy reform and the call for scientific rigor*. New York: Routledge.

Barton, J. A. (1968). Bringing society back in: Survey research and macro-methodology. *American Behavioral Scientist, 12*, 1–9.

Baumgarten, S. A. (1975). The innovative communicator in the diffusion process. *Journal of Marketing Research, 12*, 12–18.

Becker, G. S. (1964/1993). *Human capital*. Chicago: University of Chicago Press.

Bercovici, J. (2012). Is Twitter's user growth slowing down already? *Forbes.com*. Retrieved from http://www.forbes.com/sites/jeffbercovici/2012/05/31/is-twitters-user-growth-slowing-down-already/

Berends, M. (2000). Teacher-reported effects of New American School designs: Exploring relationships to teacher background and school context. *Educational Evaluation and Policy Analysis, 22*, 65–82.

Bernard, H. R., & Killworth, P. D. (1977). Informant accuracy in social network data II. *Human Communications Research, 4*, 3–18.

Bernard, H. R., Killworth, P. D., & Sailer, L. (1980). Informant accuracy in social network data IV: A comparison of clique-level structure in behavioral and cognitive network data. *Social Networks, 2*, 191–218.

Bignami-VanAssche, S. (2005). Network stability in longitudinal data: A case-study from rural Malawi. *Social Networks, 27*(3), 231–247.

Blau, P. M. (1964). *Exchange and power in social life.* New York: Wiley.

Bonacich, P. (1972). Technique for analyzing overlapping memberships. *Sociological Methodology, 4*, 176–185.

Bonacich, P. (1987). Power and centrality: A family of measures. *American Journal of Sociology, 92*, 1170–1182.

Booth, W. C., Colomb, G. C., & Williams, J. M. (2008). *The craft of research* (3rd ed.). Chicago: University of Chicago Press.

Borgatti, S. P. (2006). *E-Net software package for ego-network analysis.* Lexington, KY: Analytic Technologies.

Borgatti, S. P., Carley, K., & Krackhardt, D. (2006). Robustness of centrality measures under conditions of imperfect data. *Social Networks, 28*, 124–136.

Borgatti, S. P., & Everett, M. G. (1992a). Notions of position in social network analysis. *Sociological Methodology, 22*, 1–35.

Borgatti, S. P., & Everett, M. G. (1992b). Regular blockmodels of multiway, multimode matrices. *Social Networks, 19*(3), 243–269.

Borgatti, S. P., & Everett, M. G. (1997). Network analysis of 2-mode data. *Social Networks, 19*(3), 243–269.

Borgatti, S. P., & Everett, M. G. (2006). A graph-theoretic framework for classifying centrality measures. *Social Networks, 28*(4), 466–484.

Borgatti, S. P., Everett, M. G., & Freeman, L. (2006). UCINET VI for Windows (Version 6.286). Lexington, KY: Analytic Technologies.

Borgatti, S. P., & Foster, P. (2003). The network paradigm in organizational research: A review and typology. *Journal of Management, 29*(6), 991–1013.

Borgatti, S. P., & Halgin, D. S. (2011). Analyzing affiliation networks. In J. Scott & P. J. Carrington (Eds.), *The Sage handbook of Social Network Analysis* (pp. 417–433). Los Angeles: Sage Publications.

Borgatti, S. P., & Lopez-Kidwell, V. (2011). Network theory. In J. Scott & P. J. Carrington (Eds.), *The Sage handbook of social network analysis.* Thousand Oaks, CA: Sage Publications.

Borgatti, S. P., & Molina, J. L. (2005). Toward ethical guidelines for network research in organizations. *Social Networks, 27*(2), 107–117.

Borgatti, S. P., & Ofem, B. (2010). Overview: Social network theory and analysis. In A. Daly (Ed.), *Social network theory and educational change.* Cambridge, MA: Harvard Education Press.

Bourdieu, P. (1986). The forms of capital. In J. G. Richardson (Ed.), *Handbook of theory and research for the sociology of education* (pp. 241–258). Westport, CT: Greenwood Press.

Bourdieu, P. (1990). *The logic of practice.* Cambridge, MA: Polity.

Bourdieu, P., & Wacquant, L. J. D. (1992). *An invitation to reflexive sociology.* Chicago: University of Chicago Press.

Boyack, K. W., Börner, K., & Klavens, R. (2009). Mapping the structure and evolution of chemistry research. *Scientometrics, 79*(1), 45–60.

Breiger, R. L. (1974). The duality of persons and groups. *Social Forces, 53,* 181–190.

Breiger, R. L. (2004). The analysis of social networks. In M. Hardy & Bryman (Eds.), *Handbook of data analysis* (pp. 505–526). London: Sage Publications.

Breiger, R. L., Boorman, S. A., & Arabie, P. (1975). An algorithm for clustering relational data with applications to social network analysis and comparison with multidimensional scaling. *Journal of Mathematical Psychology, 12,* 328–383.

Bryk, A. S., & Raudenbush, S. W. (1992). Hierarchical linear models in social and behavioral research: Applications and data analysis methods (1st ed.). Newbury Park, CA: Sage Publications.

Bryk, A. S., & Schneider, B. L. (2002). *Trust in schools: A core resource for improvement.* New York: Russell Sage Foundation.

Burt, R. S. (1984). Network items and the General Social Survey. *Social Networks, 6*(4), 293–339.

Burt, R. S. (1987). Social contagion and innovation: Cohesion versus structural equivalence. *American Journal of Sociology, 92,* 1287–1335.

Burt, R. S. (1992). *Structural holes: The social structure of competition.* Cambridge, MA: Harvard University Press.

Burt, R. S. (1997). A note on missing network data in the general social survey. *Social Networks, 9*(1), 63–73.

Burt, R. S. (2001). Structural holes versus network closure as social capital. In N. Lin, K. Cook, & R. S. Burt (Eds.), *Social capital: Theory and research* (pp. 31–56). New York: Walter de Gruyter.

Burt, R. S. (2004). Structural holes and good ideas. *American Journal of Sociology, 110*(2), 349–399.

Butts, C. T. (2008). Social networks: A methodological introduction. *Asian Journal of Social Psychology, 11*(1), 13–41.

Cairns, R. B., Leung, M.-C., Buchanan, L., & Cairns, B. D. (1995). Friendships and social networks in childhood and adolescence: Fluidity, reliability, and interrelations. *Child Development, 66,* 1330–1345.

Carley, K. M. (2004). Linking capabilities to needs. In R. Breiger, K. M. Carley, & P. Pattison (Eds.), *Dynamic social network modeling and analysis: Summary and Papers* (pp. 324–344). Washington DC: National Academies Press.

Carolan, B. V. (2008a). The structure of educational research: The role of multivocality in promoting cohesion in an article interlock network. *Social Networks, 30*(1), 69–82.

Carolan, B. V. (2008b). Institutional pressures and isomorphic change: The case of New York City's Department of Education. *Education and Urban Society, 40,* 428–451.

Carolan, B. V. (2010). Estimating the effects of students' social networks: Does attending a norm-enforcing school pay off? *Urban Review, 42*(5), 422–440.

Carolan, B. V. (2012). An examination of the relationship among high school size, social capital, and adolescents' mathematics achievement. *Journal of Research on Adolescence.* doi: 10.1111/j.1532-7795.2012.00779.x

Coburn, C. E., Choi, L., & Mata, W. (2010). "I would go to her because her mind is math:" Network formation in the context of a district-based mathematics reform. In A. Daly (Ed.), *Social network theory and educational change.* Cambridge, MA: Harvard Education Press.

Coburn, C. E., & Russell, J. L. (2008). District policy and teachers' social networks. *Educational Evaluation and Policy Analysis, 30*(3), 203–235.

Cole, R. P., & Weinbaum, E. H. (2010). Changes in attitude: Peer influence in high school reform. In A. Daly (Ed.), *Social network theory and educational change.* Cambridge, MA: Harvard Education Press.

Coleman, J. S. (1986). Social theory, social research, and a theory of action. *American Journal of Sociology, 91*(6), 1309–1335.

Coleman, J. S. (1988). Social capital in the creation of human capital. *American Journal of Sociology, 94,* S95–S121.

Coleman, J. S. (1990). *Foundations of social theory.* Cambridge, MA: Harvard University Press.

Coleman, J. S., & Hoffer, T. (1987). *Public and private high schools: The impact of communities.* New York: Basic Book.

Coleman, J. S., Katz, E., & Menzel, H. (1966). *Medical innovation: A diffusion study.* New York: Bobbs Merrill.

Cook, K. S., & Emerson, R. M. (1978). Power, equity, and commitment in exchange networks. *American Sociological Review, 43,* 712–739.

Cook, K. S., Emerson, R. M., Gilmore, M. R., & Yamagishi, T. (1983). The distribution of power in exchange networks: Theory and experimental results. *American Journal of Sociology, 89,* 275–305.

Corten, R., & Buskens, V. (2010). Co-evolution of conventions and networks: An experimental study. *Social Networks, 32*(1), 4–15.

Costenbader, E., & Valente, T. W. (2003). The stability of centrality measures when networks are sampled. *Social Networks, 25,* 283–307.

Croninger, R. G., & Lee, V. E. (2001). Social capital and dropping out of high school. Benefits to at-risk student of teachers' support and guidance. *Teachers College Record, 103,* 548–581.

Crosnoe, R., & Needham, B. (2004). Holism, contextual variability, and the study of friendships in adolescent development. *Child Development, 75,* 264–279.

Crosnoe, R., Riegle-Crumb, C., Field, S., Frank, K., & Muller, C. (2008). Peer contexts of girls' and boys' academic experiences. *Child Development, 79,* 139–155.

Cross, R., & Parker, A. (2004). The hidden power of social networks: Understanding how work really gets done in organizations. Cambridge, MA: Harvard Business School Press.

Cuban, L. (2001). *Oversold and underused: Computers in schools 1980–2000.* Cambridge, MA: Harvard University Press.

Cyram. (2009). *NetMiner.* Seoul: Cyram Co.

Daly, A. (2010). Surveying the terrain ahead: Social network theory and education change. In A. Daly (Ed.), *Social network theory and educational change* (pp. 259–274). Cambridge, MA: Harvard Education Press.

Daly, A. (2012). Data, dyads, and dynamics: Exploring data use and social networks in educational improvement. *Teachers College Record, 114*(11). Retrieved from http://www.tcrecord.org/content.asp?contentid=16811

Daly, A., & Finnigan, K. S. (2010). The ebb and flow of social network ties between district leaders under high-stakes accountability. *American Educational Research Journal, 48*(1), 39–79.

Daly, A. J., Der-Martirosian, C., Ong-Dean, C., Park, V., & Wishard-Guerra, A. (2011). Leading under sanction: Principals' perceptions of threat rigidity, efficacy, and leadership in underperforming schools. *Leadership and Policy in Schools, 10*(2), 171–206.

Davis, A., Gardner, B. B., & Gardner, M. R. (1941). *Deep south.* Chicago: University of Chicago Press.

Davis, J. A. (1967). Clustering and structural balance in graphs. *Human Relations, 20*, 181–187.

de Lima, J. A. (2010). Studies of networks in education: Methods for collecting and managing high-quality data. In A. Daly (Ed.), *Social network theory and educational change* (pp. 243–258). Cambridge, MA: Harvard Education Press.

de Nooy, W., Mrvar, A., & Batagelj, V. (2005). *Exploratory social network analysis with Pajek*. New York: Cambridge University Press.

Dekker, D., Krackhardt, D., & Snijders, T. A. (2007). Sensitivity of MRQAP tests to collinearity and autocorrelation conditions. *Psychometrika, 72*(4), 563–581.

Doreian, P., Batagelj, V., & Ferligoj, A. (2005). *Generalized blockmodeling*. New York: Cambridge University Press.

Eagle, N., & Pentland, A. (2006). Reality mining: Sensing complex social systems. *Personal and Ubiquitous Computing, 10*(4), 255–268.

Earp, J. A., Eng, E., O'Malley, M. S., Altpeter, M., Rauscher, G., Mayne, L., et al. (2002). Increasing use of mammography among older, rural African American women: Results from a community trial. *American Journal of Public Health, 92*, 646–654.

Elmore, R. F., Peterson, P. L., & McCarthey, S. J. (1996). *Restructuring in the classroom: Teaching, learning, and school organization*. San Francisco: Jossey-Bass.

Emirbayer, M. (1997). Manifesto for a relational sociology. *American Journal of Sociology, 103*(2), 281–317.

Epple, D., & Romano, R. (2008). Educational vouchers and cream skimming. *International economic review, 49*(4), 1395–1435.

Farmer, T. W., Hall, C. M., Leung, M.-C., Estell, D. B., & Brooks, D. (2011). Social prominence and the heterogeneity of rejected status in late elementary school. *School Psychology Quarterly, 26*(4), 260–274.

Faust, K. (2008). Triadic configurations in limited choice sociometric networks: Empirical and theoretical results. *Social Networks, 30*, 273–282.

Feick, L. F., & Price, L. L. (1987). The market maven: A diffuser of marketplace information. *Journal of Marketing, 51*, 83–97.

Feld, S., & Carter, W. C. (2002). Detecting measurement bias in respondent reports of personal networks. *Social Networks, 24*, 365–383.

Feldman, L. P., & Armstrong, G. M. (1975). Identifying buyers of a major automotive innovation. *Journal of Marketing, 39*, 47–53.

Ferligoj, A., Doreian, P., & Batagelj, V. (2011). Positions and roles. In J. Scott & P. J. Carrington (Eds.), *The Sage handbook of social network analysis* (pp. 434–446). Thousand Oaks, CA: Sage Publications.

Ferligoj, A., & Hlebec, V. (1999). Evaluation of social network measurement instruments. *Social Networks, 21*, 111–130.

Festinger, L. (1954). A theory of social comparison processes. *Human Relations, 7*, 117–140.

Field, S., Frank, K. A., Schiller, K., Riegle-Crumb, C., & Muller, C. (2006). Identifying positions from affiliation networks: Preserving the duality of people and events. *Social Networks, 28*(2), 97–123.

Frank, K. A. (1995). Identifying cohesive subgroups. *Social Networks, 17*(1), 27–56.

Frank, K. A. (1996). Mapping interactions within and between cohesive subgroups. *Social Networks, 18*(2), 93–119.

Frank, K. A. (1998). The social context of schooling: Quantitative methods. *Review of Research in Education, 23,* 171–216.

Frank, K. A. (2009). KliqueFinder for Windows (Version 0.11). East Lansing: Michigan State University.

Frank, O., & Strauss, D. (1986). Markov graphs. *Journal of the American Statistical Association, 81*(395), 832–842.

Frank, K. A., Kim, C. M., & Belman, D. (2010). Utility theory, social networks, and teacher decision making: Modeling networks' influences on teacher attitudes and practices. In A. Daly (Ed.), *Social network theory and educational change* (pp. 223–242). Cambridge, MA: Harvard Education Press.

Frank, K. A., Zhao, Y., & Borman, K. (2004). Social capital and the diffusion of innovations within organizations: The case of computer technology in schools. *Sociology of Education, 77,* 148–171.

Frank, K. A., Zhao, Y., Penuel, W. R., Ellefson, N., & Porter, S. (2011). Focus, fiddle, and friends: Experiences that transform knowledge for the implementation of innovations. *Sociology of Education, 84*(2), 137–156.

Frank, O. (1981). A survey of statistical methods for graph analysis. In S. Leinhardt (Ed.), *Sociological methodology 1981* (pp. 110–155). San Francisco: Jossey-Bass.

Freeman, L. C. (1977). A set of measures of centrality based on betweenness. *Sociometry, 40*(1), 35–41.

Freeman, L. C. (1979). Centrality in social networks. *Social Networks, 1,* 215–239.

Freeman, L. C. (2004). The development of social network analysis: A study in the sociology of science. Vancouver: Empirical Press.

Freeman, L. C. (2011). The development of social network analysis—with an emphasis on recent events. In J. Scott & P. J. Carrington (Eds.), *The Sage handbook of social network analysis* (pp. 26–39). Thousand Oaks, CA: Sage Publications.

Freeman, L. C., & Romney, A. K. (1987). Words, deeds, and social structure: A preliminary study of the reliability of informants. *Human Organization, 46*(4), 330–334.

Friedkin, N. E. (1984). Structural cohesion and equivalence explanations of social homogeneity. *Sociological Methods and Research, 12,* 235–261.

Friedkin, N. E. (1998). *A structural theory of social influence.* New York: Cambridge University Press.

Friedkin, N. E., & Johnsen, E. C. (2011). *Social influence network theory: A sociological investigation of small group dynamics.* New York: Cambridge University Press.

Gates, G., & Kennedy, S. (1989). Peer educators reach college students with nutrition information. *Journal of American College Health, 35,* 95–96.

Gest, S. D. (2006). Teacher reports of children's friendships and social groups: Agreement with peer reports and implications for studying peer similarity. *Social Development, 15*(2), 248–259.

Gest, S. D., Farmer, T. W., Cairns, B. D., & Xie, H. (2003). Identifying children's peer social networks in school classrooms: Links between peer reports and observed interactions. *Social Development, 12*(4), 513–529.

Girvan, M., & Newman, M. E. J. (2002). Community structure in social and biological networks. *Proceedings of the National Academy of Science, 99*(12), 7921–7826.

Gladwell, M. (2000). *The tipping point: How little things can make a big difference.* New York: Little, Brown, and Company.

Goldenberg, A., Zheng, A., Fienberg, S., & Airoldi, E. (2009). A survey of statistical network models. *Foundations and Trends in Machine Learning, 2*(2), 129–233.

Goldhaber, D., & Eide, E. (2003). Methodological thoughts on measuring the impact of private sector competition on the educational workplace. *Educational Evaluation and Policy Analysis, 25*(2), 217–232.

Goodreau, S. M., Kitts, J. M., & Morris, M. (2009). Birds of a feather, or friend of a friend? Using exponential random graph models to investigate adolescent social networks. *Demography, 46*(1), 103–125.

Gould, J., & Fernandez, J. (1989). Structures of mediation: A formal approach to brokerage in transaction networks. *Sociological Methodology* (19), 89–126.

Granovetter, M. (1973). The strength of weak ties. *American Journal of Sociology, 81*, 1287–1303.

Hallinan, M. T., & Sorenson, A. B. (1985). Ability grouping and student friendships. *American Educational Research Journal, 22*, 485–499.

Hallinan, M. T., & Williams, R. A. (1990). Students' characteristics and the peer-influence process. *Sociology of Education, 63*, 122–132.

Handcock, M. A., Raftery, A. E., & Tantrum, J. M. (2007). Model-based clustering for social networks. With discussion. *Journal of the Royal Statistical Society A, 170*(2), 301–354.

Hanneman, R. A., & Riddle, M. (2005). *Introduction to social network methods.* Retrieved from http://faculty.ucr.edu/~hanneman/

Hanneman, R. A., & Riddle, M. (2011a). A brief introduction to analyzing social network data. In J. Scott & P. J. Carrington (Eds.), *The Sage handbook of social network analysis* (pp. 331–339). Thousand Oaks, CA: Sage Publications.

Hanneman, R. A., & Riddle, M. (2011b). Concepts and measures for basic network analysis. In J. Scott & P. J. Carrington (Eds.), *The Sage handbook of social network analysis* (pp. 340–369). Thousand Oaks, CA: Sage Publications.

Hansen, W. B., & Reese, E. L. (2008). *Network genie.* Greensboro, NC: Tanglewood Research.

Hare, P. A., & Hare, J. R. (1996). *J. L. Moreno.* London: Sage Publications.

Harris, K. M., Halpern, C. T., Whitsel, E., Hussey, J., Tabor, J., Entzel, P., & Udry, J. R. (2009). *The national longitudinal study of adolescent health: Research design.* Retrieved from http://www.cpc.unc.edu/projects/addhealth/design

Haythornthwaite, C., & Wellman, B. (1996). Using SAS to convert ego-centered networks to whole networks. *Bulletin de Methode Sociologique, 50*, 71–78.

Heider, F. (1946). Attitudes and cognitive organization. *Journal of Psychology, 21*, 107–112.

Heider, F. (1958). *The psychology of interpersonal relations.* New York: John Wiley and Sons.

Holland, P. W., & Leinhardt, S. (1973). The structural implications of measurement error in sociometry. *Journal of Mathematical Sociology, 3*(1), 85–111.

Holland, P. W., & Leinhardt, S. (1979). *Perspectives on social network research.* New York: Academic Press.

Holland, P. W., & Leinhardt, S. (1981). An exponential family of probability distributions for directed graphs. *Journal of the American Statistical Association, 76*(373), 33–50.

Hollstein, B. (2011). Qualitative approaches. In J. Scott & P. J. Carrington (Eds.), *The Sage handbook of social network analysis* (pp. 404–416). Thousand Oaks, CA: Sage Publications.

Homans, G. C. (1950). *The human group.* New York: Harcourt Brace.

Horvat, E. M., Weininger, E. B., & Lareau, A. (2003). From social ties to social capital: Class differences in the relations between schools and parent networks. *American Educational Research Journal, 40*, 319–351.

Hubert, L. J. (1987). *Assignment methods in combinatorial data analysis*. New York: Marcel Dekker.

Huisman, M., & van Duijn, M. A. J. (2011). A reader's guide to SNA software. In J. Scott & P. J. Carrington (Eds.), *The Sage handbook of social network analysis* (pp. 578–600). Thousand Oaks, CA: Sage Publications.

Ingels, S. J., Pratt, D. J., Rogers, J., Siegel, P. H., & Stutts, E. S. (2004). *Education longitudinal study of 2002: Base year data file user's manual*. Washington DC: National Center for Education Statistics, Institute of Education Sciences, U.S. Department of Education.

Jackson, M. O. (2008). *Social and economic networks*. Princeton, NJ: Princeton University Press.

John, P. (2005). The contribution of volunteering, trust, and networks to educational performance. *Policy Studies Journal, 33*.

Johnson, C. A. (2010). Do public libraries contribute to social capital? A preliminary investigation into the relationship. *Library & Information Science Research, 32*(2), 147–155.

Kadushin, C. (2004). Too much investment in social capital? *Social Networks, 26*, 75–90.

Kadushin, C. (2005). Who benefits from network analysis: Ethics of social network research. *Social Networks, 27*(2), 139–153.

Kamada, T., & Kawai, S. (1989). An algorithm for drawing undirected graphs. *Information Processing Letters, 31*(1), 7–15.

Katz, L. (1953). A new index derived from sociometric data analysis. *Psychometrika, 18*, 39–43.

Katz, L., & Powell, J. H. (1955). Measurement and the tendency toward reciprocation of choice. *Sociometry, 18*, 659–665.

Katz, N., Lazer, D., Arrow, H., & Contractor, N. (2004). Network theory and small groups. *Small Group Research, 35*(3), 307–332.

Klovdahl, A. S., Potterat, J. J., Woodhouse, D., Muth, S. Q., Muth, J., & Darrow, W. W. (1994). Social networks and infectious disease: The Colorado Springs study. *Social Science and Medicine, 56*, 79–88.

Knoke, D., & Rogers, D. L. (1979). A blockmodel analysis of interorganizational networks. *Sociology and Social Research, 64*, 28–52.

Knoke, D., & Yang, S. (2008). *Network analysis* (2nd ed.). Thousand Oaks, CA: Sage Publications.

Kogovsek, T., & Ferligoj, A. (2005). Effects on reliability and validity of egocentered network measurements. *Social Networks, 27*, 205–229.

Kosfeld, M. (2004). Networks in the laboratory: A survey. *Review of Network Economics, 3*, 20–41.

Kossinets, G. (2006). Effects of missing data in social networks. *Social Networks, 28*, 247–268.

Kowalski, R. M., & Limber, S. E. (2007). Electronic bullying among middle school students. *Journal of Adolescent Health, 41*, S22–S30.

Krackhardt, D. (1987a). Cognitive social structures. *Social Networks, 9*(2), 109–134.

Krackhardt, D. (1987b). QAP partialling as a test of spuriousness. *Social Networks, 92*(2), 171–186.

Krackhardt, D. (1996). Social networks and the liability of newness for managers. In C. L. Cooper & D. M. Rousseau (Eds.), *Trends in organizational behavior* (Vol. 3, pp. 159–173). New York: John Wiley & Sons.

Kreager, D. A., & Haynie, D. L. (2011). Dangerous liaisons? Dating and drinking diffusion in adolescent peer networks. *American Sociological Review, 76*, 737–763.

Krempel, L. (2011). Network visualization. In J. Scott & P. J. Carrington (Eds.), *The Sage handbook of social network analysis* (pp. 558–577). Thousand Oaks, CA: Sage Publications.

Kuhn, T. S. (1962). *The structure of scientific revolutions*. Chicago: University of Chicago Press.

Laumann, E. O., Marsden, P. V., & Prensky, D. (1989). The boundary specification problem in network analysis. In L. C. Freeman, D. R. White, & A. K. Romney (Eds.), *Research methods in social network analysis* (pp. 61–87). Fairfax, VA: George Mason University Press.

Lazarfeld, P. F., & Merton, R. K. (1954). Friendship as a social process: A substantive and methodological analysis. In M. Berger, T. Abel, & C. H. Page (Eds.), *Freedom and control in modern society*. New York: Van Nostrand.

Levine, J. H. (1999). We can count, but what do the numbers mean? In J. Abu-Lughod (Ed.), *Sociology for the twenty-first century: Continuities and cutting edges* (pp. 83–93). Chicago: University of Chicago Press.

Lin, N. (2001a). Building a network theory of social capital. In N. Lin, K. Cook, & R. S. Burt (Eds.), *Social capital: Theory and research* (pp. 3–30). New York: Walter de Gruyter.

Lin, N. (2001b). *Social capital: A theory of social structure in action*. New York: Cambridge University Press.

Lin, N., Fu, Y.-C., & Hsung, R.-M. (2001). The position generator: Measurement techniques for investigations of social capital. In N. Lin, K. Cook, & R. S. Burt (Eds.), *Social capital: Theory and research* (pp. 57–81). New York: Aldine de Gruyter.

Lomas, J., Enkin, M., Anderson, G. M., Hannah, W. J., Vayda, E., & Singer, J. (1991). Opinion leaders vs. audit feedback to implement practice guidelines: Delivery after previous cesarean section. *Journal of the American Medical Association, 265*, 2202–2207.

Lorrain, F. P., & White, H. C. (1971). Structural equivalence of individuals in social networks. *Journal of Mathematical Sociology, 1*, 49–80.

Marin, A., & Wellman, B. (2011). Social network analysis: An introduction. In J. Scott & P. J. Carrington (Eds.), *The Sage handbook of social network analysis* (pp. 11–25). Thousand Oaks, CA: Sage Publications.

Maroulis, S., & Gomez, L. M. (2008). Does "connectedness" matter? Evidence from a social network analysis within a small-school reform. *Teachers College Record, 110*(9), 1901–1929.

Maroulis, S., Guimera, R., Petry, H., Gomez, L., Amaral, L. A. N., & Wilensky, U. (2010). Complex systems view on educational policy research. *Science, 300*(6000), 38–39.

Marsden, P. V. (2011). Survey methods for network data. In J. Scott & P. J. Carrington (Eds.), *The Sage handbook of social network analysis* (pp. 370–388). Thousand Oaks, CA: Sage Publications.

Marsden, P. V., & Friedkin, N. E. (1993). Network studies of social influence. *Sociological Methods and Research, 22*, 127–151.

Martin, J. L. (2003). What is field theory? *American Journal of Sociology, 109*, 1–49.

Marx, K. (1933/1849). *Wage-labour and capital*. New York: International Publishers.

Mazur, A. (1971). Comments on Davis' graph model. *American Sociological Review, 36*, 308–311.

McCarty, C. (2003). EgoNet: Sourceforge.net.

McFarland, D. A. (2001). Student resistance: How the formal and informal organization of classrooms facilitate everyday forms of student defiance. *American Journal of Sociology, 107*(3), 612–678.

McFarland, D. A., Diehl, D., & Rawlings, C. (2011). Methodological transactionalism and the sociology of education. In M. T. Hallinan (Ed.), *Frontiers in sociology of education* (pp. 87–109). New York: Springer-Verlag.

McNeal, R. B. (1999). Parental involvement as social capital: Differential effectiveness on science achievement, truancy, and dropping out. *Social Forces, 78*, 117–144.

McNulty, T. L., & Bellair, P. E. (2003). Explaining racial and ethnic differences in adolescent violence: Structural disadvantage, family well-being, and social capital. *Justice Quarterly, 20*, 1–31.

Mercken, L., Snijders, T. A. B., Steglich, C., Vartiainen, E., & de Vries, H. (2009). Dynamics of adolescent friendship networks and smoking behavior. *Social Networks, 32*, 72–81.

Mische, A. (2011). Relational sociology, culture, and agency. In J. Scott & P. J. Carrington (Eds.), *The Sage handbook of social network analysis* (pp. 80–97). Thousand Oaks, CA: Sage Publications.

Moody, J. (2006). Fighting a hydra: A note on the network embeddedness of the war on terror. *Structure and Dynamics: eJournal of Anthropological and Related Sciences, 1*(2), article 9.

Moody, J., & White, D. R. (2003). Structural cohesion and embeddedness: A hierarchical concept of social groups. *American Sociological Review, 68*, 103–27.

Moolenaar, N. M. (2010). *Ties with potential: Nature, antecedents, and consequences of social networks in school teams*. Amsterdam, the Netherlands: University of Amsterdam.

Moolenaar, N. M., Daly, A. J., & Sleegers, P. J. (2011). Ties with potential: Social network structure and innovative climate in Dutch schools. *Teachers College Record, 113*(9), 1983–2017.

Moolenaar, N. M., & Sleegers, P. J. C. (2010). Social networks, trust, and innovation: The role of relationships in supporting an innovative climate in Dutch schools. In A. Daly (Ed.), *Social network theory and educational change* (pp. 97–114). Cambridge, MA: Harvard Education Press.

Moreno, J. (1934). *Who shall survive?* Washington DC: Nervous and Mental Disease Publishing Company.

Morgan, D. L., Neal, M. B., & Carder, P. (1997). The stability of core and periphery networks over time. *Social Networks, 19*(1), 9–25.

Morgan, S. L., & Sorenson, A. B. (1999). A test of Coleman's social capital explanation of school effects. *American Sociological Review, 64*, 661–681.

Morgan, S. L., & Todd, J. J. (2008). Intergenerational closure and academic achievement in high school: A new evaluation of Coleman's conjecture. *Sociology of Education, 82*, 267–286.

Müller, C., Wellman, B., & Marin, A. (1999). How to use SPSS to study ego-centered networks. *Bulletin de Methode Sociologique, 69*, 83–100.

Natarajan, M. (2000). Understanding the structure of a drug trafficking organization: A conversational analysis. In M. Natarajan & M. Hough (Eds.), *Illegal drug markets: From research to policy, crime prevention studies* (pp. 273–298). Monsey, NY: Criminal Justice Press.

Newcomb, T. M. (1961). *The acquaintance process*. New York: Holt, Rhinehart, and Winston.

Newman, M. E. J., & Girvan, M. (2004). Finding and evaluating community structure in networks. *Physics Review, E69*, 1–16.

Noh, J. D., & Rieger, H. (2004). Random walks on complex networks. *Physical Review Letters, 92*, eprint.

Ogbu, J. (1997). Variability in minority school performance: A problem in search of an explanation. *Anthropology and Education Quarterly 18*, 213–334.

Optimice. (2012). *ONA surveys*. Sydney, Australia: Optimice Pty.

Otte, E., & Rousseau, R. (2002). Social network analysis: A powerful strategy, also for the information sciences. *Journal of Information Science, 28*(6), 443–455.

Pattison, P. E., & Wasserman, S. (1999). Logit models and logistic regressions for social networks, II. Multivariate relations. *British Journal of Mathematical and Statistical Psychology, 52*, 169–194.

Pearson, M., Steglich, C., & Snijders, T. A. B. (2006). Homophily and assimilation among sport-active adolescent substance users. *Connections, 27*(1), 51–67.

Penuel, W. R., Frank, K. A., & Krause, A. (2010). Between leaders and teachers: Using social network analysis to examine effects of distributed leadership. In A. Daly (Ed.), *Social network theory and educational change* (pp. 159–178). Cambridge, MA: Harvard Education Press.

Penuel, W. R., Frank, K. A., Sun, M., Kim, C. M., & Singleton, C. (2013). The organization as a filter of institutional diffusion. *Teachers College Record, 115*(1).

Penuel, W. R., Riel, M., Krause, A. E., & Frank, K. A. (2009). Analyzing teachers' professional interactions in a school as social capital: A social network approach. *Teachers College Record, 111*(1), 124–163.

Perry, C. L., Komro, K. A., Beblen-Mortenson, S., Bosma, L. M., Farbakhsh, K., Munson, K. A., et al. (2003). A randomized controlled trial of the middle and junior high schools D.A.R.E. and D.A.R.E. plus programs. *Archives of Pediatric Adolescent Medicine, 157*, 178–184.

Pittinsky, M., & Carolan, B. V. (2008). Behavioral vs. cognitive classroom friendship networks: Do teacher perceptions agree with student reports? *Social Psychology of Education, 11*, 133–147.

Plank, S. (2000). Finding one's place: Teaching styles and peer relations in diverse classrooms. New York: Teachers College Press.

Portes, A. (1998). Social capital: Its origins and applications in modern sociology. *Annual Review of Sociology, 24*, 1–24.

Powell, J. J. W., Bernhard, N., & Graf, L. (2012). The emergent European model in skill formation: Comparing higher education and vocational training in the Bologna and Copenhagen processes. *Sociology of Education, 85*, 240–258.

Prell, C. (2012). *Social network analysis: History, theory, and methodology*. Thousand Oaks, CA: Sage Publications.

Putnam, R. D. (2000). Bowling alone: The collapse and revival of American community. New York: Simon & Schuster.

Ream, R., & Rumberger, R. (2008). Student engagement, peer social capital, and school dropout among Mexican American and non–Latino White students. Sociology of Education, 81(2), 109–139.

Ream, R. K., & Stanton-Salazar, R. (2007). The mobility/social capital dynamic: Understanding Mexican-American families and students. In S. J. Paik & H. Walberg (Eds.), *Narrowing the achievement gap: Strategies for educating Latino, black, and Asian students* (pp. 67–89). New York: Springer.

Remler, D. K., & Van Ryzin, G. G. (2010). *Research methods in practice: Strategies for description and causation*. Thousand Oaks, CA: Sage Publications.

Renzulli, L. A., & Roscigno, V. J. (2005). Charter school policy, implementation, and diffusion across the United States. *Sociology of Education, 78*, 344–366.

Rhodes, C. J., & Keefe, E. M. J. (2007). Social network topology: A Bayesian approach. *Journal of the Operational Research Society 58*, 1605–1611.

Richards, W. D., & Seary, A. J. (2009). *MultiNet*. Burnaby, Canada: Simon Fraser University.

Ripley, R. M., & Snijders, T. A. B. (2010). RSiena (Version 4.0). Oxford, UK: University of Oxford.

Robins, G. (2011). Exponential random graph models for social networks. In J. Scott & P. J. Carrington (Eds.), *The Sage handbook of social network analysis* (pp. 484–500). Los Angeles: Sage Publications.

Robins, G., Pattison, P., Kalish, Y., & Lusher, D. (2007). An introduction to exponential random graph (p) models for social networks. *Social Networks, 29*, 173–191.

Roethlisberger, F. J., & Dickson, W. J. (1939). *Management and the worker: An account of a research program conducted by the Western Electric Company, Hawthorne Works, Chicago.* Cambridge, MA: Harvard University Press.

Roger, E. M., & Kincaid, D. L. (1981). *Communication networks: A new paradigm for research.* New York: Free Press.

Rogers, E. M. (1962/2003). *Diffusion of innovations* (1st and 5th eds.). New York: The Free Press.

Romney, A. K., & Weller, S. C. (1984). Predicting informant accuracy from patterns of recall among individuals. *Social Networks, 4,* 59–77.

Ryan, R., & Gross, N. (1943). The diffusion of hybrid seed corn in two Iowa communities. *Rural Sociology, 8,* 15–24.

Salganick, M. J., & Heckathorn, D. D. (2004). Sampling and estimation in hidden populations using respondent-drive sampling. *Sociological Methodology, 34,* 193–239.

Sampson, R., McAdam, D., MacIndoe, H., & Weffer, S. (2005). Civil society reconsidered: The durable nature and community structure of collective civic action. *American Journal of Sociology, 111,* 673–714.

Sandefur, G. D., Meier, A. M., & Campbell, M. E. (2006). Family resources, social capital, and college attendance. *Social Science Research, 35,* 525–553.

Schelling, T. (1978). *Micromotives and macrobehavior.* New York: Norton.

Schweinberger, M., & Snijders, T. A. B. (2003). Settings in social networks. *Sociological Methodology, 33*(1), 307–341.

Scott, J. (2000). *Social network analysis: A handbook* (2nd ed.). Thousand Oaks, CA: Sage Publications.

Sikkema, K. J., Kelly, J. A., Winett, R. A., Solomon, L. J., Cargill, V. A., & Roffman, R. A. (2000). Outcomes of a randomized community-level HIV prevention intervention for women living in 19 low-income housing developments. *American Journal of Public Health, 90,* 57–63.

Simmel, G. (1908/1950). *The sociology of Georg Simmel* (K. H. Wolff, Trans.). Glencoe, IL: The Free Press.

Smith, T. M., Desimone, L. M., Zeidner, T. L., Dunn, A. C., Bhatt, M., & Rumyantseva, N. L. (2007). Inquiry-oriented instruction in science: Who teaches that way. *Educational Evaluation and Policy Analysis, 29,* 169–199.

Snijders, T. A. B., & Baerveldt, C. (2003). A multilevel network study of the effects of delinquent behavior on friendship evolution. *Journal of Mathematical Sociology, 27,* 123–151.

Snijders, T. A. B., & Bosker, R. J. (1999). *Multilevel analysis: An introduction to basic and advanced multilevel modeling.* Thousand Oaks, CA: Sage Publications.

Snijders, T. A. B., van de Bunt, G., & Steglich, C. (2010). Introduction to stochastic actor-based models for network dynamics. *Social Networks, 32,* 44–60.

Song, L. (2012). Raising network resources while raising children? Access to social capital by parenthood status, gender, and marital status. *Social Networks, 34*(2), 241–252.

Spillane, J. P., Healey, K., & Kim, C. M. (2010). Leading and managing instruction: Formal and informal aspects of elementary school organization. In A. Daly (Ed.), *Social network theory and educational change.* Cambridge, MA: Harvard Education Press.

Steglich, C., Snijders, T. A. B., & West, P. (2006). Applying SIENA. Methodology: European Journal of Research Methods for the Behavioral and Social Sciences, 2(1), 48–56.

Story, M., Lytle, L. A., Birnbaum, A. S., & Perry, C. L. (2002). Peer-led, school-based nutrition education for young adolescents: Feasibility and process evaluation of the TEENS study. *Journal of School Health, 72,* 121–127.

Suárez, D. F., Ramirez, F. O., & Koo, J.-W. (2009). UNESCO and the Associated Schools Project: Symbolic affirmation of world community, international understanding, and human rights. *Sociology of Education, 82*, 197–216.

Summers, J. O. (1970). The identity of women's clothing fashion opinion leaders. *Journal of Marketing Research, 7*, 178–185.

Tilly, C. (2004). Observations of social processes and their formal representations. *Sociological Theory, 22*, 595–602.

Tindall, D. B., Cormier, J., & Diani, M. (2012). Network social capital as an outcome of social movement mobilization: Using the position generator as an indicator of social network diversity. *Social Networks.* doi: http://dx.doi.org/10.1016/j.socnet.2011.12.007

Tourangeau, K., Nord, C., Lê, T., Sorongon, A. G., & Najarian, M. (2009). Early Childhood Longitudinal Study, kindergarten class of 1998–99 (ECLS-K), combined user's manual for the ECLS-K eighth-grade and K–8 full sample data files and electronic codebooks. Washington, DC: National Center for Education Statistics, Institute of Education Sciences.

Tschannen-Moran, M., & Gareis, C. (2004). Principals' sense of efficacy: Assessing a promising construct. *Journal of Educational Administration, 42*, 573–585.

Tschannen-Moran, M., & Hoy, W. K. (2003). The conceptualization and measurement of faculty trust in schools: The omnibus *T*-Scale. In W. K. Hoy & C. G. Miskel (Eds.), *Studies in leading and organizing schools* (pp. 181–208). Greenwich: CT: Information Age Publishing.

Turner, R. J., & Marino, F. (1994). Social support and social structure: A descriptive epidemiology. *Journal of Health and Social Behavior, 35*(3), 193–212.

Tutzauer, F. (2007). Entropy as a measure of centrality in networks characterized by path-transfer flow. *Social Networks, 29*, 249–265.

Tyack, D., & Cuban, L. (1995). *Tinkering toward utopia*. Cambridge, MA: Harvard University Press.

Uzzi, B. (1996). The sources and consequences of embeddedness for the economic performance of organizations: The network effect. *American Sociological Review, 61*(4), 674–698.

Uzzi, B., & Spiro, J. (2005). Collaboration and creativity: The small-world problem. *American Journal of Sociology, 111*, 447–504.

Valente, T., Gallaher, P., & Mouttapa, M. (2004). Using social networks to understand and prevent substance use: A transdisciplinary perspective. *Substance Use and Misuse, 39*, 1685–1712.

Valente, T. W. (1993). Diffusion of innovations and policy decision-making. *Journal of Communication, 43*, 30–41.

Valente, T. W. (2005). Models and methods for innovation diffusion. In P. J. Carrington, J. Scott & S. Wasserman (Eds.), *Models and methods in social network analysis* (pp. 98–116). New York: Cambridge University Press.

Valente, T. W. (2010). *Social networks and health: Models, methods, and applications*. New York: Oxford University Press.

Valente, T. W., Hoffman, B. R., Ritt-Olson, A., Lichtman, K., & Johnson, C. A. (2003). The effects of a social network method for group assignment strategies on peer-led tobacco prevention programs in schools. *American Journal of Public Health, 93*, 1837–1843.

Valente, T. W., & Pumpuang, P. (2007). Identifying opinion leaders to promote behavior change. *Health Education & Behavior, 34*, 881–896.

Valente, T. W., & Rogers, E. M. (1995). The origins and development of the diffusion of innovations paradigm as an example of scientific growth. *Science Communication: An Interdisciplinary Social Science Journal, 16*, 238–269.

Valente, T. W., & Vlahov, D. (2001). Selective risk taking among needle exchange participants in Baltimore: Implications for supplemental interventions. *American Journal of Public Health, 91*, 406–411.

Van der Gaag, M. P. J., & Snijders, T. A. B. (2005). The resource generator: Measurement of individual social capital with concrete items. *Social Networks, 27*, 1–29.

Van der Gaag, M. P. J., Snijders, T. A. B., & Flap, H. D. (2004). *Position generator measures and their relationship to other social capital measures.* Retrieved from http://gaag.home.xs4all.nl/work/PG_comparison.pdf

van Duijn, M. A. J., & Huisman, M. (2011). Statistical models for ties and actors. In J. Scott & P. J. Carrington (Eds.), *The Sage handbook of social network analysis* (pp. 459–483). Los Angeles: Sage Publications.

Wang, P., Robins, G., & Pattison, P. (2008). *PNet: Program for the simulation and estimation of p exponential random graph models.* Melbourne, Australia: University of Melbourne.

Wasserman, S., & Faust, K. (1994). *Social network analysis: Methods and applications.* New York: Cambridge University Press.

Wasserman, S., & Robins, G. L. (2005). An introduction to random graphs, dependence graphs, and p. In P. J. Carrington, J. Scott, & S. Wasserman (Eds.), *Models and methods in social network analysis* (pp. 148–161). New York: Cambridge University Press.

Watts, D. (1999). Networks, dynamics, and the small-world phenomenon. *American Journal of Sociology, 105*(2), 493–527.

Watts, D. (2003). *Six degrees: The science of a connected age.* New York: W. W. Norton & Company.

Watts, D. J. (2004). The "new" science of networks. *Annual Review of Sociology, 30*, 243–270.

Watts, D. J., & Strogatz, S. H. (1998). Collective dynamics of "small-world" networks. *Nature, 393*, 409–410.

Wellman, B. (1988). Structural analysis: From method and metaphor to theory and substance. In B. Wellman & S. D. Berkowitz (Eds.), *Social structures: A network approach* (pp. 19–61). New York: Cambridge University Press.

White, H. C., Boorman, S. A., & Breiger, R. L. (1976). Social structure from multiple networks I: Blockmodels of roles and positions. *American Journal of Sociology, 81*, 730–781.

White, K., & Watkins, S. C. (2000). Accuracy, stability and reciprocity in informal conversational networks in rural Kenya. *Social Networks, 22*, 337–355.

Whyte, W. F. (1943). *Street corner society: The social structure of an Italian slum.* Chicago: University of Chicago Press.

Willis, P. (1977). *Learning to labor: How working-class kids get working-class jobs.* New York: Columbia University Press.

Windschitl, M., & Sahl, K. (2002). Tracing teachers' use of technology in a laptop computer school: The interplay of teacher beliefs, social dynamics, and institutional culture. *American Educational Research Journal, 39*, 165–205.

Wolfe, A. W. (1978). The rise of network thinking in anthropology. *Social Networks, 1*, 53–64.

Zhao, Y., Pugh, K., Sheldon, S., & Byers, J. (2002). Conditions for classroom technology innovations. *Teachers College Record, 104*, 482–515.

AUTHOR INDEX

SUBJECT INDEX

◉SAGE research**methods**

The essential online tool for researchers from the world's leading methods publisher

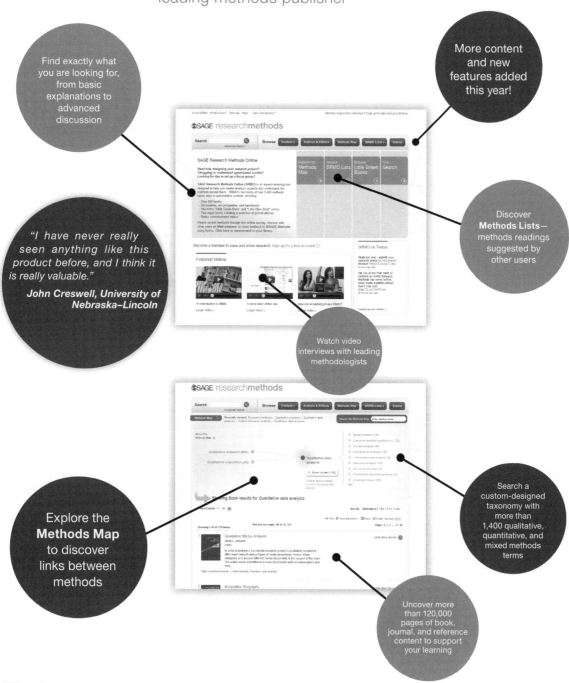

Find exactly what you are looking for, from basic explanations to advanced discussion

More content and new features added this year!

"I have never really seen anything like this product before, and I think it is really valuable."
John Creswell, University of Nebraska–Lincoln

Discover Methods Lists—methods readings suggested by other users

Watch video interviews with leading methodologists

Explore the Methods Map to discover links between methods

Search a custom-designed taxonomy with more than 1,400 qualitative, quantitative, and mixed methods terms

Uncover more than 120,000 pages of book, journal, and reference content to support your learning

Find out more at
www.sageresearchmethods.com